D1194957

AUDUBON

NOVEMBER, 1843

From the portrait by John Woodhouse Audubon

AUDUBON AND HIS JOURNALS

BY

MARIA R. AUDUBON

WITH ZOÖLOGICAL AND OTHER NOTES

BY

ELLIOTT COUES

ILLUSTRATED

VOLUME I.

Dover Publications, Inc.
New York

Published in Canada by General Publishing Company, Ltd., 30 Lesmill Road, Don Mills, Toronto, Ontario.

Published in the United Kingdom by Constable and Company, Ltd., 10 Orange Street, London WC2H 7EG.

This Dover edition, first published in 1986, is an unabridged republication of the 1960 Dover edition, which was a republication of the first edition originally published by Charles Scribner's Sons, New York, in 1897.

Manufactured in the United States of America
Dover Publications, Inc., 31 East 2nd Street, Mineola, N.Y. 11501

Library of Congress Cataloging in Publication Data

Audubon, John James, 1785-1851.
Audubon and his journals.

Reprint. Originally published: New York : Scribner, 1897.
Includes index.
1. Audubon, John James, 1785-1851. 2. Birds—North America. 3. Naturalists—United States—Biography. 1. Audubon, Maria Rebecca, 1843-1925. II. Title.
QL31.A9A2 1986 598.092'4 [B] 85-29258
ISBN 0-486-25143-8 (v. 1)
ISBN 0-486-25144-6 (v. 2)

In Loving Memory

OF MY FATHER,

JOHN WOODHOUSE AUDUBON,

AND OF

HIS LOVE AND ADMIRATION FOR HIS FATHER,

JOHN JAMES AUDUBON,

THIS BOOK WAS WRITTEN.

PREFACE

IT is customary at the close of a Preface to make some acknowledgment of the services rendered by others in the preparation of a volume; but in my case this aid has been so generous, so abundant, and so helpful, that I must reverse the order of things and begin by saying that my heartiest thanks are due to the many who have assisted me in a work which for many years has been my dream.

Without the very material aid, both by pen and advice, of Dr. Elliott Coues, these pages would have lost more than I care to contemplate. All the zoölogical notes are his, and many of the geographical, besides suggestions too numerous to mention; moreover, all this assistance was most liberally given at a time when he personally was more than busy; and yet my wishes and convenience have always been consulted.

Next to the memory of my father, Mr. Ruthven Deane has been the motive power which has caused these volumes to be written. For many years he has urged me to attempt it, and has supplied me with some valuable material, especially regarding Henderson. During the months that I have been working on much that I have felt incompetent to deal with, his encouragement has helped me over many a difficulty.

To my sisters Harriet and Florence, and my cousin M. Eliza Audubon, I am especially indebted. The first and last have lent me of their choicest treasures; letters, journals, and other manuscripts they have placed unconditionally in my hands, besides supplying many details from other sources; and my sister Florence has been my almost hourly assistant in more ways than I can specify.

The arrangement of the papers and journals was suggested by the late Dr. G. Brown Goode; and many names come to mind of friends who have helped me in other ways. Among them are those of Mr. W. H. Wetherill, Messrs. Richard R. and William Rathbone, my aunt, Mrs. James Hall, Dr. Arthur T. Lincoln, Mr. Morris F. Tyler, Mr. Joseph Coolidge, Rev. A. Gordon Bakewell, and Mr. George Bird Grinnell.

I wish also to say that without the loving generosity of my friend the late Miss M. Louise Comstock, I should never have had the time at my command which I have needed for this work; and last, but by no means least, I thank my mother for her many memories, and for her wise criticisms.

There came into my hands about twelve years ago some of these journals, — those of the Missouri and Labrador journeys; and since then others have been added, all of which had been virtually lost for years. The story of how I heard of some, and traced others, is too long to tell here, so I will only say that these journals have formed my chief sources of information. So far as has been possible I have verified and supplemented them by every means. Researches have been made in San Domingo, New Orleans, and France; letters and journals have been consulted which prove this or that statement; and from the mass of papers I have accumulated, I have used perhaps one fifth.

"The Life of Audubon the Naturalist, edited by Mr. Robert Buchanan from material supplied by his widow," covers, or is supposed to cover, the same ground I have gone over. That the same journals were used is obvious; and besides these, others, destroyed by fire in Shelbyville, Ky., were at my grandmother's command, and more than all, her own recollections and voluminous diaries. Her manuscript, which I never saw, was sent to the English publishers, and was not returned to the author by them or by Mr. Buchanan. How much of it was valuable, it is impossible to say; but the fact remains that Mr. Buchanan's book is so mixed up, so interspersed with anecdotes and episodes, and so interlarded with derogatory remarks of his own, as to be practically useless to the world, and very unpleasant to the Audubon family. Moreover, with few exceptions everything about birds has been left out. Many errors in dates and names are apparent, especially the date of the Missouri River journey, which is ten years later than he states. However, if Mr. Buchanan had done his work better, there would have been no need for mine; so I forgive him, even though he dwells at unnecessary length on Audubon's vanity and selfishness, of which I find no traces.

In these journals, nine in all, and in the hundred or so of letters, written under many skies, and in many conditions of life, by a man whose education was wholly French, one of the journals dating as far back as 1822, and some of the letters even earlier, — there is not one sentence, one expression, that is other than that of a refined and cultured gentleman. More than that, there is not one utterance of " anger, hatred or malice." Mr. George Ord and Mr. Charles Waterton were both my grandfather's bitter enemies, yet one he rarely mentions, and of the latter, when he says, " I had a scrubby letter from Waterton," he has said his worst.

But the journals will speak for themselves better than I can, and so I send them forth, believing that to many they will be of absorbing interest, as they have been to me.

M. R. A.

CONTENTS

Volume I

LIST OF ILLUSTRATIONS.

Vol. I.

AUDUBON

INTRODUCTION

IN the brief biography of Audubon which follows, I have given, I believe, the only correct account that has been written, and as such I present it. I am not competent to give an opinion as to the merits of his work, nor is it necessary. His place as naturalist, woodsman, artist, author, has long since been accorded him, and he himself says: "My enemies have been few, and my friends numerous."

I have tried only to put Audubon *the man* before my readers, and in his own words so far as possible, that they may know what he was, not what others *thought* he was.

M. R. A.

AUDUBON

THE village of Mandeville in the parish of St. Tammany, Louisiana, is about twenty miles from New Orleans on the north shore of Lake Ponchartrain. Here, on the plantation of the same name, owned by the Marquis de Mandeville de Marigny, John James Laforest Audubon[1] was born, the Marquis having lent his home, in the generous southern fashion, to his friend Admiral Jean Audubon, who, with his Spanish Creole wife, lived here some months. In the same house, towards the close of the last century, Louis Philippe found refuge for a time with the ever hospitable Marigny family, and he named the beautiful plantation home "Fontainebleau." Since then changes innumerable have come, the estate has other owners, the house has gone, those who once dwelt there are long dead, their descendants scattered, the old landmarks obliterated.

Audubon has given a sketch of his father in his own words in "Myself," which appears in the pages following; but of his mother little indeed is known. Only within the year, have papers come into the hands of her great-grandchildren, which prove her surname to have been *Rabin*. Audubon himself tells of her tragic death, which was not, however, in the St. Domingo insurrection of 1793, but in one of the local uprisings of the slaves which were of

1 "My name is John James Laforest Audubon. The name Laforest I never sign except when writing to my wife, and she is the only being, since my father's death, who calls me by it." (Letter of Audubon to Mrs. Rathbone, 1827.) All Mrs. Audubon's letters to her husband address him as Laforest.

frequent occurrence in that beautiful island, whose history is too dark to dwell upon. Beyond this nothing can be found relating to the mother, whom Audubon lost before he was old enough to remember her, except that in 1822 one of the family Marigny told my father, John Woodhouse Audubon, then a boy of ten, who with his parents was living in New Orleans, that she was "une dame d'une beauté incomparable et avec beaucoup de fierté." It may seem strange that nothing more can be found regarding this lady, but it is to be remembered these were troublous days, when stormy changes were the rule; and the roving and adventurous sailor did not, I presume, encumber himself with papers. To these circumstances also it is probably due that the date of Audubon's birth is not known, and must always remain an open question. In his journals and letters various allusions are made to his age, and many passages bearing on the matter are found, but with one exception no two agree; he may have been born anywhere between 1772 and 1783, and in the face of this uncertainty the date usually given, May 5, 1780, may be accepted, though the true one is no doubt earlier.

The attachment between Audubon and his father was of the strongest description, as the long and affectionate, if somewhat infrequent letters, still in the possession of the family, fully demonstrate. When the Admiral was retired from active service, he lived at La Gerbétière in France with his second wife, Anne Moynette, until his death, on February 19, 1818, at the great age of ninety-five.

In this home near the Loire, Audubon spent his happy boyhood and youth, dearly beloved and loving, and receiving the best education time and place afforded. As the boy grew older and more advantages were desired for him, came absences when he was at school in La Rochelle and Paris; but La Gerbétière was his home till in early manhood he returned to America, the land he loved above all others, as his journals show repeatedly. The impress of the years in France was never lost; he always had a strong French accent, he possessed in a marked degree the adaptability to circumstances which is a trait of that nation, and his disposition inherited from both parents was elated or depressed by a trifle. He was quick-tempered, enthusiastic, and romantic, yet affectionate, forgiving, and with unlimited industry and perseverance; he was generous to every one with time, money, and possessions; nothing was too good for others, but his own personal requirements were of the simplest character. His life shows all this and more, better than words of mine can tell; and as the only account of his years till he left Henderson, Ky., in 1819, is in his own journal, it is given here in full.[1]

MYSELF.[2]

The precise period of my birth is yet an enigma to me, and I can only say what I have often heard my father repeat to me on this subject, which is as follows: It seems that my father had large properties in Santo Domingo, and was in the habit of visiting frequently that portion of our Southern States called, and known by the name of, Louisiana, then owned by the French Government.

During one of these excursions he married a lady of Spanish extraction, whom I have been led to understand was as beautiful as she was wealthy, and otherwise attractive, and who bore my father three sons and a daughter, — I being the youngest of the sons and the only one who survived extreme youth. My mother, soon after my birth, accompanied my father to the estate of Aux Cayes, on the island of Santo Domingo, and she was one of the victims during the ever-to-be-lamented period of the negro insurrection of that island.

[1] This manuscript was found in an old book which had been in a barn on Staten Island for years.

[2] Reprinted from Scribner's Magazine, March, 1893, p. 267. A few errors in names and dates are now corrected.

My father, through the intervention of some faithful servants, escaped from Aux Cayes with a good portion of his plate and money, and with me and these humble friends reached New Orleans in safety. From this place he took me to France, where, having married the only mother I have ever known, he left me under her charge and returned to the United States in the employ of the French Government, acting as an officer under Admiral Rochambeau. Shortly afterward, however, he landed in the United States and became attached to the army under La Fayette.

The first of my recollective powers placed me in the central portion of the city of Nantes, on the Loire River, in France, where I still recollect particularly that I was much cherished by my dear stepmother, who had no children of her own, and that I was constantly attended by one or two black servants, who had followed my father from Santo Domingo to New Orleans and afterward to Nantes.

One incident which is as perfect in my memory as if it had occurred this very day, I have thought of thousands of times since, and will now put on paper as one of the curious things which perhaps did lead me in after times to love birds, and to finally study them with pleasure infinite. My mother had several beautiful parrots and some monkeys; one of the latter was a full-grown male of a very large species. One morning, while the servants were engaged in arranging the room I was in, "Pretty Polly" asking for her breakfast as usual, "*Du pain au lait pour le perroquet Mignonne*," the man of the woods probably thought the bird presuming upon his rights in the scale of nature; be this as it may, he certainly showed his supremacy in strength over the denizen of the air, for, walking deliberately and uprightly toward the poor bird, he at once killed it, with unnatural composure. The sensations of my infant heart at this cruel sight were agony to me. I prayed the servant to beat the monkey, but he, who for some reason preferred the monkey to the parrot, refused. I uttered long and piercing cries, my mother rushed into the room, I was tranquillized, the monkey was forever afterward chained, and Mignonne buried with all the pomp of a cherished lost one.

This made, as I have said, a very deep impression on my youthful mind. But now, my dear children, I must tell you somewhat of *my* father, and of his parentage.

John Audubon, my grandfather, was born and lived at the small village of Sable d'Olhonne, and was by trade a very humble fisherman. He appears to have made up for the want of wealth by the number of his children, twenty-one of whom he actually raised to man and womanhood. All were sons, with one exception; my aunt, one uncle, and my father, who was the twentieth son, being the only members of that extraordinary numerous family who lived to old age. In subsequent years, when I visited Sable d'Olhonne, the old residents assured me that they had seen the whole family, including both parents, at church many times.

When my father had reached the age of twelve years, his father presented him with a shirt, a dress of coarse material, a stick, and his blessing, and urged him to go and seek means for his future support and sustenance.

Some *kind* whaler or cod-fisherman took him on board as a "Boy." Of his life during his early voyages it would be useless to trouble you; let it suffice for me to say that they were of the usual most uncomfortable nature. How many trips he made I cannot say, but he told me that by the time he was seventeen he had become an able seaman before the mast; when twenty-one he commanded a fishing-smack, and went to the great Newfoundland Banks; at twenty-five he owned several small crafts, all fishermen, and at twenty-eight sailed for Santo Domingo with his little flotilla heavily loaded with the produce of the deep. "Fortune," said he to me one day, "now began to smile upon me. I did well in this enterprise, and after a few more voyages of the same sort gave up the sea, and purchased a small estate on the Isle à Vaches;[1] the prosperity of Santo Domingo was at its zenith, and in the course of ten years I had realized something very considerable. The then Governor gave me an appointment which called me to France, and having received some favors there, I became once more a seafaring man, the government having granted me the command of a small vessel of war."[2]

[1] Isle à Vache, eight miles south of Aux Cayes.

[2] This vessel was the "Annelle."

How long my father remained in the service, it is impossible for me to say. The different changes occurring at the time of the American Revolution, and afterward during that in France, seem to have sent him from one place to another as if a foot-ball; his property in Santo Domingo augmenting, however, the while, and indeed till the liberation of the black slaves there.

During a visit he paid to Pennsylvania when suffering from the effects of a sunstroke, he purchased the beautiful farm of Mill Grove, on the Schuylkill and Perkiomen streams. At this place, and a few days only before the memorable battle (*sic*) of Valley Forge, General Washington presented him with his portrait, now in my possession; and highly do I value it as a memento of that noble man and the glories of those days.[1] At the conclusion of the war between England and her child of the West, my father returned to France and continued in the employ of the naval department of that country, being at one time sent to Plymouth, England, in a seventy-five-gun ship to exchange prisoners. This was, I think, in the short peace that took place between England and France in 1801. He returned to Rochefort, where he lived for several years, still in the employ of government. He finally sent in his resignation and returned to Nantes and La Gerbétière. He had many severe trials and afflictions before his death, having lost my two older brothers early in the French Revolution; both were officers in the army. His only sister was killed by the Chouans of La Vendée,[2] and the only brother he had was not on good terms with him. This brother resided at

[1] The family still own this portrait, of which Victor G. Audubon writes: "This portrait is probably the *first* one taken of that great and good man, and although the drawing is hard, the coloring and costume are correct, I have no doubt. It was copied by Greenough, the sculptor, when he was preparing to model his 'Washington' for the Capitol, and he considered it as a valuable addition to the material already obtained. This portrait was painted by an artist named Polk, but who or what he was, I know not."

[2] There still remain those who recall how Audubon would walk up and down, snapping his fingers, a habit he had when excited, when relating how he had seen his aunt tied to a wagon and dragged through the streets of Nantes in the time of Carrier.

Bayonne, and, I believe, had a large family, none of whom I have ever seen or known.[1]

In personal appearance my father and I were of the same height and stature, say about five feet ten inches, erect, and with muscles of steel; his manners were those of a most polished gentleman, for those and his natural understanding had been carefully improved both by observation and by self-education. In temper we much resembled each other also, being warm, irascible, and at times violent; but it was like the blast of a hurricane, dreadful for a time, when calm almost instantly returned. He greatly approved of the change in France during the time of Napoleon, whom he almost idolized. My father died in 1818, regretted most deservedly on account of his simplicity, truth, and perfect sense of honesty. Now I must return to myself.

My stepmother, who was devotedly attached to me, far too much so for my good, was desirous that I should be brought up to live and die "like a gentleman," thinking that fine clothes and filled pockets were the only requisites needful to attain this end. She therefore completely spoiled me, hid my faults, boasted to every one of my youthful merits, and, worse than all, said frequently in my presence that I was the handsomest boy in France. All my wishes and idle notions were at once gratified; she went so far as actually to grant me *carte blanche* at all the confectionery shops in the town, and also of the village of Couëron, where during the summer we lived, as it were, in the country.

My father was quite of another, and much more valuable description of mind as regarded my future welfare; he believed not in the power of gold coins as efficient means to render a man happy. He spoke of the stores of the mind, and having suffered much himself through the want of education, he ordered that I should be put to school, and have teachers at home. "Revolutions," he was wont to say, "too often take place in the lives of individuals, and they are apt to lose in one day the fortune they before possessed; but talents and knowledge, added to sound mental training, assisted by honest industry, can never fail, nor be

[1] This brother left three daughters; only one married, and her descen dants, if any, cannot be traced.

taken from any one once the possessor of such valuable means." Therefore, notwithstanding all my mother's entreaties and her tears, off to a school I was sent. Excepting only, perhaps, military schools, none were good in France at this period; the thunders of the Revolution still roared over the land, the Revolutionists covered the earth with the blood of man, woman, and child. But let me forever drop the curtain over the frightful aspect of this dire picture. To think of these dreadful days is too terrible, and would be too horrible and painful for me to relate to you, my dear sons.

The school I went to was none of the best; my private teachers were the only means through which I acquired the least benefit. My father, who had been for so long a seaman, and who was then in the French navy, wished me to follow in his steps, or else to become an engineer. For this reason I studied drawing, geography, mathematics, fencing, etc., as well as music, for which I had considerable talent. I had a good fencing-master, and a first-rate teacher of the violin; mathematics was hard, dull work, I thought; geography pleased me more. For my other studies, as well as for dancing, I was quite enthusiastic; and I well recollect how anxious I was then to become the commander of a corps of dragoons.

My father being mostly absent on duty, my mother suffered me to do much as I pleased; it was therefore not to be wondered at that, instead of applying closely to my studies, I preferred associating with boys of my own age and disposition, who were more fond of going in search of birds' nests, fishing, or shooting, than of better studies. Thus almost every day, instead of going to school when I ought to have gone, I usually made for the fields, where I spent the day; my little basket went with me, filled with good eatables, and when I returned home, during either winter or summer, it was replenished with what I called curiosities, such as birds' nests, birds' eggs, curious lichens, flowers of all sorts, and even pebbles gathered along the shore of some rivulet.

The first time my father returned from sea after this my room exhibited quite a show, and on entering it he was so pleased to see my various collections that he complimented me on my taste for such things: but when he inquired what else I had done, and I, like a culprit, hung my head, he left me without saying another word. Dinner over he asked my sister for some music, and, on her playing for him, he was so pleased with her improvement that he presented her with a beautiful book. I was next asked to play on my violin, but alas! for nearly a month I had not touched it, it was stringless; not a word was said on that subject. "Had I any drawings to show?" Only a few, and those not good. My good father looked at his wife, kissed my sister, and humming a tune left the room. The next morning at dawn of day my father and I were under way in a private carriage; my trunk, etc., were fastened to it, my violin-case was under my feet, the postilion was ordered to proceed, my father took a book from his pocket, and while he silently read I was left entirely to my own thoughts.

After some days' travelling we entered the gates of Rochefort. My father had scarcely spoken to me, yet there was no anger exhibited in his countenance; nay, as we reached the house where we alighted, and approached the door, near which a sentinel stopped his walk and presented arms, I saw him smile as he raised his hat and said a few words to the man, but so low that not a syllable reached my ears.

The house was furnished with servants, and everything seemed to go on as if the owner had not left it. My father bade me sit by his side, and taking one of my hands calmly said to me: "My beloved boy, thou art now safe. I have brought thee here that I may be able to pay constant attention to thy studies; thou shalt have ample time for pleasures, but the remainder *must* be employed with industry and care. This day is entirely thine own, and as I must attend to my duties, if thou wishest to see the docks, the fine ships-of-war, and walk round the wall, thou may'st accompany me." I accepted, and off together we went; I was presented to every officer we met, and they noticing me more or less, I saw much that day, yet still I perceived that I was like a prisoner-of-war on parole in the city of Rochefort.

My best and most amiable companion was the son of Admiral, or Vice-Admiral (I do not precisely recollect his rank) Vivien, who lived nearly opposite to the house where my father and I then resided; his company I much enjoyed, and with him all my leisure hours were spent. About this time my father was sent to England in a corvette with a view to exchange prisoners, and he sailed on board the man-of-war "L'Institution" for Plymouth. Previous to his sailing he placed me under the charge of his secretary, Gabriel Loyen Dupuy Gaudeau, the son of a fallen nobleman. Now this gentleman was of no pleasing nature to me; he was, in fact, more than too strict and severe in all his prescriptions to me, and well do I recollect that one morning, after having been set to a very arduous task in mathematical problems, I gave him the slip, jumped from the window, and ran off through the gardens attached to the Marine Secrétariat. The unfledged bird may stand for a while on the border of its nest, and perhaps open its winglets and attempt to soar away, but his youthful imprudence may, and indeed often does, prove inimical to his prowess, as some more wary and older bird, that has kept an eye toward him, pounces relentlessly upon the young adventurer and secures him within the grasp of his more powerful talons. This was the case with me in this instance. I had leaped from the door of my cage and thought myself quite safe, while I rambled thoughtlessly beneath the shadow of the trees in the garden and grounds in which I found myself; but the secretary, with a side glance, had watched my escape, and, ere many minutes had elapsed, I saw coming toward me a corporal with whom, in fact, I was well acquainted. On nearing me, and I did not attempt to escape, our past familiarity was, I found, quite evaporated; he bid me, in a severe voice, to follow him, and on my being presented to my father's secretary I was at once ordered on board the pontoon in port. All remonstrances proved fruitless, and on board the pontoon I was conducted, and there left amid such a medley of culprits as I cannot describe, and of whom, indeed, I have but little recollection, save that I felt vile myself in their vile company. My father returned in due course, and released me from these floating and most disagreeable lodgings, but not without a rather severe reprimand.

Shortly after this we returned to Nantes, and later to La

Gerbétière. My stay here was short, and I went to Nantes to study mathematics anew, and there spent about one year, the remembrance of which has flown from my memory, with the exception of one incident, of which, when I happen to pass my hand over the left side of my head, I am ever and anon reminded. 'T is this: one morning, while playing with boys of my own age, a quarrel arose among us, a battle ensued, in the course of which I was knocked down by a round stone, that brought the blood from that part of my skull, and for a time I lay on the ground unconscious, but soon rallying, experienced no lasting effects but the scar.

During all these years there existed within me a tendency to follow Nature in her walks. Perhaps not an hour of leisure was spent elsewhere than in woods and fields, and to examine either the eggs, nest, young, or parents of any species of birds constituted my delight. It was about this period that I commenced a series of drawings of the birds of France, which I continued until I had upward of two hundred drawings, all bad enough, my dear sons, yet they were representations of birds, and I felt pleased with them. Hundreds of anecdotes respecting my life at this time might prove interesting to you, but as they are not in my mind at this moment I will leave them, though you may find some of them in the course of the following pages.

I was within a few months of being seventeen years old, when my stepmother, who was an earnest Catholic, took into her head that I should be confirmed; my father agreed. I was surprised and indifferent, but yet as I loved her as if she had been my own mother, — and well did she merit my deepest affection, — I took to the catechism, studied it and other matters pertaining to the ceremony, and all was performed to her liking. Not long after this, my father, anxious as he was that I should be enrolled in Napoleon's army as a Frenchman, found it necessary to send me back to my own beloved country, the United States of America, and I came with intense and indescribable pleasure.

On landing at New York I caught the yellow fever by walking to the bank at Greenwich to get the money to which my father's letter of credit entitled me. The kind man who commanded the ship that brought me from France, whose name was a common one, John Smith, took particular charge of me, removed me to Morristown, N. J., and placed me under the care of two Quaker ladies who kept a boarding-house. To their skilful and untiring ministrations I may safely say I owe the prolongation of my life. Letters were forwarded by them to my father's agent, Miers Fisher of Philadelphia, of whom I have more to say hereafter. He came for me in his carriage and removed me to his villa, at a short distance from Philadelphia and on the road toward Trenton. There I would have found myself quite comfortable had not incidents taken place which are so connected with the change in my life as to call immediate attention to them.

Miers Fisher had been my father's trusted agent for about eighteen years, and the old gentlemen entertained great mutual friendship; indeed it would seem that Mr. Fisher was actually desirous that I should become a member of his family, and this was evinced within a few days by the manner in which the good Quaker presented me to a daughter of no mean appearance, but toward whom I happened to take an unconquerable dislike. Then he was opposed to music of all descriptions, as well as to dancing, could not bear me to carry a gun, or fishing-rod, and, indeed, condemned most of my amusements. All these things were difficulties toward accomplishing a plan which, for aught I know to the contrary, had been premeditated between him and my father, and rankled the heart of the kindly, if somewhat strict Quaker. They troubled me much also; at times I wished myself anywhere but under the roof of Mr. Fisher, and at last I reminded him that it was his duty to install me on the estate to which my father had sent me.

One morning, therefore, I was told that the carriage was ready to carry me there, and toward my future home he and I went. You are too well acquainted with the position of Mill Grove for me to allude to that now; suffice it to say that we reached the former abode of my father about sunset. I was presented to our tenant, William Thomas, who also was a Quaker, and took possession under certain restrictions, which amounted to my not receiving more than enough money per quarter than was

MILL GROVE MANSION ON THE PERKIOMEN CREEK.

FROM A PHOTOGRAPH FROM W. H. WETHERILL, ESQ.

considered sufficient for the expenditure of a young gentleman.

Miers Fisher left me the next morning, and after him went my blessings, for I thought his departure a true deliverance; yet this was only because our tastes and educations were so different, for he certainly was a good and learned man. Mill Grove was ever to me a blessed spot; in my daily walks I thought I perceived the traces left by my father as I looked on the even fences round the fields, or on the regular manner with which avenues of trees, as well as the orchards, had been planted by his hand. The mill was also a source of joy to me, and in the cave, which you too remember, where the Pewees were wont to build, I never failed to find quietude and delight.

Hunting, fishing, drawing, and music occupied my every moment; cares I knew not, and cared naught about them. I purchased excellent and beautiful horses, visited all such neighbors as I found congenial spirits, and was as happy as happy could be. A few months after my arrival at Mill Grove, I was informed one day that an English family had purchased the plantation next to mine, that the name of the owner was Bakewell, and moreover that he had several very handsome and interesting daughters, and beautiful pointer dogs. I listened, but cared not a jot about them at the time. The place was within sight of Mill Grove, and Fatland Ford, as it was called, was merely divided from my estate by a road leading to the Schuylkill River. Mr. William Bakewell, the father of the family, had called on me one day, but, finding I was rambling in the woods in search of birds, left a card and an invitation to go shooting with him. Now this gentleman was an Englishman, and I such a foolish boy that, entertaining the greatest prejudices against all of his nationality, I did not return his visit for many weeks, which was as absurd as it was ungentlemanly and impolite.

Mrs. Thomas, good soul, more than once spoke to me on the subject, as well as her worthy husband, but all to no import; English was English with me, my poor childish mind was settled on that, and as I wished to know none of the race the call remained unacknowledged.

Frosty weather, however, came, and anon was the ground covered with the deep snow. Grouse were abundant along the fir-covered ground near the creek, and as I was in pursuit of game one frosty morning I chanced to meet Mr. Bakewell in the woods. I was struck with the kind politeness of his manner, and found him an expert marksman. Entering into conversation, I admired the beauty of his well-trained dogs, and, apologizing for my discourtesy, finally promised to call upon him and his family.

Well do I recollect the morning, and may it please God that I may never forget it, when for the first time I entered Mr. Bakewell's dwelling. It happened that he was absent from home, and I was shown into a parlor where only one young lady was snugly seated at her work by the fire. She rose on my entrance, offered me a seat, and assured me of the gratification her father would feel on his return, which, she added, would be in a few moments, as she would despatch a servant for him. Other ruddy cheeks and bright eyes made their transient appearance, but, like spirits gay, soon vanished from my sight; and there I sat, my gaze riveted, as it were, on the young girl before me, who, half working, half talking, essayed to make the time pleasant to me. Oh! may God bless her! It was she, my dear sons, who afterward became my beloved wife, and your mother. Mr. Bakewell soon made his appearance, and received me with the manner and hospitality of a true English gentleman. The other members of the family were soon introduced to me, and "Lucy" was told to have luncheon produced. She now arose from her seat a second time, and her form, to which I had previously paid but partial attention, showed both grace and beauty; and my heart followed every one of her steps. The repast over, guns and dogs were made ready.

Lucy, I was pleased to believe, looked upon me with some favor, and I turned more especially to her on leaving. I felt that certain "*je ne sais quoi*" which intimated that, at least, she was not indifferent to me.

To speak of the many shooting parties that took place with Mr. Bakewell would be quite useless, and I shall merely say that he was a most excellent man, a great shot, and possessed of extraordinary learning — aye, far beyond my comprehension. A few days after this first interview with the family the Perkiomen chanced to be bound with ice, and many a one from the neighborhood was playing pranks on the glassy surface of that lovely stream. Being somewhat of a skater myself, I sent a note to the inhabitants of Fatland Ford, inviting them to come and partake of the simple hospitality of Mill Grove farm, and the invitation was kindly received and accepted. My own landlady bestirred herself to the utmost in the procuring of as many pheasants and partridges as her group of sons could entrap, and now under my own roof was seen the whole of the Bakewell family, seated round the table which has never ceased to be one of simplicity and hospitality.

After dinner we all repaired to the ice on the creek, and there in comfortable sledges, each fair one was propelled by an ardent skater. Tales of love may be extremely stupid to the majority, so that I will not expatiate on these days, but to me, my dear sons, and under such circumstances as then, and, thank God, now exist, every moment was to me one of delight.

But let me interrupt my tale to tell you somewhat of other companions whom I have heretofore neglected to mention. These are two Frenchmen, by name Da Costa and Colmesnil. A lead mine had been discovered by my tenant, William Thomas, to which, besides the raising of fowls, I paid considerable attention; but I knew nothing of mineralogy or mining, and my father, to whom I communicated the discovery of the mine, sent Mr. Da Costa as a partner and partial guardian from France. This fellow was intended to teach me mineralogy and mining engineering, but, in fact, knew nothing of either; besides which he was a covetous wretch, who did all he could to ruin my father, and indeed swindled both of us to a large amount. I had to go to France and expose him to my father to get rid of him, which I fortunately accomplished at first sight of my kind parent. A greater scoundrel than Da Costa never probably existed, but peace be with his soul.

The other, Colmesnil, was a very interesting young Frenchman with whom I became acquainted. He was very poor, and I invited him to come and reside under my roof. This he did, remaining for many months, much to my delight. His appearance was typical of what he was, a perfect gentleman; he was handsome in form, and possessed of talents far above my own. When introduced to your mother's family he was much thought of, and at one time he thought himself welcome to my Lucy; but it was only a dream, and when once undeceived by her whom I too loved, he told me he must part with me. This we did with mutual regret, and he returned to France, where, though I have lost sight of him, I believe he is still living.

During the winter connected with this event your uncle Thomas Bakewell, now residing in Cincinnati, was one morning skating with me on the Perkiomen, when he challenged me to shoot at his hat as he tossed it in the air, which challenge I accepted with great pleasure. I was to pass by at full speed, within about twenty-five feet of where he stood, and to shoot only when he gave the word. Off I went like lightning, up and down, as if anxious to boast of my own prowess while on the glittering surface beneath my feet; coming, however, within the agreed distance the signal was given, the trigger pulled, off went the load, and down on the ice came the hat of my future brother-in-law, as completely perforated as if a sieve. He repented, alas! too late, and was afterward severely reprimanded by Mr. Bakewell.

Another anecdote I must relate to you on paper, which I have probably too often repeated in words, concerning my skating in those early days of happiness; but, as the world knows nothing of it, I shall give it to you at some length. It was arranged one morning between your young uncle, myself, and several other friends of the same age, that we should proceed on a duck-shooting excursion up the creek, and, accordingly, off we went after an early breakfast. The ice was in capital order wherever no air-holes existed, but of these a great number interrupted our course, all of which were, however, avoided as we proceeded upward along the glittering, frozen bosom of the stream. The day was spent in much pleasure, and the game collected was not inconsiderable.

FATLAND FORD MANSION, LOOKING TOWARD VALLEY FORGE.

FROM A PHOTOGRAPH FROM W. H. WETHERILL, ESQ.

On our return, in the early dusk of the evening, I was bid to lead the way; I fastened a white handkerchief to a stick, held it up, and we all proceeded toward home as a flock of wild ducks to their roosting-grounds. Many a mile had already been passed, and, as gayly as ever, we were skating swiftly along when darkness came on, and now our speed was increased. Unconsciously I happened to draw so very near a large air-hole that to check my headway became quite impossible, and down it I went, and soon felt the power of a most chilling bath. My senses must, for aught I know, have left me for a while; be this as it may, I must have glided with the stream some thirty or forty yards, when, as God would have it, up I popped at another air-hole, and here I did, in some way or another, manage to crawl out. My companions, who in the gloom had seen my form so suddenly disappear, escaped the danger, and were around me when I emerged from the greatest peril I have ever encountered, not excepting my escape from being murdered on the prairie, or by the hands of that wretch S—— B——, of Henderson. I was helped to a shirt from one, a pair of dry breeches from another, and completely dressed anew in a few minutes, if in motley and ill-fitting garments; our line of march was continued, with, however, much more circumspection. Let the reader, whoever he may be, think as he may like on this singular and, in truth, most extraordinary escape from death; it is the truth, and as such I have written it down as a wonderful act of Providence.

Mr. Da Costa, my tutor, took it into his head that my affection for your mother was rash and inconsiderate. He spoke triflingly of her and of her parents, and one day said to me that for a man of my rank and expectations to marry Lucy Bakewell was out of the question. If I laughed at him or not I cannot tell you, but of this I am certain, that my answers to his talks on this subject so exasperated him that he immediately afterward curtailed my usual income, made some arrangements to send me to India, and wrote to my father accordingly. Understanding from many of my friends that his plans were fixed, and finally hearing from Philadelphia, whither Da Costa had gone, that he had taken my passage from Philadelphia to Canton, I walked to Philadelphia, entered his room quite unexpectedly, and asked him for such an amount of money as would enable me at once to sail for France and there see my father.

The cunning wretch, for I cannot call him by any other name, smiled, and said: "Certainly, my dear sir," and afterward gave me a letter of credit on a Mr. Kauman, a half-agent, half-banker, then residing at New York. I returned to Mill Grove, made all preparatory plans for my departure, bid a sad adieu to my Lucy and her family, and walked to New York. But never mind the journey; it was winter, the country lay under a covering of snow, but withal I reached New York on the third day, late in the evening.

Once there, I made for the house of a Mrs. Palmer, a lady of excellent qualities, who received me with the utmost kindness, and later on the same evening I went to the house of your grand-uncle, Benjamin Bakewell, then a rich merchant of New York, managing the concerns of the house of Guelt, bankers, of London. I was the bearer of a letter from Mr. Bakewell, of Fatland Ford, to this brother of his, and there I was again most kindly received and housed.

The next day I called on Mr. Kauman; he read Da Costa's letter, smiled, and after a while told me he had nothing to give me, and in plain terms said that instead of a letter of credit, Da Costa — that rascal! — had written and advised him to have me arrested and shipped to Canton. The blood rose to my temples, and well it was that I had no weapon about me, for I feel even now quite assured that his heart must have received the result of my wrath. I left him half bewildered, half mad, and went to Mrs. Palmer, and spoke to her of my purpose of returning at once to Philadelphia and there certainly murdering Da Costa. Women have great power over me at any time, and perhaps under all circumstances. Mrs. Palmer quieted me, spoke religiously of the cruel sin I thought of committing, and, at last, persuaded me to relinquish the direful plan. I returned to Mr. Bakewell's low-spirited and mournful, but said not a word about all that had passed. The next morning my sad visage showed something was wrong, and I at last gave vent to my outraged feelings.

Benjamin Bakewell was a *friend* of his brother (may you ever be so toward each other). He comforted me much, went with me to the docks to seek a vessel bound to France, and offered me any sum of money I might require to convey me to my father's house. My passage was taken on board the brig "Hope," of New Bedford, and I sailed in her, leaving Da Costa and Kauman in a most exasperated state of mind. The fact is, these rascals intended to cheat both me and my father. The brig was bound direct for Nantes. We left the Hook under a very fair breeze, and proceeded at a good rate till we reached the latitude of New Bedford, in Massachusetts, when my captain came to me as if in despair, and said he must run into port, as the vessel was so leaky as to force him to have her unloaded and repaired before he proceeded across the Atlantic. Now this was only a trick; my captain was newly married, and was merely anxious to land at New Bedford to spend a few days with his bride, and had actually caused several holes to be bored below water-mark, which leaked enough to keep the men at the pumps. We came to anchor close to the town of New Bedford; the captain went on shore, entered a protest, the vessel was unloaded, the apertures bunged up, and after a week, which I spent in being rowed about the beautiful harbor, we sailed for La Belle France. A few days after having lost sight of land we were overtaken by a violent gale, coming fairly on our quarter, and before it we scudded at an extraordinary rate, and during the dark night had the misfortune to lose a fine young sailor overboard. At one part of the sea we passed through an immensity of dead fish floating on the surface of the water, and, after nineteen days from New Bedford, we had entered the Loire, and anchored off Painbœuf, the lower harbor of Nantes.

On sending my name to the principal officer of the customs, he came on board, and afterward sent me to my father's villa, La Gerbétière, in his barge, and with his own men, and late that evening I was in the arms of my beloved parents. Although I had written to them previous to leaving America, the rapidity of my voyage had prevented them hearing of my intentions, and to them my appearance was sudden and unexpected. Most welcome, however, I was; I found my father hale and hearty, and *chère maman* as fair and good as ever. Adored *maman*, peace be with thee!

I cannot trouble you with minute accounts of my life in France for the following two years, but will merely tell you that my first object being that of having Da Costa disposed of, this was first effected; the next was my father's consent to my marriage, and this was acceded to as soon as my good father had received answers to letters written to your grandfather, William Bakewell. In the very lap of comfort my time was happily spent; I went out shooting and hunting, drew every bird I procured, as well as many other objects of natural history and zoölogy, though these were not the subjects I had studied under the instruction of the celebrated David.

It was during this visit that my sister Rosa was married to Gabriel Dupuy Gaudeau, and I now also became acquainted with Ferdinand Rozier, whom you well know. Between Rozier and myself my father formed a partnership to stand good for nine years in America.

France was at that time in a great state of convulsion; the republic had, as it were, dwindled into a half monarchical, half democratic era. Bonaparte was at the height of success, overflowing the country as the mountain torrent overflows the plains in its course. Levies, or conscriptions, were the order of the day, and my name being French my father felt uneasy lest I should be forced to take part in the political strife of those days.

I underwent a mockery of an examination, and was received as midshipman in the navy, went to Rochefort, was placed on board a man-of-war, and ran a short cruise. On my return, my father had, in some way, obtained passports for Rozier and me, and we sailed for New York. Never can I forget the day when, at St. Nazaire, an officer came on board to examine the papers of the many passengers. On looking at mine he said: "My dear Mr. Audubon, I wish you joy; would to God that I had such papers; how thankful I should be to leave unhappy France under the same passport."

About a fortnight after leaving France a vessel gave us chase. We were running before the wind under all sail, but the unknown gained on us at a great rate, and after a while stood to the windward of our ship, about half a mile off. She fired a gun, the ball passed within a few yards of our bows; our captain heeded not, but kept on his course, with the United States flag displayed and floating in the breeze. Another and another shot was fired at us; the enemy closed upon us; all the passengers expected to receive her broadside. Our commander hove to: a boat was almost instantaneously lowered and alongside our vessel;[1] two officers leaped on board, with about a dozen mariners; the first asked for the captain's papers, while the latter with his men kept guard over the whole.

The vessel which had pursued us was the "Rattlesnake" and was what I believe is generally called a privateer, which means nothing but a pirate; every one of the papers proved to be in perfect accordance with the laws existing between England and America, therefore we were not touched nor molested, but the English officers who had come on board robbed the ship of almost everything that was nice in the way of provisions, took our pigs and sheep, coffee and wines, and carried off our two best sailors despite all the remonstrances made by one of our members of Congress, I think from Virginia, who was accompanied by a charming young daughter. The "Rattlesnake" kept us under her lee, and almost within pistol-shot, for a whole day and night, ransacking the ship for money, of which we had a good deal in the run beneath a ballast of stone. Although this was partially removed they did not find the treasure. I may here tell you that I placed the gold belonging to Rozier and myself, wrapped in some clothing, under a cable in the bow of the ship, and there it remained snug till the "Rattlesnake" had given us leave to depart, which you may be sure we did without thanks to her commander or crew; we were afterward told the former had his wife with him.

After this rencontre we sailed on till we came to within about thirty miles of the entrance to the bay of New York,[2] when we

[1] "The Polly," Captain Sammis commander. [2] May 26, 1806.

passed a fishing-boat, from which we were hailed and told that two British frigates lay off the entrance of the Hook, had fired an American ship, shot a man, and impressed so many of our seamen that to attempt reaching New York might prove to be both unsafe and unsuccessful. Our captain, on hearing this, put about immediately, and sailed for the east end of Long Island Sound, which we entered uninterrupted by any other enemy than a dreadful gale, which drove us on a sand-bar in the Sound, but from which we made off unhurt during the height of the tide and finally reached New York.

I at once called on your uncle Benjamin Bakewell, stayed with him a day, and proceeded at as swift a rate as possible to Fatland Ford, accompanied by Ferdinand Rozier. Mr. Da Costa was at once dismissed from his charge. I saw my dear Lucy, and was again my own master.

Perhaps it would be well for me to give you some slight information respecting my mode of life in those days of my youth, and I shall do so without gloves. I was what in plain terms may be called extremely extravagant. I had no vices, it is true, neither had I any high aims. I was ever fond of shooting, fishing, and riding on horseback; the raising of fowls of every sort was one of my hobbies, and to reach the maximum of my desires in those different things filled every one of my thoughts. I was ridiculously fond of dress. To have seen me going shooting in black satin smallclothes, or breeches, with silk stockings, and the finest ruffled shirt Philadelphia could afford, was, as I now realize, an absurd spectacle, but it was one of my many foibles, and I shall not conceal it. I purchased the best horses in the country, and rode well, and felt proud of it; my guns and fishing-tackle were equally good, always expensive and richly ornamented, often with silver. Indeed, though in America, I cut as many foolish pranks as a young dandy in Bond Street or Piccadilly.

I was extremely fond of music, dancing, and drawing; in all I had been well instructed, and not an opportunity was lost to confirm my propensities in those accomplishments. I was, like most young men, filled with the love of amusement, and not a ball, a skating-match, a house or riding party took place without me.

Withal, and fortunately for me, I was not addicted to gambling; cards I disliked, and I had no other evil practices. I was, besides, temperate to an *intemperate* degree. I lived, until the day of my union with your mother, on milk, fruits, and vegetables, with the addition of game and fish at times, but never had I swallowed a single glass of wine or spirits until the day of my wedding. The result has been my uncommon, indeed iron, constitution. This was my constant mode of life ever since my earliest recollection, and while in France it was extremely annoying to all those round me. Indeed, so much did it influence me that I never went to dinners, merely because when so situated my peculiarities in my choice of food occasioned comment, and also because often not a single dish was to my taste or fancy, and I could eat nothing from the sumptuous tables before me. Pies, puddings, eggs, milk, or cream was all I cared for in the way of food, and many a time have I robbed my tenant's wife, Mrs. Thomas, of the cream intended to make butter for the Philadelphia market. All this time I was as fair and as rosy as a girl, though as strong, indeed stronger than most young men, and as active as a buck. And why, have I thought a thousand times, should I not have kept to that delicious mode of living? and why should not mankind in general be more abstemious than mankind is?

Before I sailed for France I had begun a series of drawings of the birds of America, and had also begun a study of their habits. I at first drew my subjects dead, by which I mean to say that, after procuring a specimen, I hung it up either by the head, wing, or foot, and copied it as closely as I possibly could.

In my drawing of birds only did I interest Mr. Da Costa. He always commended my efforts, nay he even went farther, for one morning, while I was drawing a figure of the *Ardea herodias*,[1] he assured me the time might come when I should be a great American naturalist. However curious it may seem to the scientific world that these sayings from the lips of such a man should affect me, I assure you they had great weight with me, and I felt a certain degree of pride in these words even then.

Too young and too useless to be married, your grandfather

[1] Great Blue Heron.

William Bakewell advised me to study the mercantile business; my father approved, and to insure this training under the best auspices I went to New York, where I entered as a clerk for your great-uncle Benjamin Bakewell, while Rozier went to a French house at Philadelphia.

The mercantile business did not suit me. The very first venture which I undertook was in indigo; it cost me several hundred pounds, the whole of which was lost. Rozier was no more fortunate than I, for he shipped a cargo of hams to the West Indies, and not more than one-fifth of the cost was returned. Yet I suppose we both obtained a smattering of business.

Time passed, and at last, on April 8th, 1808, your mother and I were married by the Rev. Dr. Latimer, of Philadelphia, and the next morning left Fatland Ford and Mill Grove for Louisville, Ky. For some two years previous to this, Rozier and I had visited the country from time to time as merchants, had thought well of it, and liked it exceedingly. Its fertility and abundance, the hospitality and kindness of the people were sufficiently winning things to entice any one to go there with a view to comfort and happiness.

We had marked Louisville as a spot designed by nature to become a place of great importance, and, had we been as wise as we now are, I might never have published the "Birds of America;" for a few hundred dollars laid out at that period, in lands or town lots near Louisville, would, if left to grow over with grass to a date ten years past (this being 1835), have become an immense fortune. But young heads are on young shoulders; it was not to be, and who cares?

On our way to Pittsburg, we met with a sad accident, that nearly cost the life of your mother. The coach upset on the mountains, and she was severely, but fortunately not fatally hurt. We floated down the Ohio in a flatboat, in company with several other young families; we had many goods, and opened a large store at Louisville, which went on prosperously when I attended to it; but birds were birds then as now, and my thoughts were ever and anon turning toward them as the objects of my greatest delight. I shot, I drew, I looked on nature only; my days were happy beyond human conception, and beyond this I really cared not.

Victor was born June 12, 1809, at Gwathway's Hotel of the Indian Queen. We had by this time formed the acquaintance of many persons in and about Louisville; the country was settled by planters and farmers of the most benevolent and hospitable nature; and my young wife, who possessed talents far above par, was regarded as a gem, and received by them all with the greatest pleasure. All the sportsmen and hunters were fond of me, and I became their companion; my fondness for fine horses was well kept up, and I had as good as the country — and the country was Kentucky — could afford. Our most intimate friends were the Tarascons and the Berthouds, at Louisville and Shippingport. The simplicity and whole-heartedness of those days I cannot describe; man was man, and each, one to another, a brother.

I seldom passed a day without drawing a bird, or noting something respecting its habits, Rozier meantime attending the counter. I could relate many curious anecdotes about him, but never mind them; he made out to grow rich, and what more could *he* wish for?

In 1810 Alexander Wilson the naturalist — not the *American* naturalist — called upon me.[1] About 1812 your uncle Thomas W. Bakewell sailed from New York or Philadelphia, as a partner of mine, and took with him all the disposable money which I had at that time, and there [New Orleans] opened a mercantile house under the name of "Audubon & Bakewell."

Merchants crowded to Louisville from all our Eastern cities. None of them were, as I was, intent on the study of birds, but all were deeply impressed with the value of dollars. Louisville did not give us up, but we gave up Louisville. I could not bear to give the attention required by my business, and which, indeed, every business calls for, and, therefore, my business abandoned me. Indeed, I never thought of it beyond the ever-engaging journeys which I was in the habit of taking to Philadelphia or New York to purchase goods; these journeys I greatly enjoyed,

[1] This visit passed into history in the published works of each of the great ornithologists, who were never friends. See "Behind the Veil," by Dr. Coues in Bulletin of Nuttall Ornithological Club, Oct., 1880, p. 200.

as they afforded me ample means to study birds and their habits as I travelled through the beautiful, the darling forests of Ohio, Kentucky, and Pennsylvania.

Were I here to tell you that once, when travelling, and driving several horses before me laden with goods and dollars, I lost sight of the pack-saddles, and the cash they bore, to watch the motions of a warbler, I should only repeat occurrences that happened a hundred times and more in those days. To an ordinary reader this may appear very odd, but it is as true, my dear sons, as it is that I am now scratching this poor book of mine with a miserable iron pen. Rozier and myself still had some business together, but we became discouraged at Louisville, and I longed to have a wilder range; this made us remove to Henderson, one hundred and twenty-five miles farther down the fair Ohio. We took there the remainder of our stock on hand, but found the country so very new, and so thinly populated that the commonest goods only were called for. I may say our guns and fishing-lines were the principal means of our support, as regards food.

John Pope, our clerk, who was a Kentuckian, was a good shot and an excellent fisherman, and he and I attended to the procuring of game and fish, while Rozier again stood behind the counter.

Your beloved mother and I were as happy as possible, the people round loved us, and we them in return; our profits were enormous, but our sales small, and my partner, who spoke English but badly, suggested that we remove to St. Geneviève, on the the Mississippi River. I acceded to his request to go there, but determined to leave your mother and Victor at Henderson, not being quite sure that our adventure would succeed as we hoped. I therefore placed her and the children under the care of Dr. Rankin and his wife, who had a fine farm about three miles from Henderson, and having arranged our goods on board a large flatboat, my partner and I left Henderson in the month of December, 1810, in a heavy snow-storm. This change in my plans prevented me from going, as I had intended, on a long expedition. In Louisville we had formed the acquaintance of Major Croghan (an old friend of my father's), and of General Jonathan

Clark, the brother of General William Clark, the first white man who ever crossed the Rocky Mountains. I had engaged to go with him, but was, as I have said, unfortunately prevented. To return to our journey. When we reached Cash Creek we were bound by ice for a few weeks; we then attempted to ascend the Mississippi, but were again stopped in the great bend called Tawapatee Bottom, where we again planted our camp till a thaw broke the ice.[1] In less than six weeks, however, we reached the village of St. Geneviève. I found at once it was not the place for me; its population was then composed of low French Canadians, uneducated and uncouth, and the ever-longing wish to be with my beloved wife and children drew my thoughts to Henderson, to which I decided to return almost immediately. Scarcely any communication existed between the two places, and I felt cut off from all dearest to me. Rozier, on the contrary, liked it; he found plenty of French with whom to converse. I proposed selling out to him, a bargain was made, he paid me a certain amount in cash, and gave me bills for the residue. This accomplished, I purchased a beauty of a horse, for which I paid dear enough, and bid Rozier farewell. On my return trip to Henderson I was obliged to stop at a humble cabin, where I so nearly ran the chance of losing my life, at the hands of a woman and her two desperate sons, that I have thought fit since to introduce this passage in a sketch called "The Prairie," which is to be found in the first volume of my "Ornithological Biography."

Winter was just bursting into spring when I left the land of lead mines. Nature leaped with joy, as it were, at her own new-born marvels, the prairies began to be dotted with beauteous flowers, abounded with deer, and my own heart was filled with happiness at the sights before me. I must not forget to tell you that I crossed those prairies on foot at another time, for the purpose of collecting the money due to me from Rozier, and that I walked one hundred and sixty-five miles in a little over three days, much of the time nearly ankle deep in mud and water, from which I suffered much afterward by swollen feet. I reached Henderson in early March, and a few weeks later the lower portions of Kentucky

[1] Episode "Breaking of the Ice."

and the shores of the Mississippi suffered severely by earthquakes. I felt their effects between Louisville and Henderson, and also at Dr. Rankin's. I have omitted to say that my second son, John Woodhouse, was born under Dr. Rankin's roof on November 30, 1812; he was an extremely delicate boy till about a twelvemonth old, when he suddenly acquired strength and grew to be a lusty child.

Your uncle, Thomas W. Bakewell, had been all this time in New Orleans, and thither I had sent him almost all the money I could raise; but notwithstanding this, the firm could not stand, and one day, while I was making a drawing of an otter, he suddenly appeared. He remained at Dr. Rankin's a few days, talked much to me about our misfortunes in trade, and left us for Fatland Ford.

My pecuniary means were now much reduced. I continued to draw birds and quadrupeds, it is true, but only now and then thought of making any money. I bought a wild horse, and on its back travelled over Tennessee and a portion of Georgia, and so round till I finally reached Philadelphia, and then to your grandfather's at Fatland Ford. He had sold my plantation of Mill Grove to Samuel Wetherell, of Philadelphia, for a good round sum, and with this I returned through Kentucky and at last reached Henderson once more. Your mother was well, both of you were lovely darlings of our hearts, and the effects of poverty troubled us not. Your uncle T. W. Bakewell was again in New Orleans and doing rather better, but this was a mere transient clearing of that sky which had been obscured for many a long day.

Determined to do something for myself, I took to horse, rode to Louisville with a few hundred dollars in my pockets, and there purchased, half cash, half credit, a small stock, which I brought to Henderson. *Chemin faisant*, I came in contact with, and was accompanied by, General Toledo, then on his way as a revolutionist to South America. As our flatboats were floating one clear moonshiny night lashed together, this individual opened his views to me, promising me wonders of wealth should I decide to accompany him, and he went so far as to offer me a colonelcy on what he was pleased to call "his Safe Guard." I listened, it is true, but looked more at the heavens than on his face, and in the former found so much more of peace than of war that I concluded not to accompany him.

When our boats arrived at Henderson, he landed with me, purchased many horses, hired some men, and coaxed others, to accompany him, purchased a young negro from me, presented me with a splendid Spanish dagger and my wife with a ring, and went off overland toward Natchez, with a view of there gathering recruits.

I now purchased a ground lot of four acres, and a meadow of four more at the back of the first. On the latter stood several buildings, an excellent orchard, etc., lately the property of an English doctor, who had died on the premises, and left the whole to a servant woman as a gift, from whom it came to me as a freehold. The pleasures which I have felt at Henderson, and under the roof of that log cabin, can never be effaced from my heart until after death. The little stock of goods brought from Louisville answered perfectly, and in less than twelve months I had again risen in the world. I purchased adjoining land, and was doing extremely well when Thomas Bakewell came once more on the tapis, and joined me in commerce. We prospered at a round rate for a while, but unfortunately for me, he took it into his brain to persuade me to erect a steam-mill at Henderson, and to join to our partnership an Englishman of the name of Thomas Pears, now dead.

Well, up went the steam-mill at an enormous expense, in a country then as unfit for such a thing as it would be now for me to attempt to settle in the moon. Thomas Pears came to Henderson with his wife and family of children, the mill was raised, and worked very badly. Thomas Pears lost his money and we lost ours.

It was now our misfortune to add other partners and petty agents to our concern; suffice it for me to tell you, nay, to assure you, that I was gulled by all these men. The new-born Kentucky banks nearly all broke in quick succession; and again we started with a new set of partners; these were your present uncle N. Berthoud and Benjamin Page of Pittsburg. Matters, however, grew worse every day; the times were what men called "bad," but I am fully persuaded the great fault was ours, and the building of that accursed steam-mill was, of all the follies of man, one of the greatest, and to your uncle and me the worst of all our pecuniary misfortunes. How I labored at that infernal mill! from dawn to dark, nay, at times all night. But it is over now; I am old, and try to forget as fast as possible all the different trials of those sad days. We also took it into our heads to have a steamboat, in partnership with the engineer who had come from Philadelphia to fix the engine of that mill. This also proved an entire failure, and misfortune after misfortune came down upon us like so many avalanches, both fearful and destructive.

About this time I went to New Orleans, at the suggestion of your uncle, to arrest T—— B——, who had purchased a steamer from us, but whose bills were worthless, and who owed us for the whole amount. I travelled down to New Orleans in an open skiff, accompanied by two negroes of mine; I reached New Orleans one day too late; Mr. B—— had been compelled to surrender the steamer to a prior claimant. I returned to Henderson, travelling part way on the steamer "Paragon," walked from the mouth of the Ohio to Shawnee, and rode the rest of the distance. On my arrival old Mr. Berthoud told me that Mr. B—— had arrived before me, and had sworn to kill me. My affrighted Lucy forced me to wear a dagger. Mr. B—— walked about the streets and before my house as if watching for me, and the continued reports of our neighbors prepared me for an encounter with this man, whose violent and ungovernable temper was only too well known. As I was walking toward the steam-mill one morning, I heard myself hailed from behind; on turning, I observed Mr. B—— marching toward me with a heavy club in his hand. I stood still, and he soon reached me. He complained of my conduct to him at New Orleans, and suddenly raising his bludgeon laid it about me. Though white with wrath, I spoke nor moved not till he had given me twelve severe blows, then, drawing my dagger with my left hand (unfortunately my right was disabled and in a sling, having been caught and

AUDUBON'S MILL AT HENDERSON, KENTUCKY.

NOW OWNED BY MR. DAVID CLARK.

much injured in the wheels of the steam-engine), I stabbed him and he instantly fell. Old Mr. Berthoud and others, who were hastening to the spot, now came up, and carried him home on a plank. Thank God, his wound was not mortal, but his friends were all up in arms and as hot-headed as himself. Some walked through my premises armed with guns; my dagger was once more at my side, Mr. Berthoud had his gun, our servants were variously armed, and our carpenter took my gun "Long Tom." Thus protected, I walked into the Judiciary Court, that was then sitting, and was blamed, *only*,—for not having killed the scoundrel who attacked me.

The "bad establishment," as I called the steam-mill, worked worse and worse every day. Thomas Bakewell, who possessed more brains than I, sold his town lots and removed to Cincinnati, where he has made a large fortune, and glad I am of it.

From this date my pecuniary difficulties daily increased; I had heavy bills to pay which I could not meet or take up. The moment this became known to the world around me, that moment I was assailed with thousands of invectives; the once wealthy man was now nothing. I parted with every particle of property I held to my creditors, keeping only the clothes I wore on that day, my original drawings, and my gun.

Your mother held in her arms your baby sister Rosa, named thus on account of her extreme loveliness, and after my own sister Rosa. *She* felt the pangs of our misfortunes perhaps more heavily than I, but never for an hour lost her courage; her brave and cheerful spirit accepted all, and no reproaches from her beloved lips ever wounded my heart. With her was I not always rich?

Finally I paid every bill, and at last left Henderson, probably forever, without a dollar in my pocket, walked to Louisville alone, by no means comfortable in mind, there went to Mr. Berthoud's, where I was kindly received; they were indeed good friends.

My plantation in Pennsylvania had been sold, and, in a word, nothing was left to me but my humble talents. Were those talents to remain dormant under such exigencies? Was I to see my beloved Lucy and children suffer and want bread, in the abundant State of Kentucky? Was I to repine because I had acted like an honest man? Was I inclined to cut my throat in foolish despair? No!! I *had* talents, and to them I instantly resorted.

To be a good draughtsman in those days was to me a blessing; to any other man, be it a thousand years hence, it will be a blessing also. I at once undertook to take portraits of the human "head divine," in black chalk, and, thanks to my master, David, succeeded admirably. I commenced at exceedingly low prices, but raised these prices as I became more known in this capacity. Your mother and yourselves were sent up from Henderson to our friend Isham Talbot, then Senator for Kentucky; this was done without a cent of expense to me, and I can never be grateful enough for his kind generosity.

In the course of a few weeks I had as much work to do as I could possibly wish, so much that I was able to rent a house in a retired part of Louisville. I was sent for four miles in the country, to take likenesses of persons on their death-beds, and so high did my reputation suddenly rise, as the best delineator of heads in that vicinity, that a clergyman residing at Louisville (I would give much now to recall and write down his name) had his dead child disinterred, to procure a fac-simile of his face, which, by the way, I gave to the parents as if still alive, to their intense satisfaction.

My drawings of birds were not neglected meantime; in this particular there seemed to hover round me almost a mania, and I would even give up doing a head, the profits of which would have supplied our wants for a week or more, to represent a little citizen of the feathered tribe. Nay, my dear sons, I thought that I now drew birds far better than I had ever done before misfortune intensified, or at least developed, my abilities. I received an invitation to go to Cincinnati,[1] a flourishing place, and which you now well know to be a thriving town in the State of Ohio. I was presented to the president of the Cincinnati College, Dr. Drake, and immediately formed an engagement to stuff birds for the museum there, in concert with Mr. Robert Best, an Englishman

[1] 1819.

of great talent. My salary was large, and I at once sent for your mother to come to me, and bring you. Your dearly beloved sister Rosa died shortly afterward. I now established a large drawing-school at Cincinnati, to which I attended thrice per week, and at good prices.

The expedition of Major Long[1] passed through the city soon after, and well do I recollect how he, Messrs. T. Peale,[2] Thomas Say,[3] and others stared at my drawings of birds at that time.

So industrious were Mr. Best and I that in about six months we had augmented, arranged, and finished all we could do for the museum. I returned to my portraits, and made a great number of them, without which we must have once more been on the starving list, as Mr. Best and I found, sadly too late, that the members of the College museum were splendid promisers and very bad paymasters.

In October of 1820 I left your mother and yourselves at Cincinnati, and went to New Orleans on board a flat-boat commanded and owned by a Mr. Haromack. From this date my journals are kept with fair regularity, and if you read them you will easily find all that followed afterward.

In glancing over these pages, I see that in my hurried and broken manner of laying before you this very imperfect (but perfectly correct) account of my early life I have omitted to tell you that, before the birth of your sister Rosa, a daughter was born at Henderson, who was called, of course, Lucy. Alas! the poor, dear little one was unkindly born, she was always ill and suffering; two years did your kind and unwearied mother nurse her with all imaginable care, but notwithstanding this loving devotion she died, in the arms which had held her so long, and so tenderly.

[1] Stephen Harriman Long, Corps of Engineers, U. S. Army, who was then on his way to explore the region of the upper Mississippi and Minnesota Rivers.

[2] Titian R. Peale, afterward naturalist of the U. S. Exploring Expedition, under Commodore Wilkes. Later in life he was for many years an examiner in the Patent Office at Washington, and died at a very advanced age. He was a member of the eminent Peale family of artists, one of whom established Peale's Museum in Philadelphia. — E. C.

[3] The distinguished naturalist of that name. — E. C.

This infant daughter we buried in our garden at Henderson, but after removed her to the Holly burying-ground in the same place.

Hundreds of anecdotes I could relate to you, my dear sons, about those times, and it may happen that the pages that I am now scribbling over may hereafter, through your own medium, or that of some one else be published. I shall try, should God Almighty grant me life, to return to these less important portions of my history, and delineate them all with the same faithfulness with which I have written the ornithological biographies of the birds of my beloved country.

Only one event, however, which possesses in itself a lesson to mankind, I will here relate. After our dismal removal from Henderson to Louisville, one morning, while all of us were sadly desponding, I took you both, Victor and John, from Shippingport to Louisville. I had purchased a loaf of bread and some apples; before we reached Louisville you were all hungry, and by the river side we sat down and ate our scanty meal. On that day the world was with me as a blank, and my heart was sorely heavy, for scarcely had I enough to keep my dear ones alive; and yet through these dark ways I was being led to the development of the talents I loved, and which have brought so much enjoyment to us *all*, for it is with deep thankfulness that I record that you, my sons, have passed your lives almost continuously with your dear mother and myself. But I will here stop with one remark.

One of the most extraordinary things among all these adverse circumstances was that I never for a day gave up listening to the songs of our birds, or watching their peculiar habits, or delineating them in the best way that I could; nay, during my deepest troubles I frequently would wrench myself from the persons around me, and retire to some secluded part of our noble forests; and many a time, at the sound of the wood-thrush's melodies have I fallen on my knees, and there prayed earnestly to our God.

This never failed to bring me the most valuable of thoughts and always comfort, and, strange as it may seem to you, it was often necessary for me to exert my will, and compel myself to return to my fellow-beings.

To speak more fully on some of the incidents which Audubon here relates, I turn to one of the two journals which are all that fire has spared of the many volumes which were filled with his fine, rather illegible handwriting previous to 1826. In the earlier of these journals I read: "I went to France not only to escape Da Costa, but even more to obtain my father's consent to my marriage with my Lucy, and this simply because I thought it my moral and religious duty to do so. But although my request was immediately granted, I remained in France nearly two years. As I told you, Mr. Bakewell considered my Lucy too young (she was then but seventeen), and me too unbusiness-like to marry; so my father decided that I should remain some months with him, and on returning to America it was his plan to associate me with some one whose commercial knowledge would be of value to me.

"My father's beautiful country seat, situated within sight of the Loire, about mid-distance between Nantes and the sea, I found quite delightful to my taste, notwithstanding the frightful cruelties I had witnessed in that vicinity, not many years previously. The gardens, greenhouses, and all appertaining to it appeared to me then as if of a superior cast; and my father's physician was above all a young man precisely after my own heart; his name was D'Orbigny, and with his young wife and infant son he lived not far distant. The doctor was a good fisherman, a good hunter, and fond of all objects in nature. Together we searched the woods, the fields, and the banks of the Loire, procuring every bird we could, and I made drawings of every one of them — very bad, to be sure, but still they were of assistance to me. The lessons which I had received from the great David[1] now proved all-important to me, but what I wanted, and what I had the good fortune to stumble upon a few years later, was the

[1] Jacques Louis David (1748–1825), court painter to Louis XVI. and afterwards to Napoleon I.

knowledge of putting up my models, in true and good positions according to the ways and habits of my beautiful feathered subjects. During these happy years I managed to make drawings of about two hundred species of birds, all of which I brought to America and gave to my Lucy.[1]

"At last my father associated me with Ferdinand Rozier, as you already know, and we were fairly smuggled out of France; for he was actually an officer attached to the navy of that country, and though I had a passport stating I was born at New Orleans, my French name would have swept that aside very speedily. Rozier's passport was a Dutch one, though he did not understand a single word in that language. Indeed, our passengers were a medley crowd; two days out two monks appeared among us from the hold, where our captain had concealed them."

This same "medley crowd" appears to have comprised many refugees from the rule of Napoleon, this being about 1806, and the amusements were varied, including both gaming and dancing. To quote again: "Among the passengers was a handsome Virginian girl, young and graceful. She was constantly honored by the attentions of two Frenchmen who belonged to the nobility; both were fine young fellows, travelling, as was not uncommon then, under assumed names. One lovely day the bonnet of the fair lady was struck by a rope and knocked overboard. One of the French chevaliers at once leaped

[1] In 1836, Audubon wrote to Dr. John Bachman: "Some of my early drawings of European birds are still in our possession, but many have been given away, and the greatest number were destroyed, not by the rats that gnawed my collection of the "Birds of America," but by the great fire in New York, as these drawings were considered my wife's special property and seldom out of her sight. Would that the others had been under her especial care also! Yet, after all, who can say that it was not a material advantage, both to myself and to the world, that the Norway rats destroyed those drawings?"

into the ocean, captured the bonnet, and had the good fortune to be picked up himself by the yawl. On reaching the deck he presented the bonnet with a graceful obeisance and perfect *sang froid*, while the rival looked at him as black as a raven. No more was heard of the matter till dawn, when reports of firearms were heard; the alarm was general, as we feared pirates. On gaining the deck it was found that a challenge had been given and accepted, a duel had positively taken place, ending, alas! in the death of the rescuer of the bonnet. The young lady felt this deeply, and indeed it rendered us all very uncomfortable."

The voyage ended, Audubon returned to Mill Grove, where he remained some little time before his marriage to Lucy Bakewell. It was a home he always loved, and never spoke of without deep feeling. His sensitive nature, romantic if you will, was always more or less affected by environment, and Mill Grove was a most congenial spot to him.

This beautiful estate in Montgomery Co., Pa., lies in a lovely part of the country. The house, on a gentle eminence, almost a natural terrace, overlooks, towards the west, the rapid waters of Perkiomen Creek, which just below empties into the Schuylkill river, across which to the south is the historic ground of Valley Forge. The property has remained in the Wetherill family nearly ever since Audubon sold it to Samuel Wetherill in 1813. The present owner[1] delights to treasure every trace of the bird lover, and not only makes no changes in anything that he can in the least degree associate with him, but has added many photographs and engravings of Audubon which adorn his walls.

The house, of the usual type of those days, with a hall passing through the centre and rooms on either side, was built of rubble-stone by Roland Evans in 1762, and in

[1] Mr. W. H. Wetherill, of Philadelphia.

1774 was sold to Admiral Audubon, who in the year following built an addition, also of rubble-stone. This addition is lower than the main house, which consists of two full stories and an attic with dormer windows, where, it is said, Audubon kept his collections. The same Franklin stove is in the parlor which stood there giving out its warmth and cheer when the young man came in from the hunting and skating expeditions on which he loved to dwell. The dense woods which once covered the ground are largely cut down, but sufficient forest growth remains to give the needed shade and beauty; the hemlocks in particular are noticeable, so large and of such perfect form.

Going down a foot-path to Perkiomen Creek, a few steps lead to the old mill which gave the place its name. Built of stone and shaded by cottonwood trees, the stream rushing past as in days long gone, the mill-wheel still revolves, though little work is done there now.

When I saw Mill Grove[1] the spring flowers were abundant; the soft, pale blossom of the May-apple (*Podophyllum peltatum*) held its head above the blue of many violets, the fingers of the potentilla with their yellow stars crept in and out among the tangled grass and early undergrowth; the trilliums, both red and white, were in profusion; in the shade the wood anemones, with their shell pink cups grew everywhere, while in damp spots by the brook yet remained a few adder's-tongues, and under the hemlocks in the clefts of the rocks the delicate foliage of the Dutchmen's breeches (*Dicentra cucullaria*) with a few late blossoms; all these and many more which I do not now recall, Audubon has pictured with the birds found in the same regions, as his imperishable tribute to the home he loved — Mill-Grove Farm on the Perkiomen Creek.

Fatland Ford, to the south of Mill Grove, is a far larger and grander mansion than that of the modest Quaker Evans; as one approaches, the white columns of the

[1] April 28, 1893.

imposing entrance are seen for some distance before entering the avenue which leads to the front of the mansion. Like Mill Grove it stands on a natural terrace, and has an extensive outlook over the Schuylkill and Valley Forge. This house was built by James Vaux in 1760. He was a member of the Society of Friends and an Englishman, but in sympathy with the colonists. One end of Sullivan's Bridge was not far from the house; the spot where it once stood is now marked by the remains of a red-sandstone monument.[1] Washington spent a night in the mansion house with Mr. Vaux, and left only twelve hours in advance of the arrival of Howe, who lodged there the following night.[2] The old walled garden still remains, and the stable with accommodation for many horses. A little withdrawn from all these and on the edge of a wood are "the graves of a household," not neglected, as is so often the case, but preserved and cared for by those who own Fatland Farm[3] as well as Mill Grove.

Dear as Mill Grove was to Audubon, he left it with his young bride the day following their wedding, which took place at Fatland Ford on April 8, 1808, and departed for Louisville, Ky., where he and Rozier, his partner, had previously done some business. Though they had both lost money they liked the place, which reason seemed quite sufficient to decide them to return and lose more money, as they promptly did. They remained at Louisville till 1810,

1 "I have often seen the red-sandstone monument placed to mark the terminal of the Sullivan Bridge on our side of the river, but the curiosity hunters have so marred it that only 'livans' and part of the date remain." (Extract from letter of Mr. W. H. Wetherill, Aug. 12, 1893.)

2 This statement is from the "Pennsylvania Magazine of History and Biography," vol. xiv., No. 2, page 218, July, 1890.

3 "Under the will of Col. Jno. Macomb Wetherill, late owner of Fatland Farm, 40 feet square were deeded out of the farm, and placed in trust, and $1000 trusteed to keep the grove and lot in order. A granite curb and heavy iron rail surround this plot; Col. Wetherill was buried there and his remains lie with those of your ancestors." (Extract from letter of W. H. Wetherill, May 10, 1897.)

when they moved to Henderson, where Rozier did what business was done, and Audubon drew, fished, hunted, and rambled in the woods to his heart's content, but his purse's depletion. He describes this life in the episode "Fishing in the Ohio," and in these rushing times such an Arcadian existence seems impossible. Small wonder that his wife's relatives, with their English thrift, lost patience with him, could not believe he was aught but idle, because he did not work their way. I doubt not many would think, as they did, that he wasted his days, when in truth he was laying up stores of knowledge which later in life brought him a rich harvest. Waiting times are always long, longest to those who do not understand the silent inner growth which goes on and on, yet makes no outward sign for months and even years, as in the case of Audubon.

Henderson was then a tiny place, and gains being small if any, Rozier and Audubon, in December, 1810, started for St. Geneviève, spent their winter in camp, and reached their destination when the ice broke up. On April 11, 1811, they dissolved partnership, and wrote each as they felt, Audubon saying: "Rozier cared only for money and liked St. Geneviève;" Rozier writing: "Audubon had no taste for commerce, and was continually in the forest."

Once more, however, he went to St. Geneviève to try to get money Rozier owed him, and returned to Henderson on foot, still unpaid, in February or March of 1812. He had gone with a party of Osage Indians, but his journey back was made alone. He writes in his journal, simply with date of April, 1812: —

"Bidding Rozier good-bye, I whistled to my dog, crossed the Mississippi and went off alone and on foot, bent on reaching Shawanee Town as soon as possible; but little had I foreseen the task before me, for soon as I had left the river lands and reached the prairies, I found them covered with water, like large lakes; still nothing would have made me retrace my steps, and the thoughts of my

Lucy and my boy made me care little what my journey might be. Unfortunately I had no shoes, and my moccasins constantly slipping made the wading extremely irksome; notwithstanding, I walked forty-five miles and swam the Muddy River. I only saw two cabins that day, but I had great pleasure in viewing herds of Deer crossing the prairie, like myself ankle deep in water. Their beautiful movements, their tails spread to the breeze, were perceivable for many miles. A mound covered with trees through which a light shone, gave me an appetite, and I made for it. I was welcomed kindly by the woman of the house, and while the lads inspected my fine double-barrelled gun, the daughters bustled about, ground coffee, fried venison, boiled some eggs, and made me feel at once at home.

"Such hospitality is from the heart, and when the squatter came in, his welcome was not less genuine than that of his family. Night fell; I slept soundly on some bearskins, but long before day was ready to march. My hostess was on the alert; after some breakfast she gave me a small loaf and some venison in a clean rag, and as no money would be received, I gave the lads a flask of gunpowder, a valuable article in those days to a squatter.

"My way lay through woods, and many small crossroads now puzzled me, but I walked on, and must have travelled another forty-five miles. I met a party of Osage Indians encamped, and asked in French to stay with them. They understood me, and before long I had my supper of boiled bear's-fat and pecan-nuts, of which I ate heartily, then lay down with my feet to the fire, and slept so soundly that when I awoke my astonishment was great to find all the Indians had gone hunting, and only left two dogs to keep the camp free from wolves.

"I walked off gayly, my dog full of life, but met no one till four o'clock when I passed the first salt well, and thirty minutes more brought me to Shawanee Town. As I entered the inn I was welcomed by several whom I knew, who had come to purchase salt. I felt no fatigue, ate heartily, slept soundly without being rocked, and having come forty miles had only forty-seven more to walk to reach my home. Early next morning I pursued my way; the ferry boat took me from Illinois to Kentucky, and as night came I found myself with my wife beside me, my child on my knee."

The time from now till 1819 was the most disastrous period of Audubon's life, as regarded his finances. With his brother-in-law, Thomas W. Bakewell, he engaged in various ventures in which, whatever others did, he lost money at every turn. The financial affairs of Kentucky were, it is true, not on a very sound basis, but Audubon frankly acknowledges the fault in many cases was his own. Thomas W. Bakewell was often in New Orleans, where they had a mercantile establishment, and Audubon spent not only days, but weeks and months, at his favorite pursuits. On his journeys to Philadelphia to procure goods he wandered miles in all directions from the main route; when in Henderson he worked, at times, very hard in the mill, for, indeed, he never did anything except intensely; but the cry of the wild geese overhead, the sound of the chattering squirrel, the song of the thrush, the flash of the humming-bird with its jewelled throat, were each and all enough to take him from work he hated as he never hated anything else.

When first in Henderson he bought land, and evidently had some idea of remaining there permanently; for, "on March 16, 1816, he and Mr. Bakewell took a ninety-five years' lease of a part of the river front between First and Second Sts., intending to erect a grist and saw mill, which mill was completed in 1817, and yet stands, though now incorporated in the factory of Mr. David Clark. The weather-boarding whip-sawed out of yellow poplar is still intact on three sides, the joists are of unhewn logs, and the foundation walls of pieces of flat broken rock are four and a half feet thick. For those days it was built on a large scale, and did the sawing for the entire country." [1]

It has been said that the inside walls had many drawings of birds on them, but this, while quite likely, has never been proved; what was proved conclusively is that, from his woodcutters, whose labors were performed on a tract of forest land of about 1200 acres, which Audubon purchased from the government, to those who were his partners, by far the greater number had the advantage of him. The New Orleans venture has a similar record; money left him by his father was lost by the failure of the merchant who held it until Audubon could prove his right to it, and finally he left Henderson absolutely penniless. He writes: "Without a dollar in the world, bereft of all revenues beyond my own personal talents and acquirements, I left my dear log house, my delightful garden and orchards with that heaviest of burdens, a heavy heart, and turned my face toward Louisville. This was the saddest of all my journeys, — the only time in my life when the Wild Turkeys that so often crossed my path, and the thousands of lesser birds that enlivened the woods and the prairies, all looked like enemies, and I turned my eyes from them, as if I could have wished that they had never existed."

From Louisville Audubon went almost at once to Shippingport, where he was kindly received by his friends Nicholas Berthoud, who was also his brother-in-law, and the Tarascon family. Here he was joined by his wife and two sons, Victor Gifford and John Woodhouse, and again I quote from Audubon's own words: "As we were straitened to the very utmost, I undertook to draw portraits at the low price of five dollars per head, in black chalk. I drew a few gratis, and succeeded so well that ere many days had elapsed I had an abundance of work;

[1] From "History of Henderson County, Kentucky," by E. L. Starling, page 794.

and being industrious both by nature and habit I produced a great number of those black-chalk sketches."
This carried him on for some months, but the curse, or blessing, of the "wandering foot" was his, and as soon as money matters were a little ahead, off he went again to the forests. It was during these years, that is from 1811 to 1819, that many months were passed hunting with the Indians, the Osage tribe being the one whose language Audubon spoke. Late in life he wrote: "Of all the Indian tribes I know, the Osage are by far the superior." With them he delighted to track the birds and quadrupeds as only an Indian or one of like gifts, can; from them he learned much woodcraft; with them he strengthened his already iron constitution; and in fearlessness, endurance, patience, and marvellously keen vision, no Indian surpassed him.

He had a wonderful gift of making and retaining friends, and even in these days of poverty and depression he never seemed too poor to help others; and certainly from others he received much kindness, which he never ceased to remember and acknowledge. Through one of these friends — I believe a member of the Tarascon family — he was offered a position in the Museum at Cincinnati. Without delay, or any written agreement, Audubon and his family were again (1818) in new surroundings, and the work being congenial, he entered heartily into it with Mr. Robert Best. The promised salary was large, but being never paid Audubon began drawing classes to support his modest household. In Cincinnati he first met Mr. Daniel Mallory (whose second daughter afterwards married Victor G. Audubon) and Captain Samuel Cummings. This latter gentleman had many tastes similar to Audubon's, and later went with him to New Orleans.

The life at Cincinnati was one of strict economy. Mrs. Audubon was a woman of great ability and many re-

[1] Of these many sketches few can be traced, and none purchased.

John J. Audubon

FROM THE MINIATURE BY F. CRUIKSHANK, PUBLISHED BY ROBERT HAVELL,
January 12, 1835.

sources, and with one less gifted her unpractical husband would have fared far worse than he did. To quote again: "Our living here [Cincinnati] is extremely moderate; the markets are well supplied and cheap, beef only two and a half cents a pound, and I am able to provide a good deal myself; Partridges are frequently in the streets, and I can shoot Wild Turkeys within a mile or so; Squirrels and Woodcock are very abundant in the season, and fish always easily caught."

Even with these advantages, Audubon, receiving no money[1] from Dr. Drake, president of the Museum, decided on going to New Orleans. He had now a great number of drawings and the idea of publishing these had suggested itself both to him and his wife. To perfect his collection he planned going through many of the Southern States, then pushing farther west, and thence returning to Cincinnati. On Oct. 12, 1820, he left Cincinnati with Captain Samuel Cummings for New Orleans, but with a long pause at Natchez, did not reach that city before mid-winter, where he remained with varying success until the summer of 1821, when he took a position as tutor in the family of Mrs. Charles Percy of Bayou Sara. Here, in the beloved Louisiana whose praises he never wearied of singing, whose magnolia woods were more to him than palaces, whose swamps were storehouses of treasures, he stayed till autumn, when, all fear of yellow fever being over, he sent for his wife and sons. Many new drawings had been made in this year of separation from them, and these were by far the greater part of the furniture in the little house in Dauphine St., to which he took his family on their arrival in December, 1821.

The former life of drawing portraits, giving lessons, painting birds, and wandering through the country, began again, though there was less of this last, Audubon realizing

[1] Mrs. Audubon afterwards received four hundred dollars, of the twelve hundred dollars due; the remainder was never paid.

that he *must* make money. He had had to use strong persuasions to induce Mrs. Audubon to join him in New Orleans. She had relatives in Cincinnati, as well as many friends, and several pupils brought her a small income. Who, recalling her early married life, can wonder that she hesitated before leaving this home for the vicissitudes of an unknown city? She and her husband were devotedly attached to each other, but she thought more of the uncertainty for her sons than for herself. They were now boys of twelve and nine years old, and their mother, whose own education was far beyond the average, realized how unwise a thing for them the constant change was. Audubon was most anxious also that his "Kentucky lads," as he often called them, should be given every advantage, but he had the rare quality of being able to work equally well in any surroundings, in doors or out, and he failed to understand why others could not, just as he failed to see why his wife should ever doubt the desirability of going anywhere, at any time, under any conditions. He thus writes to her in a letter, dated New Orleans, May 3, 1821: "Thou art not, it seems, as daring as I am about leaving one place to go to another, without the means. I am sorry for that. I never will fear want as long as I am well; and if God will grant me health with the little talents I have received from Nature, I would dare go to England or anywhere, without one cent, one single letter of introduction to any one."

This, as we know, was no empty boast, but the principle on which Audubon proceeded numberless times in his life. His own courage, or persuasions, brought his wife, as has been said, to join him in the Crescent City, and here as elsewhere that noble woman proved her courage and endurance fully equal to his, although perhaps in another line.

Under the date of January 1, 1822, Audubon writes: "Two months and five days have elapsed before I could venture to dispose of one hundred and twenty-five cents to pay for this book, that probably, like all other things in the world, is ashamed to find me so poor." On March 5th of the same year: "During January my time was principally spent in giving lessons in painting and drawing, to supply my family and pay for the schooling of Victor and Johnny at a Mr. Branards', where they received notions of geography, arithmetic, grammar, and writing, for six dollars per month each. Every moment I had to spare I drew birds for my ornithology, in which my Lucy and myself alone have faith. February was spent in drawing birds strenuously, and I thought I had improved much by applying coats of water-color under the pastels, thereby preventing the appearance of the paper, that in some instances marred my best productions. I discovered also many imperfections in my earlier drawings, and formed the resolution to redraw the whole of them; consequently I hired two French hunters, who swept off every dollar that I could raise for specimens. I have few acquaintances; my wife and sons are more congenial to me than all others in the world, and we have no desire to force ourselves into a society where every day I receive fewer bows."

This winter (1821–1822) in New Orleans, proved to Audubon that his wife's judgment was correct; it was not the place for them to make either a permanent income or home. True, they had been able to live with extreme simplicity, and to send the boys to school; they had had their own pleasures, as the worn, brown volume, the journal of 1822–24, with its faded entries, bears witness. There are accounts of walks and of musical evenings when they were joined by one or two friends of like tastes and talents. Both played well, she on the piano, and he on a variety of instruments, principally the violin, flute, and flageolet. For over two months a fifth inmate was added to the home circle in Mr. Matabon, a former friend, whom Audubon found one morning in the market, in a state of great poverty. He at once took him to his house and kept him as a guest, till, like Micawber, "something turned up" for him to do. When this gentleman left, this entry is made: "Mr. Matabon's departure is regretted by us all, and we shall sorely miss his beautiful music on the flute."

Summer approaching, when those who purchased pictures and took drawing-lessons were about to leave the city, Audubon accepted a position as tutor in the household of a Mr. Quaglas near Natchez. Mrs. Audubon, who had for some time been teaching in the family of Mr. Brand, removed to that gentleman's house with her sons; they, however, were almost immediately sent to school at Washington, nine miles from Natchez, Audubon's salary enabling him to do this, and in September he was joined by his wife.

While at Natchez, the long summer days permitted the drawing of birds as well as the teaching, which was conscientiously performed, and the hope of eventually publishing grew stronger. In the autumn of this year (1822), Audubon met a portrait painter named John Steen or Stein, from Washington, Pa., and thus writes, December, 1822: "He gave me the first lesson in painting in oils I ever took in my life; it was a copy of an Otter from one of my water-colors. Together we painted a full length portrait of Père Antonio, which was sent to Havana."

January, 1823, brought fresh changes. Mrs. Audubon, with her son John, went to Mrs. Percy's plantation, Beechwoods, to teach not only Marguerite Percy, but also the daughters of the owners of the neighboring plantations, and Audubon, with Victor and Mr. Steen, started on a tour of the Southern States in a dearborn, intending to paint for their support. The journal says, March, 1823; "I regretted deeply leaving my Natchez friends, especially Charles Carré and Dr. Provan. The many birds I had collected to take to France I made free; some of the doves had become so fond of me that I was obliged to chase them to the woods, fearing the wickedness of the boys, who would, no doubt, have with pleasure destroyed them." So it would seem boys then were much the same as now. Jackson and other places were visited, and finally New Orleans, whence Audubon started for Louisville with Victor, May 1. The whole of this summer (1823) was one of enjoyment in many ways to the naturalist. He felt his wife was in a delightful home (where she remained many years), beloved by those around her; Victor now was nearly fourteen, handsome, strong, and very companionable, old for his years, and as his father was always young for his, they were good comrades, and till both were attacked by yellow fever, the days passed smoothly on. Nursed through this malady by the ever devoted wife and mother, who had come to them at once on hearing they were ill, some time was spent at the Beechwoods to recuperate, and on October 1, 1823, Audubon with Victor departed for Kentucky by boat. The water being low, their progress was greatly delayed; he became impatient and at Trinity left the boat with his son and two gentlemen, and walked to Louisville. This walk, of which we have a full published account[1] began on October 15, and on the 21st they reached Green River, when Victor becoming weary, the remaining distance was performed in a wagon. It was on this journey, which Audubon undertook fearing, so he says, that he should not have enough money to provide for himself and Victor in Louisville beyond a few weeks, that he relates this incident: "The squatter had a Black Wolf, perfectly gentle, and completely under the control of his master; I put my hand in my pocket and took out a hundred-dollar bill, which I offered for it, but it was refused. I respected the man for his attachment to the wolf, for I doubted if he had ever seen a hundred dollars before."

Louisville was speedily quitted for Shippingport, where

[1] See Episode: "A Tough Walk for a Youth."

Audubon engaged a room for Victor and himself, and painted all winter (1823–24) at birds, landscapes, portraits, and even signs.

Shippingport was then a small village with mills, and was largely owned by the Tarascons and Berthouds, the latter living in the mansion of the place, and possessed of a very beautiful garden. Steamers and boats for the river traffic were built here, and it was a stirring place for its size, situated on the Falls of the Ohio, about two miles from Louisville then, but now part of that city. With forests and river to solace his anxieties, another season was passed by the man whose whole energies were now bent on placing his work before the best judges in Europe. This winter too, he lost one of his best and dearest friends, Madame Berthoud; how he felt this parting his own words best tell: "January 20, 1824. I arose this morning by that transparent light which is the effect of the moon before dawn, and saw Dr. Middleton passing at full gallop towards the white house; I followed — alas! my old friend was dead! What a void in the world for me! I was silent; many tears fell from my eyes, accustomed to sorrow. It was impossible for me to work; my heart, restless, moved from point to point all round the compass of my life. Ah, Lucy! what have I felt to-day! how can I bear the loss of our truest friend? This has been a sad day, most truly; I have spent it thinking, thinking, learning, weighing my thoughts, and quite sick of life. I wished I had been as quiet as my venerable friend, as she lay for the last time in her room."

As I turn over the pages of this volume [1] from which only a few extracts have been taken, well do I understand the mental suffering of which it tells so constantly. Poverty for himself, Audubon did not mind, but for those he loved it was a great and bitter trial to him. His keenly sensitive nature was wounded on every hand; no one but

[1] The before-mentioned journal, 1822–24.

his wife, from whom he was now absent, had any faith in him or his genius. He never became indifferent, as most of us do, to the coldness of those who had in earlier days sought him, not for what he *was*, but for what he *had.* Chivalrous, generous, and courteous to his heart's core, he could not believe others less so, till painful experiences taught him; then he was grieved, hurt, but never imbittered; and more marvellous yet, with his faith in his fellows as strong as ever, again and again he subjected himself to the same treatment. This was not stupidity, nor dulness of perception; it was that always, even to the end, Audubon kept the freshness of childhood; he was one of those who had "the secret of youth;" he was "old in years only, his heart was young. The earth was fair; plants still bloomed, and birds still sang for him."[1] It has been hard for me to keep from copying much from this journal, but I have felt it too sacred. Some would see in it the very heart of the man who wrote it, but to others — and the greater number — it would be, as I have decided to leave it, a sealed book.

Early in March, 1824, Audubon left Shippingport for Philadelphia, Victor remaining in the counting-house of Mr. Berthoud. He had some money, with which he decided to take lessons in painting either from Rembrandt Peale or Thomas Sully. He much preferred the latter both as artist and friend, and he remained in Philadelphia from April until August of the same year. This visit was marked by his introduction to Charles Lucien Bonaparte[2]

[1] (With slight alterations) from "Bird Life," by F. M. Chapman, 1897, p. 13.

[2] Prince of Musignano, and subsequently a distinguished ornithologist. In March, 1824, Bonaparte was just publishing his "Observations on the Nomenclature of Wilson's Ornithology," which ran through the "Journal of the Academy of Natural Sciences," of Philadelphia, from April 5, 1824, to Aug. 25, 1825, in five parts. This was preliminary to Bonaparte's "American Ornithology," which appeared in four quarto vols., 1825–33, to his "Synopsis," of 1828, and to his "Comparative List," of 1838. — E. C.

and Edward Harris, both of whom became life-long friends, especially Mr. Harris, with whom he corresponded frequently when they were separated, and with whom he made many journeys, the most prolonged and important being that to the Yellowstone in 1843. To copy again: "April 10, 1824. I was introduced to the son of Lucien Bonaparte, nephew of Napoleon, a great ornithologist, I was told. He remained two hours, went out, and returned with two Italian gentlemen, and their comments made me very contented." That evening he was taken to the Philosophical Academy[1] where the drawings were greatly admired, and their author says: "*I* do not think much of them except when in the very act of drawing them." At this meeting Mr. George Ord met Audubon and objected strongly to the birds and plants being drawn together, "but spoke well of them otherwise." Mr. Ord was one of those (of the very few, I might say) who disliked the naturalist from first to last,[2] who was perhaps, his bitterest enemy. In later years Dr. John Bachman resented his conduct, and wrote a very trenchant reply[3] to one of Mr. Ord's published articles about Audubon; but there is no word of anger anywhere in the letters or journals, only of regret or pain.[4]

Of Mr. Harris we find this: "July 12, 1824. I drew for Mr. Fairman a small grouse to be put on a bank-note belonging to the State of New-Jersey; this procured me the acquaintance of a young man named Edward Harris of Moorestown, an ornithologist, who told me he had seen

[1] Probably the Academy of Natural Sciences.

[2] Ord had edited the posthumous vols. viii. and ix. of "Wilson's Ornithology," which appeared in 1814; and in 1824 was engaged upon that edition of Wilson which was published in 3 vols. 8vo, in 1828–29, with a folio atlas of 76 plates. This is probably enough to account for his attitude toward Audubon. — E. C.

[3] "Defence of Audubon," by John Bachman. "Bucks Co. Intelligencer," 1835, and other papers.

[4] Almost the only other enemy Audubon appears to have ever had in public print was Charles Waterton, who vehemently assailed him in "Lou-

some English Snipes[1] within a few days, and that they bred in the marshes about him." And also: "July 19th. Young Harris, God bless him, looked at the drawings I had for sale, and said he would take them *all*, at my prices. I would have kissed him, but that it is not the custom in this icy city."

Other friends were made here, almost as valuable as Mr. Harris, though not as well *loved*, for these two were truly congenial souls, who never wearied of each other, and between whom there was never a shadow of difference. Thomas Sully, the artist, Dr. Richard Harlan,[2] Reuben

don's Magazine of Natural History," vi. 1833, pp. 215–218, and vii., 1834, pp. 66–74. Audubon was warmly defended by his son Victor in the same magazine, vi. 1833, p. 369, and at greater length by "R. B.," *ibid.*, pp. 369–372. Dr. Coues characterizes Waterton's attack as "flippant and supercilious animadversion," in "Birds of the Colorado Valley," 1878, p. 622.

The present is hardly the occasion to bring up the countless reviews and notices of Audubon's published life-work; but a few references I have at hand may be given. One of the earliest, if not the first, appeared in the "Edinburgh Journal of Science," vi. p. 184 (1827). In 1828, Audubon himself published "An Account of the Method of Drawing Birds," etc., in the same Journal, viii., pp. 48–54. The "Report of a Committee appointed by the Lyceum of Natural History of New York to examine the splendid work of Mr. Audubon," etc., appeared in "Silliman's Journal," xvi., 1829, pp. 353, 354. His friend William Swainson published some highly commendatory and justly appreciative articles on the same subject in "Loudon's Magazine," i., 1829, pp. 43–52, and in the "Edinburgh New Philosophical Journal," x., 1831, pp. 317–332, under the pseudonym "Ornithophilus." Another anonymous review, highly laudatory, appeared in the same Journal, xviii., 1834, pp. 131–144. Dr. John Bachman defended the truthfulness of Audubon's drawings in the "Journal of the Boston Society of Natural History," i. 1834, pp. 15–31. One of the most extended notices appeared anonymously in the "North American Review," July, 1835, pp. 194–231; and another signed "B," in "Loudon's Magazine," viii., 1835, pp. 184–190. In Germany, "Isis von Oken" contained others, xxx., 1837, pp. 922-928, xxxv., 1842, pp. 157, 158; and xxxvii., 1844, pp. 713–718. "Silliman's Journal" again reviewed the work in xlii., 1842, pp. 130–136. — E. C.

[1] That is the species now known as Wilson's Snipe, *Gallinago delicata.*

[2] Dr. Richard Harlan is the author of the well-known "Fauna Americana," 8vo, Philadelphia, 1825, and of many scientific papers. Audubon dedicated to him the Black Warrior, *Falco harlani*, a large, dark hawk of the genus *Buteo*, shot at St. Francisville, La., Nov. 18, 1829.

Haines, Le Sueur,[1] Dr. Mease, and many another honored name might be given.

In August Philadelphia was quitted, and another period of travel in search of birds was begun. Of this next year, 1825, no record whatever can be found besides the episodes of "Niagara" and "Meadville," and two detached pages of journal. Audubon went to New York, up the Hudson, along the Great Lakes, then to Pittsburg, and finally to Bayou Sara, where, having decided to go to England, he made up his mind to resume at once his classes in drawing, music, and dancing, to make money for the European journey, for which he never ceased to accumulate pictures of his beloved birds. Reaching Bayou Sara in December, 1825, this work at once began by giving lessons in dancing to the young ladies under my grandmother's care; and Judge Randolph, a near neighbor, had his sons take lessons in fencing. In these branches Audubon was so successful that the residents of the village of Woodville, fifteen miles distant, engaged him for Friday and Saturday of each week, and here he had over sixty pupils. From the account of this class I take the following: "I marched to the hall with my violin under my arm, bowed to the company assembled, tuned my violin; played a cotillon, and began my lesson by placing the gentlemen in a line. Oh! patience support me! how I labored before I could promote the first appearance of elegance or ease of motion; in doing this I first broke my bow, and then my violin; I then took the ladies and made them take steps, as I sang in time to accompany their movements."

These lessons continued three months, and were in every sense a success, Audubon realizing about $2000

[1] Charles Alexandre Le Sueur, 1778–1846, distinguished French naturalist. Best biography in Youman's "Pioneers of Science in America," 8vo, N. Y., 1896, pp. 128–139, with portrait. The same volume contains a biographical sketch of Audubon, pp. 152–166, with portrait after the oil painting by George P. A. Healy, belonging to the Boston Society of Natural History. — E. C.

from his winter's work. With this, and the greater part of the savings of his wife, which she had hoarded to forward this journey, so long the goal of their hopes, another farewell was taken, the many valued drawings packed up, and on April 26, 1826, the vessel with the naturalist and his precious freight left New Orleans for England.

The journals from this date, until May 1, 1829, are kept with the usual regularity, and fortunately have escaped the destruction which has befallen earlier volumes. They tell of one of the most interesting periods of Audubon's life, and are given beyond, — not entire, yet so fully that I pass on at once to the last date they contain, which marks Audubon's return to America, May 5, 1829.

His time abroad had seen the publication of the "Birds of America"[1] successfully begun, had procured him sub-

[1] Of the great folios, parts i.–v., containing plates 1–25, were originally published at successive dates (not ascertained) in 1827; parts vi.–x., plates 26–50, appeared in the course of 1828, — all in London. The whole work was completed in 1838; it is supposed to have been issued in 87 parts of 5 plates each, making the actual total of 435 plates, giving 1065 figures of birds. On the completion of the series, the plates were to be bound in 4 vols. Vol. i., pll. 1–100, 1827–30; vol. ii., pll. 101–200, 1831–34; vol. iii., pll. 201–300, 1834–35; vol. iv., pll. 301–435, 1835–38 (completed June 30). These folios had no text except the title-leaf of each volume. The original price was two guineas a part; a complete copy is now worth $1,500 to $2,000, according to condition of binding, etc., and is scarce at any price. The text to the plates appeared under the different title of "Ornithological Biography," in 5 large 8vo volumes, Edinburgh, 1831–39; vol. i., 1831; vol. ii., 1834; vol. iii., 1835; vol. iv., 1838; vol. v., 1839. In 1840–44, the work reappeared in octavo, text and plates together, under the original title of "Birds of America;" the text somewhat modified by the omission of the "Delineations of American Scenery and Manners," the addition of some new matter acquired after 1839, and change in the names of many species to agree with the nomenclature of Audubon's Synopsis of 1839; the plates reduced by the camera lucida, rearranged and renumbered, making 500 in all. The two original works, thus put together and modified, became the first octavo edition called "Birds of America," issued in 100 parts, to be bound in 7 volumes, 1840–44. There have been various subsequent issues, partial or complete, upon which I cannot here enlarge. For full bibliographical data see Dr. Coues' "Birds of the

scribers enough to warrant his continuing the vast undertaking, and had given him many friends. His object now was to make drawings of birds which he had not yet figured for the completion of his work, and then to take his wife, and possibly his sons with him to England. During these years Mrs. Audubon was latterly alone, as John had taken a position with Victor and was in Louisville. Victor, meantime, had worked steadily and faithfully, and had earned for himself a position and a salary far beyond that of most young men of his age. Both parents relied on him to an extent that is proof in itself of his unusual ability; these words in a letter from his father, dated London, Dec. 23, 1828, "Victor's letters to me are highly interesting, full of candor, sentiment, and sound judgment, and I am very proud of him," are certainly testimony worth having. As the years went on both sons assisted their father in every way, and to an extent that the world has never recognized.

Great as was Audubon's wish to proceed without delay to Louisiana, he felt it due to his subscribers to get to work at once, and wrote to his wife under date of New York, May 10, 1829: "I have landed here from on board the packet ship Columbia after an agreeable passage of thirty-five days from Portsmouth. I have come to America to remain as long as consistent with the safety of the continuation of my publication in London without my personal presence. According to future circumstances I shall return to England on the 1st of October next, or, if possible, not until April, 1830. I wish to employ and devote every moment of my sojourn in America to drawing such birds and plants as I think necessary to enable me to give my publication throughout the degree of perfection that I am told exists in that portion already published. I have left my business going on quite well; my

Colorado Valley," Appendix, 1878, pp. 612, 618, 625, 629, 644, 661, 666, 669 and 686. — E. C.

engraver[1] has in his hands all the drawings wanted to complete this present year, and those necessary to form the first number of next year. I have finished the two first years of publication, the two most difficult years to be encountered." To Victor he writes from Camden, N. J., July 10, 1829: "I shall this year have issued ten numbers, each containing five plates, making in all fifty.[2] I cannot publish more than five numbers annually, because it would make too heavy an expense to my subscribers, and indeed require more workmen than I could find in London. The work when finished will contain eighty numbers,[3] therefore I have seventy to issue, which will take fourteen years more. It is a long time to look forward to, but it cannot be helped. I think I am doing well; I have now one hundred and forty-four subscribers."

All this summer and early fall, until October 10th, Audubon spent in the neighborhood of New Jersey and Pennsylvania, working as few can work, four hours continuing to be his allowance for sleep. Six weeks in September and October were spent in the Great Pine Swamp, or Forest,[4] as he called it, his permanent lodgings being at Camden, N. J. Here he writes, October 11, 1829: "I am at work and have done much, but I wish I had eight pairs of hands, and another body to shoot the specimens; still I am delighted at what I have accumulated

[1] Referring to Mr. Robert Havell, of No. 77 Oxford St., London. His name will be recalled in connection with *Sterna havellii*, the Tern which Audubon shot at New Orleans in 1820, and dedicated to his engraver in "Orn. Biogr." v., 1839, p. 122, "B. Amer.," 8vo, vii., 1844, p. 103, pl. 434. It is the winter plumage of the bird Nuttall called *S. forsteri* in his "Manual," ii., 1834, p. 274. See Coues, "Proceedings of the Philadelphia Academy of Science," 1862, p. 543. — E. C.

[2] See previous note on p. 59, where it is said that plates 1–25 appeared in 1827, and plates 26–50 in 1828 — in attestation of which the above words to Victor Audubon become important. — E. C.

[3] It actually ran to 87 numbers, as stated in a previous note.

[4] See Episodes "Great Egg Harbor" and "Great Pine Swamp."

in drawings this season. Forty-two drawings in four months, eleven large, eleven middle size, and twenty-two small, comprising ninety-five birds, from Eagles downwards, with plants, nests, flowers, and sixty different kinds of eggs. I live alone, see scarcely any one, besides those belonging to the house where I lodge. I rise long before day and work till nightfall, when I take a walk, and to bed.

"I returned yesterday from Mauch Chunk; after all, there is nothing perfect but *primitiveness*, and my efforts at copying nature, like all other things attempted by us poor mortals, fall far short of the originals. Few better than myself can appreciate this with more despondency than I do."

Very shortly after this date Audubon left for Louisiana, crossed the Alleghanies to Pittsburg, down the Ohio by boat to Louisville, where he saw Victor and John. "Dear boys!" he says; "I had not seen Victor for nearly five years, and so much had he changed I hardly knew him, but he recognized me at once. Johnny too had much grown and improved." Remaining with his sons a few days, he again took the boat for Bayou Sara, where he landed in the middle of the night. The journal says: "It was dark, sultry, and I was quite alone. I was aware yellow fever was still raging at St. Francisville, but walked thither to procure a horse. Being only a mile distant, I soon reached it, and entered the open door of a house I knew to be an inn; all was dark and silent. I called and knocked in vain, it was the abode of Death alone! The air was putrid; I went to another house, another, and another; everywhere the same state of things existed; doors and windows were all open, but the living had fled. Finally I reached the home of Mr. Nübling, whom I knew. He welcomed me, and lent me his horse, and I went off at a gallop. It was so dark that I soon lost my way, but I cared not, I was about to rejoin my wife, I was in the woods, the woods of Louisiana, my heart was bursting with joy! The first glimpse of dawn set me on my road, at six o'clock I was at Mr. Johnson's house;[1] a servant took the horse, I went at once to my wife's apartment; her door was ajar, already she was dressed and sitting by her piano, on which a young lady was playing. I pronounced her name gently, she saw me, and the next moment I held her in my arms. Her emotion was so great I feared I had acted rashly, but tears relieved our hearts, once more we were together."

Audubon remained in Louisiana with his wife till January, 1830, when together they went to Louisville, Washington, Philadelphia, and New York, whence they sailed for England in April. All his former friends welcomed them on their arrival, and the kindness the naturalist had received on his first visit was continued to his wife as well as himself. Finding many subscribers had not paid, and others had lapsed, he again painted numerous pictures for sale, and journeyed hither and yon for new subscribers as well as to make collections.

Mrs. Audubon, meanwhile, had taken lodgings in London, but that city being no more to her taste than to her husband's, she joined him, and they travelled together till October, when to Audubon's joy he found himself at his old lodgings at 26 George St., Edinburgh, where he felt truly at home with Mrs. Dickie ; and here he began the "Ornithological Biography," with many misgivings, as the journal bears witness: "Oct. 16, 1830. I know that I am a poor writer, that I scarcely can manage to scribble a tolerable English letter, and not a much better one in French, though that is easier to me. I know I am not a scholar, but meantime I am aware that no man living knows better than I do the habits of our birds; no man living has studied them as much as I have done, and with the assistance of my old journals and memorandum-books which were written on the spot, I can at least put down plain truths, which may be useful and perhaps

[1] Mr. Garrett Johnson, where Mrs. Audubon was then teaching.

interesting, so I shall set to at once. I cannot, however, give *scientific* descriptions, and here must have assistance."

His choice of an assistant would have been his friend Mr. William Swainson, but this could not be arranged, and Mr. James Wilson recommended Mr. William MacGillivray.[1] Of this gentleman Mr. D. G. Elliot says:[2] "No better or more fortunate choice could have been made. Audubon worked incessantly, MacGillivray keeping abreast of him, and Mrs. Audubon re-wrote the entire manuscript to send to America, and secure the copyright there." The happy result of this association of two great men, so different in most respects as Audubon and MacGillivray, is characterized by Dr. Coues in the following terms ("Key to North American Birds," 2d ed., 1884, p. xxii): "Vivid and ardent was his genius, matchless he was both with pen and pencil in giving life and spirit to the beautiful objects he delineated with passionate love; but there was a strong and patient worker by his side,—William MacGillivray, the countryman of Wilson, destined to lend the sturdy Scotch fibre to an Audubonian epoch.[3] The brilliant French-American Naturalist was little of a 'scientist.' Of his work the magical beauties of form and color and movement are all his; his page is redolent of Nature's fragrance; but MacGillivray's are the bone and sinew, the hidden anatomical parts beneath the lovely face, the nomenclature, the classification,—in a word, the technicalities of the science."

[1] There has been much question as to the spelling of MacGillivray's name, Professor Newton and most others writing it Macgillivray, but in the autograph letters we own the capital "G" is always used.

[2] Address at the special meeting of the New York Academy of Sciences, April 26, 1893.

[3] Referring to one of the six "epochs" into which, in the same work, Dr. Coues divided the progress of American Ornithology. His "Audubon epoch" extends from 1824 to 1853, and one of the four periods into which this epoch is divided is the "Audubonian period," 1834–1853.

MRS. AUDUBON.

FROM THE MINIATURE BY F. CRUIKSHANK, 1835.

Though somewhat discouraged at finding that no less than three editions of Alexander Wilson's "American Ornithology" were about to be published, Audubon went bravely on. My grandmother wrote to her sons: "Nothing is heard, but the steady movement of the pen; your father is up and at work before dawn, and writes without ceasing all day. Mr. MacGillivray breakfasts at nine each morning, attends the Museum four days in the week, has several works on hand besides ours, and is moreover engaged as a lecturer in a new seminary on botany and natural history. His own work[1] progresses slowly, but surely, for he writes until far into the night."

The first volume of "Ornithological Biography" was finished, but no publisher could be found to take it, so Audubon published it himself in March, 1831.[2] During this winter an agreement had been made with Mr. J. B. Kidd to copy some of the birds, put in backgrounds, sell them, and divide the proceeds. Eight were finished and sold immediately, and the agreement continued till May, 1, 1831, when Audubon was so annoyed by Mr. Kidd's lack of industry that the copying was discontinued. Personally, I have no doubt that many of the paintings which are said to be by Audubon are these copies. They are all on mill-board, — a material, however, which grandfather

[1] Descriptions of the Rapacious Birds of Great Britain. By William MacGillivray, A. M., Edinburgh, 1836, 1 vol. small 8vo. This valuable treatise is dedicated "To John James Audubon, in admiration of his talents as an ornithologist, and in gratitude for many acts of friendship." Mr. MacGillivray also had then in preparation or contemplation his larger "History of British Birds," 3 volumes of which appeared in 1837–40, but the 4th and 5th volumes not till 1852. — E. C.

[2] The completed volume bears date of MDCCCXXXI. on the titlepage and the publisher's imprint of "Adam Black, 55, North Bridge, Edinburgh." The collation is pp. i–xxiv, 1–512, + 15 pp. of Prospectus, etc. This is the text to plates I.–C. (1–100) of the elephant folios. Other copies are said to bear the imprint of "Philadelphia, E. L. Carey and A. Hart, MDCCCXXXI." — E. C.

Audubon wrote to Dr. Richard Harlan on March 13, 1831, "I have sent a copy of the first volume to you to-day."

used himself, so that, as he rarely signed an oil painting,[1] the mill-board is no proof of identity one way or the other.

On April 15, 1831, Mr. and Mrs. Audubon left Edinburgh for London, then went on to Paris, where there were fourteen subscribers. They were in France from May until the end of July, when London again received them. On August 2d they sailed for America, and landed on September 4th. They went to Louisville at once, where Mrs. Audubon remained with her sons, and the naturalist went south, his wish being to visit Florida and the adjacent islands. It was on this trip that, stopping at Charleston, S. C., he made the acquaintance of the Rev. John Bachman[2] in October, 1831. The two soon became the closest friends, and this friendship was only severed by death. Never were men more dissimilar in character, but both were enthusiastic and devoted naturalists; and herein was the bond, which later was strengthened by the marriages of Victor and John to Dr. Bachman's two eldest daughters.[3]

The return from Florida in the spring of 1832 was followed by a journey to New Brunswick and Maine, when, for the first time in many years, the whole family travelled together. They journeyed in the most leisurely manner, stopping where there were birds, going on when they found none, everywhere welcomed, everywhere finding those willing to render assistance to the "American backwoodsman" in his researches. Audubon had the simplicity and charm of manner which interested others at once, and his old friend Dr. Bachman understood this when he

[1] We only possess one oil painting signed "Audubon."

[2] John Bachman, D. D., LL. D., Ph. D., Feb. 4, 1790–April 24, 1874. Author of many works, scientific, zoölogical, and religious. For sixty years he was pastor of St. John's Lutheran Church, Charleston, S. C.

[3] Both these daughters died young, — Maria, the eldest, who married John, before she was twenty-four; Eliza, who married Victor, still younger, during the first year of her wedded life.

wrote: "Audubon has *given* to him what nobody else can *buy*." On this Maine journey, the friendship between the Lincolns at Dennysville, begun in the wanderer's earlier years, was renewed, and with this hospitable family Mrs. Audubon remained while her husband and sons made their woodland researches.

In October of 1832, Victor sailed for England, to superintend the publishing of the work; his father remained in America drawing and re-drawing, much of the time in Boston, where, as everywhere, many friends were made, and where he had a short, but severe illness — an unusual experience with him. In the spring of 1833, the long proposed trip to Labrador was planned and undertaken. The schooner "Ripley," Captain Emery commanding, was chartered. Audubon was accompanied by five young men, all under twenty-four years of age, namely: Joseph Coolidge, George C. Shattuck, William Ingalls, Thomas Lincoln and John Woodhouse, the naturalist's younger son. On June 6 they sailed for the rocky coasts and storm-beaten islands, which are so fully described in the Labrador Journal, now first published entire in the present work.

Victor was still in England, and to him his father wrote, on May 16, 1833, a long letter filled with careful directions as to the completion of the work now so far accomplished, and which was so dear — as it is to-day — to all the family. The entire letter is too long and too personal to give beyond a few extracts: "Should the Author of all things deprive us of our lives, work for and comfort the dear being who gave you birth. Work for her, my son, as long as it may be the pleasure of God to grant her life; never neglect her a moment; in a word, prove to her that you are truly *a son!* Continue the publication of our work to the last; you have in my journals all necessary facts, and in yourself sufficient ability to finish the letter-press, with the assistance of our worthy friend John Bachman, as well as MacGillivray. If you should deem it wise to remove the publication of the work to this country, I advise you to settle in Boston; *I have faith in the Bostonians.* I entreat you to be careful, industrious, and persevering; pay every one most punctually, and never permit your means to be over-reached. May the blessings of those who love you be always with you, supported by those of Almighty God."

During the Labrador voyage, which was both arduous and expensive, many bird-skins (seventy-three) were prepared and brought back, besides the drawings made, a large collection of plants, and other curiosities. Rough as the experience was, it was greatly enjoyed, especially by the young men. Only one of these[1] is now living (1897), and he bears this testimony to the character of the naturalist, with whom he spent three months in the closest companionship. In a letter to me dated Oct. 9, 1896, he says: "You had only to meet him to love him; and when you had conversed with him for a moment, you looked upon him as an old friend, rather than a stranger. . . . To this day I can see him, a magnificent gray-haired man, childlike in his simplicity, kind-hearted, noble-souled, lover of nature and lover of youth, friend of humanity, and one whose religion was the golden rule."

The Labrador expedition ended with summer, and Mr. and Mrs. Audubon went southward by land, John going by water to meet them at Charleston, S. C., — Victor meanwhile remaining in London. In the ever hospitable home of the Bachmans part of the winter of 1833–34 was spent, and many a tale is told of hunting parties, of camping in the Southern forests, while the drawings steadily increased in number. Leaving Charleston, the travels were continued through North and South Carolina and

[1] Mr. Joseph Coolidge, formerly of Maine, now of San Francisco, Cal. Two others are known by name to every ornithologist through Audubon's *Emberiza shattuckii* and *Fringilla lincolnii*; for these birds see notes beyond. — E. C.

northward to New York, when the three sailed for Liverpool April 16, and joined Victor in London, in May, 1834.

It has been erroneously stated that Audubon kept no journals during this second visit to England and Scotland, for the reasons that his family — for whom he wrote — was with him, and also that he worked so continuously for the "Ornithological Biography;" but this is a mistake. Many allusions to the diaries of these two years from April, 1834, until August, 1836, are found, and conclusive proof is that Victor writes: "On the 19th of July last, 1845, the copper-plates from which the "Birds of America" had been printed were ruined by fire,[1] though not entirely destroyed, as were many of my father's journals, — most unfortunately those which he had written during his residence in London and Edinburgh while writing and publishing the letter-press."

It was at this time that Victor and John went to the Continent for five months, being with their parents the remainder of the time, both studying painting in their respective branches, Victor working at landscapes, John at portraits and birds.

In July, 1836, Audubon and John returned to America, to find that nearly everything in the way of books, papers, the valuable and curious things collected both at home and abroad, had been destroyed in New York in the fire of 1835, Mr. Berthoud's warehouse being one of those blown up with gunpowder to stay the spread of the fire. Mrs. Audubon and Victor remained in London, in the house where they had lived some time, 4 Wimpole St., Cavendish Square. After a few weeks in New York, father and son went by land to Charleston, pausing at Washington and other cities; and being joined by Mr. Edward Harris in the spring of 1837, they left Dr. Bachman's where they had spent the winter, for the purpose

[1] The offices 34 Liberty St., New York, were burned at this time.

of exploring part of the coast of the Gulf of Mexico. This expedition they were assisted in making by Col. John Abert,[1] who procured them the Revenue cutter "Campbell." Fire having afterward (in 1845) destroyed the journals of this period, only a few letters remain to tell us of the coasting voyage to Galveston Bay, Texas, though the ornithological results of this journey are all in the "Birds of America." It was during this visit to Charleston that the plans were begun which led to the "Quadrupeds of North America," under the joint authorship of Audubon and Bachman.[2]

In the late summer of 1837, Audubon, with John and his wife, — for he had married Maria, Dr. Bachman's eldest daughter, — returned to England, his last voyage there, and remained abroad until the autumn of 1839, when the family, with the addition of the first grandchild,[3] once more landed in America, and settled, if such wanderers can ever be said to settle, in New York, in the then uptown region of 86 White St.

The great ornithological work had been finished, abso-

[1] John James Abert, who was in 1837 brevet lieutenant-colonel of Topographical Engineers, U. S. Army, and afterward chief of his corps. Abert's Squirrel, *Sciurus aberti*, forms the subject of plate 153, fig. 1, of Audubon and Bachman's "Quadrupeds."

[2] This important and standard work on American Mammalogy was not, however, finished till many years afterward, nor did Audubon live to see its completion. Publication of the colored plates in oblong folio, without text, began at least as early as 1840, and with few exceptions they first appeared in this form. They were subsequently reduced to large octavo size, and issued in parts with the text, then first published. The whole, text and plates, were then gathered in 3 volumes: vol. i., 1846; vol. ii., 1851; vol. iii., to page 254 and pl. 150, 1853; vol. iii., p. 255 to end, 1854. There are in all 155 plates; 50 in vol. i., 50 in vol. ii., 55 in vol. iii.; about half of them are from Andubon's brush, the rest by John Woodhouse. The exact character of the joint authorship does not appear; but no doubt the technical descriptions are by Dr. Bachman. Publication was made in New York by Victor Audubon; and there was a reissue of some parts of the work at least, as vol. i. is found with copyright of 1849, and date 1851 on the title. — E. C.

[3] Lucy, now Mrs. Delancey B. Williams.

lutely completed,[1] in the face of incredible delays and difficulties, and representing an amount of work which in these days of easy travel it is hard to comprehend. The "Synopsis" also was published in this year, and the indefatigable worker began at once the octavo edition of the "Birds," and the drawings of the quadrupeds. For this edition of the "Birds" Victor attended almost wholly to the printing and publishing, and John reduced every drawing to the required size with the aid of the camera lucida, Audubon devoting his time to the coloring and obtaining of subscribers.

Having fully decided to settle in New York City, and advised their friends to that effect, Audubon found he could not live in any city, except, as he writes, "perhaps fair Edinburgh;" so in the spring of 1842, the town house was sold, and the family moved to "Minniesland," now known as Audubon Park, in the present limits of New York City. The name came from the fact that my father and uncle always used the Scotch name "Minnie" for mother. The land when bought was deeded to her, and always spoken of as *Minnie's land,* and this became the name which the Audubons gave it, by which to day those of us who are left recall the lovely home where their happy childhood was spent; for here were born all but three of the fourteen grandchildren.

No railroad then separated the lawn from the beach where Audubon so often hauled the seine; the dense

[1] Victor Audubon wrote in reply to a question as to how many copies of the "Birds" were in existence: "About 175 copies; of these I should say 80 were in our own country. The length of time over which the work extended brought many changes to original subscribers, and this accounts for the odd volumes which are sometimes offered for sale."

In stating that the work had been "absolutely completed" in 1838, I must not omit to add that when the octavo reissue appeared it contained a few additional birds chiefly derived from Audubon's fruitful voyage up the Missouri in 1843, which also yielded much material for the work on the Quadrupeds. The appearance of the "Synopsis" in 1839 marks the interval between the completion of the original undertaking and the beginning of plans for its reduction to octavo. — E. C.

woods all around resounded to the songs of the birds he so loved; many animals (deer, elk, moose, bears, wolves, foxes, and smaller quadrupeds) were kept in enclosures — never in cages — mostly about a quarter of a mile distant from the river, near the little building known as the "painting house." What joyous memories are those of the rush out of doors, lessons being over, to the little brook, following which one gathered the early blossoms in their season, or in the autumn cleared out leaves, that its waters might flow unimpeded, and in winter found icicles of wondrous shape and beauty; and just beyond its source stood the painting house, where every child was always welcome,[1] where the wild flowers from hot little hands were painted in the pictures of what we called "the animals," to the everlasting pride and glory of their finder.

It was hoped that only shorter trips would now be taken, and a visit to Canada as far as Quebec was made in August and September of 1842.

But even in this home after his own tastes, where hospitality and simplicity ruled, Audubon could not stay, for his heart had always been set on going farther west, and though both family and friends thought him growing too old for such a journey, he started in March, 1843, for St. Louis, and thence up the Missouri on the steamboat "Omega" of the American Fur Company, which left on its annual trip April 25, 1843, taking up supplies of all sorts, and returning with thousands of skins and furs. Here again Audubon speaks for himself, and I shall not now anticipate his account with words of mine, as the Missouri journal follows in full. He was accompanied on this trip by Mr. Edward Harris, his faithful friend of many years, John G. Bell as taxidermist, Isaac Sprague

[1] "These little folk, of all sizes, sit and play in my room and do not touch the specimens." (Letter of Dr. Bachman, May 11, 1848, to his family in Charleston.)

as artist, and Lewis Squires as secretary and general assistant. With the exception of Mr. Harris, all were engaged by Audubon, who felt his time was short, his duties many, while the man of seventy (?) had no longer the strength of youth.

November of 1843 saw him once more at Minniesland, and the *long* journeys were forever over; but work on the "Quadrupeds" was continued with the usual energy. The next few years were those of great happiness. His valued friend Dr. Thomas M. Brewer, of Boston, visited him in 1846. Writing of him Dr. Brewer says: [1] "The patriarch had greatly changed since I had last seen him. He wore his hair longer, and it now hung down in locks of snowy whiteness on his shoulders. His once piercing gray eyes, though still bright, had already begun to fail him. He could no longer paint with his wonted accuracy, and had at last, most reluctantly, been forced to surrender to his sons the task of completing the illustrations to the "Quadrupeds of North America." Surrounded by his large family, including his devoted wife, his two sons with their wives,[2] and quite a troop of grandchildren, his enjoyments of life seemed to leave him little to desire. . . . A pleasanter scene, or a more interesting household it has never been the writer's good fortune to witness."

Of this period one of his daughters-in-law [3] speaks in her journal as follows: "Mr. Audubon was of a most kindly nature; he never passed a workman or a stranger of either sex without a salutation, such as, 'Good-day, friend,' 'Well, my good man, how do you do?' If a boy, it was, 'Well, my little man,' or a little girl, 'Good morning, lassie, how are you to-day?' All were noticed,

[1] Harper's Monthly Magazine, October, 1880, p. 665.

[2] Both sons had married a second time. Victor had married Georgiana R. Mallory of New York, and John, Caroline Hall of England.

[3] Mrs. V. G. Audubon.

and his pleasant smile was so cordial that all the villagers and work-people far and near, knew and liked him. He painted a little after his return from the Yellowstone River, but as he looked at his son John's animals, he said: 'Ah, Johnny, no need for the old man to paint any more when you can do work like that.' He was most affectionate in his disposition, very fond of his grandchildren, and it was a pleasant sight to see him sit with one on his knee, and others about him, singing French songs in his lively way. It was sweet too, to see him with his wife; he was always her lover, and invariably used the pronouns 'thee' and 'thou' in his speech to her. Often have I heard him say, 'Well, sweetheart! always busy; come sit thee down a few minutes and rest.'"

My mother has told me that when the picture of the Cougars came from Texas, where my father had painted it, my grandfather's delight knew no bounds. He was beside himself with joy that "his boy Johnny" could paint a picture he considered so fine; he looked at it from every point, and could not keep quiet, but walked up and down filled with delight.

Of these years much might be said, but much has already been written of them, so I will not repeat.[1] Many characteristics Audubon kept to the last; his enthusiasm, freshness, and keenness of enjoyment and pain were never blunted. His ease and grace of speech and movement were as noticeable in the aged man as they had been in the happy youth of Mill Grove. His courteous manners to all, high and low, were always the same; his chivalry, generosity, and honor were never dimmed, and his great personal beauty never failed to attract attention; always he was handsome. His stepmother writes from Nantes to her husband in Virginia: "He is the handsomest boy in Nantes, but perhaps not the most studious." At Mill

[1] Reminiscences of Audubon, Scribner's Monthly, July, 1876, p. 333; Turf, Field, and Farm, Nov. 18, 1881.

AUDUBON.

DATE UNKNOWN. FROM A DAGUERREOTYPE OWNED BY M. ELIZA AUDUBON.

Grove Mr. David Pawling wrote in January, 1805: "To-day I saw the swiftest skater I ever beheld; backwards and forwards he went like the wind, even leaping over large air-holes fifteen or more feet across, and continuing to skate without an instant's delay. I was told he was a young Frenchman, and this evening I met him at a ball, where I found his dancing exceeded his skating; all the ladies wished him as partner; moreover, a handsomer man I never saw, his eyes alone command attention; his name, Audubon, is strange to me."

Abroad it was the same; Mr. Rathbone speaks of "his beautiful expressive face," as did Christopher North, and so on until the beauty of youth and manhood passed into the "magnificent gray-haired man."

But "the gay young Frenchman who danced with all the girls," was an old man now, not so much as the years go, but in the intensity of his life. He had never done anything by halves; he had played and worked, enjoyed and sorrowed, been depressed and elated, each and all with his highly strung nature at fever heat, and the end was not far. He had seen the accomplishment of his hopes in the "Birds," and the "Quadrupeds" he was content to leave largely to other hands; and surely no man ever had better helpers. From first to last his wife had worked, in more ways than one, to further the aim of his life; Victor had done the weary mechanical business work; John had hunted, and preserved specimens, taken long journeys — notably to Texas and California — and been his father's travelling companion on more than one occasion. Now the time had come when he no longer led; Victor had full charge of the publication of the "Quadrupeds," besides putting in many of the backgrounds, and John painted a large proportion of the animals. But I think that none of them regarded their work as individual, — it was always *ours*, for father and sons were comrades and friends; and with Dr. Bachman's invaluable aid this last work was finished, but not during Audubon's life. He travelled more or less in the interests of his publications during these years, largely in New England and in the Middle States.

In 1847 the brilliant intellect began to be dimmed; at first it was only the difficulty of finding the right word to express an idea, the gradual lessening of interest, and this increased till in May, 1848, Dr. Bachman tells the pathetic close of the enthusiastic and active life: "Alas, my poor friend Audubon! The outlines of his beautiful face and form are there, but his noble mind is all in ruins. It is indescribably sad."

Through these last years the devotion of the entire household was his. He still loved to wander in the woods, he liked to hear his wife read to him, and music was ever a delight. To the very last his daughter-in-law, Mrs. Victor G. Audubon, sang a little Spanish song to him every evening, rarely permitting anything to interfere with what gave him so much pleasure, and evening by evening he listened to the *Buenas Noches*, which was so soon to be his in reality.

His grandchildren, also, were a constant source of enjoyment to him, and he to them, for children always found a friend in him; and thus quietly did he pass through that valley which had no shadows for him.

I wish to wholly correct the statement that Audubon became blind. His sight became impaired by old age, as is usually the case; he abhorred spectacles or glasses of any kind, would not wear them except occasionally, and therefore did not get the right focus for objects near by; but his far-sight was hardly impaired. That wonderful vision which surprised even the keen-eyed Indian never failed him.

Well do I remember the tall figure with snow-white hair, wandering peacefully along the banks of the beautiful Hudson. Already he was resting in that border land

AUDUBON MONUMENT IN TRINITY CHURCH CEMETERY, NEW YORK.

The reverse of the base bears the inscription—

Erected to the Memory of
JOHN JAMES AUDUBON
In the year 1893, by subscriptions raised by the
New York Academy of Science.

which none can fathom, and it could not have been far to go, no long and weary journey, when, after a few days of increasing feebleness, for there was no illness, just as sunset was flooding the pure, snow-covered landscape with golden light, at five o'clock on Monday, January 27, 1851, the "pard-like spirit, beautiful and swift, . . . outsoared the shadow of our night."

. . . .

In a quiet spot in Trinity Church Cemetery, not far from the home where Audubon spent his last years, the remains of the naturalist were laid with all honor and respect, on the Thursday following his death. Time brought changes which demanded the removal of the first burial-place, and a second one was chosen in the same cemetery, which is now marked by the beautiful monument erected by the New York Academy of Sciences.[1]

Now wife and sons have joined him; together they rest undisturbed by winter storms or summer heat; the river they loved so well flows past their silent home as in days long gone when its beauties won their hearts.

Truly the place where they dwelt shall know them no more, but "while the melody of the mocking-bird is heard in the cypress forests of Louisiana, and the squirrel leaps from its leafy curtain like a thing of beauty, the name of Audubon will live in the hearts of coming generations."

[1] Unveiled April 26, 1893, on which occasion eulogies were pronounced by Mr. D. G. Elliot, ex-president of the American Ornithologists' Union, and Prof. Thomas Egleston of Columbia College.

THE EUROPEAN JOURNALS

1826–1829

THE EUROPEAN JOURNALS

1826–1829

ON *the 26th April*, 1826, I left my beloved wife Lucy Audubon, and my son John Woodhouse with our friends the Percys at Bayou Sara. I remained at Doctor Pope's at St. Francisville till Wednesday at four o'clock P. M., when I took the steamboat "Red River," Captain Kemble, for New Orleans, which city I reached at noon on Wednesday, 27th. Visited many vessels for my passage to England, and concluded to go in the ship "Delos" of Kennebunk, Captain Joseph Hatch, bound to Liverpool, and loaded entirely with cotton. During my stay in New Orleans, I lived at G. L. Sapinot's, and saw many of my old friends and acquaintances, but the whole time of waiting was dull and heavy. I generally walked from morning till dusk. New Orleans, to a man who does not trade in dollars or other such stuff, is a miserable spot. Finally, discovering that the ship would not be ready for sea for several days longer, I ascended the Mississippi again in the "Red River," and arrived at Mrs. Percy's at three o'clock in the morning, having had a dark ride through the Magnolia woods. I remained two days, left at sunrise, and breakfasted with my good friend Augustin Bourgeat. Arrived at New Orleans, I called on the governor, who gave me a letter bearing the seal of the State, obviating the necessity of a passport. I received many letters of introduction from different persons which will be of use to me. Also I wrote to Charles Bonaparte, apprising him of the box of bird skins forwarded to him.

On the *17th of May*, my baggage was put on board, I following, and the steamboat "Hercules" came alongside at seven P. M., and in ten hours put the "Delos" to sea. I was immediately affected with sea-sickness, which, however, lasted but a short time; I remained on deck constantly, forcing myself to exercise. We calculated our day of departure to be May 18, 1826, at noon, when we first made an observation. It is now the 28th; the weather has been generally fair with light winds. The first objects which diverted my thoughts from the dear ones left behind me, were the beautiful Dolphins that glided by the vessel like burnished gold by day, and bright meteors by night. Our captain and mate proved experts at alluring them with baited hooks, and dexterous at piercing them with a five-pronged instrument, generally called by seamen "grain." If hooked, the Dolphin flounces desperately, glides off with all its natural swiftness, rises perpendicularly out of the water several feet, and often shakes off the hook and escapes; if, however, he is well hooked, he is played about for a while, soon exhausted, and hauled into the ship. Their flesh is firm, dry, yet quite acceptable at sea. They differ much in their sizes, being, according to age, smaller or larger; I saw some four and a half feet long, but a fair average is three feet. The paunch of all we caught contained more or less small fishes of different varieties, amongst which the flying-fish is most prevalent. Dolphins move in companies of from four or five to twenty or more. They chase the flying-fish, that with astonishing rapidity, after having escaped their sharp pursuer a while in the water, emerge, and go through the air with the swiftness of an arrow, sometimes in a straight course, sometimes forming part of a circle; yet frequently the whole is unavailing, for the Dolphin bounds from the sea in leaps of fifteen or twenty feet, and so moves rapidly towards his prey, and the little fish falls, to be swallowed by his antagonist. You must not suppose, however, that the Dolphin moves through the seas without risk or danger; he, as well as others has vigilant and powerful enemies. One is the Barracouta, in shape much like a Pike, growing sometimes to a large size; one of these cut off upwards of a foot of a Dolphin's tail, as if done with an axe, as the Dolphin made for a baited hook; and I may say we about divided the bounty. There is a degree of sympathy existing between Dolphins quite remarkable; the moment one of them is hooked or grained, all those in company immediately make towards him, and remain close to him till the unfortunate is hauled on board, then they move off and will rarely bite. The skin of the fish is a tissue of small scales, softer in their substance than is generally the case in scaley fishes of such size; the skin is tough.

We also caught a Porpoise about seven feet in length. This was accomplished during the night, when the moon gave me a full view of all that happened. The fish, contrary to custom, was *grained* instead of harpooned, but grained in such a way and so effectually, through the forehead, that it was then held and suffered to flounce and beat about the bow of the ship, until the man who had first speared it gave the line holding the grain to our captain, slid along the bobstay with a rope, then, after some little time and perhaps some difficulty, the fish was secured immediately about its tail, and hoisted with that part upwards. Arrived at the deck it gave a deep groan, much like the last from a dying hog, flapped heavily once or twice, and died. I had never before examined one of these closely, and the duck-bill-like snout, and the curious disposition of the tail, with the body, were new and interesting matters of observation to me. The large, sleek, black body, the quantity of warm, black blood issuing from the wound, the blowing apertures placed over the forehead, — all attracted my attention. I requested it might be untouched till the next morning, and my wish was granted. On opening it the intestines were still warm (say eight hours after death), and resembled very much those of a hog. The paunch contained several cuttle-fish partly decayed. The flesh was removed from the skeleton and left the central bone supported on its sides by two horizontal, and one perpendicular bone, giving it the appearance of a four-edged cutting instrument; the lower jaw, or as I would prefer writing it, mandible, exceeds the upper about three-fourths of an inch. Both were furnished with single rows of divided conical teeth, about one-half an inch in length, so parted as to admit those of the upper jaw between each of those of the lower. The fish might weigh about two hundred pounds. The eyes were small in proportion to the size of the animal, and having a breathing aperture above, of course it had no gills. Porpoises move in large companies, and generally during spring and early summer go in pairs. I have seen a parcel of them leap perpendicularly about twenty feet, and fall with a heavy dash in the sea. Our captain told us that there were instances when small boats had been sunk by one of these heavy fish falling into them. Whilst I am engaged with the finny tribe (of which, however, I know little or nothing), I may as well tell you that one morning when moving gently, two miles per hour, the captain called me to show me some pretty little fishes just caught from the cabin window. These measured about three inches, were broad, and moved very quickly through the water. We had pin-hooks, and with these, in about two hours, three hundred and seventy were caught; they were sweet and good as food. They are known ordinarily as Rudder-fish, and always keep on the lee side of the rudder, as it affords them a strong eddy to support them, and enable them to follow the vessel in that situation; when calm they disperse about the bow and sides, and then will not bite. The least breeze brings them all astern again in a compact body, when they seize the baited hook the moment it reaches the water.

We have also caught two Sharks, one a female about seven feet long, that had ten young, alive, and able to swim well; one of them was thrown overboard and made off as if well accustomed to take care of himself. Another was cut in two, and the head half swam off out of our sight. The remainder, as well as the parent, were cut in pieces for bait for Dolphins, which are extremely partial to that meat. The weather being calm and pleasant, I felt desirous to have a view of the ship from a distance and Captain Hatch politely took me in the yawl and had it rowed all round the "Delos." This was a sight I had not enjoyed for twenty years, and I was much pleased with it; afterwards having occasion to go out to try the bearings of the current, I again accompanied him, and bathed in the sea, not however without some fears as to Sharks. To try the bearings of the current we took an iron pot fastened to a line of one hundred and twenty fathoms, and made a log-board out of a barrel's head leaded on one side to make it sink perpendicularly on its edge, and tried the velocity of the current with it fixed to a line *by the help of a second glass*,[1] whilst our iron pot acted as an anchor.

Let me change my theme, and speak of birds awhile. Mother Carey's Chickens (*Procellaria*) came about us, and I longed to have *at least one* in my possession. I had watched their evolutions, their gentle patting of the sea when on the wing, with the legs hanging and the web extended, seen them take large and long ranges in search of food, and return for bits of fat thrown overboard for them, I had often looked at different figures given by scientific men; but all this could not diminish for a moment the long-wished for pleasure of possessing one in the flesh. I fired, and dropped the first one that came alongside, and the captain most courteously sent for it with the yawl. I made two drawings of it; it proved to be a female with eggs, numerous, but not larger than grains of fine powder,

[1] This sounds involved, but is copied verbatim.

inducing me to think that these birds must either breed earlier, or much later, than any in our southern latitude. I should be inclined to think that the specimen I inspected had not laid this season, though I am well satisfied that it was an old bird. During many succeeding weeks I discovered that numbers flew mated side by side, and occasionally, particularly on calm, pleasant days caressed each other as Ducks are known to do.

May 27, 1826. Five days ago we saw a small vessel with all sails set coming toward us; we were becalmed and the unknown had a light breeze. It approached gradually; suspicions were entertained that it might be a pirate, as we had heard that same day reports, which came undoubtedly from cannon, and from the very direction from which this vessel was coming. We were well manned, tolerably armed, and were all bent on resistance, knowing well that these gentry gave no quarter, to purses at least, and more or less uneasiness was perceptible on every face. Night arrived, a squally breeze struck us, and off we moved, and lost sight of the pursuing vessel in a short time. The next day a brig that had been in our wake came near us, was hailed, and found to be the "Gleaner," of Portland, commanded by an acquaintance of our commander, and bound also to Liverpool. This vessel had left New Orleans five days before us. We kept close together, and the next day Captain Hatch and myself boarded her, and were kindly received; after a short stay her captain, named Jefferson, came with us and remained the day. I opened my drawings and showed a few of them. Mr. Swift was anxious to see some, and I wanted to examine in what state they kept, and the weather being dry and clear I feared nothing. It was agreed the vessels should keep company until through the Gulf Stream, for security against pirates. So fine has the weather been so far, that all belonging to the cabin have constantly slept on deck; an awning has been extended to protect from the sun by day and the dampness by night. When full a hundred leagues at sea, a female Rice Bunting came on board, and remained with us one night, and part of a day. A Warbler also came, but remained only a few minutes, and then made for the land we had left. It moved while on board with great activity and sprightliness; the Bunting, on the contrary, was exhausted, panted, and I have no doubt died of inanition.

Many Sooty Terns were in sight during several days. I saw one Frigate Pelican high in air, and could only judge it to be such through the help of a telescope. Flocks of unknown birds were also about the ship during a whole day. They swam well, and preferred the water to the air. They resembled large Phalaropes, but I could not be certain. A small Alligator, that I had purchased for a dollar in New Orleans, died at the end of nine days, through my want of knowledge, or thought, that salt matter was poisonous to him. In two days he swelled to nearly double his natural size, breathed hard, and, as I have said, died.

In latitude 24°, 27′, a Green Heron came on board, and remained until, becoming frightened, it flew towards the brig "Gleaner;" it did not appear in the least fatigued. The captain of the brig told me that on a former voyage from Europe to New Orleans, when about fifty leagues from the Balize, a fully grown Whooping Crane came on board his vessel during the night, passing over the length of his deck, close over his head, over the helmsman, and fell in the yawl; the next morning the bird was found there completely exhausted, when every one on board supposed it had passed on. A cage was made for it, but it refused food, lingered a few days, and then died. It was plucked and found free from any wound, and in good condition; a very singular case in birds of the kind, that are inured to extensive journeys, and, of course liable to spend much time without the assistance of food.

June 4. We are a few miles south of the Line, for the second time in my life. Since I wrote last we have parted from our companion the "Gleaner," and are yet in the Gulf of Mexico. I have been at sea three Sundays, and yet we have not made the shores of Cuba. Since my last date I have seen a large Sword-fish, but *only* saw it, two Gannets, caught a live Warbler, and killed a Great-footed Hawk. This bird, after having alighted several times on our yards, made a dash at a Warbler which was feeding on the flies about the vessel, seized it, and ate it in our sight, *on the wing*, much like a Mississippi Kite devouring the Red-throated Lizards. The warbler we caught was a nondescript, which I named "The Cape Florida Songster." We also saw two Frigate Pelicans at a great height, and a large species of Petrel, entirely unknown to me. I have read Byron's "Corsair" with much enjoyment.

June 17. A brig bound to Boston, called the "Andromache," came alongside, and my heart rejoiced at the idea that letters could be carried by her to America. I set to, and wrote to my wife and to Nicholas Berthoud. A sudden squall separated us till quite late, but we boarded her, I going with the captain; the sea ran high, and the tossing of our light yawl was extremely disagreeable to my feelings. The brig was loaded with cotton, extremely filthy, and I was glad to discover that with all *our* disagreeables we were comparatively comfortable on the "Delos." We have been in sight of Cuba four days; the heat excessive. I saw three beautiful White-headed Pigeons, or Doves, flying about our ship, but after several rounds they shaped their course towards the Floridas and disappeared. The Dolphins we catch here are said to be poisonous; to ascertain whether they are or not, a piece of fish is boiled with a silver dollar till quite cooked, when if the coin is not tarnished or green, the fish is safe eating. I find bathing in the sea water extremely refreshing, and enjoy this luxury every night and morning. Several vessels are in sight.

June 26. We have been becalmed many days, and I should be dull indeed were it not for the fishes and birds, and my pen and pencil. I have been much interested in the Dusky Petrels; the mate killed four at one shot, so plentiful were they about our vessel, and I have made several drawings from these, which were brought on board for that purpose. They skim over the sea in search of what is here called Gulf Weed, of which there are large patches, perhaps half an acre in extent. They flap the wings six or seven times, then soar for three or four seconds, the tail spread, the wings extended. Four or five of these birds, indeed sometimes as many as fifteen or twenty, will alight on this weed, dive, flutter, and swim with all the gayety of ducks on a pond, which they have reached after a weary journey. I heard no note from any of them. No sooner have the Petrels eaten or dispersed the fish than they rise and extend their wings for flight, in search of more. At times, probably to rest themselves, they alighted, swam lightly, dipping their bills frequently in the water as Mergansers and fishy Ducks do when trying, by tasting, if the water contains much fish. On inspection of the body, I found the wings powerfully muscular and strong for the size of the bird, a natural requisite for individuals that have such an extent of water to traverse, and frequently heavy squalls to encounter and fight against. The stomach, or pouch, resembled a leather purse of four inches in length and was much distended by the contents, which were a compound of fishes of different kinds, some almost entire, others more or less digested. The gullet was capable of great extension. Fishes two and a half inches by one inch were found nearly fresh. The flesh of these Petrels smelt strong, and was tough and not fit to eat. I tasted some, and found it to resemble the flesh of the Porpoise. There was no difference in the sexes, either in size or color; they are sooty black above, and snowy white below. The exact measurements are in my memorandum-book.

June 29. This morning we came up with the ship "Thalia," of Philadelphia, Captain John R. Butler, from Havana to Minorca up the Mediterranean, with many passengers, Spaniards, on board. The captain very politely offered us some fruit, which was gladly accepted, and in return we sent them a large Dolphin, they having caught none. I sent a Petrel, stuffed some days previously, as the captain asked for it for the Philadelphia Society of Sciences.

June 30. Whilst sailing under a gentle breeze last night, the bird commonly called by seamen "Noddy" alighted on the boom of the vessel, and was very soon caught by the mate. It then uttered a rough cry, not unlike that of a young crow when taken from the nest. It bit severely and with quickly renewed movement of the bill, which, when it missed the object in view, snapped like that of our larger Flycatchers. I found it one of the same species that hovered over the seaweeds in company with the large Petrel. Having kept it alive during the night, when I took it in hand to draw it it was dull looking and silent. I know nothing of this bird more than what our sailors say, that it is a Noddy, and that they often alight on vessels in this latitude, particularly in the neighborhood of the Florida Keys. The bird was in beautiful plumage, but poor. The gullet was capable of great extension, the paunch was empty, the heart large for the bird, and the liver uncommonly so.

A short time before the capture of the above bird, a vessel of war, a ship that we all supposed to be a South American Republican, or Columbian, came between us and the "Thalia," then distant from us about one and a half miles astern, fired a gun, and detained her for some time, the reason probably being that the passengers were

Spaniards, and the cargo Spanish property; however, this morning both vessels were in view making different routes. The man-of-war deigned not to come to us, and none of us were much vexed at this mark of inattention. This day has been calm; my drawing finished, I caught four Dolphins; how much I have gazed at these beautiful creatures, watching their last moments of life, as they changed their hue in twenty varieties of richest arrangement of tints, from burnished gold to silver bright, mixed with touches of ultramarine, rose, green, bronze, royal purple, quivering to death on our hard, broiling deck. As I stood and watched them, I longed to restore them to their native element in all their original strength and vitality, and yet I felt but a few moments before a peculiar sense of pleasure in catching them with a hook to which they were allured by false pretences.

We have at last entered the Atlantic Ocean this morning and with a propitious breeze; the land birds have left us, and I — I leave my beloved America, my wife, my children, my friends. The purpose of this voyage is to visit not only England, but the continent of Europe, with the intention of publishing my work on the "Birds of America." If not sadly disappointed my return to these shores, these happy shores, will be the brightest day I have ever enjoyed. Oh! wife, children, friends, America, farewell! farewell!

July 9. At sea. My leaving America had for some time the feelings of a dream; I could scarce make up my mind fixedly on the subject. I thought continually I still saw my beloved friends, and my dear wife and children. I still felt every morning when I awoke that the land of America was beneath me, and that I would in a short time throw myself on the ground in her shady woods, and watch for, and listen to the many lovely warblers. But now that I have positively been at sea since *fifty-one* days, tossing to and fro, without the sight or the touch of those dear to me, I feel fully convinced, and look forward with an anxiety such as I never felt before, when I calculate that not less than four months, the third of a year, must elapse before my wife and children can receive any tidings of my arrival on the distant shores to which I am bound. When I think that many more months must run from the Life's sand-glass allotted to my existence before I can think of returning, and that my re-union with my friends and country is yet an unfolded and unknown event, I am filled with sudden apprehensions which I cannot describe nor dispel.

Our fourth of July was passed near the Grand Banks, and how differently from any that I can recollect. The weather was thick, foggy, and as dull as myself; not a sound of rejoicing reached my ears, not once did I hear "Hail Columbia! Happy land." My companion passengers lay about the deck and on the cotton-bales, basking like Crocodiles, while the sun occasionally peeped out of the smoky haze that surrounded us; yet the breeze was strong, the waves moved majestically, and thousands of large Petrels displayed their elegant, aerial movements. How much I envied their power of flight to enable me to be here, there, and all over the globe comparatively speaking, in a few moments, throwing themselves edgeways against the breeze, as if a well sharpened arrow shot with the strength and grace of one sprung from the bow of an Apollo. I had remarked a regular increase in the number of these Petrels ever since the capes of Florida were passed; but here they were so numerous, and for part of a day flew in such succession towards the west and southwest, that I concluded they were migrating to some well known shore to deposit their eggs, or perhaps leading their young. These very seldom alighted; they were full the size of a common gull, and as they flew they showed in quick alternations the whole upper and under part of their bodies, sometimes skimming low, sometimes taking immense curves, then dashing along the deep trough of the sea, going round our vessel (always out of gun-reach) as if she had been at anchor. Their lower parts are white, the head all white, and the upper part of the body and wings above sooty brown. I would imagine that one of these Petrels flies over as much distance in one hour, as one of the little black Petrels in our wake does in twelve. Since we have left the neighborhood of the Banks, these birds have gradually disappeared, and now in latitude 44°, 53′ I see none. Our captain and sailors speak of them as companions in storms, as much as their little relations Mother Carey's chickens.

As suddenly as if we had just turned the summit of a mountain dividing a country south of the equator from Iceland, the weather altered in the present latitude and longitude. My light summer clothing was not sufficient, and the dews that fell at night rendered the deck, where I always slept, too damp to be comfortable. This, however, of two evils I preferred, for I could not endure the more disagreeable odors of the cabin, where now the captain, officers, and Mr. Swift, eat their meals daily. The length of the days has increased astonishingly; at nine o'clock I can easily read large print. Dawn comes shortly after 2 A.M., and a long day is before us.

At Sea — July, 1826. We had several days a stiff breeze that wafted us over the deep fully nine miles an hour. This was congenial to my wishes, but not to my feelings. The motion of the vessel caused violent headaches, far more distressing than any seasickness I had ever experienced. Now, for the third or fourth time, I read Thomson's " Seasons," and I believe enjoyed them better than ever.

Among our live stock on board, we had a large hen. This bird was very tame and quite familiar with the ins and outs of the vessel, and was allowed all the privileges of the deck. She had been hatched on board, and our cook, who claimed her as his property, was much attached to her, as was also the mate. One morning she imprudently flew overboard, while we were running three miles an hour. The yawl was immediately lowered, four men rowed her swiftly towards the floating bird that anxiously looked at her place of abode gliding from her; she was picked up, and her return on board seemed to please every one, and I was gratified to see such kind treatment to a bird; it assured me, had I needed that assurance, that the love of animals develops the better side of all natures. Our hen, however, ended her life most distressingly not long after this narrow escape; she again flew over the side, and the ship moving at nine knots, the sea very high and rough, the weather rainy and squally, the captain thought it imprudent to risk the men for the fowl; so, notwithstanding the pleadings of the cook, we lost sight of the adventurous bird in a few moments. We have our long boat as usual lashed to the deck; but instead of being filled with lumber as is usually the case, it now contained three passengers, all bound to Europe to visit friends, with the intention of returning to America in the autumn. One has a number of books which he politely offered me; he plays most sweetly on the flute, and is a man superior to his apparent situation. We have a tailor also; this personage is called a deck hand, but the fact is, that two thirds of his time is spent sleeping on the windlass. This man, however, like all others in the world, is useful in his way. He works whenever called on, and will most cheerfully put a button or a patch on any one's clothing; his name is Crow, and during the entire voyage, thus far, he has lived solely on biscuit and raw bacon. We now see no fish except now and then a shoal of porpoises. I frequently long for the beautiful Dolphins in the Gulf of Mexico; Whales have been seen by the sailors, but not by me. During this tedious voyage I frequently sit and watch our captain at his work; I do not remember ever to have seen a man more industrious or more apt at doing nearly everything he needs himself. He is a skilful carpenter and turner, cooper, tin and black smith, and an excellent tailor; I saw him making a pair of pantaloons of fine cloth with all the neatness that a city brother of the cross-legged faculty could have used. He made a handsome patent swift for his wife, and a beautiful plane for his own use, manufactured out of a piece of beech-wood that probably grew on the banks of the Ohio, as I perceived it had been part of a flat-boat, and brought on board to be used for fuel. He can plait straw in all sorts of ways, and make excellent bearded fishhooks out of common needles. He is an excellent sailor, and the more stormy it becomes, the gayer he is, even when drenched to the skin. I was desirous of understanding the means of ascertaining the latitude on land, and also to find the true rising of the sun whilst travelling in the uninhabited parts of America; this he showed me with pleasure, and I calculated our latitude and longitude from this time, though not usually fond of mathematics. To keep busy I go often about the deck pencil in hand, sketching the different attitudes of the sailors, and many a laugh is caused by these rough drawings. Both the mates have shown a kindness towards me that I cannot forget. The first mate is S. L. Bragdon from Wells, the second Wm. Hobart from Kennebunk.

To-day we came in with a new set and species of Petrels, resembling those in the Gulf of Mexico, but considerably larger; between fifty and sixty were at one time close to the vessel, catching small fish that we guessed to be herrings; the birds swam swiftly over the water, their wings raised, and now and then diving and dipping after the small fry; they flew heavily, and with apparent reluctance, and alighted as soon as we passed them. I was satisfied that several in our wake had followed us from the Gulf of Mexico; the sudden change in the weather must have been seriously felt by them.

July 12. I had a beautiful view of a Whale about five hundred yards from the vessel when we first perceived it; the water thrown from his spiracles had the appearance of a small, thick cloud, twelve or fourteen feet wide. Never have I felt the weather so cold in July. We are well wrapped up, and yet feel chilly in the drizzling rain.

July 15. Yesterday-night ended the ninth Sunday passed at sea; the weather continues cold, but the wind is propitious. We are approaching land, and indeed I thought I smelt the "land smell." We have had many Whales near us during the day, and an immense number of Porpoises; our captain, who prefers their flesh to the best of veal, beef, or mutton, said he would give five dollars for one; but our harpoon is broken, and although several handles were fastened for a while to the grain, the weapon proved too light, and the fish invariably made their escape after a few bounces, probably to go and die in misery. European Hawks were seen, and two Curlews; these gave me hope that we might see the long desired land shortly.

July 18, 1826. The sun is shining clear over Ireland; that land was seen at three o'clock this morning by the man at the helm, and the mate, with a stentorian voice, announced the news. As we approached the coast a small boat neared us, and came close under our lee; the boat looked somewhat like those employed in bringing in heavy loads to New Orleans, but her sails were more tattered, her men more fair in complexion. They hailed us and offered for sale fresh fish, new potatoes, fresh eggs. All were acceptable, I assure thee. They threw a light line to us most dexterously. Fish, potatoes, and eggs were passed to us, in exchange for whiskey, salt pork, and tobacco, which were, I trust, as acceptable to them as their wares were to us. I thought the exchange a fair one, but no!—they called for rum, brandy, whiskey, more of everything. Their expressions struck me with wonder; it was

"Here 's to your Honor," — "Long life to your Honor," — "God bless your Honor," — *Honors* followed with such rapidity that I turned away in disgust. The breeze freshened and we proceeded fast on our way. Perhaps to-morrow may see me safe on land again — perhaps to-morrow may see us all stranded, perishing where the beautiful "Albion" went ashore.

St. George's Channel, Thursday, July 20. I am approaching very fast the shores of England, indeed Wales is abreast of our ship, and we can plainly distinguish the hedges that divide the fields of grain; but what nakedness the country exhibits, scarce a patch of timber to be seen; our fine forests of pine, of oak, of heavy walnut-trees, of magnificent magnolias, of hickories or ash or maple, are represented here by a diminutive growth called "furze." But I must not criticise so soon! I have not seen the country, I have not visited any of the historic castles, or the renowned parks, for never have I been in England nor Scotland, that land made famous by the entrancing works of Walter Scott. We passed yesterday morning the Tuskar, a handsome light on a bare rock. This morning we saw Holyhead, and we are now not more than twenty-five miles from Liverpool; but I feel no pleasure, and were it not for the sake of my Lucy and my children, I would readily embark to-morrow to return to America's shores and all they hold for me. . . . The pilot boat that came to us this morning contained several men all dressed in blue, with overcoats of oiled linen, — all good, hearty, healthy-looking men. . . . I have been on deck, and from the bow the land of England is plainly distinguishable; the sight around us is a beautiful one, I have counted fifty-six vessels with spreading sails, and on our right are mountains fading into the horizon; my dull thoughts have all abandoned me, I am elated, my heart is filled with hope. To-morrow we shall land at the city of Liverpool, but when I think of Custom House officials, acceptancy of Bills, hunting up lodgings, — again my heart fails me; I must on deck.

Mersey River opposite Liverpool, 9.30 P. M. The night is cloudy, and we are at anchor! The lights of the city show brightly, for we are not more than two hundred yards distant from them.

Liverpool, July 21. This morning when I landed it was raining, yet the appearance of the city was agreeable; but no sooner had I entered it than the smoke became so oppressive to my lungs that I could hardly breathe; it affected my eyes also. All was new to me. After a breakfast at an inn with Mr. Swift for 2/6, we went to the Exchange Buildings, to the counting-house of Gordon and Forstall, as I was anxious to deliver my letters to Mr. Gordon from Mr. Briggs. I also presented during the morning my bill of exchange. The rest of the day was spent in going to the Museum, gazing about, and clearing my brains as much as possible; but how lonely I feel, — not a soul to speak to freely when Mr. Swift leaves me for Ireland. We took lodgings at the Commercial Inn not far from the Exchange Buildings; we are well fed, and well attended to, although, to my surprise, altogether by women, neatly dressed and modest. I found the persons of whom I enquired for different directions, remarkably kind and polite; I had been told this would not be the case, but I have met with only real politeness from all.

Liverpool, July 22. The Lark that sings so sweetly, and that now awakened me from happy dreams, is nearly opposite my table, prisoner in a cage hanging by a window where from time to time a young person comes to look on the world below; I think of the world of the West and — but the Lark, delightful creature, sings sweetly, yet in a cage!

The Custom House suddenly entered my head, and after considerable delay there, my drawings went through a regular, strict, and complete examination. The officers were all of opinion that they were free of duty, but the law was looked at and I was obliged to pay two pence on each drawing, as they were water-colored. My books being American, I paid four pence *per pound*, and when all was settled, I took my baggage and drawings, and went to my lodgings. The noise of pattens on the sidewalk startles me very frequently; if the sound is behind me I often turn my head expecting to see a horse, but instead I observe a neat, plump-looking maid, tripping as briskly as a Killdeer. I received a polite note from Mr. Rathbone [1] this morning, inviting me to dine next Wednesday with him and Mr. Roscoe.[2] I shall not forget the appointment.

Sunday, July 23. Being Sunday I must expect a long and lonely day; I woke at dawn and lay for a few moments only, listening to the sweet-voiced Lark; the day was beautiful; thermometer in the sun 65°, in the shade 41°; I might say 40°, but I love odd numbers, — it is a foolish superstition with me. I spent my forenoon with Mr. Swift and a friend of his, Mr. R. Lyons, who was afterwards kind enough to introduce us to the Commercial Reading Room at the Exchange Buildings. In the afternoon we went across the Mersey. The country is somewhat dull; we returned to supper, sat chatting in the coffee room, and the day ended.

July 24, Monday. As early as I thought proper I

[1] Mr. Wm. Rathbone, of the firm of Rathbone Bros. & Co., to whom Audubon had a letter from Mr. Vincent Nolté. To Messrs. Wm. and Richard Rathbone, and their father Wm. Rathbone, Sr., Audubon was more deeply indebted than to any other of his many kind friends in England. Their hospitality was only equalled by their constant and valuable assistance in preparing for the publication of the "Birds," and when this was an assured fact, they were unresting in their efforts to aid Audubon in procuring subscribers. It is with pleasure that Audubon's descendants to-day acknowledge this indebtedness to the "family Rathbone," which is ever held in grateful remembrance.

[2] William Roscoe, historical, botanical, and miscellaneous writer, 1753-1831.

turned my steps to No. 87 Duke Street, where the polite English gentleman, Mr. Richard Rathbone,[1] resides. My locks blew freely from under my hat in the breeze, and nearly every lady I met looked at them with curiosity. Mr. Rathbone was not in, but was at his counting-house, where I soon found myself. A full dozen of clerks were at their separate desks, work was going on apace, letters were being thrown into an immense bag belonging to a packet that sailed this day for the shores where I hope my Lucy is happy — dearest friend! My name was taken to the special room of Mr. Rathbone, and in a moment I was met by one who acted towards me as a brother. He did not give *his card* to poor Audubon, he gave his hand, and a most cordial invitation to be at his house at two o'clock, which hour found me there. I was ushered into a handsome dining-room, and Mr. Rathbone almost immediately entered the same, with a most hearty greeting. I dined with this hospitable man, his charming wife and children. Mrs. Rathbone is not only an amiable woman,

[1] In a charming letter written to me by Mr. Richard R. Rathbone, son of this gentleman, dated Glan y Menai, Anglesey, May 14, 1897, he says: "To us there was a halo of romance about Mr. Audubon, artist, naturalist, quondam backwoodsman, and the author of that splendid work which I used to see on a table constructed to hold the copy belonging to my Uncle William, opening with hinges so as to raise the bird portraits as if on a desk. But still more I remember his amiable character, though tinged with melancholy by past sufferings; and his beautiful, expressive face, kept alive in my memory by his autograph crayon sketch thereof, in profile, with the words written at foot, 'Audubon at Green Bank. *Almost* happy, 9th September, 1826.' Mr. Audubon painted for my father, as a gift, an Otter (in oils) caught by the fore-foot in a steel trap, and after vainly gnawing at the foot to release himself, throwing up his head, probably with a yell of agony, and displaying his wide-open jaws dripping with blood. This picture hung on our walls for years, until my mother could no longer bear the horror of it, and persuaded my father to part with it. We also had a full-length, life-sized portrait of the American Turkey, striding through the forest. Both pictures went to a public collection in Liverpool. I have also a colored sketch by Mr. Audubon of a Robin Redbreast, shot by him at Green Bank, which I saw him pin with long pins into a bit of board to fix it into position for the instruction of my mother."

but a most intelligent and highly educated one. Mr. Rathbone took me to the Exchange Buildings in order to see the American consul, Mr. Maury, and others. Introduction followed introduction; then I was taken through the entire building, the mayor's public dining-hall, etc. I gazed on pictures of royalty by Sir Thomas Lawrence and others, mounted to the dome and looked over Liverpool and the harbor that Nature formed for her. It was past five when I went to keep my appointment with Mr. Swift.

July 25. The day has passed quickly. In the morning I made a crayon portrait of Mr. Swift — or rather began it — for his father, then took a walk, and on my return found a note from Mr. Richard Rathbone awaiting me. He desired me to come at once with one of my portfolios to Duke Street. I immediately took a hackney coach and found Mr. and Mrs. Rathbone with Mr. James Pyke awaiting me, to take me to the home of Mr. Rathbone, Sr., who lives some miles out of Liverpool.[1] Their youngest boy, Basil, a sweet child, took a fancy to me and I to him, and we made friends during our drive. The country opened gradually to our view, and presently passing up an avenue of trees we entered the abode of the venerable pair, and I was heartily made welcome. I felt painfully awkward, as I always do in new company, but so much kindness and simplicity soon made me more at ease. I saw as I entered the house a full and beautiful collection of the birds of England, well prepared and arranged. What sensations I had whilst I helped to untie the fastenings of my portfolio! I knew by all around me that these good friends were possessed of both taste and judgment, and I did not know that I should please. I was panting like the winged Pheasant, but ah! these kind people praised *my Birds*, and I felt the praise to be honest; once more I breathed freely. My portfolio thoroughly

[1] At Green Bank.

examined, we returned to Liverpool, and later the Rev. Wm. Goddard, rector of Liverpool, and several ladies called on me, and saw some drawings; *all* praised them. Oh! what can I hope, my Lucy, for thee and for us all?

July 26. It is very late, and I am tired, but I will not omit writing on that account. The morning was beautiful, but for some reason I was greatly depressed, and it appeared to me as if I could not go on with the work before me. However, I recollected that the venerable Mr. Maury must not be forgotten. I saw him; Mr. Swift left for Dublin with his crayon portrait; I called at the post-office for news from America, but in vain. I wrote for some time, and then received a call from Mr. Rathbone with his brother William; the latter invited me to dine on Friday at his house, which I promised to do, and this evening I dined with Mr. Rd. Rathbone. I went at half-past six, my heart rather failing me, entered the corridor, my hat was taken, and going upstairs I entered Mr. Rathbone's drawing-room. I have frequently thought it strange that my *observatory nerves* never give way, no matter how much I am overcome by *mauvaise honte*, nor did they now. Many pictures embellished the walls, and helped, with Mr. Rathbone's lively mien, to remove the misery of the moment. Mr. Edward Roscoe came in immediately, — tall, with a good eye under a well marked brow. Dinner announced, we descended to the room I had entered on my first acquaintance with this charming home, and I was conducted to the place of honor. Mr. Roscoe sat next, Mr. Barclay of London, and Mr. Melly opposite with Consul Maury; the dinner was enlivened with mirth and *bon mots*, and I found in such good company infinite pleasure. After we left the table Mrs. Rathbone joined us in the parlor, and I had now again to show my drawings. Mr. Roscoe, who had been talking to me about them at dinner, would not give me any hopes, and I felt unusually gloomy as one by one I slipped them from their case; but after looking at a few only, the great man said heartily: "Mr. Audubon, I am filled with surprise and admiration." On bidding me adieu he invited me to dine with him to-morrow, and to visit the Botanical Gardens. Later Mrs. Rathbone showed me some of her drawings, where talent has put an undeniable stamp on each touch.

July 27. I reached Mr. Roscoe's place, about one and a half miles distant from Liverpool, about three o'clock, and was at once shown into a little drawing-room where all was nature. Mr. Roscoe was drawing a very handsome plant most beautifully. The room was ornamented with many flowers, receiving from his hands the care and treatment they required; they were principally exotics from many distant and different climes. His three daughters were introduced to me, and we then started for the Gardens. Mr. Roscoe and I rode there in what he called his little car, drawn by a pony so small that I was amazed to see it pull us both with apparent ease. Mr. Roscoe is a *come-at-able* person, who makes me feel at home immediately, and we have much in common. I was shown the whole of the Gardens, which with the hot-house were in fine order. The ground is level, well laid out, and beautifully kept; but the season was, so Mr. Roscoe said, a little advanced for me to see the place to the best advantage. On our return to the charming *laboratoire* of Mr. Roscoe the large portfolio is again in sight. I will not weary you with the details of this. One of the daughters draws well, and I saw her look closely at me very often, and she finally made known her wish to take a sketch of my head, to which I gave reluctant consent for some future time. Mr. Roscoe is very anxious I should do well, and says he will try to introduce me to Lord Stanley, and assured me nothing should be left undone to meet my wishes; he told me that the honorable gentleman "is rather shy." It was nine o'clock when I said good-night, leaving my drawings with him at his request. On my return to Dale Street I found the following note: "Mr. Martin, of the Royal Institution of Liverpool, will do himself the pleasure to wait upon Mr. Ambro to-morrow at eleven o'clock." Why do people make such errors with my simple name?

July 28. A *full grown man* with a scarlet vest and breeches, black stockings and shoes for the coloring of his front, and a long blue coat covering his shoulders and back reminds me somewhat of our summer red bird (*Tanagra rubra*). Both man and bird attract the eye, but the scientific appellation of the *man* is unknown to me. At eleven Mr. Martin (who I expect is secretary to the Royal Institution) called, and arranged with me a notice to the members of the Institution, announcing that I would exhibit my drawings for two hours on the mornings of Monday, Tuesday, and Wednesday following, at the Institution. Later, feeling lonely and sad, I called on Mrs. R. Rathbone, whom I found putting away in a little box, a dissected map, with which, *Edgeworth-like*, she had been transmitting knowledge with pleasure. She is so truly delightful a companion that had it been possible I should have made my call long instead of short, but I walked home by a roundabout way, and found a note from Mr. Wm. Rathbone reminding me of my promise to dine with him, and adding that he wished me to meet a brother-in-law of his from London who may be of use to me, so will I bring a few drawings? At the hour named I found myself in Abercrombie Street and in the parlor with two little daughters of my host, the elder about thirteen, extremely handsome. Mrs. Rathbone soon entered and greeted me as if she had known me all my life; her husband followed, and the guests, all gentlemen, collected. Mr. Hodgson, to whom I had a letter from Mr. Nolté[1] was particularly kind to me, but every one seemed desirous I should succeed in England. A Swiss gentleman urged me not to waste time here, but proceed at once to Paris, but he was

[1] Vincent Nolté, born at Leghorn, 1779, traveller, merchant, adventurer.

not allowed to continue his argument, and at ten I left with Mr. Pyke for my lodgings.

July 29. To-day I visited Mr. Hunt,[1] the best landscape painter of this city. I examined much of his work and found some beautiful representations of the scenery of Wales. I went to the Royal Institution to judge of the light, for naturally I wish my work to have every possible advantage. I have not found the population of Liverpool as dense as I expected, and except during the evenings (that do not at this season commence before eight o'clock) I have not been at all annoyed by the elbowings of the crowd, as I remember to have been in my youth, in the large cities of France. Some shops here are beautifully supplied, and have many customers. The new market is in my opinion an object worth the attention of all travelers. It is the finest I have ever seen — it is a large, high and long building, divided into five spacious avenues, each containing its specific commodities. I saw here viands of all descriptions, fish, vegetables, game, fruits, — both indigenous and imported from all quarters of the globe, — bird sellers, with even little collections of stuffed specimens, cheeses of enormous size, butter in great abundance, immense crates of hen's-eggs packed in layers of oats imported from Ireland, twenty-five for one shilling. This market is so well lighted with gas that this evening at ten o'clock I could plainly see the colors of the irids of living pigeons in cages. The whole city is lighted with gas; each shop has many of these illuminating fires, and fine cambric can be looked at by good judges. Mr. A. Hodgson called on me, and I am to dine with him on Monday; he has written to Lord Stanley about me. He very kindly asked if my time passed heavily, gave me a note of admittance for the Athenæum, and told me he would do all in his power for me. I dined at the inn to-day for the second time only since my arrival.

[1] William Henry Hunt (1790–1864).

July 30. It is Sunday again, but not a dull one; I have become better acquainted, and do not feel such an utter stranger. I went to the church of the Asylum for the Blind. A few steps of cut stone lead to an iron gate, and under a colonnade; at the inner gate you pay whatever you please *over* sixpence. Near the entrance is a large picture of Christ healing the blind. The general structure is a well proportioned oblong; ten light columns support the flat ceiling. A fine organ is placed over the entrance in a kind of upper lobby, which contains also the musicians, who are blind. All is silent, and the mind is filled with heavenly thoughts, when suddenly the sublime music glides into one's whole being, and the service has begun. Nowhere have I ever seen such devotion in a church. In the afternoon the Rev. Wm. Goddard took me to some institutions for children on the Lancastrian system; all appeared well dressed, clean, and contented. I dined with Mr. and Mrs. Gordon;[1] Anne advised me to have my hair cut, and to buy a fashionable coat.

July 31. This day has been one of trial to me. At nine of the morning I was quite busy, arranging and disposing in sets my drawings, that they might be inspected by the public. The doors were thrown open at noon, and the ladies flocked in. I knew but one, Mrs. Richard Rathbone, but I had many glances to meet and questions to answer. The time passed, however, and at two the doors were closed. At half-past four I drove with Mr. Adam Hodgson to his cottage, where I was introduced to Mrs. Hodgson, a tall young woman with the freshness of spring, who greeted me most kindly; there were three other guests, and we passed a quiet evening after the usual excellent dinner. Soon after ten we retired to our rooms.

August 1. I arose to listen to the voice of an English Blackbird just as the day broke. It was a little after three, I dressed; and as silently as in my power moved

[1] Mrs. Alexander Gordon was Mrs. Audubon's sister Anne.

downstairs carrying my boots in my hand, gently opened the door, and was off to the fields and meadows. I walked a good deal, went to the seashore, saw a Hare, and returned to breakfast, after which and many invitations to make my kind hosts frequent visits, I was driven back to town, and went immediately to the Institution, where I met Dr. Traill[1] and many other persons of distinction. Several gentlemen attached to the Institution, wished me to be remunerated for exhibiting my pictures, but though I am poor enough, God knows, I do not think I should do that, as the room has been given to me gratis. Four hundred and thirteen persons were admitted to see my drawings.

August 2. I put up this day two hundred and twenty-five of my drawings; the *coup d'œil* was not bad, and the room was crowded. Old Mr. Roscoe did me the honor to present me to Mr. Jean Sismondi,[2] of Geneva. Mr. and Mrs. Rathbone had gone to their country home, "Green Bank," but I sent a note telling them how many pictures I had added to the first day's exhibition. I have decided to collect what letters I can for London, and go there as soon as possible. I was introduced to Mr. Booth of Manchester, who promised me whatever aid he could in that city. After a call at Mr. Roscoe's, I went, with a gentleman from Charleston, S. C., to the theatre, as I was anxious to see the renowned Miss Foote. Miss Foote has been pretty, nay, handsome, nay, beautiful, but — she *has been.* The play was good, the playhouse bad, and the audience numerous and fashionable.

August 4. I had no time to write yesterday; my morning was spent at the Institution, the room was again crowded, I was wearied with bowing to the many to

[1] Thomas Stewart Traill, M. D., Scottish naturalist, born in Orkney, 1781; edited the eighth edition of the "Enclyclopædia Britannica," was associated with the Royal Institute at Liverpool; he died 1862.

[2] The Swiss historian, born at Geneva, 1773, died 1842.

whom I was introduced. Some one was found copying one of the pictures, but the doorkeeper, an alert Scotchman, saw his attempt, turned him out, and tore his sketch. Mr. A. Hodgson invited me to dine with Lord Stanley to-morrow in company with Mr. Wm. Roscoe, Sr. Mr. Sismondi gave me a letter to Baron von Humboldt, and showed me a valuable collection of insects from Thibet, and after this I took tea with Mr. Roscoe.

This morning I breakfasted with Mr. Hodgson, and met Mrs. Wm. Rathbone somewhat later at the Institution; never was a woman better able to please, and more disposed to do so; a woman possessed of beauty, good sense, great intelligence, and rare manners, with a candor and sweetness not to be surpassed. Mr. William Roscoe sent his carriage for me, and I again went to his house, where quite a large company had assembled, among others two botanists who knew every plant and flower, and were most obliging in giving me much delightful information. Having to walk to "Green Bank," the home of Mr. William Rathbone, Sr., I left Mr. Roscoe's at sunset (which by the way was beautiful). The evening was calm and lovely, and I soon reached the avenue of trees leading to the house I sought. Almost immediately I found myself on the lawn with a group of archers, and was interested in the sport; some of the ladies shot very well. Mr. Rathbone, Sr., asked me much about Indians, and American trees, the latter quite unknown here, and as yet I have seen none larger than the saplings of Louisiana. When the other guests had left, I was shown the new work on the Birds of England; I did not like it as well as I had hoped; I much prefer Thomas Bewick. Bewick is the Wilson of England.

August 5. Miss Hannah Rathbone[1] drove me into Liverpool with great speed. Two little Welsh ponies, well matched, drew us beautifully in a carriage which is

[1] Daughter of Mr. William Rathbone, Sr.; married Dr. William Reynolds.

the young lady's special property. After she left me my head was full of Lord Stanley. I am a very poor fool, to be sure, to be troubled at the idea of meeting an English *gentleman*, when those I have met have been in kindness, manners, talents, all I could desire, far more than I expected. The Misses Roscoe were at the Institution, where they have been every day since my pictures were exhibited. Mrs. Wm. Rathbone, with her daughter — her younger self — at her side, was also there, and gave me a packet of letters from her husband. On opening this packet later I found the letters were contained in a handsome case, suitable for my pocket, and a card from Mr. Rathbone asking me to use it as a token of his affectionate regard. In the afternoon I drove with Mr. Hodgson to his cottage, and while chatting with his amiable wife the door opened to admit Lord Stanley.[1] I have not the least doubt that if my head had been looked at, it would have been thought to be the body, globularly closed, of one of our largest porcupines; all my hair — and I have enough — stood straight on end, I am sure. He is tall, well formed, made for activity, simply but well dressed; he came to me at once, bowing to Mrs. Hodgson as he did so, and taking my hand in his, said: "Sir, I am glad to see you." Not the words only, but his manner put me at once at my ease. My drawings were soon brought out. Lord Stanley is a great naturalist, and in an instant he was exclaiming over my work, "Fine!" "Beautiful!" and when I saw him on his knees, having spread my drawings on the floor, the better to compare them, I forgot he was Lord Stanley, I knew only he too loved Nature. At dinner I looked at him closely; his manner reminded me of Thomas Sully, his forehead would have suited Dr.

[1] Edward, fourteenth Earl of Derby, 1799–1869. Member of Parliament, Chief Secretary for Ireland, Secretary for the Colonies, First Lord of the Treasury, and Prime Minister. Translated Homer's Iliad into blank verse. His was a life of many interests: literature, art, society, public affairs, sportsmanship, and above all "the most perfect orator of his day."

Harlan, his brow would have assured that same old friend of his great mental powers. He cordially invited me to call on him in Grosvenor Street in *town* (thus he called London), shook hands with me again, and mounting a splendid hunter rode off. I called to thank Mr. Rathbone for his letters and gift, but did so, I know, most awkwardly. Oh! that I had been flogged out of this miserable shyness and *mauvaise honte* when I was a youth.

August 6, Sunday. When I arrived in this city I felt dejected, miserably so; the uncertainty as to my reception, my doubts as to how my work would be received, all conspired to depress me. Now, how different are my sensations! I am well received everywhere, my works praised and admired, and my poor heart is at last relieved from the great anxiety that has for so many years agitated it, for I know now that I have not worked in vain. This morning I went to church; the sermon was not to my mind, but the young preacher may improve. This afternoon I packed up Harlan's "Fauna" for Mr. E. Roscoe, and went to the Institution, where Mr. Munro was to meet me and escort me to Mr. Wm. Roscoe, Jr., where I was to take tea. Mr. Munro was not on hand, so, after a weary waiting, I went alone to Mr. Roscoe's habitation. It was full of ladies and gentlemen, all his own family, and I knew almost every one. I was asked to imitate the calls of some of the wild birds, and though I did not wish to do so, consented to satisfy the curiosity of the company. I sat between Mr. Wm. Roscoe and his son Edward, and answered question after question. Finally, the good old gentleman and I retired to talk about my plans. He strongly advises me not to exhibit my works without remuneration. Later more guests came in, and more questions were asked; they appeared surprised that I have no wonderful tales to tell, that, for instance, I have not been devoured at least six times by *tigers*, bears, wolves, foxes; no, I never was troubled by any larger animals than ticks and mosquitoes, and that is quite enough. At last one after another took leave. The *well bred* society of England is the perfection of manners; such tone of voice I never heard in America. Indeed, thus far, I have great reason to like England. My plans now are to go to Manchester, to Derbyshire to visit Lord Stanley (Earl of Derby), Birmingham, London for three weeks, Edinburgh, back to London, and then to France, Paris, Nantes, to see my venerable stepmother, Brussels, and return to England. I am advised to do this by men of learning and excellent judgment, who say this will enable me to find where my work may be published with greatest advantage. I have letters given me to Baron Humboldt, General La Fayette, Sir Walter Scott, Sir Humphry Davy, Miss Hannah More, Miss Edgeworth, Sir Thomas Lawrence, etc., etc. How I wish Victor could be with me; what an opportunity to see the best of this island; few ordinary individuals ever enjoyed the same reception. Many persons of distinction have begged drawing lessons of me at a guinea an hour. I am astonished at the plainness of the ladies' dress; in the best society there are no furbelows and fandangoes.

August 7. I am just now from the society of the learned Dr. Traill, and have greatly enjoyed two hours of his interesting company; to what perfection men like him can rise in this island of instruction. I dined at Mr. Edward Roscoe's, whose wife wished me to draw something for her while she watched me. I drew a flower for her, and one for Miss Dale, a fine artist. I am grieved I could not reach "Green Bank" this evening to enjoy the company of my good friends, the Rathbones; they with the Roscoes and Hodgsons have done more for me in every way than I can express. I must have walked twenty miles to-day on these pavements; that is equal to forty-five in the woods, where there is so much to see.

August 8. Although I am extremely fatigued and it is past midnight, I will write. Mr. Roscoe spoke much of my exhibiting my drawings for an admission fee, and he, as well as Dr. Traill and others, have advised me so strongly to do so that I finally consented, though not quite agreeable to me, and Mr. Roscoe drew a draft of a notice to be inserted in the papers, after which we passed some charming hours together.

August 9. The Committee of the Royal Institution met to-day and *requested* me to exhibit my drawings by ticket of admission. This request must and will, I am sure, take off any discredit attached to the tormenting feeling of showing my work for money.

August 10. The morning was beautiful, and I was out very early; the watchmen have, however, ceased to look upon me with suspicion, and think, perhaps, I am a harmless lunatic. I walked to the "Mound" and saw the city and the country beyond the Mersey plainly; then I sat on the grass and watched four truant boys rolling marbles with great spirit; how much they brought before me my younger days. I would have liked them still better had they been *clean;* but they were not so, and as I gave them some money to buy marbles, I recommended that some of it be spent in soap. I begin to feel most powerfully the want of occupation at drawing and studying the habits of the birds that I see about me; and the little Sparrows that hop in the streets, although very sooty with coal smoke, attract my attention greatly; indeed, I watched one of them to-day in the dust of the street, with as much pleasure as in far different places I have watched the play of finer birds. All this induced me to begin. I bought water colors and brushes, for which I paid dearer than in New Orleans. I dined with Mr. Edward Roscoe. As you go to Park Place the view is extensive up and down the Mersey; it gives no extraordinary effects, but is a calming vision of repose to the eyes wearied with the bustle of the streets. There are plenty of steam vessels, but not to be compared to those on the Ohio; these look like smoky, dirty dungeons. Immediately opposite Mr. Roscoe's dwelling is a pond where I have not yet seen a living thing, not even a frog. No moccasin nor copper-headed snake is near its margin; no snowy Heron, no Rose-colored Ibis ever is seen here, wild and charming; no sprightly trout, nor waiting gar-fish, while above hovers no Vulture watching for the spoils of the hunt, nor Eagle perched on dreary cypress in a gloomy silence. No! I am in England, and I cannot but long with unutterable longing for America, charming as England is, and there is nothing in England more charming than the Roscoe family. Our dinner is simple, therefore healthful. Two ladies and a gentleman came in while we were at dessert, and almost as soon as we left the table tea was announced. It is a singular thing that in England dinner, dessert, wines, and tea drinking follow each other so quickly that if we did not remove to another room to partake of the last, it would be a constant repast. I walked back to Liverpool, and more than once my eyes were shocked whilst crossing the fields, to see signs with these words: "Any person trespassing on these grounds will be prosecuted with the rigor of the law." This must be a mistake, certainly; this cannot be English freedom and liberty, surely. Of this I intend to know more hereafter; but that I saw these words painted on boards there is really no doubt.

Sunday, August 13. I am greatly disappointed that not yet have I had letters from home, though several vessels have arrived; perhaps to-morrow may bring me what I long for inexpressibly. This morning I went again to the church for the blind, and spent the remainder of the day at my kind friend's, Mr. Wm. Roscoe.

August 14. This day I have passed with the delightful Rathbone family at Green Bank; I have been drawing for Mrs. Rathbone,[1] and after dinner we went through the

[1] Mrs. Wm. Rathbone, Sr., whom Audubon often calls "Lady Rathbone," and also "The Queen Bee."

greenhouse and *jardin potager*. How charming is Green Bank and the true hospitality of these English friends. It is a cold night, the wind blowing like November; it has been the first day of my exhibition of pictures per card, and one hundred and sixty-four persons were admitted.

August 15. Green Bank, three miles from Liverpool. I am now at this quiet country home; the morning passed in drawing, and this afternoon I took a long walk with Miss Rathbone and her nephew; we were accompanied by a rare dog from Kamschatka. How I did wish *I* could have conducted them towards the beech woods where we could move wherever fancy led us; but no, it could not be, and we walked between dreary walls, without the privilege of advancing towards any particular object that might attract the eye. Is it not shocking that while in England all is hospitality *within*, all is so different *without?* No one dare *trespass*, as it is called. Signs of *large dogs* are put up; steel traps and spring guns are set up, and even *eyes* are kept out by high walls. Everywhere we meet beggars, for England though rich, has poverty gaping every way you look, and the beggars ask for *bread*, — yes, absolutely for food. I can only pray, May our Heavenly Father have mercy on them.

August 17. Green Bank. This morning I lay on the grass a long time listening to the rough voice of a Magpie; it is not the same bird that we have in America. I drove to the Institution with the *Queen Bee* of Green Bank, and this afternoon began a painting of the Otter in a trap, with the intention to present it (if it is good) to my friend Mr. Roscoe's wife. This evening dined at Mr. Wm. Rathbone's, and there met a Quaker lady, Mrs. Abigail ——, who talked much and well about the present condition of England, her poor, her institutions, etc. It is dreadful to know of the want of bread here; will it not lead to the horrors of another revolution? The children of the very poor are often forced by their parents to collect daily a certain

FLYCATCHERS. (*Heretofore unpublished.*)

From a drawing made by Audubon in 1826, and presented to Mrs. Rathbone of Green Bank, Liverpool.
Still in the possession of the Rathbone family.

amount by begging, or perhaps even stealing; failing to obtain this they are cruelly punished on their return home, and the tricks they resort to, to gain their ends, are numberless and curious. The newspapers abound with such accounts, and are besides filled with histories of murders, thefts, hangings, and other abominable acts; I can scarce look at them.

August 19. Dined with Mr. A. Melly in Grenville St. The dinner was quite *à la française*, all gayety, witticism, and good cheer. The game, however, was what I call *highly tainted*, the true flavor for the lords of England.

August 21. I painted many hours this day, finished my Otter; it was viewed by many and admired. I was again invited to remove to Green Bank, but declined until I have painted the Wild Turkey cock for the Royal Institution, say three days more.

September 4. Having been too busy to write for many days, I can only relate the principal facts that have taken place. I have been to two very notable suppers, one at Dr. Traill's in company with the French consul and two other French gentlemen; I was much encouraged, and urged to visit France at once. The other at the house of Mr. Molineux; there indeed my ears were feasted; such entertaining conversation, such delightful music; Mr. Clementi[1] and Mr. Tomlinson from London were present. Many persons came to my painting room, they wonder at the rapidity of my work and that I can paint fourteen hours without fatigue. My Turkeys are now framed, and hung at the Institution which is open daily, and paying well. I have made many small drawings for different friends. All my Sundays are alike, — breakfast with Mr. Melly, church with the blind, dinner with Mr. Roscoe. Every one is surprised at my habits of early rising, and at my rarely touching meat, except game.

[1] Muzio Clementi, composer and pianist, born in Rome, 1752, died in London, 1832. Head of the piano firm of that name.

Green Bank, September 6. When I reached this place I was told that Lady Isabella Douglass, the sister of Lord Selkirk, former governor of Canada, was here; she is unable to walk, and moves about in a rolling chair. At dinner I sat between her and Mrs. Rathbone, and I enjoyed the conversation of Lady Douglass much, her broad Scotch accent is agreeable to me; and I amused her by eating some tomatoes raw; neither she, nor any of the company had ever seen them on the table without being cooked.

September 9. Dr. Traill has ordered all my drawings to be packed by the curator of the Institution, so that has given me no trouble whatever. It is hard to say farewell to all those in town and country who have been so kind, so hospitable to me, but to-morrow I leave for Manchester, where Mr. Roscoe advises me to go next.

Manchester, County of Lancashire, September 10, 1826. I must write something of my coming here. After bidding adieu to many friends, I went to Dr. Traill, who most kindly insisted on my taking Mr. Munro with me for two days to assist me, and we left by coach with my portfolios, my trunk to follow by a slower conveyance. I paid one pound for our inside seats. I felt depressed at leaving all my good friends, yet Mr. Munro did all in his power to interest me. He made me remark Lord Stanley's domains, and I looked on the Hares, Partridges, and other game with a thought of apprehension that the apparent freedom and security they enjoyed was very transient. I thought it more cruel to permit them to grow tame and gentle, and then suddenly to turn and murder them by thousands, than to give them the fair show that our game has in our forests, to let them be free and as wild as nature made them, and to let the hunter pay for them by the pleasure and work of pursuing them. We stopped, I thought frequently, to renew the horses, and wherever we stopped a neatly dressed maid offered cakes, ale, or other refreshments for sale. I remarked little shrubs in many parts of the meadows that concealed traps for moles and served as beacons for the persons who caught them. The road was good, but narrow, the country in a high degree of cultivation. We crossed a canal conducting from Liverpool here; the sails moving through the meadows reminded me of Rochester, N. Y. I am, then, now at Manchester, thirty-eight miles from Liverpool, and nearly six thousand from Louisiana.

Manchester, September 12. Yesterday was spent in delivering my letters to the different persons to whom I was recommended. The American consul, Mr. J. S. Brookes, with whom I shall dine to-morrow, received me as an American gentleman receives another, most cordially. The principal banker here, Arthur Heywood, Esq., was equally kind; indeed *everywhere* I meet a most amiable reception. I procured, through these gentlemen, a good room to exhibit my pictures, in the Exchange buildings, had it cleared, cleaned, and made ready by night. At five this morning Mr. Munro (the curator of the Institution at Liverpool and a most competent help) with several assistants and myself began putting up, and by eleven all was ready. Manchester, as I have seen it in my walks, seems a miserably laid out place, and the smokiest I ever was in. I think I ought not to use the words "laid out" at all. It is composed of an astonishing number of small, dirty, narrow, crooked lanes, where one cart can scarce pass another. It is full of noise and tumult; I thought last night not one person could have enjoyed repose. The postilion's horns, joined to the cry of the watchmen, kept my eyelids asunder till daylight again gave me leave to issue from the King's Arms. The population appears denser and worse off than in Liverpool. The vast number of youth of both sexes, with sallow complexions, ragged apparel, and downcast looks, made me feel they were not as happy as the slaves of Louisiana. Trade is slowly improving, but the times are dull. I have heard the *times* abused ever since my earliest recollections. I saw to-day several members of the Gregg family.

September 13, Wednesday. I have visited the Academy of Sciences; my time here was largely spoiled by one of those busybodies who from time to time rise to the surface, — a dealer in stuffed specimens, and there ends his history. I wished him in Hanover, or Congo, or New Zealand, or Bombay, or in a bomb-shell *en route* to eternity. Mr. Munro left me to-day, and I removed from the hotel to the house of a Mrs. Edge, in King Street, who keeps a circulating library; here I have more quietness and a comfortable parlor and bedroom. I engaged a man named Crookes, well recommended, to attend as money receiver at the door of my exhibition room. I pay him fifteen shillings per week; he finds himself, and copies letters for me. Two men came to the exhibition room and inquired if I wished a band of music to entertain the visitors. I thanked them, but do not consider it necessary in the company of so many songsters. My pictures here must depend on their *real* value; in Liverpool I *knew* I was supported by my particular friends. . . . It is eleven o'clock, and I have just returned from Consul Brookes' dinner. The company were all gentlemen, among whom were Mr. Lloyd, the wealthy banker, and Mr. Garnet. Our host is from Boston, a most intelligent and polite man. Judge of my surprise when, during the third course, I saw on the table a dish of Indian corn, purposely for me. To see me eat it buttered and salted, held as if I intended gagging myself, was a matter of much wonder to the English gentlemen, who did not like the vegetable. We had an English dinner Americanized, and the profusion of wines, and the quantity drank was uncomfortable to me; I was constantly obliged to say, "No." The gentleman next me was a good naturalist; much, of course, was said about my work and that of Charles Bonaparte. The conversation turned on politics, and Mr. Brookes and myself, the only Americans present, ranged ourselves and toasted "Our enemies in war, but our friends in peace." I am particularly fond of a man who speaks well of his country, and the peculiar warmth of Englishmen on this subject is admirable. I have had a note from Lord de Tabelay, who is anxious to see my drawings and me, and begs me to go to his domain fourteen miles distant, on my way to Birmingham. I observed that many persons who visited the exhibition room investigated my style more closely than at Liverpool. A Dr. Hulme spent several hours both yesterday and to-day looking at them, and I have been asked many times if they were for sale. I walked some four miles out of the town; the country is not so verdant, nor the country seats so clean-looking, as Green Bank for instance. The funnels raised from the manufactories to carry off the smoke appear in hundreds in every direction, and as you walk the street, the whirring sound of machinery is constantly in your ears. The changes in the weather are remarkable; at daylight it rained hard, at noon it was fair, this afternoon it rained again, at sunset was warm, and now looks like a severe frost.

September 14, Thursday. I have dined to-day at the home of Mr. George W. Wood, about two miles from the town. He drove me thither in company with four gentlemen, all from foreign countries, Mexico, Sumatra, Constantinople, and La Guayra; all were English and had been travelling for business or pleasure, not for scientific or literary purposes. Mrs. Wood was much interested in her gardens, which are very fine, and showed me one hundred bags of black gauze, which she had made to protect as many bunches of grapes from the wasps.

September 15. FROST. This morning the houses were covered with frost, and I felt uncommonly cold and shivery. My exhibition was poorly attended, but those who came seemed interested. Mr. Hoyle, the eminent chemist, came with four very pretty little daughters, in little gray satin bonnets, gray silk spencers, and white petticoats, as befitted them, being Quakers; also Mr. Heywood, the banker, who invited me to dine next Sunday. I spent the evening at the Rev. James I. Taylor's, in company with himself, his wife, and two gentlemen, one a Parisian. I cannot help expressing my surprise that the people of England, generally speaking, are so unacquainted with the customs and localities of our country. The principal conversation about it always turns to Indians and their ways, as if the land produced nothing else. Almost every lady in England draws in water-colors, many of them extremely well, very much better than I ever will do, yet few of them dare to show their productions. Somehow I do not like Manchester.

September 17, Sunday. I have been thinking over my stay in Liverpool; surely I can never express, much less hope to repay, my indebtedness to my many friends there, especially the Roscoes, the three families of Rathbone, and Dr. Thomas S. Traill. My drawings were exhibited for four weeks without a cent of expense to me, and brought me £100. I gave to the Institution a large piece, the wild Turkey Cock; to Mrs. Rathbone, Sr., the Otter in a trap, to Mr. Roscoe a Robin, and to many of my other friends some small drawing, as mementos of one who will always cherish their memories. I wrote a long letter to my son John Woodhouse urging him to spend much of his time at drawing *from nature only*, and to keep every drawing with the date, that he may trace improvement, if any, also to speak French constantly, that he may not forget a language in which he is now perfect. I have also written to the Governor of New York, his Excellency De Witt Clinton, to whose letters I am indebted for much of my cordial reception here. At two I started for Clermont, Mr. Heywood's residence, where I was to dine. The grounds are fine, and on a much larger scale than Green Bank, but the style is wholly different. The house is immense, but I was kindly received and felt at ease at once. After dinner the ladies left us early. We soon retired to the library to drink tea, and Miss Heywood showed me her portfolio of drawings, and not long after I took my leave.

September 18, Monday. Mr. Sergeant came for me at half-past three and escorted me to his house. I am delighted with him — his house — his pictures — his books — his guns — and his dogs, and very much so with a friend of his from London, who dined with us. The weather has been beautiful, and more persons than usual at my rooms.

September 19, Tuesday. I saw Mr. Melly this morning at the Exchange; he had not long arrived from Liverpool. He had been to my door-keeper, examined the *Book of Income*, and told me he was sorry and annoyed at my want of success, and advised me to go at once to London or Paris. He depressed me terribly, so that I felt really ill. He invited me to dine with him, but I told him I had already engaged to go to Mr. Samuel Gregg[1] at Quarry Bank, fourteen miles distant, to pass the night. Mr. Gregg, who is the father of a large family, met me as if he had known me fifty years; with him came his brother William and his daughter, the carriage was ready, and off we drove. We crossed a river in the course of our journey nearly fifty feet wide. I was told it was a stream of great importance: the name I have forgotten,[2] but I know it is seven miles from Manchester *en route* to Derbyshire. The land is highly improved, and grows wheat principally; the country is pretty, and many of the buildings are really beautiful. We turn down a declivity to Quarry Bank, a most enchanting spot, situated on the edge of the same river we had crossed, — the grounds truly picturesque, and cultivated to the greatest possible extent. In the drawing-room I met three ladies, the daughters of Mr. Gregg, and

[1] Relative of Mr. Wm. Rathbone, Sr. [2] The Irwell.

the second daughter of Mr. Wm. Rathbone. After tea I drew a dog in charcoal, and rubbed it with a cork to give an idea of the improvement over the common stumps ordinarily used. Afterwards I accompanied the two brothers to a debating club, instituted on their premises for the advancement of their workmen; on the way we passed a chapel and a long row of cottages for the work-people, and finally reached the schoolroom, where about thirty men had assembled. The question presented was "Which was the more advantageous, the discovery of the compass, or that of the art of printing?" I listened with interest, and later talked with the men on some of the wonders of my own country, in which they seemed to be much interested.

Quarry Bank, September 20. Though the weather was cloudy and somewhat rainy, I rose early, took an immense walk, up and down the river, through the gardens, along the road, and about the woods, fields, and meadows; saw a flock of Partridges, and at half-past eight had done this and daubed in a sketch of an Esquimau in a sledge, drawn by four dogs. The offer was made me to join a shooting party in the afternoon; all was arranged, and the pleasure augmented by the presence of Mr. Shaw, the principal game-keeper of Lord Stanford, who obligingly promised to show us many *birds* (so are Partridges called). Our guns are no longer than my arm, and we had two good dogs. Pheasants are not to be touched till the first of October, but an exception was made for me and one was shot, and I picked it up while his eye was yet all life, his feathers all brilliancy. We had a fine walk and saw the Derbyshire hills. Mr. Shaw pocketed five shillings, and we the game. This was my first hunting on English soil, on Lord Stanford's domain, where every tree — such as we should call saplings — was marked and numbered, and for all that I know pays either a tax to the government or a tithe to the parish. I am told that a Partridge which crosses the river, or a road, or a boundary, and alights on ground other than Lord Stanford's, is as safe from his gun as if in Guinea.

September 21. I returned to town this morning with my Pheasant. Reached my exhibition room and received miserable accounts. I see plainly that my expenses in Manchester will not be repaid, in which case I must move shortly. I called on Dr. Hulme and represented the situation, and he went to the Academy of Natural History and ordered a committee to meet on Saturday, to see if the Academy could give me a room. Later I mounted my pheasant, and all is ready for work to-morrow.

September 22. I have drawn all day and am fatigued. Only twenty people to see my birds; sad work this. The consul, Mr. Brookes, came to see me, and advised me to have a subscription book for my work. I am to dine with him at Mr. Lloyd's at one next Sunday.

September 23. My drawing this morning moved rapidly, and at eleven I walked to the Exchange and met Dr. Hulme and several other friends, who told me the Committee had voted unanimously to grant me a room gratis to exhibit my drawings. I thanked them most heartily, as this greatly lessens my expenses. More people than usual came to my rooms, and I dined with Mr. Samuel Gregg, Senior, in Fountain Street. I purchased some chalk, for which I paid more than four times as much as in Philadelphia, England is so overdone with duty. I visited the cotton mills of George Murray, Esq., where fifteen hundred souls are employed. These mills consist of a square area of about eight acres, built round with houses five, six, and seven stories high, having in the centre of the square a large basin of water from the canal. Two engines of forty and forty-five horse-power are kept going from 6 A. M. to 8 P. M. daily. Mr. Murray himself conducted me everywhere. This is the largest establishment owned by a single individual in Manchester. Some others, belonging to companies, have as many as twenty-five hundred hands, as poor, miserable, abject-looking wretches as ever worked in the mines of Golconda. I was asked to spend Monday night at Mr. Robert Hyde Gregg's place, Higher Ardwick, but I have a ticket for a fine concert, and I so love music that it is doubtful if I go. I took tea at Mr. Bartley's, and promised to write on his behalf for the bones of an alligator of a good size. Now we shall see if he gets one as quickly as did Dr. Harlan. I have concluded to have a "Book of Subscriptions" open to receive the names of all persons inclined to have the best illustrations of American birds yet published; but alas! I am but a beginner in depicting the beautiful works of God.

Sunday, September 24. I drew at my Pheasant till near eleven o'clock, the weather warm and cloudy. Then I went to church and then walked to Mr. Lloyd's. I left the city and proceeded two miles along the turnpike, having only an imperfect view of the country; I remarked, however, that the foliage was deeply colored with autumnal tints. I reached the home of Mr. Brookes, and together we proceeded to Mr. Lloyd's. This gentleman met us most kindly at the entrance, and we went with him through his garden and hot-houses. The grounds are on a declivity affording a far view of agreeable landscape, the gardens most beautifully provided with all this wonderful island affords, and the hot-houses contain abundant supplies of exotics, flower, fruit, and shrub. The coffee-tree was bearing, the banana ripening; here were juicy grapes from Spain and Italy, the sensitive plant shrunk at my touch, and all was growth, blossom, and perfume. Art here helps Nature to produce her richest treasures at will, and man in England, *if rich*, may be called the God of the present day. Flower after flower was plucked for me, and again I felt how perfectly an English gentleman makes a stranger feel at home. We were joined by Mr. Thomas Lloyd and Mr. Hindley as we moved towards the house, where we met Mrs. Lloyd, two daughters, and a lady whose name escapes me. We were, of course, surrounded by all that is rich, comfortable, pleasing to the eye. Three men servants in livery trimmed with red on a white ground moved quietly as Killdeers; everything was choice and abundant; the conversation was general and lively; but we sat at the table *five hours*, two after the ladies left us, and I grew restless; unless drawing or out of doors I like not these long periods of repose. After joining the ladies in the library, tea and coffee were served, and in another hour we were in a coach *en route* for Manchester.

September 25. Who should come to my room this morning about seven whilst I was busily finishing the ground of my Pheasant but a handsome Quaker, about thirty years of age and very neatly dressed, and thus he spoke: "My friends are going out of Manchester before thee opens thy exhibition rooms; can we see thy collection at nine o'clock?" I answer, "Yes," and show him my drawing. Now were all the people here Quakers, I might perhaps have some encouragement, but really, my Lucy, my times are dull, heavy, long, painful, and my mind much harassed. Five minutes before nine I was standing waiting for the Quaker and his friends in the lobby of the Exchange, when two persons came in and held the following discourse. "Pray, have you seen Mr. Audubon's collections of birds? I am told it is well worth a shilling; suppose we go now." "Pah! it is all a hoax; save your shilling for better use. I *have* seen them; the fellow ought to be drummed out of town." I dared not raise my head lest I might be known, but depend upon it I wished myself in America. The Quakers, however, restored my equilibrium, for they all praised my drawings so much that I blushed in spite of my old age. I took my drawing of the Pheasant to Mr. Fanetti's (?) shop and had it put in a good light. I have made arrangements to have my pictures in my new place in King Street, and hope to do better next week. At four I took down two hundred and forty drawings and packed them ready for removal. Now for the concert. It was six o'clock and raining when I left for Fountain Street, where already carriages had accumulated to a great number. I presented my ticket, and was asked to write my name and residence, for this is not exactly a public affair, but most select; so I am told. The room is full of red, white, blue, and green turbans well fitted to the handsome heads of the ladies. I went to one side where my ear and my intellect might be well satisfied, and where I should not be noticed; but it would not do, my long hair and unfashionable garments were observed far more than was agreeable to me. But the music soon began, and I forgot all else for the time; still between the various performances I felt myself gazed at through lorgnettes, and was most ill at ease. I have passed many uncomfortable evenings in company, and this one may be added.

Quarry Bank, September 26. Whilst putting up my pictures in my newly granted "apartment" I received a note from Mrs. Gregg inviting me here for the night to meet Professor Smyth.[1] He is a tall, fine-looking gentleman from Cambridge, full of knowledge, good taste, and kindness. At dinner the Professor sat opposite the Woodsman, and America was largely the topic of conversation. One evening spent with people such as these is worth a hundred fashionable ones.

Wednesday, September 27. It is a strange atmosphere, warm, damp, rainy, then fair again, all in less than two hours, which was the time consumed by my early walk. On my return soon after eight I found four of the ladies all drawing in the library; that in this country is generally the sitting-room. At about ten we had breakfast, when we talked much of duels, and of my friend Clay[2] and

[1] William Smyth, 1766–1849, poet, scholar, and Professor of Modern History at Cambridge.

[2] Henry Clay.

crazy Randolph.[1] Much is unknown about our country, and yet all are deeply interested in it. To-morrow I am off to Liverpool again; how much I shall enjoy being once again with the charming Rathbones.

Green Bank, near Liverpool, September 28. At five this morning I left Manchester and its smoke behind me; but I left there the labors of about ten years of my life, fully one half of my collection. The ride was a wet one, heavy rain falling continuously. I was warmly welcomed by my good Liverpool friends, and though completely drenched I felt it not, so glad was I to be in Liverpool again. My being here is soon explained. I felt it best to see Dr. Traill and Mr. Roscoe, and I dined with the latter; we talked of Manchester and our friends there, and Mr. Roscoe thought well of the subscription book. From here to Green Bank, where I am literally *at home.* Mr. Rathbone and Mr. Roscoe will both aid me in the drawing up of a prospectus for my work.

Green Bank, September 29. It rained during the night and all the early portion of the day. I breakfasted early, and at half-past nine Mr. Rathbone and I drove in the gig to Mrs. Wm. S. Roscoe.[2] After a little conversation we decided nothing could be done about the prospectus without more definite knowledge of what the cost of publication would be, and I was again referred to Dr. Traill. It happened that here I met a Mr. Bohn, from London, not a publisher, but a bookseller with an immense establishment, two hundred thousand volumes as a regular stock. He advised me to proceed at once to London, meet the principal naturalists of the day, and through them to see the best engravers, colorists, printers, paper-merchants, etc., and thus form some idea of the cost; then to proceed to Paris, Brussels, and possibly Berlin,

[1] John Randolph of Roanoke, 1773–1833, American orator and statesman.

[2] William S. Roscoe, son of William Roscoe, 1781–1843.

with proper letters, and follow the same course, thereby becoming able to judge of the advantages and disadvantages attached to each country and *to determine myself when, where, and how* the work should be undertaken; to be during this time, through the medium of friends, correspondence, and scientific societies, announced to the world in some of the most widely read periodical publications. "Then, Mr. Audubon, issue a prospectus, and bring forth one number of your work, and I think you will succeed and do well; but remember my observations on the *size* of your book, and be governed by this fact, that at present productions of taste are purchased with delight, by persons who receive much company particularly, and to have your book laid on the table as a pastime, or an evening's entertainment, will be the principal use made of it, and that if it needs so much room as to crowd out other things or encumber the table, it will not be purchased by the set of people who now are the very life of the trade. If large public institutions only and a few noblemen purchase, instead of a thousand copies that may be sold if small, not more than a hundred will find their way out of the shops; the size must be suitable for the *English market*" (such was his expression), "and ought not to exceed that of double Wilson." This conversation took place in the presence of Dr. Traill, and both he and Mr. Roscoe are convinced it is my only plan. Mr. Bohn told Dr. Traill, as well as myself, that exhibiting my pictures would not do well; that I might be in London a year before I should be known at all, but that through the scientific periodicals I should be known over Europe in the same time, when probably my first number would be published. He strongly advised me to have the work printed and finished in Paris, bring over to England say two hundred and fifty copies, to have it bound and the titlepage printed, to be issued to the world of England as an English publication. *This I will not do;* no work of

FROM A PENCIL SKETCH OF AUDUBON.

DRAWN BY HIMSELF FOR MRS. RATHBONE.

Now in the possession of Mr. Richard R. Rathbone, Glan-y-Menai, Anglesey.

mine shall be other than true metal — if copper, copper, if gold, gold, but not copper gilded. He admitted it would be a great undertaking, and immensely laborious, but, he added, my drawings being so superior, I might rest assured success would eventually be mine. This plan, therefore, I will pursue with the same perseverance that since twenty-five years has not wavered, and God's will be done. Having now determined on this I will return to Manchester after a few days, visit thy native place, gaze on the tombs of thy ancestors in Derby and Leicester, and then enter London with a head humbly bent, but with a heart intently determined to conquer. On returning to this abode of peace, I was overtaken by a gentleman in a gig, unknown to me quite, but who offered me a seat. I thanked him, accepted, and soon learned he was a Mr. Dearman. He left me at Green Bank, and the evening was truly delightful.

September 30, Woodcroft. I am now at Mr. Richard Rathbone's; I did not leave Green Bank this morning till nearly noon. The afternoon was spent with Dr. Traill, with whom I dined; there was only his own family, and I was much entertained by Dr. Traill and his son. A man of such extensive and well digested knowledge as Dr. Traill cannot fail to be agreeable. About eight his son drove me to Woodcroft, where were three other guests, Quakers. The remainder of the evening was spent with a beautiful microscope and a Diamond Beetle. Mr. Rathbone is enthusiastic over my publishing plans, and I will proceed with firm resolution to attempt the being an author. It is a terrible thing to me; far better am I fitted to study and delineate in the forest, than to arrange phrases with suitable grammatical skill. For the present the public exhibiting of my work will be laid aside, — *I* hope, forever. I now intend going to Matlock, and from there to my Lucy's native place, pass through Oxford, and so reach the great London, and once more become the man of business. From there to France, but, except to see my venerable mother, I shall not like France, I am sure, as I *now* do England; and I sincerely hope that this country may be preferred to that, on financial grounds, for the production of my work. Yet I love France most truly, and long to enter my old garden on the Loire and with rapid steps reach my mother, — yes, my mother! the only one I truly remember; and no son ever had a better, nor more loving one. Let no one speak of her as my "stepmother." I was ever to her as a son of her own flesh and blood, and she to me a true mother. I have written to Louisiana to have forwarded from Bayou Sara six segments of magnolia, yellow-poplar, beech, button-wood or sycamore, sassafras, and oak, each about seven or eight inches in thickness of the largest diameter that can be procured in the woods; to have each segment carefully handled so as not to mar the bark, and to have each name neatly painted on the face, with the height of the tree. These are for the Liverpool Royal Institution.

Green Bank, October 1. Though the morning was bright it was near four before I left my room and stepped into the fresh air, where I could watch the timid birds fly from bush to bush before me. I turned towards the Mersey reflecting the calm, serene skies, and listened to the voice of the Quail, here so shy. I walked to the tide-beaten beach and watched the Solan Goose in search of a retreat from the destroyer, man. Suddenly a poorly dressed man, in somewhat of a sailor garb, and carrying a large bag dashed past me; his movement suggested flight, and instinctively I called, "Stop thief!" and made towards him in a style that I am sure he had never seen used by the gentlemen of the customs, who at this hour are doubtless usually drowsy. I was not armed, but to my surprise he turned, fell at my feet, and with eyes starting from his head with apprehension, begged for mercy, said the bag only contained a few leaves of rotten tobacco, and it was the first time he had ever smuggled. This, then, was a smuggler! I told him to rise, and as he did so I perceived the boat that had landed him. There were five men in it, but instead of landing and defending their companion, they fled by rowing, like cowards, swiftly away. I was astonished at such conduct from Englishmen. I told the abject creature to bring his bag and open it; this he did. It was full of excellent tobacco, but the poor wretch looked ill and half starved, and I never saw a human being more terrified. He besought me to take the tobacco and let him go, that it was of the rarest quality. I assured him I never had smoked a single cigar, nor did I intend to, and told him to take care he did not offend a second time. One of my pockets was filled with the copper stuff the shop-keepers here give, which they call penny. I gave them all to him, and told him to go. He thanked me many times and disappeared through a thick hedge. The bag must have contained fifty pounds of fine tobacco and two pistols, which were not loaded, or so he said. I walked back to Green Bank thinking of the smuggler. When I told Mr. Rathbone of my adventure he said I had been extremely rash, and that I might have been shot dead on the spot, as these men are often desperadoes. Well! I suppose I might have thought of this, but dear me! one cannot always think over every action carefully before committing it. On my way back I passed a man digging potatoes; they were small and indifferently formed. The season has been uncommonly dry and hot — so the English say; for my part I am almost freezing most of the time, and I have a bad cough.

October 2. This morning Mrs. Rathbone asked me if I would draw her a sketch of the Wild Turkey, about the size of my thumb-nail. I assured her I would with pleasure, but that I could perhaps do better did I know for what purpose. She colored slightly, and replied after a moment that it was for something she desired to have made; so after I had reached the Institution and finished my business there, I sat opposite my twenty-three hours' picture and made the diminutive sketch in less than twenty-three minutes. The evening was spent at Woodcroft, and Mr. Rathbone sent his servant to drive me in the gig to Green Bank, the night being cold and damp. The man was quite surprised I did not make use of a great coat which had been placed at my disposal. How little he knew how often I had lain down to rest, wet, hungry, harassed and full of sorrow, with millions of mosquitoes buzzing round me as I lay awake listening to the Chuckmill's Widow, the Horned Owl, and the hoarse Bull-frog, impatiently awaiting the return of day to enable me to hunt the forests and feast my eyes on their beautiful inhabitants. I thought of all this and then moved the scene to the hunter's cabin. Again wet, harassed, and hungry, I felt the sudden warmth of the "Welcome, stranger!" saw the busy wife unhook dry clothes from the side of the log hut, untie my moccasins, and take my deerskin coat; I saw the athletic husband wipe my gun, clean the locks, hang all over the bright fire; the eldest boy pile on more wood, whilst my ears were greeted with the sound of the handmill crushing the coffee, or the rye, for my evening drink; I saw the little ones, roused by the stranger's arrival, peeping from under the Buffalo robe, and then turn over on the Black Bear skin to resume their slumbers. I *saw* all this, and then arrived at Green Bank to meet the same hearty welcome. The squatter is rough, true, and hospitable; my friends here polished, true, and generous. Both give what they have, freely, and he who during the tough storms of life can be in such spots may well say he has known happiness.

Green Bank, October 3. To-day I have visited the jail at Liverpool. The situation is fine, it is near the mouth of the estuary that is called the river Mersey, and from its

AUDUBON IN INDIAN DRESS.

From a pencil sketch drawn by himself for Miss Rathbone, 1826. Now in the possession of Mrs. Abraham Dixon (*née* Rathbone), London, England.

walls is an extensive view of the Irish Channel. The area owned by this institution is about eight acres. It is built almost circular in form, having gardens in the court in the centre, a court of sessions on one side and the main entrance on the other. It contains, besides the usual cells, a chapel, and yards in which the prisoners take exercise, kitchens, store-rooms, etc., besides treadmills. The treadmills I consider infamous; conceive a wild Squirrel in a round cage constantly moving, without progressing. The labor is too severe, and the true motive of correction destroyed, as there are no mental resources attached to this laborious engine of shame. Why should not these criminals — if so they are — be taught different trades, enabling them when again thrown into the world to earn their living honestly? It would be more profitable to the government, and the principle would be more honorable. It is besides injurious to health; the wheel is only six feet in diameter, therefore the motion is rapid, and each step must be taken in quick succession, and I know a quick, short step is more fatiguing than a long one. The emaciated bodies of the poor fellows proved this to my eyes, as did my powers of calculation. The circulation of air was much needed; it was painful to me to breathe in the room where the mill was, and I left it saddened and depressed. The female department is even more lamentable, but I will say no more, except that my guide and companion was Miss Mary Hodgson, a Quakeress of great benevolence and solid understanding, whose labors among these poor unfortunates have been of immense benefit. I dined with her, her sister and brother, the latter a merchant of this busy city.

Manchester, October 6. This morning after four hours' rest I rose early. Again taking my boots in my hand, I turned the latch gently, and found myself alone in the early dawn. It was one of those mornings when not sufficiently cold for a frost; the dew lay in large drops on each object, weighing down the points of every leaf, every blade of grass. The heavens were cloudless, all breezes hushed, and the only sound the twitterings of the Red-breasted Warbler. I saw the Blackbird mounted on the slender larch, waiting to salute the morning sun, the Thrush on the grass by the mulberry tree, and the Lark unwilling to bid farewell to summer. The sun rose, the Rook's voice now joined with that of the Magpie. I saw a Stock Pigeon fly over me, and I started and walked swiftly into Liverpool. Here, arriving before six, no one was up, but by repeated knockings I aroused first Mr. Pillet, and then Mr. Melly. On my return to the country I encountered Mr. Wm. Roscoe, also out for an early walk. For several days past the last Swallows have flown toward the south, frosts have altered the tints of the foliage, and the mornings have been chilly; and I was rubbing my hands to warm them when I met Mr. Roscoe. "A fine, warm morning this, Mr. Audubon." "Yes," I replied, "the kind of morning I like a fire with half a cord of wood." He laughed and said I was too tropical in my tastes, but I was glad to keep warm by my rapid walking. At eleven I was on my way to Manchester, this time in a private carriage with Mrs. Rathbone and Miss Hannah. We changed horses twelve miles from Green Bank; it was done in a moment, up went a new postilion, and off we went. Our luncheon had been brought with us, and was really *well served* as we rolled swiftly along. After plenty of substantials, our dessert consisted of grapes, pears, and a melon, this last by no means so frequently seen here as in Louisiana. We reached smoky Manchester and I was left at the door of the Academy of Natural History, where I found the man I had left in charge much intoxicated. Seldom in my life have I felt more vexed. When he is sober I shall give him the opportunity of immediately finding a new situation.

Quarry Bank, October 7, Saturday. From Green Bank to Quarry Bank from one pleasure to another, is not like the butterfly that skips from flower to flower and merely sees their beauties, but more, I hope, as a bee gathering honeyed stores for future use. My cold was still quite troublesome, and many remedies were offered me, but I never take physic, and will not, even for kind Mrs. Gregg.

Sunday, October 8. I went to church at Mr. Gregg's chapel; the sermon was good, and the service being over, took Miss Helen a long ramble through the gardens, in which even now there is much of beauty.

October 9. As soon as possible a male Chaffinch was procured, and I sat to draw it to give an idea of what Mrs. Gregg calls " my style." The Chaffinch was outlined, daubed with water-colors, and nearly finished when we were interrupted by callers, Dr. Holland among them, with whom I was much pleased and interested, though I am neither a craniologist nor a physiognomist. Lord Stanford's gamekeeper again came for us, and we had a long walk, and I killed a Pheasant and a Hare.

October 10. To-day I returned to Manchester to meet Mr. Bohn. We went to the Academy together, and examined my drawings. Mr. Bohn was at first simply surprised, then became enthusiastic, and finally said they must be published the full size of life, and he was *sure* they would pay. God grant it! He strongly advised me to leave Manchester, and go to London, where he knew I should at once be recognized. I dined at the good Quaker's, Mr. Dockray, where my friends Mrs. and Miss Rathbone are visiting; there is a large and interesting family. I sketched an Egret for one, a Wild Turkey for another, a Wood Thrush for a third.

Bakewell, October 11. I am at last, my Lucy, at the spot which has been honored with thy ancestor's name. Though dark and rainy I have just returned from a walk in the churchyard of the village, where I went with Miss Hannah Rathbone, she and her mother having most kindly accompanied me hither. It was perhaps a strange place to go first, but we were attracted by the ancient Gothic edifice. It seemed to me a sort of illusion that made me doubt whether I lived or dreamed. When I think how frequently our plans have been laid to come here, and how frequently defeated, it is no great wonder that I find it hard to believe I am here at last. This morning at breakfast, Lady Rathbone spoke of coming to Matlock, and in a few moments all was arranged. She, with her niece, Mrs. Dockray, and Miss Hannah, with several of the children and myself, should leave in two chaises at noon. I spent the time till then in going over Mr. Dockray's wool mill. He procures the wool rough from the sheep, and it is cloth when he disposes of it; he employs about seventy weavers, and many other people in the various departments. I was much interested in the dyeing apparatus. I packed up a few of my drawings to take with me. We started, seven of us, in two chaises; all was new, and therefore interesting. We reached Stockport, a manufacturing town lying between two elongated hillsides, where we changed horses, and again at Chapel En-La-Frith, thirty miles from the point of departure. I saw a good deal of England that I admired very much. The railways were new to me, but the approach of the mountains dampened my spirits; the aridity of the soil, the want of hedges, and of course of birds, the scarcity of cattle, and the superabundance of stone walls cutting the hills in all sorts of distorted ways, made me a very unsocial companion, but the comfortable inn, and our lively evening has quite restored my cheerfulness.

Matlock, October 12. This morning I was out soon after sunrise; again I walked round the church, remarked its decaying state, and that of all the thatched roofs of the humble cottages. I ascended the summit of the hill, crossing a bridge which spanned a winding stream, and had a lovely view of the country just lighted by the sun's first beams, and returned to the inn, the Rutland Arms, in time for the hour of departure, seven. The weather was now somewhat fitful, but the road good, and the valley charming. We passed the seat of the Duke of Devonshire, and Matlock opened to our eyes in all its beauty, the hills dotted with cottages and gentlemen's seats, the autumnal tints diversifying the landscape and enriching beautiful nature; the scenery reminds me of that part of America on the river called the Clear Juniata. All is remarkably clean; we rise slowly to more elevated ground, leave the river and approach the New Baths Hotel, where our host, Mr. Saxton, has breakfast ready. After this we took a long walk, turning many times to view the delightful scenery, though the weather had become quite rainy. We visited the celebrated cave, each carrying a lighted candle, and saw the different chambers containing rich minerals and spars; the walls in many places shone like burnished steel. On our return, which was down-hill, I heard with much pleasure the repeated note of the Jackdaws that constantly flew from hole to hole along the rocky declivities about us. After dinner, notwithstanding the rain, we rowed in a boat down the stream, to a dam and a waterfall, where we landed, walked through the woods, gathered some beautiful mosses, and saw some Hares, heard a Kestrell just as if in America, returned to our boat and again rowed, but this time up-stream, and so left the Derwent River.

Matlock, October 13. Still rainy, but I found a sheltered spot, and made this sketch. We entered part of the grounds of Sir Thomas Arkwright, saw his castle, his church, and his meadows. The Rooks and Jackdaws were over our heads by hundreds. The steep banks of the Derwent were pleasantly covered with shrubby trees; the castle on the left bank, on a fine elevation, is too regular to be called (by me) well adapted to the rich natural scenery about it. We passed along a canal, by a large manufactory, and a coal-yard to the inn, the Crumford, and the rest of the day was employed in drawing. The sketch I took was from "The Heights of Abraham," and I copied it for Miss Hannah. About sunset we visited the Rutland Cave, which surpassed all my expectations; the natural chambers sparkled with brilliancy, and lights were placed everywhere. I saw there some little fishes which had not seen the daylight for three years, and yet were quite sprightly. A certain portion of the roof represented a very good head of a large tiger. I imitated, at Mrs. Rathbone's request, the Owl's cry, and the Indian yell. This latter music never pleased my fancy much, and I well know the effects it produces previous to and during an attack whilst the scalping knife is at work. We had a pleasant walk back to the inn, for the evening was calm and clear, and the moon shone brightly; so after a hasty tea we all made for the river, took a boat, and seated ourselves to contemplate the peace around us. I rowed, and sung many of the river songs which I learned in scenes far from quiet Matlock.

Manchester, October 14, Mr. Dockray's House, Hardwick. By five o'clock this morning I was running by the Derwent; everything was covered with sparkling congealed dew. The fog arising from the little stream only permitted us to see its waters when they made a ripple against some rock. The vale was all mist, and had I not known where I was, and heard the notes of the Jackdaws above my head, I might have conceived myself walking through a subterraneous passage. But the sun soon began to dispel the mist, and gradually the tops of the trees, the turrets of the castle, and the church pierced through, and stood as if suspended above all objects below. All was calm till a bell struck my ear, when I soon saw the long files of women and little girls moving towards Arkwright's Mills. Almost immediately we started for Bakewell, and breakfasted at the Rutland Arms. Proceeding we changed our route, and made for the well known watering place, Buxton, still in Derbyshire. The country here is barren, rocky, but so picturesque that the want of trees is almost atoned for. The road winds along a very narrow valley for several miles, bringing a vast variety of detached views before us, all extremely agreeable to the sight. The scantiness of vegetable growth forces the cattle to risk much to obtain food, and now and then when seeing a bull, on bent knee with outstretched neck, putting out his tongue to seize the few grasses hanging over the precipices, I was alarmed for his safety. The Hawk here soars in vain; after repeated rounds he is forced to abandon the dreary steep, having espied only a swift Kingfisher. Suddenly the view was closed, a high wall of rock seemed to put an end to our journey, yet the chaise ran swiftly down-hill, and turning a sharp angle afforded delight to our eyes. Here we alighted and walked to view the beauties around at our leisure, and we reached the large inn, the Crescent, where I met the American consul, my friend Mr. Maury, who has visited this place regularly for twenty-five years. We had what my friends called a luncheon; I considered it an excellent dinner, but the English eat heartily. On our resuming our journey a fine drizzle set in, and as we neared Manchester the air became thick with coal smoke, the carts, coaches, and horsemen gradually filled the road, faces became less clean and rosy, and the children had none of the liveliness found amongst those in the Derbyshire Hills. I dreaded returning to the town, yet these days among the beauties of England in such delightful society are enough to refresh one after years of labor.

Manchester, October 15, Sunday. I went to the Unitarian Chapel to hear a sermon from the Rev. John Taylor, but to my regret he had gone to preach elsewhere, and I was obliged to content myself with another, — not quite so practical a sermon as I care for. I dined and spent the night at Mr. Bentley's; after retiring to my room I was surprised at a knock; I opened my door and there stood Mr. Bentley, who said he thought he heard me asking for something as he passed by. I told him I prayed aloud every night, as had been my habit from a child at my mother's knees in Nantes. He said nothing for a moment, then again wished me good-night, and was gone.

October 18. This evening I was to dine with Dr. Hulme and (as he said) "*a few friends;*" so when at four o'clock I entered his sitting-room, I was surprised to find it filled with ladies and gentlemen, and felt awkward for a moment. Some of my drawings were asked for, and at five we went to dinner; after the ladies had retired, wine and wit flowed till a late hour.

Quarry Bank, 12 miles from Manchester, October 19. At five, my cane in hand, I made my way from Manchester, bound on foot for Quarry Bank; the morning was pleasant and I enjoyed my walk very much, but found myself quite out of the right road; therefore, instead of twelve miles, I measured sixteen, and was hungry enough when I reached my destination. I was soon put at my drawing, and drew the whole day; in the afternoon I began a sketch of Mr. Gregg, and felt quite satisfied with my work, but not so everybody else. Faults were found, suggestions made, and I enjoyed the criticisms very much, especially those of an Irish nephew of Mr. Gregg's, who, after several comments, drew me confidentially aside, and asked who it was intended to represent; after this, amid hearty laughter, I concluded to finish it next day. Later we took a walk and I entered a cottage where dwelt a silk weaver; all was clean and well arranged, and I saw the weaving going on for the first time since I left France.

October 20. Drawing again all morning, and a walk later. I was taken to a cottage, where to my great surprise I saw two cases of well stuffed birds, the work of the weaver who lived in the cottage. I was taken to the dairy, where I saw the finest cattle I have yet met with in England.

October 21. This has been a busy day. On my return from Quarry Bank I saw Mr. Bentley, Mr. Heywood, and other friends. Mr. H. gave me a letter to Professor Jameson, of Edinburgh. Called on Dr. Hulme; paid, in all, twenty visits, and dined with Mr. Bentley,[1] and with his assistance packed up my birds safe and snug, though much fatigued; it was late when we parted; he is a brother Mason and has been most kind to me. I wrote down for Mrs. Rathbone a brief memorandum of the flight of birds, with a few little pencil sketches to make my figures more interesting: Swallows, two and a half miles a minute; Wild Pigeons, when travelling, two miles per minute; Swans, ditto two miles, Wild Turkeys, one mile and three quarters.

Manchester, October 23, 1826, Monday. This day was absolutely all spent packing and making ready for my start for Edinburgh; my seat in the coach taken and paid for,—three pounds fifteen shillings. I spent my last evening with Mr. Bentley and his family. As the coach leaves at 5 A. M., I am sleeping at the inn to be ready when called. I am leaving Manchester much poorer than I was when I entered it.

Carlisle, Tuesday, October 24. The morning was clear and beautiful, and at five I left Manchester; but as no dependence can be placed on the weather in this country, I prepared for rain later. I was alone in the coach, and had been regretting I had no companion, when a very tall gentleman entered, but after a few words, he said he was much fatigued and wished to sleep; he composed himself therefore and soon slept soundly. How I envied him! We rolled on, however, and arrived at the village of Preston, where we breakfasted as quickly as if we had been Kentuckians. The coaches were exchanged, packages transferred, and I entered the conveyance and met two

[1] I believe Mr. Robert Bentley, the publisher.

new gentlemen whose appearance I liked; we soon commenced to chat, and before long were wandering all over America, part of India, and the Atlantic Ocean. We discussed the emancipation of the slaves, and the starvation of the poor in England, the Corn Law, and many other topics, the while I looked frequently from the windows. The approach to Lancaster is beautiful; the view of the well placed castle is commanding, and the sea view bounded by picturesque shores. We dined at Kendal, having passed through Bolton and Burton, but before this my two interesting companions had been left behind at a place where we stopped to change horses, and only caught up with the coach by running across some fields. This caused much altercation between them, the driver, and the guard; one of the proprietors of the coach who was on board interfered, and being very drunk made matters worse, and a complaint was lodged against driver and guard. The tall gentleman was now wide awake; he introduced himself as a Mr. Walton, and knew the other gentlemen, who were father and son, the Messrs. Patison from Cornwall; all were extremely polite to me, a stranger in their land, but so have I ever found the *true English gentleman.*

We now entered a most dreary country, poor beyond description, immense rolling hills in constant succession, dotted here and there with miserable cots, the residences of poor shepherds. No game was seen, the weather was bleak and rainy, and I cannot say that I now enjoyed the ride beyond the society of my companions. We passed through Penrith and arrived at Carlisle at half-past nine, having ridden one hundred and twenty-two miles. I was told that in hard winters the road became impassable, so choked with snow, and that when not entirely obstructed it was customary to see posts painted black at the top, every hundred yards or so, to point out the road surely. We had a miserable supper, but good beds, and I enjoyed mine, for I felt very wearied, my cold and cough having been much increased from my having ridden outside the coach some thirty miles, to see the country.

Edinburgh, Scotland, October 25, Wednesday. We breakfasted at Carlisle, left there at eight, but I was sadly vexed at having to pay twelve shillings for my trunk and portfolio, as I had been positively assured at Manchester that no further charge would be made. For perhaps ten miles we passed through an uncommonly flat country, meandering awhile along a river, passed through a village called Longtown, and entered *Scotland* at ten minutes before ten. I was then just six miles from the spot where runaway matches are rendered lawful. The country changed its aspect, and became suddenly quite woody; we ran along, and four times crossed a beautiful little stream like a miniature Mohawk; many little rapids were seen in its windings. The foliage was about to fall, and looked much as it does with us about our majestic western streams, only much less brilliant. This scenery, however, lasted only one stage of perhaps twelve miles, and again we entered country of the same dreariness as yesterday, mere burnt mountains, which were not interesting. The number of sheep grazing on these hills was very great, and they all looked well, though of a very small species; many of them had black heads and legs, the body white, with no horns; others with horns, and still others very small, called here "Cheviots." The shepherds were poor, wrapped up in a thin piece of plaid, and did not seem of that noble race so well painted by Sir Walter Scott. I saw the sea again to-day. We dined at Hawick on excellent sea fish, and for the first time in my life, I tasted Scotch whiskey. It appeared very potent, so after a few sips I put it down, and told Mr. Patison I suspected his son of wishing to make me tipsy; to which he replied that probably it was to try if I would in such a case be as good-natured as I was before. I took this as quite a compliment and forgave the son. The conversation at dinner was very agreeable, several Scotch gentlemen having joined us; some of them drank their native whiskey pure, as if water, but I found it both smoky and fiery; so much for habit. We passed through Selkirk, having driven nearly the whole day through the estates of the young Duke of ——, a young fellow of twenty who passes his days just now shooting Black-cock; he has something like two hundred thousand pounds per annum. Some of the shepherds on this astonishing estate have not probably more than two hundred pounds of oatmeal, a terrible contrast. We passed so near Sir Walter Scott's seat that I stood up and stretched my neck some inches to see it, but in vain, and who knows if I shall ever see the home of the man to whom I am indebted for so much pleasure? We passed a few miles from Melrose; I had a great wish to see the old abbey, and the gentleman to whom Dr. Rutter had given me a letter, but the coach rolled on, and at ten o'clock I entered this splendid city. I have seen yet but a very small portion of it, and that by gaslight, yet I call it a splendid city! The coach stopped at the Black Bull Hotel, but it was so full no room could be procured, so we had our baggage taken to the Star. The clerk, the guard, the driver, all swore at my baggage, and said that had I not paid at Carlisle, I would have been charged more here. Now it is true that my trunk is large and heavy, and so is the portfolio I carry with me, but to give an idea of the charges and impositions connected with these coaches (or their owners) and the attendants, remark the price I paid; to begin with,—

at Manchester,	£3	15	00,	
at Carlisle,		12	00,	and during the
two days to drivers and guards,		18	06,	
	£5	5	06,	

nearly twenty-seven dollars in our money for two days' travelling from Manchester to Edinburgh. It is not so much the general amount, although I am sure it is quite enough for two hundred and twelve miles, but the beggarly manners used to obtain about one half of it; to see a fellow with a decent coat on, who calls himself an independent free-born Englishman, open the door of the coach every ten or twelve miles, and beg for a shilling each time, is detestable, and quite an abuse; but this is not all: they never are satisfied, and if you have the appearance of wealth about you, they hang on and ask for more. The porters here were porters indeed, carrying all on their backs, the first I have seen in this island. At the Star we had a good supper, and chatted a long time, and it was near one before the Messrs. Patison and I parted; Mr. Walton had gone on another course. I thought so much of the multitude of learned men that abound in this place, that I dreaded the delivery of my letters to-morrow.

George St., Edinburgh, October 26. It was ten o'clock when I breakfasted, because I wished to do so with the Patisons, being so much pleased with their company. I was much interested in the different people in the room, which was quite full, and the waiters were kept skipping about with the nimbleness of Squirrels. My companions, who knew Edinburgh well, offered to accompany me in search of lodgings, and we soon entered the second door in George Street, and in a few minutes made an arrangement with Mrs. Dickie for a fine bedroom and a well furnished sitting-room. I am to pay her one guinea per week, which I considered low, as the situation is fine, and the rooms clean and comfortable. I can see, from where I am now writing, the Frith, and the boats plying on it. I had my baggage brought by a man with a tremendous beard, who imposed on me most impudently by bringing a brass shilling, which he said he would swear I had given him. I gave him another, threw the counterfeit in the fire, and promised to myself to pay some little attention hereafter to what kind of money I give or receive. I walked to

Professor Jameson's[1] in the Circus, — not at home; to James Hall, Advocate, 128 George St., — absent in the country. Dr. Charles Henry of the Royal Infirmary was sought in vain, Dr. Thompson was out also, and Professor Duncan[2] could not be seen until six o'clock. I only saw Dr. Knox in Surgeon's Square, and Professor Jameson at the college. This latter received me, I thought, rather coolly; said that Sir Walter Scott was now quite a recluse, and was busy with a novel and the Life of Napoleon, and that probably I should not see him. "*Not see Walter Scott?*" thought I; "I SHALL, if I have to crawl on all-fours for a mile!" But I was a good deal surprised when he added it would be several days before *he* could pay me a visit, that his business was large, and must be attended to; but I could not complain, as I am bent on doing the same towards myself; and besides, why should I expect any other line of conduct? I have been spoiled by the ever-to-be-remembered families of Roscoes and Rathbones. Dr. Knox came at once to see me, dressed in an overgown and with bloody fingers. He bowed, washed his hands, read Dr. Traill's letter, and promised me at once to do all in his power for me and my drawings, and said he would bring some scientific friends to meet me, and to examine my drawings. Dr. Knox is a distinguished anatomist, and a great student; Professor Jameson's special science is mineralogy. I walked a good deal and admired the city very much, the great breadth of the streets, the good pavements and footways, the beautiful buildings, their natural gray coloring, and wonderful cleanliness; perhaps all was more powerfully felt, coming direct from dirty

[1] Robert Jameson, the eminent Scotch naturalist, 1774–1854. Regius Professor of Natural History in the University of Edinburgh. Founder of the Wernerian Society of that city, and with Sir David Brewster originated the "Edinburgh Philosophical Review." Wrote many works on geology and mineralogy.

[2] Andrew Duncan, M. D., 1745–1828. Lecturer in the University of Edinburgh.

Manchester, but the picturesqueness of the *toute ensemble* is wonderful. A high castle here, another there, on to a bridge whence one looks at a second city below, here a rugged mountain, and there beautiful public grounds, monuments, the sea, the landscape around, all wonderfully put together indeed; it would require fifty different views at least to give a true idea, but I will try from day to day to describe what I may see, either in the old or new part of the town. I unpacked my birds and looked at them with pleasure, and yet with a considerable degree of fear that they would never be published. I felt very much alone, and many dark thoughts came across my mind; I felt one of those terrible attacks of depression to which I so often fall a prey overtaking me, and I forced myself to go out to destroy the painful gloom that I dread at all times, and of which I am sometimes absolutely afraid. After a good walk I returned more at ease, and looked at a pair of stuffed pheasants on a large buffet in my present sitting-room, at the sweetly scented geraniums opposite to them, the black hair-cloth sofa and chairs, the little cherubs on the mantelpiece, the painted landscape on my right hand, and the mirror on my left, in which I saw not only my own face, but such strong resemblance to that of my venerated father that I almost imagined it was he that I saw; the thoughts of my mother came to me, my sister, my young days, — all was at hand, yet how far away. Ah! how far is even the last moment, that is never to return again.

Edinburgh, October 27, 1826. I visited the market this morning, but to go to it I first crossed the New Town into the Old, over the north bridge, went down many flights of winding steps, and when at the desired spot was positively *under* the bridge that has been built to save the trouble of descending and mounting from one side of Edinburgh to the other, the city being mostly built on the slopes of two long ranges of high, broken hills. The vegetable market was well arranged, and looked, as did the sections for meats and fruits, attractive; but the situation, and the narrow booths in which the articles were exhibited, was, compared with the Liverpool market, nothing. I ascended the stairs leading to the New Town, and after turning to the right, saw before me the monument in honor of Nelson, to which I walked. Its elevated situation, the broken, rocky way along which I went, made it very picturesque; but a tremendous shower of rain accompanied by a heavy gust of cold wind made me hurry from the spot before I had satisfied myself, and I returned *home* to breakfast. I was struck with the resemblance of the women of the lower classes to our Indian squaws. Their walk is precisely the same, and their mode of carrying burdens also; they have a leather strap passed over the forehead attached to large baskets without covers, and waddle through the streets, just like the Shawanees, for instance. Their complexion, if fair, is beyond rosy, partaking, indeed, of purple — dull, and disagreeable. If dark, they are dark indeed. Many of the men wear long whiskers and beards, and are extremely uncouth in manners, and still more so in language. I had finished breakfast when Messrs. Patison came to see my drawings, and brought with them a Miss Ewart, who was said to draw beautifully. She looked at one drawing after another, but remained mute till I came to the doves; she exclaimed at this, and then told me she knew Sir Walter Scott well, "and," she added, "he will be delighted to see your magnificent collection." Later I called again at Dr. Thompson's, but as he was not at home, left the letter and my card; the same at Professor Duncan's. I then walked to the fish market, where I found Patrick Neill, Esq.,[1] at his desk, after having passed between two long files of printers at their work. Mr. Neill shook hands cordially, gave me his home address, promised to come and see me, and accompanied me to the street, begging me not to visit

[1] Patrick Neill, 1776–1851, Scottish naturalist and horticulturalist. Was a printer in Edinburgh at this time.

the Museum until Professor Jameson had sent me a general ticket of admission. I went then to the Port of Leith, distant not quite three miles, but missing my way, reached the Frith of Forth at Trinity, a small village on the bay, from whence I could see the waters of the German Ocean; the shore opposite was distant about seven miles, and looked naked and hilly. During my walk I frequently turned to view the beautiful city behind me, rising in gradual amphitheatre, most sublimely backed by mountainous clouds that greatly improved the whole. The wind was high, the waters beat the shore violently, the vessels at anchor pitched, — all was grand. On inquiry I found this was no longer an admiral's station, and that in a few more weeks the steamboats that ply between this and London, and other parts of the north of this island, would stop their voyages, the ocean being too rough during the winter season. I followed along the shores, and reached Leith in about twenty minutes. I saw a very pretty iron jetty with three arches, at the extremity of which vessels land passengers and freight. Leith is a large village apparently, mostly connected with Hamburg and the seaports of Holland. Much business is going on. I saw here great numbers of herring-boats and the nets for capturing these fishes; also some curious drags for oysters, clams, and other shellfish. The docks are small, and contain mostly Dutch vessels, none of them large. An old one is fitted up as a chapel for mariners. I waited till after sunset before returning to my lodgings, when I told my landlady I was going to the theatre, that I might not be locked out, and went off to see "Rob Roy." The theatre not opening till half-past six, I spent some little time in a bookseller's shop, reading an account of the Palace and Chapel of Holyrood. The pit, where I sat, was crowded with gentlemen and ladies; for ladies of the second class go to the pit, the superior classes to the boxes, and those of neither class way above. The house is small but well lighted. "God save the King" was the overture, and every one rose uncovered. "Rob Roy" was represented as if *positively* in the Highlands; the characters were natural, the scenery perfectly adapted, the dress and manners quite true to the story. I may truthfully say that I saw a good picture of the great outlaw, his Ellen, and the unrelenting Dougal. I would, were it possible, always see "Rob Roy" in Edinburgh, "Le Tartuffe" in Paris, and "She Stoops to Conquer" in England. "Rob Roy," as exhibited in America, is a burlesque; we do not even know how the hardy mountaineer of this rigid country throws on his plaid, or wears his cap or his front piece, beautifully made of several tails of the red deer; neither can we render the shrill tone of the horn bugle that hangs at his side, the merry bagpipe is wanted, also the scenery. I would just as soon see "Le Tartuffe" in broken French, by a strolling company, as to see "Rob Roy" again as I have seen it in Kentucky. It is almost to be regretted that each country does not keep to its own productions; to do otherwise only leads to fill our minds with ideas far different from the truth. I did not stay to see "Rosina;" though I liked Miss Stephens pretty well, yet she is by no means equal to Miss Foote.

Edinburgh, October 28, 1826. To-day I have visited the Royal Palace of Holyrood; it is both interesting and curious, especially the chapel and the rooms where the present King of France resided during his exile. I find Professor Jameson is engaged with Mr. Selby[1] and others in a large ornithological publication, and Mr. Ed. Roscoe has written, suggesting that I try to connect myself with them; but my independent spirit does not turn to the idea with any pleasure, and I think if my work deserves the attention of the public, it must stand on its own legs, not on the reputation of men superior in education and literary acquire-

[1] Prideaux John Selby, English ornithologist, author of "British Birds" and other works; died 1867.

ments, but possibly not so in the actual observation of Nature at her best, in the wilds, as I certainly have seen her.

October 29, Sunday. With the exception of the short walk to the post-office with my letters, I have been as busy as a bee all day, for I have written much. Yesterday at ten Messrs. Patison brought twelve ladies and the Messrs. Thomas and John Todd of this city to see my drawings; they remained full two hours. Professor Duncan came in and was truly a kind friend. After my company had left, and I had been promised several letters for Sir Walter Scott, I took a walk, and entered a public garden, where I soon found myself a prisoner, and where, had I not found a pretty maid who took pity on my *étourderie,* I certainly would have felt very awkward, as I had neither letter nor pocket-book to show for my identification. I then went in search of a Scotch pebble; one attracted me, but a boy in the shop said his father could make one still handsomer. I wanted not pebbles made by man, I wanted them the result of nature, but I enquired of the lad how they were made. Without hesitation the boy answered: "by fire-heat, and whilst the pores of the pebbles are open colored infusions are impregnated." Now what will not man do to deceive his brother? I called on Mr. Jeffrey,[1] who was not in; he comes from his Hall, two and a half miles off, every day for two hours, from two to four o'clock; therefore I entered his sanctum sanctorum, sealed the letter, and wrote on my card that I would be happy to see him. What a mass of books, papers, portfolios, dirt, beautiful paintings, engravings, casts, with such parcels of unopened packages all directed "Francis Jeffrey, Esq." Whilst I looked at this mass I thought, What have *I* done, compared with what this man has done, and has to do? I much long to see the famous critic. As I came away my thoughts reverted to

[1] Lord Francis Jeffrey, 1773–1850, the distinguished Scottish critic and essayist.

Holyrood Palace. What a variety of causes has brought king after king to that spot; what horrors have been committed there! The general structure is not of a defensive nature; it lies in a valley, and has simply its walls to guard it. I was surprised that the narrow stairs which led to the small chamber where the murder was committed, communicated at once with the open country, and I was also astonished to see that the mirrors were positively much superior to those of the present day in point of intrinsic purity of reflection; the plates cannot be less than three-fourths of an inch in thickness. The furniture is all decaying fast, as well as the paintings which are set into the walls. The great room for the King's audience contains a throne by no means corresponding with the ideas *de luxe* that I had formed. The room, however, being hung in scarlet cloth, had a very warm effect, and I remember it with pleasure. I also recall the view I then had from a high hill, of the whole city of Edinburgh and the country around the sea; the more I look on Edinburgh the better I like it. To-day, as I have said, I have been in my rooms constantly, and after much writing received Dr. Knox and a friend of his. The former pronounced my drawings the finest of their kind in the world. No light praise this. They promised to see that I was presented to the Wernerian Society, and talked very scientifically, indeed quite too much so for the poor man of the woods. They assured me the ornithological work now about being published by Messrs. "Selby, Jameson, and Sir Somebody[1] and Co.," was a "job book." It is both amusing and distressing to see how inimical to each other men of science are; and why are they so?

October 30. Mr. Neill took me to a Mr. Lizars,[2] in St. James Square, the engraver for Mr. Selby, who came

[1] Sir William Jardine.

[2] W. H. Lizars, the engraver who made a few of the earliest plates of the "Birds of America."

with us to see my work. As we walked along under an umbrella he talked of nothing else than the astonishing talent of his employer, how quickly he drew and how well, until we reached my lodgings. I lost hope at every step, and I doubt if I opened my lips. I slowly unbuckled my portfolio, placed a chair for him, and with my heart like a stone held up a drawing. Mr. Lizars rose from his seat, exclaiming: "My God! I never saw anything like this before." He continued to be delighted and astonished, and said Sir William Jardine[1] must see them, and that he would write to him; that Mr. Selby must see them; and when he left at dark he went immediately to Mr. Wm. Heath, an artist from London, who came at once to see me. I had gone out and missed him; but he left a note. Not knowing who he might be, I went to see him, up three pairs of stairs, *à l'artisan;* met a brunette who was Mrs. Heath, and a moment after the gentleman himself. We talked together, he showed me some of his work and will call on me to-morrow.

October 31. So at last Professor Jameson has called on me! That warm-hearted Mr. Lizars brought him this morning, just as I was finishing a letter to Victor. He was kind to me, very kind, and yet I do not understand the man clearly; he has a look quite above my reach, I must acknowledge, but I am to breakfast with him to-morrow at nine. He says he will, with my permission, announce my work to the world, and I doubt not I shall find him an excellent friend. Dr. Thompson's sons came in, tall, slender, and well-looking, made an apology for their father, and invited me to breakfast on Thursday; and young Dr. Henry called and also invited me to breakfast. Mr. Patrick Symes, a learned Scotchman, was with me a long time, and my morning was a very agreeable one within, though outside it was cold and rained. Edin-

[1] Scottish naturalist, 1800–1874. Published "Naturalists' Library" and other works.

burgh even in the rain, for I took a walk, is surprisingly beautiful, picturesque, romantic; I am delighted with it. Mr. Lizars has invited me to call at *nine* to spend the evening with him ; now I call it much more as if going to spend the night. I met Mrs. Lizars when I stopped at his house for a moment to-day; she is the first lady to whom I have been introduced here, and is a very beautiful one. Eleven and a half o'clock and I have just returned from Mr. Lizars, where my evening has been extremely pleasant. I have seen some of Mr. Selby's original drawings, and some of Sir William Jardine's, and I no longer feel afraid. But I must to rest, for I hate late hours and love to be up before daylight.

November 1. I breakfasted at Professor Jameson's. A most splendid house, splendid everything, breakfast to boot. The professor wears his hair in three distinct, different courses; when he sits fronting the south, for instance, the hair on his forehead bends westwardly, the hair behind eastwardly, and the very short hair on top mounts directly upward, perhaps somewhat like the quills of the "fretful porcupine." But never mind the ornamental, external appendages of his skull, the sense *within* is great, and full of the nobleness which comes from a kind, generous heart. Professor Jameson to-day is no more the man I took him to be when I first met him. He showed me an uncommon degree of cordiality, and promised me his powerful assistance so forcibly that I am sure I can depend upon him. I left him and his sister at ten, as we both have much to do besides talking, and drinking hot, well creamed coffee; but our separation was not long, for at noon he entered my room with several gentlemen to see my drawings. Till four I was occupied showing one picture after another, holding each one at arm's-length, and was very tired, and my left arm once I thought had an idea of revolutionizing. When my guests had gone I walked out, took plenty of needed exercise, often hearing remarks about myself such as "That's a German physician;" "There's a French nobleman." I ended my walk at Mr. Lizars', and while with him expressed a wish to secure some views of beautiful Edinburgh; he went to another room and brought in a book of views for me to look at, which I did with interest. He then asked me to draw something for him, and as I finished a vignette he pushed the book of superb Edinburgh towards me; on the first leaf he had written, "To John J. Audubon, as a very imperfect expression of the regard entertained for his abilities as an artist, and for his worth as a friend, by William H. Lizars, engraver of the 'Views of Edinburgh.'" I saw — though by gas-light — some of Mr. Lizars' work, printing from copper, coloring with water-color and oils, etc., on the same, for the first time in my life. How little I know! how ignorant I am! but I will learn. I went to bed after reading Sir Walter's last novel till I was so pleased with the book that I put it under my pillow to dream about, as children do at Christmas time; but my dreams all went another way and I dreamed of the beech woods in my own dear land.

November 2, Thursday. I drew the bell at the door of No. 80 George Street, where lives Dr. Thompson, just as the great bell of St. Andrews struck nine, and we soon sat down to breakfast. Dr. Thompson is a good, and good-looking man, and extremely kind; at the table were also his wife, daughter, son, and another young gentleman; and just as my second cup of coffee was handed to me a certain Dr. Fox entered with the air of an old friend, and at once sat down. He had been seventeen years in France, and speaks the language perfectly, of course. After having spoken somewhat about the scrubbiness of the timber here, and the lofty and majestic trees of my country dear, I rose to welcome Mrs. Lizars, who came in with her husband and some friends. Mr. Lizars had not seen one of my largest drawings; he had been enamoured with the Mocking-birds and Rattle-snake, but, Lucy, the Turkeys — her brood, the pose of the Cock Turkey — the Hawk pouncing on seventeen Partridges, the Whooping Crane devouring alligators newly born — at these he exclaimed again and again. All were, he said, wonderful productions; he wished to engrave the Partridges; but when the Great-footed Hawks came with bloody rags at their beaks' ends, and cruel delight in the glance of their daring eyes, he stopped mute an instant, then said, "*That* I will engrave and publish." We were too numerous a party to transact business then, and the subject was adjourned. Fatigued and excited by this, I wrote for some hours, and at four walked out and paid my respects to young Dr. Henry at the Infirmary, — a nice young man, — and at five I found myself at Mr. Lizars', who at once began on the topic of my drawings, and asked why I did not publicly exhibit them. I told him how kind and generous the Institution at Liverpool had been, as well as Manchester, and that I had a letter of thanks from the Committees. He returned with me to my lodgings, read the letter, and we marched arm in arm from Mrs. Dickie's to Professor Jameson, who kept the letter, so he said, to make good use of it; I showed Mr. Lizars other letters of recommendation, and as he laid down the last he said: "Mr. Audubon, the people here don't know who you are at all, but depend upon it they *shall* know." We then talked of the engraving of the Hawks, and it seems that it will be done. Perhaps even yet fame may be mine, and enable me to provide all that is needful for my Lucy and my children. Wealth I do not crave, but comfort; and for my boys I have the most ardent desire that they may receive the best of education, far above any that I possess; and day by day science advances, new thoughts and new ideas crowd onward, there is always fresh food for enjoyment, study, improvement, and I must place them where all this may be a possession to them.

November 3, Friday. My birds were visited by many persons this day, among whom were some ladies, artists, of both ability and taste, and with the numerous gentlemen came Professor James Wilson,[1] a naturalist, an agreeable man, who invited me to dine at his cottage next week. Mr. Lizars, who is certainly *mon bon cheval de bataille,* is exerting himself greatly in my behalf. At half-past three good Mr. Neill came, and together we walked towards his little hermitage, a sweet spot, quite out of town; nice garden, hot-house filled with exotics, and house-walls peopled by thousands of sparrows secure in the luxuriant masses of ivy that only here and there suffer the eye to see that the habitat is of stone. The Heron's sharp lance lay on his downy breast while he balanced on one leg, silent and motionless; the Kittiwake Gull screamed for food; the Cormorant greedily swallowed it; whilst the waddling Gannet welcomed her master by biting his foot, the little Bantams and the great rooster leaped for the bread held out, the faithful Pigeon cooed to his timid mate, and the huge watch-dog rubbed against the owner's legs with joy. We entered the house, other guests were there, and full of gayety we sat down to a sumptuous dinner. Eyes sparkled with wit, sense, knowledge. Mr. Combe[2] who was present has a head quite like our Henry Clay. My neighbor, Mr. Bridges,[3] is all life; but after a few observations concerning the birds of our woods he retired to let the world know that many of them are arrived in Scotland. It is unanimously agreed that I must sit for my portrait to Mr. Syme,[4] and that friend Lizars must engrave it to be distributed abroad. On my return to my lodgings I was presented with some

[1] James Wilson, brother of Professor John Wilson (Christopher North), naturalist and scientific writer, 1795–1856.

[2] George Combe, an eminent phrenologist and author on that subject. Born and died in Edinburgh, 1788–1856.

[3] David Bridges, editor of one of the Edinburgh newspapers.

[4] John Syme. His portrait of Audubon was the first one ever engraved.

pears and apples of native growth, somewhat bigger than green peas; but ah! this is both ungrateful and discourteous. To-morrow I am to meet Lord Somebody, and Miss Stephens; she was called "that delicious actress" so fervently and so frequently by my learned friends that I reverse my judgment, or will at least suspend it, until I see more of her.

November 4, Saturday. Now had I the faculties of my good friend Mr. Bridges, I should be able to write all that I feel towards him and the good people of this romantic Edina's Academic Halls; I would set to, and write long accounts of all I have enjoyed this day. But, alas! poor me! I can only scratch a few words next to unintelligible, and simply say that my little room has been full all day of individuals good, great, and friendly, and I am very wearied to-night; it is now past one. I dined at Mr. Lizars', where were beauties, music, conviviality, and wit. I am working hard withal; I do with four hours' sleep, keep up a great correspondence, keep up my journal, and write many hours on the letter-press for my "Birds," which is almost done.

November 5, Sunday. At ten o'clock my room was filled with visitors. Friend Bridges came, and stayed a long time. Miss Stephens the actress and her brother also paid me a visit. Mr. Bridges insisted on my going home to dine with him at four, and I never perceived I was in my slippers till I reached the port of destination. A Mr. Hovey dined with us. Mrs. Bridges is a stately, handsome lady, and the *diner en famille* pleased me exceedingly. I saw quite a stock of pictures and engravings, well selected by my knowing friend. I returned home early and found a note from Mr. John Gregg, who came himself later bringing me a *scrubby* letter from Charles Waterton,[1] and a sweet little sketch from fair Ellen of Quarry Bank. I was delighted to see him; it seemed

[1] Charles Waterton, English naturalist and traveller, 1782–1865,—always an enemy of Audubon's.

like *old times* to me. With all this I am by no means in spirits to write, I am so alone in this strange land, so far from those I love the best, and the future rises ofttimes dark before me.

Monday, November 6. The same sad heart to-day, and but little work and much company. I was glad, however, to see those who came, among others my coach companion from Manchester, Mr. Walton, who invited me in a very friendly manner to see him often. It snowed this morning, and was quite a new sight to me, for I have not seen any for about five years — I think. The papers give such accounts of my drawings and of myself that I am quite ashamed to walk the streets; but I am dispirited and melancholy.

Sunday, November 19. I do not know when I have thus pitilessly put away my journal for nearly two weeks. My head and heart would not permit me to write, so I must try to *memorandum* now all I have *seen.* What I have *felt* is too much for me to write down, for when these attacks of depression overwhelm me life is almost unendurable. Every day I exhibited my drawings to those who came to see them. I had many noblemen, among whom I especially liked Sir Patrick Walker and his lady; but I welcomed all ladies, gentlemen, artists, and, I dare say, critics. At last the Committee of the Royal Institution invited me to exhibit publicly in their rooms; I owe this invitation, I know, to the astonishing perseverance of some unknown friends. When my pictures were removed there I was no longer "At Home." I painted from dawn to dark, closely, and perhaps more attentively than I ever have done before. The picture was large, contained a Turkey Cock, a hen, and nine young, all the size of life. Mr. Lizars and his amiable wife visited me often; often I spent the evenings with them. Mr. David Bridges, Mr. Cameron, and several others had regular admittance, and they all saw the regular progress of my work; all, apparently, admired it. I dined at many houses, was always kindly received, and as far as my isolated condition and unfortunate melancholy permitted, enjoyed myself. It was settled by Mr. Lizars that he would undertake the publication of the first number of the "Birds of America," and that was enough to put all my powers of acting and thinking at fever heat. The papers also began to be more eulogistic of the merits of myself and my productions, and I felt bewildered with alternate uncertainties of hope and fear. I have received many letters from my dear Liverpool friends, and one, most precious of all, from the wonderful "Queen Bee" of Green Bank, with a most beautiful seal of the Wild Turkey and the motto "America, my country."[1] When my drawings were exhibited to the public, professors, students, artists, spoke well of them. I forwarded by post seventy-five tickets to the principal persons who had been kind to me, and to all the artists in Edinburgh. I sat once for my portrait, but my picture kept me at home ever since. I saw, and dined, and dined again with Sir William Jardine, and like him very much. He visited me frequently, and sat and stood watching me painting during his stay in the city. The famous phrenologist George Combe visited me also; spoke much of the truth of his theory as exhibited and verified by my poor skill; begged I would allow a cast of my head to be taken, etc., etc., and sent me a card of admission to his lectures this winter. The famous Professor Wilson of "Blackwood" fame, I might almost say the author of "Blackwood's Magazine," visited me also, and was very friendly; indeed, every one is kind, most truly so. How proud I feel that in Edinburgh, the seat of learning, science, and solidity of judgment, I am liked, and am received so kindly. How much I wish my Lucy could also enjoy it, that our sons

[1] This seal Audubon always used afterwards, and it is still in the possession of the family.

might have partaken of it, this would have rendered each moment an age of pleasure. I have now determined to remain here till my first number is published, when I shall go to Liverpool again, with proofs in hand. I will forward some of this number to the friends at home as well as abroad, and will continue painting here the while, and watch the progress of the engravers and colorists; two drawings are now under the hand of the engraver, and God grant me success. I am going to try to find time to spend a week at Jardine Hall, and some days at Mrs. Fletcher's; it will remove me from the pressure and excitement to which I am hourly subjected, and be a complete change for me in every way.

November 20. Whilst my breakfast was preparing, and daylight improving, I sat at my little table to write a notice of descriptive import about my painting of the Wild Turkeys that now leaned against the wall of my room, *finished*. My breakfast came in, but my pen carried me along the Arkansas River, and so much did I long for my beloved country that not a morsel could I swallow. While writing, Mr. Bridges, who usually pays me a daily visit, happened to come in. I read my description and told him it was my intention to have it printed, or written out in a clear hand, to lay on the table of the exhibition room, for the use of the public. He advised me to go to Professor Wilson for criticism; so I went at once to his residence, and reached "Blackwood's" door about ten o'clock. I did not even ask if Professor Wilson was in; no, I simply told the man to say Mr. Audubon from America wished to speak with him. In a moment I was conducted to a room where I wished that all that had been written in it was my own to remember, to enjoy, to profit by; but I had not been here many minutes before a sweet child, a happy daughter of this great man, asked me to go upstairs, saying, "Papa will be there in a minute;" and truly, almost at once the Professor came in, with freedom and kindness of manner, life in his eye, and benevolence in his heart. My case was soon explained; he took my paper, read it, and said if I would allow him to keep it, he would make one or two alterations and return it in good time. Back to my lodgings and hungry by this time, and cooled off, my mind relieved, my painting finished, I dressed more carefully and walked to the Royal Institution, and was pleased at seeing there a good deal of company. But the disagreeable part of my day is yet to come. I had to dine at Professor Graham's,[1] it was five o'clock when I reached there, a large assembly of ladies and gentlemen were there, and I was introduced to Mrs. Graham only, by some oversight I am sure, but none the less was my position awkward. There I stood, motionless as a Heron, and when I dared, gazed about me at my surroundings, but no one came near me. There I stood and thought of the concert at Manchester; but there was this difference: *there* I was looked at rudely, *here* I was with polite company; so I waited patiently for a change of situation, and the change came. A woman, aye, an angel, spoke to me in such a quiet, easy way that in a few moments my *mal aise* was gone; then the ringing of a bell summoned us to the dining-room; I sat near the blue satin lady (for her name I do not know) who came to my rescue, and a charming young lady, Miss M——, was my companion. But the sumptuous dinners of this country are too much for me. They are so long, so long, that I recall briefer meals that I have had, with much more enjoyment than I eat the bountiful fare before me. This is not a *goûter* with friend Bourgeat on the Flat Lake, roasting the orange-fleshed Ibis, and a few sun-perch; neither is it on the heated banks of Thompson's Creek, on the Fourth of July, swallowing the roasted eggs of a large Soft-shelled Turtle; neither was I at Henderson, at good

[1] Robert Graham, Scottish physician and botanist, born at Stirling, 1786, died at Edinburgh, 1845.

Dr. Rankin's, listening to the howlings of the Wolves, while sitting in security, eating well roasted and jellied venison, — no, alas! it was far from all these dear spots, in Great King Street, No. 62, at Dr. Graham's, a distinguished professor of botany, with a dinner of so many rich dishes that I cannot remember them.

November 24. I have just finished a long letter to Mr. Wm. Rathbone, telling him of my reception in beautiful Edinburgh, and my present plans, which are to publish one number at my own expense and risk, and with it under my arm, make my way. If I can procure three hundred good substantial names of persons or associations or institutions, I cannot fail doing well for my family; but, to do this, I must abandon my life to its success, and undergo many sad perplexities, and perhaps never again — certainly not for some years — see my beloved America. The work, from what I have seen of Mr. Lizars' execution, will be equal to anything in the world at present, and of the rest the world must judge for itself. I shall superintend both engraving and coloring personally, and I pray my courage may not fail; my industry I know will not. It is true the work will be procured only at a great expense, but then, a number of years must elapse before it is completed, so that renders payment an easier task. This is what I shall *try;* if I do not succeed I can return to my woods and there in peace and quiet live and die. I am sorry that some of my friends, particularly Dr. Traill, are against the pictures being the size of life, and I must acknowledge it renders the work rather bulky, but my heart was always bent on it, and I cannot refrain from attempting it. I shall publish the letter-press in a separate book, at the same time with the illustrations, and shall accompany the descriptions of the birds with many anecdotes and accounts of localities connected with the birds themselves, and with my travels in search of them. I miss my "Wild Turkeys," on which I worked steadily and from dawn to dark, a long time here, — for sixteen days. It would be impossible for me to write down all my feelings and thoughts about my work, or my life here; it may be that in time I shall be reconciled or habituated to the life I now lead, but I can scarce believe this, and often think the woods the only place in which I truly *live.*

November 25, 1826. I have been drawing all day at some Wood Pigeons, as they are emphatically called here, though woods there are none. The day was cold, wet, and snowy. Mr. Lizars, however, called with Dr. Brewster,[1] an eminent and entertaining man. I received a note from Geo. Combe, Esq., the phrenologist, who wishes to plaster my poor head to take an impression of the bumps, ordinary and extraordinary; he also invited me to sup with him on Monday next. I was to dine at Dr. Monroe's, Craiglockhart, near Slateford, so I dressed and sent for a coach that took me *two and a half* miles for *twelve* shillings, and I had to pay one shilling toll, — a dear dinner this. I arrived and entered a house richly furnished, and was presented to three ladies, and four gentlemen. The ladies were Mrs. Monroe, Miss Maria Monroe, and Mrs. Murray; amongst the gentlemen I at once recognized the amiable and learned Staff-Surgeon Lyons. Mrs. Monroe I found a woman of most extraordinary powers, a brilliant conversationalist, highly educated, and most attractive. She sat by me, and entertained me most charmingly, and the rest of her company as well. I need not say the dinner was sumptuous, for I find no other kind in hospitable Edinburgh. After dinner we had music from Miss Monroe, a skilled songstress, and her rich voice, with the pathetic Scotch ballads which she sang so unaffectedly, brought tears to my eyes. My return to my lodgings was very cold, for snow lies all about the hills that surround this enchanting city.

[1] David Brewster, author, scientist, and philosopher, Edinburgh, 1781–

Sunday, November 26. I went to a Scotch church this morning, but it was cold and the services seemed to me cold also, but it may have been that I was unaccustomed to them. Snow lay thick on the ground and my lodgings looked cheerless, all but my picture, at which I worked on my return. I had put my work on the floor, and was standing on a chair to see the effect at a good distance, when Mrs. Lizars entered with her husband; they had come to invite me to dine with them on roasted sheep's-head (a Scotch dish), and I was glad to accept, for I was on the verge of a fit of depression, one of those severe ones when I am almost afraid to be alone in my lodgings; alone indeed I am, without one soul to whom I can open my heart. True, I have been alone before, but that was in beloved America, where the ocean did not roll between me and my wife and sons. At four, therefore, I reached James' Square and dined with these good people without pomp or ostentation; it is the only true way to live. Found the sheep's-head delicious, and spent the evening most agreeably. I was shown many beautiful sketches, and two plates of my birds well advanced. Mr. Lizars walked home with me; the weather was intensely cold, and the wind blew a gale; on turning a corner it almost threw me down, and although warmly dressed I felt the chill keenly. This morning seems a long way off, so many things have I thought of this day.

Monday, November 27. As soon as it dawned I was up and at work, and quite finished my drawing before breakfast. Mr. Syme came to see me, and was surprised to find it done. I had also outlined my favorite subject, the Otter in a trap. At twelve I went to *stand up* for my picture, and sick enough I was of it by two; at the request of Mr. Lizars I wear my wolf-skin coat, and if the head is not a strong likeness, perhaps the coat may be; but this is discourteous of me, even to my journal. Mr. Lizars brought a Mr. Key, an artist, to throw a sky over my drawing, and the gentleman did it in handsome style, giving me some hints about this kind of work for which I am grateful. I dined at home on herrings, mutton-chops, cabbage, and fritters. As I am now going to sup with Mr. George Combe, I will write to-morrow what I may hear to-night. A kind note from Professor Jameson, whom I have not seen for some time, for he is a busy man, with a card of admittance to the Museum.

Tuesday, 28th. After writing thus far I left my room and went to watch the engravers at work on my birds. I was delighted to see how faithfully copied they were, and scarcely able to conceive the great "*adroit*" required to form all the lines exactly *contrary* to the model before them. I took a cup of coffee with Mr. and Mrs. Lizars, went home to dress, and at nine was again with Mr. Lizars, who was to accompany me to Mr. Combe's, and reaching Brower Square we entered the dwelling of Phrenology! Mr. Scot, the president of that society, Mr. D. Stewart,[1] Mr. McNalahan, and many others were there, and also a German named Charles N. Weiss, a great musician. Mr. George Combe immediately asked this gentleman and myself if we had any objection to have our heads *looked at* by the president, who had not yet arrived. We both signified our willingness, and were seated side by side on a sofa. When the president entered Mr. Combe said: "I have here two gentlemen of talent; will you please tell us in what their natural powers consist?" Mr. Scot came up, bowed, looked at Mr. Weiss, felt his head carefully all over, and pronounced him possessed of musical faculty in a great degree; I then underwent the same process, and he said: "There cannot exist a moment of doubt that this gentleman is a painter, colorist, and compositor, and I would add an amiable, though quick-tempered man." Much conversation ensued, we had supper, Miss Scot

[1] Dugald Stewart, Professor of Moral Philosophy, author, etc., Edinburgh, 1753–1828.

and Miss Combe were present, the only ladies. Afterwards Mr. Weiss played most sweetly on the flute, Mr. Scot sang Scotch airs, glees and madrigals followed, and it was after one o'clock when "Music and Painting" left the company arm in arm. I soon reached my lodgings. Mr. Weiss gave me a ticket to his concert, and Mrs. Dickie, who kindly sat up for me, gave me a ship letter. I hoped it was from my Lucy, but no, it was from Governor DeWitt Clinton; it was dated thirty days previous to my receiving it.

Tuesday, 28th. The fog was so dense this morning that at nine o'clock I could hardly see to write. I put the drawing of the Stock Pigeons in the Institution, framed superbly, and it looked well, I thought, even though so dark a day. I again *stood* for my picture, two dreadfully long hours, and I am sure I hope it may prove a good resemblance to my poor self. Whilst yet in my hunting-dress, I received word that Sir Walter Scott was in the Institution and wished to see me; you may depend I was not long in measuring the distance, and reached the building quite out of breath, but to no purpose. Sir Walter had been compelled to go to preside at a meeting upstairs, and left an apology for me, and a request that unless too dark for him to see my work I would wait; but it very soon became quite dark, and I therefore abandoned all thought of meeting him this time. I dined at Mr. Lizars', and saw the first-proof impression of one of my drawings. It looked pretty well, and as I had procured one subscriber, Dr. Meikleham of Trinidad, I felt well contented.

Wednesday, 29th. The day was cloudy, and sitting for my portrait has become quite an arduous piece of business. I was positively in "durance vile" for two and a half hours. Just as I was finishing my dinner, Mrs. F——, the cousin of Mr. Gregg, called; ladies having the right to command, I went immediately, and found a woman whose features had more force and character than women generally show in their lineaments. Her eyes were very penetrating, and I was struck with the strength of all she said, though nothing seemed to be studied. She showed the effects of a long, well learned round of general information. She, of course, praised my work, but I scarce thought her candid. Her eyes seemed to reach my very soul; I knew that at one glance she had discovered my inferiority. The group of children she had with her were all fine-looking, but not so gracefully obedient as those of the beautiful Mrs. Rathbone of Woodcroft. She invited me to her home, near Roslyn, and I shall, of course, accept this courtesy, though I felt, and feel now, that she asked me from politeness more than because she liked *me*, and I must say the more I realized her intelligence the more stupid did I become. Afterwards I went to Mr. Lizars' to meet Dr. Meikleham, who wishes me to go with him to Trinidad, where I shall draw, so he says, four hundred birds for him, for a publication of "Birds of the West Indies." On Friday I go to Mrs. Isabella Murray's, to see her and some fine engravings. I have omitted to say that the first impression of the beautiful seal sent me by Mrs. Rathbone was sent to my beloved wife; the seal itself is much admired, and the workmanship highly praised. Mr. Combe has been to see me, and says my poor skull is a greater exemplification of the evidences of the truth of his system than any he has seen, except those of one or two whose great names only are familiar to me; and positively I have been so tormented about the shape of my head that my brains are quite out of sorts. Nor is this all; my eyes will have to be closed for about one hour, my face and hair oiled over, and plaster of Paris poured over my nose (a greased quill in each nostril), and a bust will be made. On the other hand, an artist quite as crazy and foolishly inclined, has said that my head was a perfect Vandyke's, and to establish this fact, my portrait is now growing under the pencil of the ablest artist of the science here. It is a strange-looking figure, with gun, strap, and buckles, and eyes that to me are more those of an enraged Eagle than mine. Yet it is to be engraved. Sir Walter Scott saw my drawings for a few moments yesterday, and I hope to meet him to-morrow when I dine with the Antiquarian Society at the Waterloo Hotel, where an annual feast is given. My work is proceeding in very good style, and in a couple of days colored plates will be at the exhibition rooms, and at the different booksellers; but with all this bustle, and my hopes of success, my heart is heavy, for *hopes* are not *facts*. The weather is dull, moist, and disagreeably cold at times, and just now the short duration of the daylight here is shocking; the lamps are lighted in the streets at half-past three o'clock P. M., and are yet burning at half-past seven A. M.

November 30. My portrait was finished to-day. I cannot say that I think it a very good resemblance, but it is a fine picture, and the public must judge of the rest. I had a bad headache this morning, which has now passed; to be ill far from home would be dreadful, away from my Lucy, who would do more for me in a day than all the doctors in Christendom in a twelvemonth. I visited the exhibition rooms for a few minutes; I would like to go there oftener, but really to be gazed at by a crowd is, of all things, most detestable to me. Mr. Gregg called about four, also Mr. Bridges and an acquaintance of the famous "Alligator Rider," and I was told that Mr. Waterton said that Joseph Bonaparte imitated the manners and habits of his brother Napoleon; that is much more than I know or saw. But St. Andrew's Day and my invitation to dine with the Antiquarians was not forgotten. At five I was at Mr. Lizars', where I found Mr. Moule and we proceeded to the Waterloo Hotel. The sitting-room was soon filled; I met many that I knew, and a few minutes after the Earl of Elgin[1] made his *entrée*, I was

[1] Thomas Bruce, seventh Earl of Elgin. 1777-1841.

presented to him by Mr. Innes of Stow; he shook hands with me and spoke in a very kind and truly complimentary manner about my pencil's productions. At six we walked in couples to the dining-room; I had the arm of my good friend Patrick Neill, Mr. Lizars sat on my other side, and there was a sumptuous dinner indeed. It at first consisted entirely of Scotch messes of old fashion, such as marrow-bones, codfish-heads stuffed with oatmeal and garlic, black puddings, sheep's-heads smelling of singed wool, and I do not know what else. Then a *second* dinner was served quite *à l'anglaise.* I finished with a bit of grouse. Then came on the toasts. Lord Elgin, being president and provided with an auctioneer's mallet, brought all the company to order by rapping smartly on the table with the instrument. He then rose, and simply said: "The King! four times four!" Every one rose to drink to the monarch's health, and the president saying, "Ip, ip, ip," sixteen cheers were loudly given. The Dukes of York, Argyle, and many others had their healths drunk, then Sir Walter Scott (who, to my great regret, was not able to be present), and so on and on, one and another, until mine was proposed by Mr. Skene,[1] the first secretary of the society. Whilst he was engaged in a handsome panegyric the perspiration poured from me, I thought I should faint; and I was seated in this wretched condition when everybody rose, and the Earl called out: "Mr. Audubon." I had seen each individual when toasted, rise, and deliver a speech; that being the case, could I remain speechless like a fool? No! I summoned all my resolution, and for the first time in my life spoke to a large assembly, saying these few words: "Gentlemen, my command of words in which to reply to your kindness is almost as humble as that of the birds hanging on the walls of your institution. I am truly obliged for your favors. Permit me to say, May God bless you all, and may this society prosper." I felt

[1] Wm. Forbes Skene, Scottish historian.

my hands wet with perspiration. Mr. Lizars poured me out a glass of wine and said: "Bravo! take this," which I gladly did. More toasts were given, and then a delightful old Scotch song was sung by Mr. Innes; the refrain was "Put on thy cloak about thee." Then Mr. McDonald sang. Wm. Allan, Esq.,[1] the famous painter, told a beautiful story, then rose, and imitated the buzzing of a bumble-bee confined in a room, and followed the bee (apparently) as if flying from him, beating it down with his handkerchief; a droll performance most admirably done. At ten, the Earl rose, and bid us farewell, and at half-past ten I proposed to Mr. Lizars to go, and we did. I was much pleased at having been a guest at this entertainment, particularly as Lord Elgin expressed a wish to see me again. I went to Mr. Lizars', where we sat chatting for an hour, when I returned to my lodgings and took myself to bed.

December 1. My portrait was hung up in the exhibition room; I prefer it to be gazed at rather than the original from which it was taken. The day was shockingly bad, wet, slippery, cold. I had to visit Lord Clancarty and his lady at noon, therefore I went. I met Mrs. M—— and her children and the eldest daughter of Mr. Monroe. Mrs. M—— began a long speech, telling me of her father, Lord S——, and his loyalty to the Stuarts; the details not only of that royal family but all the kings of England were being poured out, and I should probably be there yet, merely saying "Yes" from time to time, if a lucky interruption had not come in the form of a message from Lord Elgin, to say he desired to see me at the Institution. I soon reached that place, where I met Lord Elgin, in company with Secretary Skene and Mr. Hall the advocate, in the art room. Mr. Hall is nephew to Lady Douglas, and this gave me an opportunity to hand him her letter. But the best thing to relate is my breakfast with

[1] Afterwards Sir William Allan, historical painter; in 1833 was elected president of the Scottish Royal Academy, Edinburgh. 1782–1850.

that wonderful man David Bridges. I was at his house at a quarter before nine; a daughter was practising the piano, the son reading, his wife, well-dressed, was sewing. I conversed with her and looked at the pictures till the door opened and my friend came in, attired in his *robe de chambre*, shook my hand warmly, and taking his handkerchief from his pocket, he began whisking and wiping chimney mantel, tables, chairs, desk, etc., to my utter annoyance, for I felt for the wife whose poor housewifery was thus exposed. After breakfast we walked to see my portrait and to criticise it, for both Mr. Lizars and Mr. Bridges are connoisseurs. In the evening I visited Mr. Howe, the editor of the "Courant" and then to the theatre with Mr. Bridges to see Wairner (?) perform "Tyke" in "The School of Reform." We met at the Rainbow Tavern, and soon entered the theatre, which was thinly attended; but I was delighted with the piece, and the performance of it, though we left before it was concluded to attend Mr. Weiss's concert in the Assembly Rooms in George Street. The flute playing was admirable both in execution and tone; Mr. Bridges supped with me. It is now again one o'clock, and I am quite worn out.

December 2, Saturday. The weather was a sharp frost till evening, when it rained. I was busy painting all day, and did not put foot out of doors till I went to dine with Dr. Brown, the professor of theology.[1] Mr. Bridges went with me, and told me that Professor Wilson had prepared a notice for "Blackwood's Magazine" respecting myself and my work. I think the servant who called out my name at Dr. Brown's must have received a most capital lesson in pronunciation, for seldom in my travels did I hear my name so clearly and well pronounced. Several other guests were present, Professor Jameson among them, and we passed a most agreeable evening. I must not forget

[1] An eminent divine 1784–1858; father of Dr. John Brown, author of "Rab and his Friends," etc.

that Sir James Hall and his brother called to receive information respecting the comfort that may be expected in travelling through my dear country.

Sunday, December 3. My good friends, Mr. and Mrs. Lizars came in as usual after church; they like the Otter better than the Turkeys. It was nearly finished, to the great astonishment of Mr. Syme and Mr. Cameron, who came to announce that the rooms at the Institution were mine till the 20th inst. Mr. Cameron looked long at the picture and said: "No man in either England or Scotland could paint that picture in so short a time." Now to me this is all truly wonderful; I came to this Europe fearful, humble, dreading all, scarce able to hold up my head and meet the glance of the learned, and I am praised so highly! It is quite unaccountable, and I still fear it will not last; these good people certainly give me more merit than I am entitled to; it can only be a glance of astonishment or surprise operating on them because my style is new, and somewhat different from those who have preceded me. Mr. Bridges, who knows everybody, and goes everywhere, went with me to dine with Mr. Witham of Yorkshire. We dined—had coffee—supped at eleven. At twelve the ladies left us; I wished to leave, but it was impossible. Dr. Knox said he wished to propose me as an honorary member of the Wernerian Society; our host said he would second the motion; my health was drunk, and I finally retired with Dr. Knox, leaving Mr. Bridges and the other gentlemen making whiskey toddy from that potent Scotch liquor which as yet I cannot swallow. It was now half-past two; what hours do I keep! Am I to lead this life long? If I do I must receive from my Maker a new supply of strength, for even my strong constitution cannot stand it.

Monday, December 4. I gave early orders to Mrs. Dickie to have a particularly good breakfast ready by nine o'clock because Mr. Witham had offered last night to come and partake of it with me; I then took to my brushes and finished my Otter entirely. I had been just thirteen hours at it, and had I labored for thirteen weeks, I do not think I should have bettered it. Nine o'clock — ten o'clock — and no Mr. Witham. I was to accompany him to Dr. Knox, whose lecture on Anatomy he was to hear. At last he came with many apologies, having already breakfasted, and giving me but ten minutes for my morning meal. We then hurried off, the weather beautiful, but extremely cold. We ascended the stairs and opened the door of the lecture room, where were seated probably one hundred and fifty students; a beating of feet and clapping of hands took place that quite shocked me. We seated ourselves and each person who entered the room was saluted as we had been, and during the intervals a low beating was kept up resembling in its regularity the footsteps of a regiment on a flat pavement. Dr. Knox entered, and all was as hushed as if silence had been the principal study of all present. I am not an anatomist. Unfortunately, no! I know almost less than nothing, but I was much interested in the lecture, which lasted three quarters of an hour, when the Dr. took us through the anatomical Museum, and his dissecting-room. The sights were extremely disagreeable, many of them shocking beyond all I ever thought could be. I was glad to leave this charnel house and breathe again the salubrious atmosphere of the streets of "Fair Edina." I was engaged most certainly to dine out, but could not recollect where, and was seated trying to remember, when the Rev. W. J. Bakewell, my wife's first cousin, and the son of Robert Bakewell the famous grazier and zoölogist of Derbyshire, came in to see me. He asked many questions about the family in America, gave me his card and invited me to dine with him next Monday week, which is my first unengaged day. I had a letter from Mr. Monroe at Liverpool telling me I had been elected a member of the Literary and Philosophical Societies of that city. Not being able to recall where I was to dine, I was guilty of what must seem great rudeness to my intended hosts, and which is truly most careless on my part; so I went to Mr. Lizars, where I am always happy. The wild Turkey-cock is to be the large bird of my first number, to prove the necessity of the size of the work. I am glad to be able to retire at an early hour. It seems to me an extraordinary thing, my present situation in Edinburgh; looked upon with respect, receiving the attentions of the most distinguished people, and supported by men of science and learning. It is wonderful to me; am I, or is my work, deserving of all this?

Tuesday, December 5. After I had put my Otter in the exhibition room, I met Mr. Syme and with him visited Mr. Wm. Nicholson,[1] a portrait painter, and there saw, independent of his own work, a picture from the far-famed Snyders, intended for a Bear beset with dogs of all sorts. The picture had great effect, fine coloring, and still finer finishing, but the Bear was no Bear at all, and the dogs were so badly drawn, distorted caricatures that I am sure Snyders did not draw from specimens put in real postures, in my way. I was quite disappointed, so much had I heard of this man's pictures of quadrupeds, and I thought of Dr. Traill, who, although well acquainted with birds scientifically, told me he had an engraving of birds where both legs of each individual were put on the same side, and that he never noticed the defect till it was pointed out to him. This made me reflect how easily man can be impressed by general effect and beauty. I returned to the Institution and had the pleasure of meeting Captain Basil Hall,[2] of the Royal Navy, his wife, and Lady Hunter. They were extremely kind to me, and spoke of my dear friends the Rathbones and Greggs in terms which de-

[1] William Nicholson, First Secretary of the Scottish Academy and portrait painter. 1784–1844.

[2] Traveller and author. 1788–1844.

lighted me. The captain asked if I did not intend to exhibit by gaslight, and when I replied that the Institution had granted me so much favor already that I could not take it upon myself to speak of that, said that he should do so at once, and would let me know the answer from Mr. Skene, the secretary. I wrote the history of my picture of the Otter, and sent with a note to Professor Wilson, who had asked for it.

Wednesday, December 6. After breakfast I called on Professor Jameson, and as the Wild Turkey is to be in my first number, proposed to give him the account of the habits of the Turkey Buzzard instead; he appeared anxious to have any I would give. I spoke to him about the presentation of my name to the Wernerian Society; he said it was desirable for me to join it as it would attach me to the country, and he would give his aid gladly. I visited Captain Basil Hall of the Royal Navy; as I ascended the stairs to his parlor I heard the sweet sounds of a piano, and found Mrs. Hall was the performer. Few women have ever attracted me more at first sight; her youth and her fair face are in unison with her manners; and her husband also received me most kindly, especially when I recalled our previous slight acquaintance. I spent here a most agreeable hour. They spoke of visiting the States, and I urged them to do so. Captain Hall, a man of extraordinary talents, a great traveller, and a rich man, has made the most of all, and I found him the best of company. From thence to friend Neill's establishment in the Old Town to see at what time my memoranda must be ready for the press; to my astonishment I was told that to-morrow was my last day, and I ran home to scribble. Professor Monroe called on me with a friend and asked me what I would take to draw skulls, etc., for him; then Mr. Syme brought an engraver to consult with me on the subject of my portrait being immortalized. Young Gregg paid me a visit, and at last I dressed in a hurry and ran to Mr. Lizars' to know the way to Mr. Ritchie's, where I was to dine. Mr. Lizars sent a young man to show me the way, and I arrived at the appointed spot just one hour too late. I dined however, and dined well. Miss Scott was there, Miss Combe, Mr. Weiss, and several others; but when dinner was over and we ascended to the tea room, a crowd of ladies and gentlemen not before seen were in waiting to see the "Woodsman from America." We had music and dancing, and I did not leave till a late hour and must now write more for the printers. I must tell thee that some-one gave a false note of one pound at my exhibition rooms, and therefore *I* paid him well to see my birds. A man who met me to-day at the door of the Institution asked me if they were very well worth seeing. Dost thou think I said "Yes"? Not I! I positively said "No!" and off he went; but a few yards off I saw him stop to talk to another man, when he returned and went in.

Thursday, December 7. I wrote as hard as I could till early this morning, and finished the paper for Professor Jameson, who sent me a note desiring me to put down the University of Edinburgh as a subscriber to my work. I was highly pleased with this, being a powerful leader. I saw in this day's paper that Charles Bonaparte had arrived at Liverpool in the "Canada" from New York. How I longed to see him! Had I been sure of his remaining at Liverpool a few days, I positively would have gone there by the evening mail-coach. I saw to-day two of my drawings in proof; I was well pleased with them; indeed one of them I liked better than the first that were done. My dinner was at Mr. Howe's, the editor of the "Courant." Mr. Allan the artist came in at nine, when his lessons were just ended at the Academy of Arts, — an extremely agreeable man, full of gayety, wit, and good sense, a great traveller in Russia, Greece, and Turkey.

Friday, December 8, 1826. Men and their lives are very like the different growths of our woods; the noble magnolia, all odoriferous, has frequently the teasing nettle growing so near its large trunk as to sometimes be touched by it. Edinburgh contains a Walter Scott, a Wilson, a Jameson, but it contains also many nettles of the genus Mammalia, amongst which *men* hold a very prominent station. Now I have run into one of these latter gentry. To speak out at once, one of my drawings was gently purloined last evening from the rooms of the Institution. So runs the fact; perhaps a few minutes before the doors closed a somebody in a large cloak paid his shilling, entered the hall and made his round, and with great caution took a drawing from the wall, rolled it up, and walked off. The porter and men in attendance missed it almost immediately, and this morning I was asked if I or Mr. Lizars had taken it to be engraved. I immediately told Mr. Lizars; we went to Mr. Bridges, and by his advice to the court, where Captain Robeson — who, by the way, was at the battle of New Orleans — issued a warrant against a young man of the name of I——, deaf and dumb, who was strongly suspected. Gladly would I have painted a bird for the poor fellow, and I certainly did not want him arrested, but the Institution guards were greatly annoyed at the occurrence. However, I induced Mr. Lizars to call on the family of the youth, which is a very good one and well known in Edinburgh. I returned to my lodgings and on the stairs met a beggar woman with a child in her arms, but passed her without much notice beyond pitying her in her youth and poverty, reached my door, where I saw a roll of paper; I picked it up, walked in, opened it, and found my drawing of the Black-poll Warbler! Is not this a curious story? The thief — whoever he may be, God pardon him — had, we conceived, been terror-struck on hearing of the steps we had taken, and had resorted to this method of restoring the drawing before he was arrested. I was in time to stop the warrant, and the affair was silenced. During the afternoon I was called on twice by Capt. Basil Hall, who was so polite as to present me with a copy of his work, two volumes, on South America, with a kind note, and an invitation to dine with him on Thursday next at eight o'clock. The weather is miserable.

Saturday, December 9. I wrote closely all morning from six to twelve, only half dressed, and not stopping for breakfast beyond a cup of coffee, and while thus busily employed Mr. Hall came in and handed me a note from Lady Hunter, requesting the honor of my company on Saturday next to dine at six; he looked at me with surprise and doubtless thought me the strangest-looking man in the town. I had much running about with Professor Jameson to the printer, and with my manuscript to Mr. Lizars, who took it to Professor Brewster. We visited the Museum together, called on a Mr. Wilson, where I saw a most beautiful dead Pheasant that I longed to have to paint. Then to Dr. Lizars' lecture on anatomy, and with him to the dissecting-rooms, but one glance was enough for me, and I hastily, and I hope forever, made my escape. The day was extremely wet, and I was glad to be in my room. I hear Mr. Selby is expected next Monday night.

December 10, Sunday. My situation in Edinburgh borders almost on the miraculous. With scarce one of those qualities necessary to render a man able to pass through the throng of the learned people here, I am positively looked on by all the professors and many of the principal persons here as a very extraordinary man. I cannot comprehend this in the least. Indeed I have received here so much kindness and attention that I look forward with regret to my removal to Glasgow, fifty miles hence, where I expect to go the last of this month. Sir William Jardine has been spending a few days here purposely to see me, and I am to meet Mr. Selby, and with these two gentlemen discuss the question of a joint publication, which may possibly be arranged. It is now a month since my work was begun by Mr. Lizars; the paper is of unusual size, called "double elephant," and the plates are to be finished in such superb style as to eclipse all of the same kind in existence. The price of each number, which will contain five prints, is two guineas, and all individuals have the privilege of subscribing for the whole, or any portion of it. The two plates now finished are truly beautiful. This number consists of the Turkey-cock, the Cuckoos on the pawpaws, and three small drawings, which in the centre of the large sheet have a fine effect, and an air of richness, that I think must ensure success, though I do not yet feel assured that all will go well. Yet on the other hand, all things bear a better aspect than I expected to see for many months, if ever. I think that if my work takes in Edinburgh, it will anywhere. I have strong friends here who interest themselves in me, but I must wait patiently till the first number is finished. Mr. Jameson, the first professor of this place, and the conductor of the "Philosophical Journal," gives a beautiful announcement of my work in the present number, with an account, by me, of the Turkey Buzzard. Dr. Brewster also announces it, with the introductory letter to my work, and Professor Wilson also, in "Blackwood's Magazine." These three journals print upwards of thirty thousand copies, so that my name will spread quickly enough. I am to deliver lectures on Natural History at the Wernerian Society at each of the meetings while I am here, and Professor Jameson told me I should soon be made a member of all the other societies here, and that would give my work a good standing throughout Europe. Much as I find here to enjoy, the great round of company I am thrown in has become fatiguing to me in the extreme, nor does it agree with my early habits. I go out to dine at six, seven, or even eight o'clock in the evening, and it is often one or two when the party breaks up; then painting all day, with my immense correspondence which increases daily, makes my head feel like an immense hornet's-nest, and my body wearied beyond all calculation; yet it has to be done; those who have my interests at heart tell me I must not refuse a single invitation.

December 11, Monday. Though I awoke feeling much depressed, my dull feelings were soon dissipated by letters from my sweet wife and sons. What joy to know them well and happy on the 14th and 27th of September. My day was a busy one, and at seven I went to Mr. Lizars', having engaged to go with him to the Antiquarian Society, where I met many of my friends, saw a gun-barrel and other things that had belonged to the Spanish Armada, and heard a curious and interesting account of that vast fleet read by Dr. Hibbert, and saw the Scottish antiquities belonging to the society.

Tuesday, December 12. This morning at ten I went to the house of Dr. Brewster, whom I found writing in a large room with several fine pictures on the walls. He received me very kindly, and in a few minutes I began reading my paper on the habits of the Carrion Crow, *Vultur atratus.* About midway my nervousness affected my respiration; I paused a moment, and he was good enough to say it was highly interesting. I resumed, and went on to the end, much to my relief. He who has been brought up an auctioneer, or on the boards of some theatre, with all the knowledge of the proper usage of the voice, and all the *aplomb* such a life would give, knows nothing of the feelings of bashfulness which agitated me, a man who never looked into an English grammar and who has forgotten most of what he learned in French and Spanish ones — a man who has always felt awkward and shy in the presence of a stranger — a man habituated to ramble alone, with his thoughts usually bent on the beauties of Nature herself — this man, *me*, to be seated opposite Dr. Brewster in Edinburgh, reading one of my puny efforts at describing habits of birds that none but an Almighty Creator can ever know, was ridiculously absurd in my estimation, during all the time; besides, I also felt the penetrating looks and keen observation of the learned man before me, so that the cold sweat started from me. As I wiped my forehead on finishing my paper, a large black dog came in, caressed his master, and made a merciful diversion, and as my agitation gradually subsided I was able to talk with Dr. Brewster and was afterwards introduced to his lady, who put me soon at my ease, and told me I was to be introduced to Sir Walter Scott on Monday next at the Royal Academy. Poor me! — far from Sir Walter I could talk to him; hundreds of times have I spoken to him quite loudly in the woods, as I looked on the silvery streamlets, or the dense swamps, or the noble Ohio, or on mountains losing their peaks in gray mists. How many times have I longed for him to come to my beloved country, that he might describe, as no one else ever can, the stream, the swamp, the river, the mountain, for the sake of future ages. A century hence they will not be here as I see them, Nature will have been robbed of many brilliant charms, the rivers will be tormented and turned astray from their primitive courses, the hills will be levelled with the swamps, and perhaps the swamps will have become a mound surmounted by a fortress of a thousand guns. Scarce a magnolia will Louisiana possess, the timid Deer will exist nowhere, fish will no longer abound in the rivers, the Eagle scarce ever alight, and these millions of lovely songsters be driven away or slain by man. Without Sir Walter Scott these beauties must perish unknown to the world. To the great and good man himself I can never say this, therefore he can never know it, or my feelings towards him — but if he did? What have I to say more than a world of others who all admire him, perhaps are better able to do so, because more enlightened. Ah! Walter Scott! when I am presented to thee my head will droop, my heart will swell, my limbs will tremble, my lips will quiver, my tongue congeal; nevertheless I shall feel elevated if I am permitted to touch the hand to which the world owes so much.

December 13, Wednesday. I have spent the greater portion of this day in the company of Mr. Selby the ornithologist, who, in appearance is well formed, and in manners clever and polite, yet plain and unassuming. We were together some hours at the Institution, — he was greatly pleased with my drawings, — and we then dined at Mr. Lizars' in company with Dr. Lizars, and we all talked ornithology. I wish I possessed the scientific knowledge of the subject that Mr. Selby does. He wished to hear my paper on the "Buzzard," and after doing so, took it with him to read to Sir Wm. Jardine, to whom he goes to-morrow, but will return on Monday. Later Dr. Brewster came to my room with the proof of the paper on the "Carrion Crow." He read it, and we both corrected. He told me it was a question whether or no I could be made a member of the Royal Academy, for only *thirty* foreigners were allowed by law, and the number was already complete; still he hoped an exception would be made in my case. He thanked me very cordially for my paper, and said Sir Walter Scott wished to meet me, and would do so on Monday at the Royal Academy. Mr. Bridges gave me a very fine notice in the *Scotsman*, and has again invited me to dine with him to meet some distinguished Germans, and before that I must call at Lord Clancarty's to see Mrs. Murray.

Thursday, December 14. I paid my visit to Mrs. Murray this forenoon, but the lady was out; so I handed my card to the slender youth who had opened the door and who stood before me looking at my hair like an ass at a fine thistle, and then made off quickly to Dr. Brewster. My business was before him in an instant; I wished not to be introduced to Sir Walter in a crowd, and he promised me not to do so. Much relieved I went to the University to see Dr. Andrew Brown, Professor of Rhetoric. I found him a very polished man, and after some conversation he asked me to write him a paper on the manners and customs of Indians. But I must promise less writing of this kind, for I am too busy otherwise; however, immediately on my return home I sat down to write a long list of memoranda for a journey in America which I had promised Captain Basil Hall, and I wrote till my head ached. Mr. Daniel Lizars has invited me to dine with him on Friday at three, and has procured two cats, which he wishes me to paint. Now this suits me to a "T" — a long morning's work, a short meal, and some hours more of work; very different from to-day, for it was five minutes of seven when I reached Captain Hall's. We dined delightfully with just the company he had promised me, and I was not compelled to ask any one to take wine with me, a thing in my opinion detestable quite, a foppish art I cannot bear. I wish everybody was permitted to drink when he is thirsty, or at least only when he likes, and not when he dislikes it. The ladies having left us, the map of my native land was put on the table; I read my notes, the Captain followed the course with his pencil from New York to New Orleans, visiting besides Niagara, St. Louis, and a hundred other places. We talked of nothing but his journey in my dear country, and Mrs. Hall is delighted at the prospect. The Captain wishes to write a book, and he spoke of it with as little concern as I should say, "I will draw a duck;" is it not surprising? He said to me, "Why do not you write a little book telling what you have seen?" I cannot write at all, but if I could how could I make a *little* book, when I have seen enough to make a dozen *large* books? I will not write at all.

Friday, December 15. I have just returned from the theatre, where I saw for the first time "The Beggars' Opera" and "The Lord of the Manor." They were both badly represented, most certainly. Only one lady could sing, or act her part at all well. It was most truly a Beggars' Opera; I went with Mr. Daniel Lizars and his wife and brother-in-law. They were all desirous to see a certain Mr. St. Clair perform; but I truly think that the gentleman in question had drank too much brandy this day, or was it of the smoky whiskey which these Scots relish? I did little work this day, but walked much to refresh myself after all the hard work and constant writing I have lately done. The weather was most inviting, and as pleasant as Louisiana at this season. Upwards of two hundred people were at my exhibition, and to-morrow it closes. Baron Stokoe called whilst I was absent and left word he wished to see me, that he had heard from a friend of mine, whom I suppose to be Charles Bonaparte. Baron Stokoe was formerly a physician of eminence in the British service; when Dr. O'Meara was taken away from St. Helena, where he was physician to Napoleon, this gentleman was put in his place, but did not suit the peculiar ideas of his barbarous governor, and was also dismissed, not only from the island, but from the service, with a trifling pension. He had become acceptable to Napoleon even in the short time they were together, and when he returned from that lonely rock was employed by Joseph Bonaparte to attend his daughters from Rome to Philadelphia. I met him with Charles Bonaparte during his stay in America. So pleased was Joseph Bonaparte with his conduct that he is now one of his *pensionnaires*, and his general agent in Europe.

Saturday, December 16. I have really done much today. At half-past nine I faced the inclement weather, crossed the bridge, passed the college regretting such a curious and valuable monument was quite buried among the antiquated, narrow streets, and dismal houses that surround it, then rang the bell, and was admitted to Baron S——'s parlor. He was still snug asleep; so that I had enjoyed four and a half hours of life while he slept. He saw me at once in his bedroom and told me that if I wrote to the Prince of Musignano at London this morning, the letter would probably reach him. I returned home, wrote my letter, or rather began it, when I received several pages from my good friend Mr. Rathbone which quite depressed me. He feared my work would not succeed on account of the unusual size; and Mrs. Rathbone, Senior, refused me the pleasure of naming a bird after her, on account of the publicity, she said; yet I longed to do so, for what greater compliment could I pay any lady than to give her name to one of the most exquisite creations of the Almighty? The whole made me most dismal, but yet not in the least discouraged or disheartened about my work. If Napoleon by perseverance and energy rose from the ranks to be an emperor, why should not Audubon with perseverance and energy be able to leave the woods of America for a time and publish and sell a book? — always supposing that Audubon has *some* knowledge of his work, as Napoleon had *great* knowledge of his. No, no, I shall not cease to work for this end till old age incapacitates me. I thought long over Mr. Rathbone's letter, then finished mine to Charles and put it in the post-office. I then purchased a Pigeon, killed it, packed up my wires and hammer, and at one o'clock took these things with my "position board," called a coach, and went to the meeting of the Wernerian Society at the University. Lady Morton had joined me, hence my need for the coach. Mr. Skene met me at the door, where I parted from Lady Morton, who made me promise to visit her at Dalmahoy. She is a small, handsome woman, who speaks most excellent French. Mr. Lizars joined me, and we all entered the room of the Wernerian Society of Edinburgh! The room is a plain one; two tables, one fireplace, many long benches or seats, and a chair for the president were all the furniture I saw, except a stuffed sword-fish, which lay on one of the tables for examination that day. Many persons were already present, and I unrolled the drawing of the Buzzard for them to see. Professor Jameson came in, and the meeting began. My paper on the Buzzard was the first thing, read by Patrick Neill, —not very well, as my writing was not easy reading for him. Professor Jameson then rose, and gave quite a eulogy upon it, my works, and lastly — myself. I then had the thanks of the society, and showed them my manner of putting up my specimens for drawing birds, etc.; this they thought uncommonly ingenious. Professor Jameson then offered me as an honorary member, when arose a great clapping of hands and stamping of feet, as a mark of approbation. Then Professor Jameson desired that the usual law requiring a delay of some months between the nomination and the election be laid aside on this occasion; and again the same acclamations took place, and it was decided I should be elected at the next meeting; after which the meeting was ended, I having promised to read a paper on the habits of the Alligator at the following assembly of the society. Then came my dinner at Lady Hunter's.

At precisely six I found myself at No. 16 Hope St. I was shown upstairs, and presented to Lady Mary Clark, who knew both General Wolfe and General Montgomery, a most amiable English lady eighty-two years of age. Many other interesting people were present, and I had the pleasure of taking Mrs. Basil Hall to dinner, and was seated next her mother, Lady Hunter, and almost opposite Lady Mary Clark. I did not feel so uncomfortable as usual; all were so kind, affable, and *truly* well-bred. At nine the ladies left us, and Captain Basil Hall again attacked me about America, and hundreds of questions were put to me by all, which I answered as plainly and briefly as I could.

At eleven we joined the ladies, and tea and coffee were handed round; other guests had come in, card-tables were prepared, and we had some music. Portfolios of prints were ready for those interested in them. I sat watching all, but listening to Mrs. Hall's sweet music. This bustle does not suit me, I am not fitted for it, I prefer more solitude in the woods. I left at last with young Gregg, but I was the first to go, and we stepped out into the rainy Sunday morning, for it was long, long past midnight, and I hastened to my lodgings to commit murder, — yes, to commit murder; for the cats Mr. Daniel Lizars wished me to paint had been sent, and good Mrs. Dickie much objected to them in my rooms; her son helped me, and in two minutes the poor animals were painlessly killed. I at once put them up in fighting attitude, ready for painting when daylight appeared, which would not be long. Good-night, or good-morning; it is now nearly three o'clock.

Sunday, December 17. I painted all day, that is, during all the time I could see, and I was up at six this morning writing by candle-light, which I was compelled to use till nearly nine. Mr. Bridges called, and I dined at home on fried oysters and stewed Scotch herrings, then went to Mr. Lizars', where I nearly fell asleep; but a cup of coffee thoroughly awakened me, and I looked at some drawings of birds, which I thought miserable, by Mr. Pelletier. Mr. Lizars walked home with me to see my cats.

Monday, December 18. My painting of two cats fighting like two devils over a dead Squirrel was finished at three o'clock. I had been ten hours at it, but should not call it by the dignified title of "painting," for it is too rapidly done for the more finished work I prefer; but I cannot give more time to it now, and the drawing is good. I dressed, and took the painting — so I continue to call it — to Mrs. Lizars', who wished to see it, and it had rained so hard all day she had not been able to come to my rooms. At five I dined with George Combe, the conversation chiefly phrenology. George Combe is a delightful host, and had gathered a most agreeable company. At seven Mr. Lizars called for me, and we went to the meeting of the Royal Academy. Two of my plates were laid on the table. Dr. Brewster and Mr. Allan wished the Academy to subscribe for my work, and the committee retired to act on this and other business. The meeting was very numerous and no doubt very learned; Sir William Jardine and Mr. Selby arrived a little before the society was seated. The door of the hall was thrown open and we all marched in and seated ourselves on most slippery hair-cloth seats. The room is rich and beautiful; it is a large oblong, the walls covered with brilliant scarlet paper in imitation of morocco. The ceiling is painted to represent oak panels. The windows are immensely large, framed to correspond with the ceiling, and with green jalousies; large chandeliers, with gas, light every corner brilliantly. The president sat in a large arm-chair lined with red morocco, and after the minutes of the last meeting had been read, Professor —— gave us a long, tedious, and labored lecture on the origin of languages, their formation, etc. It seemed a very poor mess to me, though that was probably because I did not understand it. My friend Ord would have doubtless swallowed it whole, but I could make neither head nor tail of it. A few fossil bones were then exhibited, and then, thank heaven! it was over. Sir William Jardine brought some birds with him from Jardine Hall, and to-morrow will see my style of posing them for painting. As I had promised to go to supper with Dr. Russell, I left soon after ten, without knowing what decision the committee had reached as to subscribing to my work. I met several of the Academicians at Dr. Russell's, as well as others whom I knew; but I am more and more surprised to find how little these men, learned as they are, know of America beyond the situation of her principal cities. We sat down to supper at eleven, — everything magnificent; but I was greatly fatigued, for I had been at work since before five this morning, either painting or writing or thinking hard. We left the table about one, and I was glad to come home and shall now soon be asleep.

Tuesday, December 19. My writing takes me full two hours every morning, and soon as finished to-day, I dressed to go to breakfast with Sir William Jardine and Mr. Selby at Barry's Hotel. It was just nine, the morning fine and beautiful, the sun just above the line of the Old Town, the horizon like burnished gold, the walls of the Castle white in the light and almost black in the shade. All this made a beautiful scene, and I dwelt on the power of the great Creator who formed all, with a thought of all man had done and was doing, when a child, barefooted, ragged, and apparently on the verge of starvation, altered my whole train of ideas. The poor child complained of want, and, had I dared, I would have taken him to Sir William Jardine, and given him breakfast at the hotel; but the world is so strange I feared this might appear odd, so I gave the lad a shilling, and then bid him return with me to my lodgings. I looked over all my garments, gave him a large bundle of all that were at all worn, added five shillings, and went my way feeling as if God smiled on me through the face of the poor boy. The hotel was soon reached, and I was with my friends; they had brought Ducks, Hawks, and small birds for me to draw. After breakfast we all went to my room, and I showed these gentlemen how I set up my specimens, squared my paper, and soon had them both at work drawing a Squirrel. They called this a lesson. It was to me like a dream, that I, merely a woodsman, should teach men so much my superiors. They worked very well indeed, although I perceived at once that Mr. Selby was more enthusiastic, and therefore worked faster than Sir William; but he finished more closely, so that it was hard to give either the supremacy. They were delighted, especially Mr. Selby, who exclaimed, "I will paint all our quadrupeds for my own house." They both remained with me till we could see no more. At their request I read them my letter on the "Carrion Crow;" but Dr. Brewster had altered it so much that I was quite shocked at it, it made me quite sick. He had, beyond question, greatly improved the style (for I have none), but he had destroyed the matter.

I dined at Major Dodd's with a complete set of military gentry, generals, colonels, captains, majors, and, to my surprise, young Pattison, my companion in the coach from Manchester; he was Mrs. Dodd's cousin. I retired rather early, for I did not care for the blustering talk of all these warriors. Sir William Jardine and Mr. Lizars came to my lodgings and announced that I was elected by universal acclamation a member of the Society of Arts of the city of Edinburgh.

Wednesday, December 20. Phrenology was the order of the morning. I was at Brown Square, at the house of George Combe by nine o'clock, and breakfasted most heartily on mutton, ham, and good coffee, after which we walked upstairs to his *sanctum sanctorum.* A beautiful silver box containing the instruments for measuring the cranium, was now opened, — the box and contents were a present from the ladies who have attended Mr. Combe's lectures during the past two years, — and I was seated fronting the light. Dr. Combe acted as secretary and George Combe, thrusting his fingers under my hair, began searching for miraculous bumps. My skull was measured as minutely and accurately as I measure the bill or legs of a new bird, and all was duly noted by the scribe. Then with most exquisite touch each protuberance was found as numbered by phrenologists, and also put down according to the respective size. I was astounded when they both gave me the results of their labors in writing, and agreed in saying I was a strong and constant lover, an affectionate father, had great veneration for talent, would have made a brave general, that music did not equal painting in my estimation, that I was generous, quick-tempered, forgiving, and much else which I know to be true, though how they discovered these facts is quite a puzzle to me. They asked my permission to read the notes at their next meeting, to which I consented. I then went to court to meet Mr. Simpson the advocate, who was to introduce me to Francis Jeffrey. I found Mr. Simpson and a hundred others in their raven gowns, and powdered, curled wigs, but Mr. Jeffrey was not there. After doing many things and writing much, I went this evening to Mr. Lizars', and with him to Dr. Greville, the botanist.[1] He rarely leaves his house in winter and suffers much from asthma; I found him wearing a green silk night-cap, and we sat and talked of plants till 2 A. M. When I entered my rooms I found Mr. Selby had sent me three most beautiful Pheasants, and to-morrow I begin a painting of these birds attacked by a Fox for the Exhibition in London next March. Also I had a note from the Earl of Morton to spend a day and night at his home at Dalmahoy, saying he would send his carriage for me next Wednesday, one week hence.

Thursday, December 21. To-day I received letters from De Witt Clinton and Thomas Sully in answer to mine in forty-two days; it seems absolutely impossible the distance should have been covered so rapidly; yet it is so, as I see by my memorandum book. I have written already in reply to Thomas Sully, promising him a copy of my first number when finished, say a month hence, with the request that he forward it, in my name, to that Institution which thought me unworthy to be a member. There is no malice in my heart, and I wish no return or acknowledgment from them. I am now *determined* never to be a member of that Philadelphia Society, but I still think talents, no matter how humble, should be fostered in one's own country. The weather is clear, with a sharp frost. What a number of Wild Ducks could I shoot on a morning like this, with a little powder and plenty of shot; but I had

[1] Robert Kaye Greville, author of "Plants of Edinburgh" and other botanical works, 1794–1866.

other fish to fry. I put up a beautiful male Pheasant, and outlined it on coarse gray paper to *pounce* it in proper position on my canvas. Sir Wm. Jardine and Mr. Selby were here drawing under my direction most of the day. My time is so taken up, and daylight so short, that though four hours is all I allow for sleep, I am behindhand, and have engaged an amanuensis. I go out so much that I frequently dress three times a day, the greatest bore in the world to me; why I cannot dine in my blue coat as well as a black one, I cannot say, but so it seems. Mrs. Lizars came with a friend, Mr. Simpson, to invite me to a phrenological supper, Dr. Charles Fox, looking very ill, and two friends of Mr. Selby; the whole morning passed away, no canvas came for me, and I could not have left my guests to work, if it had. I looked often at the beautiful Pheasant, with longing eyes, but when the canvas came and my guests had gone, daylight went with them, so I had lost a most precious day; that is a vast deal in a man's life-glass. The supper was really a phrenological party; my head and Mr. Selby's were compared, and at twelve o'clock he and I went home together. I was glad to feel the frosty air and to see the stars. I think Mr. Selby one of those rare men that are seldom met with, and when one is found it proves how good some of our species may be. Never before did I so long for a glimpse of our rich magnolia woods; I never before felt the want of a glance at our forests as I do now; could I be there but a moment, hear the mellow Mock-bird, or the Wood-thrush, to me always so pleasing, how happy should I be; but alas! I am far from those scenes. I seem, in a measure, to have gone back to my early days of society and fine dressing, silk stockings and pumps, and all the finery with which I made a popinjay of myself in my youth.

December 22, Friday. I painted a good portion to-day though it was quite dark by three of the afternoon; how I long for the fair days of summer. My room to-day was a perfect levee; it is Mr. Audubon here, and Mr. Audubon there; I only hope they will not make a conceited fool of Mr. Audubon at last. I received every one as politely as I could, palette and brushes in hand, and conducted each in his turn to the door. I was called from my work twenty-five times, but I was nevertheless glad to see one and all. I supped with Sir William Jardine, Mr. Lizars, and Mr. Moule, Sir William's uncle, at Barry's Hotel; we talked much of fish and fishing, for we were all sportsmen. I left at midnight and found at my room a long letter from Charles Bonaparte.

Saturday, December 23. I had to grind up my own colors this morning; I detest it, it makes me hot, fretful, moody, and I am convinced has a bad effect on my mind. However, I worked closely, but the day was shockingly short; I cannot see before half-past nine, and am forced to stop at three. . . .

The 24th and 25th I remained closely at my work painting; on the 24th my drawings were all taken down and my paintings also. I wrote to the president of the Royal Institution and presented that society with my large painting of the "Wild Turkeys." I should have hesitated about offering it had I not been assured it had some value, as Gally, the picture dealer, offered me a hundred guineas for it the previous day; and I was glad to return some acknowledgment of the politeness of the Institution in a handsome manner. My steady work brought on a bad headache, but I rose early, took a walk of many miles, and it has gone.

December 26. My steady painting, my many thoughts, and my brief nights, bring on me now every evening a weariness that I cannot surmount on command. This is, I think, the first time in my life when, *if needed,* I could not rouse myself from sleepiness, shake myself and be ready for action in an instant; but now I cannot do that, and I have difficulty often in keeping awake as evening comes on; this evening I had to excuse myself from a gathering at Lady Hunter's, and came home intending to go at once to bed; but I lay down on my sofa for a moment, fell asleep, and did not wake till after midnight, when I found myself both cold and hungry. I have taken some food and now will rest, though no longer sleepy, for to-morrow I go to Earl Morton's, where I wish, at least, to keep awake.

Dalmahoy, eight miles from Edinburgh, December 27, Wednesday. I am now seated at a little table in the *Yellow Bedchamber* at Earl Morton's, and will give an account of my day. After my breakfast, not anxious to begin another Pheasant, I did some writing and paid some visits, returned to my lodgings and packed a box for America with various gifts, some mementos I had received, and several newspapers, when Lord Morton's carriage was announced. My *porte-feuille* and valise were carried down, and I followed them and entered a large carriage lined with purple morocco; never was I in so comfortable a conveyance before; the ship that under easy sail glides slowly on an even sea has a more fatiguing motion; I might have been in a swinging hammock. We passed the castle, through Charlotte Square, and out on the Glasgow road for eight miles, all so swiftly that my watch had barely changed the time from one hour to another when the porter pushed open the gate of Dalmahoy. I now began to think of my meeting with the man who had been great Chamberlain to the late Queen Charlotte. I did not so much mind meeting the Countess, for I had become assured of her sweetness of disposition when we had met on previous occasions, but the Chamberlain I could not help dreading to encounter. This, however, did not prevent the carriage from proceeding smoothly round a great circle, neither did it prevent me from seeing a large, square, half Gothic building with two turrets, ornamented with great lions, and all the signs of heraldry belonging to Lord Morton. The carriage stopped, a man in livery opened the door, and I walked in, giving him my hat and gloves and my American stick (that, by the bye, never leaves me unless I leave it). Upstairs I went and into the drawing-room. The Countess rose at once and came to greet me, and then presented Lord Morton to me — yes, really not me to him; for the moment I was taken aback, I had expected something so different. I had formed an idea that the Earl was a man of great physical strength and size; instead I saw a small, slender man, tottering on his feet, weaker than a newly hatched Partridge; he welcomed me with tears in his eyes, held one of my hands and attempted speaking, which was difficult to him, the Countess meanwhile rubbing his other hand. I saw at a glance his situation and begged he would be seated, after which I was introduced to the mother of the Countess, Lady Boulcar, and I took a seat on a sofa that I thought would swallow me up, so much down swelled around me. It was a vast room, at least sixty feet long, and wide in proportion, let me say thirty feet, all hung with immense paintings on a rich purple ground; all was purple about me. The large tables were covered with books, instruments, drawing apparatus, and a telescope, with hundreds of ornaments. As I glanced at the pictures I could see the Queen of England fronting Mary of Scotland, a chamberlain here, a duke there, and in another place a beautiful head by Rembrandt. Van Dyke had not been forgotten; Claude Lorraine had some landscapes here also; while the celebrated Titian gave a lustre to the whole. I rose to take a closer view, the Countess explaining all to me, but conceive my surprise when, looking from the middle window, I saw at the horizon the castle and city of Edinburgh, a complete miniature eight miles off, a landscape of fields, water, and country between us and it. Luncheon was announced; I am sure if my friends complain tha

I eat but little, they must allow that I eat often; never were such lands for constant meals as England and Scotland. The Countess of Boulcar rolled Lord Morton in his castored chair, I gave my arm to Lady Morton, we crossed a large antechamber, into a dining-room quite rich in paintings, and at present with a sumptuous repast. Three gentlemen, also visitors, entered by another door, — Messrs. Hays, Ramsay, and a young clergyman whose name I forget. After luncheon my drawings were produced, the Earl was rolled into a good position for light, and my "Book of Nature" was unbuckled. I am not going to repeat praises again. The drawings seen, we adjourned to the drawing-room and the Countess begged me to give her a lesson to-morrow, which I shall most gladly do. The Countess is not exactly beautiful, but she is good-looking, with fine eyes, a brilliant complexion, and a good figure; she is a woman of superior intellect and conversation, and I should think about forty years of age; she was dressed in a rich crimson gown, and her mother in black satin. At six I re-entered the house, having taken a short walk with the gentlemen, and was shown to my room. "The yellow room," I heard the Countess say to the lackey who showed me the way. My valise had been unpacked, and all was most comfortable, and truly yellow in this superb apartment. The bed was hung with yellow of some rich material, and ornamented with yellow crowns, and was big enough for four of my size; a large sofa and large arm-chairs, all yellow, the curtains, dressing-table, all indeed was yellow, intensified by the glow of a bright wood fire. My evening toilet is never a very lengthy matter, — for in my opinion it is a vile loss of time to spend as many minutes in arranging a cravat as a hangman does in tying his knot, — and I was ready long before seven, when I again gave the Countess my arm, and Lord Morton was again rolled in, in his chair. The waiters, I think there were four, were powdered and dressed in deep red, almost maroon liveries, except the butler, who was in black, and who appeared to me to hand fresh plates continuously. After a dinner of somewhat more than an hour, the ladies retired with the Earl, and I remained with the three gentlemen to talk and drink wine. The conversation was entirely of antiquities. Mr. Hays is a deeply learned and interesting man, besides being quite an original. At the hour of ten we joined the Countess, the Earl having retired, and I have been much interested looking at the signatures of the kings of old, as well as that of Marie, Queen of Scots, and those of many other celebrated men and women, while two of the gentlemen were examining a cabinet of antique coins. The Countess looked very brilliant, being attired in white satin with a crimson turban. At midnight (coffee having been served about eleven), the ladies bid us good-night, and we sat down to talk, and drink, if we wished to, Madeira wine. What a life! I could not stand this ceremony daily, I long for the woods; but I hope this life will enable me to enjoy them more than ever at a future period, so I must bear it patiently. After a few moments I left the gentlemen, and came to my yellow room.

Thursday, December 28. Daylight came and I opened all my yellow curtains, and explored my room by daylight; and I have forgotten to tell thee that the dressing-room, with its large porcelain tub and abundance of clear water, opened from it, and was warm with crimson of the color of the Countess's turban. The chimney-piece was decorated with choice shells, and above it a painting representing Queen Mary in her youth. The house seemed very still, but after dressing I decided to go down, for the morning was clear and the air delightful. As I entered the drawing-room I saw two housemaids busily cleaning; the younger saw me first, and I heard her say, "The American gentleman is down already," when they both vanished. I went out to look about the grounds, and in about an hour was oined by the young clergyman, and a walk was immediately undertaken. The Hares started before our dogs, and passing through various woods, we came by a turn to the stables, where I saw four superbly formed Abyssinian horses, with tails reaching to the earth, and the legs of one no larger than those of an Elk. The riding-room was yet lighted, and the animals had been exercised that morning. The game-keeper was unkennelling his dogs; he showed me a large tame Fox.

Then through other woods we proceeded to the Manor, now the habitat of the great falconer *John Anderson* and his Hawks. He had already received orders to come to the Hall at eleven to show me these birds in their full dress. We visited next the hot-houses, where roses were blooming most sweetly, and then following a brook reached the Hall about ten. The ladies were in the drawing-room, and the Earl came in, when we went to breakfast. Neither at this meal nor at luncheon are seen any waiters. The meal over, all was bustle in the drawing-room; chalks, crayons, papers, all required was before me in a few minutes, and I began to give the Countess a most unnecessary lesson, for she drew much better than I did; but I taught her how to rub with cork, and prepare for water-color. The Earl sat by watching us, and then asked to see my drawings again. The falconer came, and I saw the Falcons ready for the chase. He held the birds on his gloved hands, with bells and hoods and crests; but the morning was not fit for a flight, so I lost that pleasure. The Countess asked for my subscription book and wrote with a steel pen, "The Countess of Morton;" she wished to pay for the first number now, but this I declined. She promised me letters for England, with which offer I was much pleased. Desiring some fresh Pheasants for my work, she immediately ordered some killed for me. After luncheon I walked out to see a herd of over a hundred brown Deer, that like sheep were feeding within a few hundred paces of the Hall. I approached quite close to them, and saw that many had shed their horns; they scampered off when they sighted me, knowing perhaps what a hunter I was! Lady Morton wished me to remain longer, but as I had promised to dine with Captain Hall I could not do so; it was therefore decided that I should return next week to spend another night and give another lesson. My ride to Edinburgh was soon over, and a letter and a book from Charles Bonaparte were at my lodgings. Captain Hall told me at dinner that he was a midshipman on board the Leander when Pierce was killed off New York, and when I was on my way from France, when our captain, seeing the British vessel, wore about round Long Island and reached New York by Hell Gate. There is a curious notice about me by Professor Wilson in "Blackwood's Magazine."

Friday, December 29. I painted all day, and did this most happily and cheerfully, for I had received two long letters from my Lucy, of October 14 and 23. The evening was spent with Captain Hall, Mr. Lizars, and his brother.

Saturday, December 30. So stormy a day that I have not been disturbed by visitors, nor have I been out, but painted all day.

Sunday, December 31. This evening I dined at Captain Hall's, especially for the purpose of being introduced to Francis Jeffrey, the principal writer in the "Edinburgh Review." Following the advice given me I did not take my watch, lest it should be stolen from me on my return, for I am told this is always a turbulent night in Edinburgh. Captain Hall and his wife received me with their usual cordiality, and we were soon joined by Mr. McCulloch, a writer on Political Economy and a plain, agreeable man. Then Francis Jeffrey and his wife entered; he is a small (not to say tiny) being, with a woman under one arm and a hat under the other. He bowed very seriously indeed, so much so that I conceived him to be fully aware of his weight in society. His looks were shrewd, but I thought his eyes almost cunning. He talked a great deal and very well, yet I did not like him; but he may prove better than I think, for this is only my first impression. Mrs. Jeffrey was nervous and very much dressed. If I mistake not Jeffrey was shy of me, and I of him, for he has used me very cavalierly. When I came I brought a letter of introduction to him; I called on him, and, as he was absent, left the letter and my card. When my exhibition opened I enclosed a card of admittance to him, with another of my own cards. He never came near me, and I never went near him; for if *he* was Jeffrey, *I* was Audubon, and felt quite independent of all the tribe of Jeffreys in England, Scotland, and Ireland, put together. This evening, however, he thanked me for my card politely. At dinner he sat opposite to me and the conversation was on various topics. America, however, was hardly alluded to, as whenever Captain Hall tried to bring that country into our talk, Mr. Jeffrey most skilfully brought up something else. After coffee had been served Mr. Jeffrey made some inquiries about my work, and at ten I took my leave, having positively seen the little man whose fame is so great both in Scotland and abroad. I walked home briskly; this was the eve of a New Year, and in Edinburgh they tell me it is rather a dangerous thing to be late in the streets, for many vagabonds are abroad at this time, and murders and other fearful deeds take place. To prevent these as far as possible, the watch is doubled, and an unusual quantity of gas-lights are afforded. I reached my room, sat down and outlined a Pheasant, to save daylight to-morrow, and was about going to bed, when Mrs. Dickie came in and begged I would wait till twelve o'clock to take some toddy with her and Miss Campbell, my American boarding companion, to wish all a happy New Year. I did so, of course, and had I sat up all night, and written, or drawn, or sat thinking by my fire, I should have done as well, for the noise kept increasing in the streets, and the confusion was such that until morning I never closed my eyes. At early morning this first day of January, 1827, I received from Captain Hall three volumes of his voyages, and from the Countess of Morton four beautiful Pheasants and a basket of rare hot-house flowers.

Edinburgh, January 1, 1827, Monday.[1] A Happy New Year to you, my book. Bless me! how fair you look this very cold day. Which way, pray, are you travelling? Travelling wherever chance or circumstance may lead you? Well, I will take you for my companion, and we will talk together on all kinds of subjects, and you will help me to remember, for my memory is bad, very bad. I never can recollect the name of an enemy, for instance; it is only my friends whom I can remember, and to write down somewhat of their kind treatment of me is a delight I love to enjoy.

January 6, Saturday. Ever since the first day of this month I have been most closely engaged at my painting of the "Pheasants Attacked by a Fox." I have, however, spent another day and night at Dalmahoy. I have written a long paper for the Wernerian Society on the habits of Alligators, and am always very weary at night.

January 7. I keep at my painting closely, and for a wonder was visited by Dr. Bridges. I have labored hard, but my work is bad; some inward feeling tells me when it is good. No one, I think, paints in my method; I, who have never studied but by piecemeal, form my pictures according to my ways of study. For instance, I am now working on a Fox; I take one neatly killed, put him up with wires, and when satisfied of the truth of the position, I take my palette and work as rapidly as possible; the

[1] This entry begins a new blank book, in shape and size like a ledger, every line of which is closely written.

same with my birds. If practicable, I finish the bird at one sitting, — often, it is true, of fourteen hours, — so that I think they are correct, both in detail and composition.

Monday, 8th. I rose this morning two and a half hours before day, and wrote much before breakfast. Thanks to my good spirit not a soul called upon me this day, and I brushed away without losing a moment of the precious light of these short days. This evening I saw my plate of the Wild Turkey, and went to hear Captain Basil Hall lecture at the Royal Society on the Trade Winds. The practical as well as theoretical knowledge of this learned man rendered this a most valuable evening to me. I was introduced to Mr. Perceval, the son of the King of England's Secretary of State,[1] who was shamefully and barbarously murdered some years since.

Tuesday, 9th. Mr. Hays, the Dalmahoy antiquarian, called on me, and brought me a copy of Bewick's "Quadrupeds." At eight this evening I went to the Society of Arts, of which I have been elected a member. Here I saw a capital air-gun, and a steam-carriage in full motion; but *I* had to operate, and showed my manner of putting up my birds with wires, and I positively shook so that I feared I should not be able to proceed to the termination; this bashfulness is dreadful, how am I ever to overcome it?

January 10. The weather has been most strange, at times so dark that I could not see to paint, and suddenly the sun shone so brightly that I was dazzled. It rained, it blew, it snowed; we have had all seasons. A Mr. Buchanan from London came to see my work, and Professor Wilson at the same time; both liked my painting, and strangely enough the two had known each other twenty years ago. I went to the theatre to see Miss Foote and Mr. Murray; both were much applauded, and the house was crowded. I am very fond of the theatre; I think it

[1] Spencer Perceval, born 1762, assassinated in the lobby of the House of Commons, May 11, 1812.

the best of all ways to spend an evening for *délassement.* I often find myself when there laughing or crying like a child.

January 11. Scarce daylight at half-past seven, but I was up and away with a coal porter and his cart into the country. I wanted some large, rough stones for my foreground; this was my reason for my excursion. I passed a small, dirty, and almost lost building, where the union between Scotland and England was ratified. At one o'clock Professor Russell called in his carriage with Mr. Lizars, then we went to see a picture of the famous Hondekoeter. To me the picture was destitute of *life;* the animals seemed to me to be drawn from poorly stuffed specimens, but the coloring, the finish, the manner, the effect, was most beautiful, and but for the lack of Nature in the animals was a picture which commanded admiration and attention. Would that I could *paint* like Hondekoeter! At eight I went to the Phrenological Society, and may safely say that never before was I in such company; the deepest philosophers in this city of learning were there, and George Combe read an essay on the mental powers of man, as illustrated by phrenological researches, that astounded me; it lasted one and a half hours, and will remain in my mind all my life.

January 12. My painting has now arrived at the difficult point. To finish highly without destroying the general effect, or to give the general effect and care not about the finishing? I am quite puzzled. Sometimes I like the picture, then a heat rises to my face and I think it a miserable daub. This is the largest piece I have ever done; as to the birds, as far as *they* are concerned I am quite satisfied, but the ground, the foliage, the sky, the distance are dreadful. To-day I was so troubled about this that at two o'clock, when yet a good hour of daylight remained, I left it in disgust, and walked off to Dr. Bridges. I passed on my way the place where a man was murdered the night before last; a great multitude of people were looking at the spot, gazing like fools, for there was nothing to be seen. How is it that our sages tell us our species is much improved? If we murder now in cool blood, and in a most terrifying way, our brother, we are not a jot forward since the time of Cain.

January 13. Painted five hours, and at two o'clock accompanied by Mr. Lizars, reached the University and entered the rooms of the Wernerian Society with a paper on the habits of Alligators in my pocket, to be read to the members and visitors present. This I read after the business of the meeting had been transacted, and, thank God, after the effort of once beginning, I went on unfalteringly to the end. In the evening I went with Mr. Lizars to see "As You Like It." Miss Foote performed and also Mr. Murray, but the house was so crowded that I could scarce see.

January 14. Could not work on my picture, for I have no white Pheasant for a key-stone of light, but Professor Jameson called and said he would write for one for me to the Duke of Buccleugh. After receiving many callers I went to Mr. O'Neill's to have a cast taken of my head. My coat and neckcloth were taken off, my shirt collar turned down, I was told to close my eyes; Mr. O'Neill took a large brush and oiled my whole face, the almost liquid plaster of Paris was poured over it, as I sat uprightly till the whole was covered; my nostrils only were exempt. In a few moments the plaster had acquired the needful consistency, when it was taken off by pulling it down gently. The whole operation lasted hardly five minutes; the only inconvenience felt was the weight of the material pulling downward over my sinews and flesh. On my return from the Antiquarian Society that evening, I found *my face* on the table, an excellent cast.

January 17 to Sunday, 21st. John Syme, the artist, asked me if I did not wish to become an associate member of the *Scottish Artists.* I answered, "Yes." I have promised to paint a picture of Black Cock for their exhibition, and with that view went to market, where for fifteen shillings I purchased two superb males and one female. I have been painting pretty much all day and every day. Among my visitors I have had the son of Smollett, the great writer, a handsome young gentleman. Several noblemen came to see my Pheasants, and all promised me a *white* one. Professor Russell called and read me a letter from Lord ——, *giving me leave* to see the pictures at his hall, but I, poor Audubon, go nowhere without an *invitation.*

January 22, Monday. I was painting diligently when Captain Hall came in, and said: "Put on your coat, and come with me to Sir Walter Scott; he wishes to see you *now.*" In a moment I was ready, for I really believe my coat and hat came to me instead of my going to them. My heart trembled; I longed for the meeting, yet wished it over. Had not his wondrous pen penetrated my soul with the consciousness that here was a genius from God's hand? I felt overwhelmed at the thought of meeting Sir Walter, the Great Unknown. We reached the house, and a powdered waiter was asked if Sir Walter were in.[1] We were shown forward at once, and entering a very small room Captain Hall said: "Sir Walter, I have brought Mr. Audubon." Sir Walter came forward, pressed my hand warmly, and said he was "glad to have the honor of meeting me." His long, loose, silvery locks struck me; he looked like Franklin at his best. He also reminded me of

[1] "Jan. 22, 1827. A visit from Basil Hall with Mr. Audubon the ornithologist, who has followed that pursuit by many a long wandering in the American forests. He is an American by naturalization, a Frenchman by birth, but less of a Frenchman than I have ever seen,—no dash, no glimmer or shine about him, but great simplicity of manners and behaviour; slight in person and plainly dressed; wears long hair which time has not yet tinged; his countenance acute, handsome, and interesting, but still simplicity is the predominant characteristic." (Journal of Sir Walter Scott, vol. i., p. 343.)

AUDUBON.

From the portrait by Henry Inman. Now in the possession of the family.

Benjamin West; he had the great benevolence of Wm. Roscoe about him, and a kindness most prepossessing. I could not forbear looking at him, my eyes feasted on his countenance. I watched his movements as I would those of a celestial being; his long, heavy, white eyebrows struck me forcibly. His little room was tidy, though it partook a good deal of the character of a laboratory. He was wrapped in a quilted morning-gown of light purple silk; he had been at work writing on the "Life of Napoleon." He writes close lines, rather curved as they go from left to right, and puts an immense deal on very little paper. After a few minutes had elapsed he begged Captain Hall to ring a bell; a servant came and was asked to bid Miss Scott come to see Mr. Audubon. Miss Scott came, black-haired and black-dressed, not handsome but said to be highly accomplished, and she is the daughter of Sir Walter Scott. There was much conversation. I talked little, but, believe me, I listened and observed, careful if ignorant. I cannot write more now. — I have just returned from the Royal Society. Knowing that I was a candidate for the electorate of the society, I felt very uncomfortable and would gladly have been hunting on Tawapatee Bottom.

January 23, Tuesday. My first visitor was Mr. Hays the antiquarian, who needed my assistance, or rather my knowledge of French in the translation of a passage relating to "le droit du seigneur." Dr. Combe called later and begged me to go to Mr. Joseph, the sculptor, with him, and through a great fall of snow we went through Windsor Street, one of the handsomest in this beautiful city. Mr. Joseph was in, and I saw an uncommonly good bust of Sir Walter, one of Lord Morton, and several others. I have powerfully in my mind to give my picture of the "Trapped Otter" to Mrs. Basil Hall, and, by Washington, I will. No one deserves it more, and I cannot receive so many favors without trying to make some return.

January 24. My second visit to Sir Walter Scott was much more agreeable than my first. My portfolio and its contents were matters on which I could speak substantially,[1] and I found him so willing to level himself with me for a while that the time spent at his home was agreeable and valuable. His daughter improved in looks the moment she spoke, having both vivacity and good sense.

January 28. Yesterday I had so many visitors that I was quite fatigued; my rooms were full all the time, yet I work away as if they were so many cabbages, except for a short time taken to show them a few drawings, give them chairs, and other civil attentions. In the evening I went to the theatre to see the "Merchant of Venice;" the night was violently stormy, the worst I remember for years. I thought of the poor sailors, what hard lives they have.

January 30, Tuesday. The days begin to show a valuable augmentation. I could this morning begin work at eight, and was still at my easel at four. A man may do a good deal on a painting in eight hours provided he has the power of laying the true tints at once, and does not muddy his colors or need glazing afterwards. Now a query arises. Did the ancient artists and colorists ever glaze their work? I sometimes think they did not, and I am inclined to think thus because their work is of great strength of standing, and extremely solid and confirmed on the canvas — a proof with me that they painted clean and bright at once, but that this *once* they repeated, perhaps, as often as three times. Glazing certainly is a beautiful way of effecting transparency, particularly over shadowy parts, but I fre-

[1] "January 24. Visit from Mr. Audubon, who brings some of his birds. The drawings are of the first order — the attitudes of the birds of the most animated character, and the situations appropriate. . . . This sojourner of the desert had been in the woods for months together. He preferred associating with the Indians to the company of the settlers; very justly, I daresay, for a civilized man of the lower order when thrust back on the savage state becomes worse than a savage." (Journal of Sir Walter Scott, vol. i., p. 345.)

quently fear the coating being so thin, and that time preys on these parts more powerfully than on those unglazed, so that the work is sooner destroyed by its application than without it. I am confident Sir Joshua Reynolds' pictures fade so much in consequence of his constant glazing. Lord Hay, who has only one arm, called this morning, and promised me White Pheasants by Saturday morning. So many people have called that I have not put a foot out to-day.

January 31, Wednesday. I had the delight of receiving letters from home to-day; how every word carried me to my beloved America. Oh, that I could be with you and see those magnificent forests, and listen to sweet Wood Thrushes and the Mock-Birds so gay!

February 1. I have just finished a picture of Black Cock sunning and dusting themselves, with a view in the background of Loch Lomond, nine feet by six, for which I am offered two hundred guineas. It will be exhibited at the Royal Institute rooms next week, and the picture of the Pheasants, the same size, at the Scottish Society of Artists, of which I am now an associate member.

February 5. None of my promised White Pheasants have come, but I have determined the picture shall be finished if I have to paint in a black Crow instead. Dr. Brewster spoke to me of a camera lucida to enable me to outline birds with great rapidity. I would like such an instrument if merely to save time in hot weather, when outlining correctly is more than half the work. At eight o'clock I entered the rooms of the Royal Society. I opened my large sheets and laid them on the table; the astonishment of every one was great, and I saw with pleasure many eyes look from them to me. The business of the society was then done behind closed doors; but when these were opened and we were called into the great room, Captain Hall, taking my hand, led me to a seat immediately opposite to Sir Walter Scott; then, Lucy, I had a perfect view of that great man, and I studied from Nature Nature's noblest work. After a lecture on the introduction of the Greek language into England, the president, Sir Walter, rose and we all followed his example. Sir Walter came to me, shook my hand cordially, and asked me how the cold weather of Edinburgh agreed with me. This mark of attention was observed by other members, who looked at me as if I had been a distinguished stranger.

February 9. I have been, and am yet, greatly depressed, yet why I am so it is impossible for me to conceive, unless it be that slight vexations, trifling in themselves, are trying to me, because, alas! I am only a very, very common man. I dined to-night at Professor Jameson's, and as my note said "with a few friends," was surprised to find thirty besides myself. The engineer, Mr. S——, was here, and many other noted men, including the famous Professor Leslie,[1] an enormous mass of flesh and an extremely agreeable man, who had been in Virginia many years ago, but recollects those days well.

February 10. I visited the Royal Institution this morning, and saw my Black Cocks over the first of the first-room doors. I know well that the birds are drawn as well as any birds ever have been; but what a difference exists between drawing one bird or a dozen and amalgamating them with a sky, a landscape, and a well adapted foreground. Who has not felt a sense of fear while trying to combine all this? I looked at my work long, then walked round the room, when my eyes soon reached a picture by Landseer, the death of a stag. I saw much in it of the style of those men who know how to handle a brush and carry a good effect; but Nature was not there, although a Stag, three dogs, and a Highlander were introduced on the canvas. The Stag had his tongue out and his mouth shut! The principal dog, a greyhound, held the Deer by one ear

[1] Sir John Leslie, 1766–1832, Scottish geometer and natural philosopher and voluminous author on these subjects.

just as if a loving friend; the young hunter has laced the Deer by one horn very prettily, and in the attitude of a ballet-dancer was about to cast the noose over the head of the animal. To me, or to my friends Dr. Pope or Mr. Bourgeat such a picture is quite a farce; not so here however. Many other pictures drew my attention, and still more so the different artists who came in with brushes and palettes *to tickle their pictures.* I was to read a paper at the Wernerian Society on the Rattlesnake, but had not had time to finish it; nevertheless I went to the society rooms, which were crowded. I was sorry I was not prepared to read to those assembled that a Rattlesnake rattled his tail, not to give knowledge to man of his presence, but because he never strikes without rattling, and that destitute of that appendage he cannot strike at all. The wind blows a doleful tune and I feel utterly alone.

Monday, February 12. Mr. Lizars insisted on my going to the Antiquarian Society, saying it was usual for a member newly elected to be present on the first occasion possible. I went, of course, but felt very sheepish withal. We had an excellent paper by Mr. Hays respecting a bell found in Argyle, of very ancient date.

Tuesday, February 13. This was the grand, long promised, and much wished-for day of the opening of the Exhibition at the rooms of the Royal Institution. At one o'clock I went, the doors were just opened, and in a few minutes the rooms were crowded. Sir Walter Scott was present; he came towards me, shook my hand cordially, and pointing to Landseer's picture said: "Many such scenes, Mr. Audubon, have I witnesssd in my younger days." We talked much of all about us, and I would gladly have joined him in a glass of wine, but my foolish habits prevented me, and after inquiring of his daughter's health, I left him, and shortly afterwards the rooms; for I had a great appetite, and although there were tables loaded with delicacies, and I saw the ladies particularly eating freely, I must say to my shame *I* dared not lay my fingers on a single thing. In the evening I went to the theatre where I was much amused by "The Comedy of Errors," and afterwards "The Green Room." I admire Miss Neville's singing very much; and her manners also; there is none of the actress about her, but much of the lady.

Tuesday, 20th. A week has passed without writing here because I have done nothing else but write — many letters for Captain Hall, and at his request a paper to be read at the Natural History Society. I pitched on the "Habits of the Wild Pigeon." I began on Wednesday, and it took me until half-past three of the morning, and after a few hours' sleep I rose to correct it, which was needed, I can assure thee. Were it not for the *facts* it contains, I would not give a cent for it, nor anybody else, I dare say. I positively brought myself so much among the Pigeons and in the woods of America that my ears were as if really filled with the noise of their wings; I was tired and my eyes ached. I dined at a Mr. Tytler's and met among the guests Mr. Cruden, brother of the compiler of the famous concordance. On Sunday I made for the seashore, and walked eight miles; the weather was extremely cold, my ears and nose I thought would drop off, yet I went on. Monday Captain Hall called to speak to me about my paper on Pigeons; he complained that I expressed the belief that Pigeons were possessed of affection and tenderest love, and that this raised the brute species to a level with man. O man! misled, self-conceited being, when wilt thou keep within the sphere of humility that, with all thy vices and wickedness about thee, should be thine. At the exhibition rooms I put up my drawing of the Wild Pigeons and Captain Hall read my paper. I was struck with the silence and attention of the audience. The president invited me to supper with him, but I was too excited, so excused myself.

February 21. I wrote again nearly all day, and in the evening went to the theatre to see "The School for Grown Children."

February 23. Young Hutchinson came about the middle of the day, and I proposed we should have an early dinner and a long walk after for the sake of exercise, that I now find much needed. We proceeded towards the village of Portobello, distant three miles, the weather delightful, the shore dotted with gentlemen on horseback galloping over the sand in all directions. The sea calm and smooth, had many fishing-boats. The village is a summer resort, built handsomely of white stone, and all was quietness. From here we proceeded across country to Duddingston, about a mile and a half, to see the skaters on the *lake*, a mere duck puddle; but the ice was too thin, and no skaters were there. We gradually ascended the hill called Arthur's Seat, and all of a sudden came in full view of the fair city. We entered in the Old Town and reached my lodgings by the North Bridge. I was quite tired, and yet I had not walked more than ten miles. I thought this strange, and wondered if it could be the same body that travelled over one hundred and sixty-five miles in four days without a shade of fatigue. The cities do not tempt me to walk, and so I lose the habit.

February 24. To the Wernerian Society at two o'clock, my drawing of the Mocking-Bird with me. The room was completely filled, and a paper on the rhubarb of commerce was read; it was short, and then Professor Jameson called my name. I rose, and read as distinctly as I could my paper on Rattlesnakes, a job of three quarters of an hour. Having finished I was cheered by all, and the thanks of the Assembly unanimously voted. My cheeks burned, and after a few questions had been put me by the president and some of the gentlemen present, I handed my manuscript to Professor Jameson, and was glad to be gone. Young Murray, the son of the London publisher, accompanied me to the Scottish Society Exhibition, but I soon left him as so many eyes were directed to me that I was miserable.

February 27. It blew and rained tremendously, and this morning I parted from Captain Hall, who goes to London. His leaving Edinburgh affects me considerably; he is a kind, substantial friend, and when we finally shook hands, I doubt not he knew the feeling in my heart. This evening was spent at Mr. Joseph's the sculptor. There were a number of guests, and music and dancing was proposed. My fame as a dancer produced, I am sure, false expectations; nevertheless I found myself on the floor with Mrs. Joseph, a lively, agreeable little lady, much my junior, and about my Lucy's age. After much dancing, during which light refreshments were served, we sat down to supper at twelve o'clock, and we did not leave till three.

February 28. I have been reading Captain Hall's "Voyages and Travels," and going much about to rest my eyes and head; but these few days of idleness have completely sickened me, and have given me what is named the Blue Devils so effectually that the sooner I drive them off the better.

March 1. Mr. Kidd,[1] the landscape artist, breakfasted with me, and we talked painting a long time. I admired him for his talents at so early a period of life, he being only nineteen. What would I have been now if equally gifted by nature at that age? But, sad reflection, I have been forced constantly to hammer and stammer as if in opposition to God's will, and so therefore am nothing now but poor Audubon. I asked him to come to me daily to eat, drink, and give me the pleasure of his company and advice. I told him my wish was so intense to improve in the delightful art of painting that I should begin a new picture to-morrow, and took down my portfolio to look for one of my drawings to copy in oil. He had

[1] Joseph B. Kidd, who later copied many of Audubon's birds.

never seen my work, and his bright eyes gazed eagerly on what he saw with admiration.

March 2. Mr. Kidd breakfasted with me, and we painted the whole day.

March 3. I painted as constantly to-day, as it snowed and blew hard outside my walls. I thought frequently that the devils must be at the handles of Æolus' bellows, and turned the cold blasts into the Scotch mists to freeze them into snow. It is full twenty years since I saw the like before. I dined at Mr. Ritchie's, reaching his house safely through more than two feet of snow.

March 4. The weather tolerably fair, but the snow lay deep. The mails from all quarters were stopped, and the few people that moved along the streets gave a fuller idea of winter in a northern clime than anything I have seen for many years. Mr. Hays called for me, and we went to breakfast with the Rev. Mr. Newbold, immediately across the street. I was trundled into a sedan chair to church. I had never been in a sedan chair before, and I like to try, as well as see, all things on the face of this strange world of ours; but so long as I have two legs and feet below them, never will I again enter one of these machines, with their quick, short, up-and-down, swinging motion, resembling the sensations felt during the great earthquake in Kentucky. But Sydney Smith preached. Oh! what a soul there must be in the body of that great man. What sweet yet energetic thoughts, what goodness he must possess. It was a sermon *to me*. He made me smile, and he made me think deeply. He pleased me at times by painting my foibles with due care, and again I felt the color come to my cheeks as he portrayed my sins. I left the church full of veneration not only towards God, but towards the wonderful man who so beautifully illustrates his noblest handiwork. After lunch Mr. Hays and I took a walk towards Portobello, tumbling and pitching in the deep snow. I saw Sky-Larks, poor things, caught in snares as easily — as men are caught. For a wonder I have done no work to-day.

March 5. As a lad I had a great aversion to anything English or Scotch, and I remember when travelling with my father to Rochefort in January, 1800, I mentioned this to him, for to him, thank God, I always told all my thoughts and expressed all my ideas. How well I remember his reply: "Laforest, thy blood will cool in time, and thou wilt be surprised to see how gradually prejudices are obliterated, and friendships acquired, towards those that at one time we held in contempt. Thou hast not been in England; I have, and it is a fine country." What has since taken place? I have admired and esteemed many English and Scotch, and therefore do I feel proud to tell thee that I am a Fellow of the Royal Society of Edinburgh. My day has been rather dull, though I painted assiduously. This evening I went to the Society of Arts, where beautiful experiments were shown by the inventors themselves; a steam coach moved with incomprehensible regularity. I am undetermined whether to go to Glasgow on my way to Dublin, or proceed overland to Newcastle, Liverpool, Oxford, Cambridge, and so on to London, but I shall move soon.

March 7. This evening I was introduced to Sydney Smith, the famous preacher of last Sunday, and his fair daughters, and heard them sing most sweetly. I offered to show them some of my drawings and they appointed Saturday at one o'clock. The wind is blowing as if intent to destroy the fair city of Edinburgh.

March 8. The weather was dreadful last night and still continues so; the snow is six feet deep in some parts of the great roads, and I was told at the Post Office that horsemen sent with the mail to London had been obliged to abandon their horses, and proceed on foot. Wrote a letter to Sir Walter Scott requesting a letter of introduction, or shall I say *endorsement*, and his servant brought me a gratifying reply at eight of the evening. At one Dr. Spence came with Miss Neville, the delightful singer at the theatre, her mother, and Miss Hamilton. They sat with me some time, and I was glad to see near-by the same Miss Neville whom I admire so much at the play. I found her possessed of good sense and modesty, and like her much; her mother asked me to spend the evening of next Saturday with them, and said her daughter would sing for me with pleasure. Had a note from Sydney Smith; the man should study economy; he would destroy more paper in a day than Franklin in a week; but all great men are more or less eccentric. Walter Scott writes a diminutive hand, very difficult to read, Napoleon a large, scrawling one, still more difficult, and Sydney Smith goes up-hill all the way with large strides.

March 9. My first work this day was to send as a present to Miss Anne Scott a copy of my first number. Professor Wilson called and promised to come again on Monday.

March 10. I visited Mr. James B. Fraser,[1] a great traveller in Asia and Africa, and saw there a large collection of drawings and views in water-colors of the scenery of these countries. The lecture at the Wernerian Society was very interesting; it was on the uses of cotton in Egypt, and the origin of the name in the English language. I dined at Mr. Neill's; among the guests was a Mr. Blair, the superintendent of the Botanical Gardens here; he has been in different parts of America frequently. There were several other gentlemen present interested in like subjects, and we talked of little else than trees and exotic plants, birds and beasts; in fact it was a naturalists' dinner, but a much better one than naturalists generally have who study in the woods. I was obliged to leave early, as I had an engagement at Miss Neville's. Tea was served, after which Miss Neville rose, and said she would open the

[1] James Baillie Fraser, 1783–1856, Scottish writer of travels.

concert. I was glad to see her simply but beautifully dressed in a plain white gown of fine muslin, with naught but her fine auburn hair loose in large curls about her neck, and a plain scarf of a light-rose color. She sang and played most sweetly; the gentlemen present were all more or less musical, and we had fine glees, duets, trios. The young lady scarcely left off singing, for no sooner was a song finished than some one asked for another; she immediately replied, "Oh, yes," and in a moment the room was filled with melody. I thought she must be fatigued, and told her so, but she replied: "Mr. Audubon, singing is like painting; it never fatigues if one is fond of it, and I am." After a handsome supper we had more singing, and it was past two o'clock when I rose, shook hands with Miss Neville, bowed to the company, and made my exit.

March 12. I can scarcely believe that this day, there is in many places six feet of snow, yet with all this no invitation is ever laid aside, and last evening I went to dinner in a coach drawn by four horses. At noon to-day I went with Mr. Lizars to the Assembly Rooms, to see the fencing. About a thousand persons, all in full dress, gathered in a few minutes, and a circle being formed, eight young men came in, and went through the first principles of fencing; we had fine martial music and a succession of fencing turns till two o'clock, when the assault began between the two best scholars. Five hits were required to win the prize — a fine sword — and it was presented to the conqueror, a Mr. Webster. At half-past six I dined at Mr. Hamilton's, where a numerous and agreeable party was assembled. At ten Miss Neville and her mother came with still others. We had dancing and singing, and here I am, quite wearied at half-past three; but I must be up early to-morrow morning.

March 13. The little I slept had a bad effect on me, for I rose cross of mind and temper. I took a long walk on the London road, returned and reached Brae House, and breakfasted with the famous Mrs. Grant,[1] an old lady very deaf, but very agreeable withal. Her son and daughter and another lady formed our party. We talked of nothing but America; Mrs. Grant is positively the only person I have met here who knows anything true about my country. I promised to call again soon. This evening I dined at Sir James Riddell's, and I do not know when I have spent a more uncomfortable evening; the company were all too high for me, though Sir James and his lady did all they could for me. The *ton* here surpassed that at the Earl of Morton's; *five gentlemen* waited on us while at table, and two of these put my cloak about my shoulders, notwithstanding all I could say to the contrary. Several of these men were quite as well dressed as their master. What will that sweet lady, Mrs. Basil Hall think of a squatter's hut in Mississippi in contrast with this? No matter! whatever may be lacking, there is usually a hearty welcome. Oh! my America, how dearly I love thy plain, simple manners.

March 14. I have been drawing all day, two Cat-birds and some blackberries for the Countess of Morton, and would have finished it had I not been disturbed by visitors. Mr. Hays came with his son; he asked me if it would not be good policy for me to cut my hair and have a fashionable coat made before I reached London. I laughed, and he laughed, and my hair is yet as God made it.

March 17. I had long wished to visit Roslyn Castle and the weather being beautiful I applied to Mrs. Dickie for a guide, and she sent her son with me. We passed over the North Bridge and followed the turnpike road, passing along the foot of the Pentland Hills, looking back frequently to view Edinburgh under its cloud of smoke, until we had passed a small eminence that completely hid it afterwards from our sight. Not an object of interest lay

[1] Mrs. Anne Grant, poetess and miscellaneous writer. Born 1755, died 1838.

in our way until we suddenly turned southeast and entered the little village of Roslyn. I say *little*, because not more than twenty houses are there, and these are all small except one. It is high, however, so much so that from it we looked down on the ruined castle, although the elevation of the castle above the country around is very great. On inquiry, we were assured that the chapel was the only remaining edifice worthy of attention. We walked down to it and entered an enclosure, when before us stood the remains of the once magnificent Chapel of Roslyn. What volumes of thoughts rushed into my mind. I, who had read of the place years before, who knew by tradition the horrors of the times subsequent to the founding of the edifice, now confronted reality. I saw the marks of sacrilegious outrage on objects silent themselves and which had been raised in adoration to God. Strange that times which produced such beautiful works of art should allow the thief and the murderer to go almost unpunished. This Gothic chapel is a superb relic; each stone is beautifully carved, and each differs from all the others. The ten pillars and five arches are covered with the finest fret-work, and all round are seen the pedestals that once supported the images that Knox's party were wont to destroy without thought or reason. I went down some mouldering steps into the Sacristy, but found only bare walls, decaying very fast; yet here a curious plant was growing, of a verdigris color. To reach the castle we went down and along a narrow ridge, on each side of which the ground went abruptly to the bottom of a narrow, steep valley, through which a small, petulant stream rushed with great rapidity over a rocky bed. This guards three sides of the promontory on which Roslyn Castle once was; for now only a few masses of rubbish were to be seen, and a house of modern structure occupies nearly the original site. In its day it must have been a powerful structure, but now, were it existing, cannon could destroy

Edinburgh
March 19th 1827.

This day my Hairs were sacrificed, and the will of God usurped by the wills of Man — as the Barber clipped them rapidly it reminded me of the horrible times of the French Revolution when the same operation was performed upon all the Victims murdered at the Guillotine — My Heart sank low.

John. J. Audubon

FACSIMILE OF ENTRY IN JOURNAL.

it in a few hours, if they were placed on the opposite hills. A large meadow lay below us, covered with bleaching linen, and the place where we stood was perfectly lonely, not even the reviving chirp of a single bird could be heard, and my heart sank low while my mind was engaged in recollections of the place. In silence we turned and left the Castle and the little village, and returned by another route to busy Edinburgh. The people were just coming out of church, and as I walked along I felt a tap on my shoulder and heard good Mr. Neill say, "Where are you going at the rate of six miles an hour?" and he took me home to dine with him, after we had been to my lodgings, where I put my feet in ice cold water for ten minutes, when I felt as fresh as ever.

March 19, 1827. This day my hair was sacrificed, and the will of God usurped by the wishes of man. As the barber clipped my locks rapidly, it reminded me of the horrible times of the French Revolution when the same operation was performed upon all the victims murdered at the guillotine; my heart sank low.

JOHN J. AUDUBON.[1]

Shortly after breakfast I received a note from Captain Hall, and another from his brother, both filled with entreaties couched in strong terms that I should *alter my hair* before I went to London. Good God! if Thy works are hated by man it must be with Thy permission. I sent for a barber, and my hair was mowed off in a trice. I knew I was acting weakly, but rather than render my good friend miserable about it, I suffered the loss patiently.

March 20. I visited Mr. Hays at his office, and had the pleasure of seeing all the curious ancient manuscripts, letters, mandates, Acts of Parliament, etc., connected with the official events of Scotland with England for upwards

[1] This entry is the only one on a large page, of which a facsimile is given. It is written in the centre, and all around the edge of the paper is a heavy black border, an inch in depth.

of three hundred years past. Large volumes are written on parchment, by hand, and must have been works of immense labor. The volumes containing the mere transfers of landed estates filed within the last forty years amounted to almost three thousand, and the parcels of ancient papers filled many rooms in bundles and in bags of leather, covered with dust, and mouldering with age. The learned antiquarian, Mr. Thompson, has been at great pains to put in order all these valuable and curious documents. The edifice of the Registry is immense, and the long, narrow passages proved a labyrinth to me. Mr. Hays' allotted portion of curiosities consists of Heraldry, and I saw the greatest display of coats of arms of all sorts, emblazoned in richest style on sleek vellum and parchment.

March 21. Called on Miss D——, the fair American. To my surprise I saw the prints she had received the evening before quite abused and tumbled. This, however, was not my concern, and I regretted it only on her account, that so little care should be taken of a book that in fifty years will be sold at immense prices because of its rarity.[1] The wind blew great guns all morning. Finding it would be some days before my business would permit me to leave, I formed an agreement to go to see the interior of the Castle, the regalia, and other curiosities of the place to-morrow. I received a valuable letter of introduction to the Secretary of the Home Department, Mr. Peel, from the Lord Advocate of Scotland, given me at the particular request of the Countess of Morton, a most charming lady; the Earl of Morton would have written himself but for the low state of his health.

March 22. After lunch the Rev. Wm. Newbold and I proceeded to the Castle; the wind blew furiously, and con-

[1] A distinguished ornithologist said of the book in 1895: "It is one of the few illustrated books, if not the only one, that steadily increases in price as the years go on."

sequently no smoke interfered with the objects I wished to see. We passed a place called the "Mound," a thrown-up mass of earth connecting now the New with the Old city of Edinburgh. We soon reached the gates of the Castle, and I perceived plainly that I was looked upon as an officer from the continent. Strange! three days ago I was taken for a priest, quick transition caused only by the clipping of my locks. We crossed the drawbridge and looked attentively at the deep and immense dried ditches below, passed through the powerful double gates, all necessary securities to such a place. We ascended continually until we reached the parapets where the King stood during his visit, bowing, I am told, to the gaping multitude below, his hat off, and proud enough, no doubt, of his *high station.* My hat was also off, but under different impulses; I was afraid that the wind would rob me of it suddenly. I did not bow to the people, but I looked with reverence and admiration on the beauties of nature and of art that surrounded me, with a pleasure seldom felt before. The ocean was rugged with agitated waves as far as the eye could reach eastwardly; not a vessel dared spread its sails, so furious was the gale. The high mountains of wild Scotland now and then faintly came to our view as the swift-moving clouds passed, and suffered the sun to cast a momentary glance at them. The coast of the Frith of Forth exhibited handsome villas, and noblemen's seats, bringing at once before me the civilization of man, and showing how weak and insignificant we all are. My eyes followed the line of the horizon and stopped at a couple of small elevations, that I knew to be the home of the Countess of Morton; then I turned to the immense city below, where men looked like tiny dwarfs, and horses smaller than sheep. To the east lay the Old Town, and now and then came to my ears the music of a band as the squall for a moment abated. I could have remained here a whole day, but my companion called, and I followed him to the room where the regalia are kept. We each wrote our names, paid our shilling, and the large padlock was opened by a red-faced, bulky personage dressed in a fanciful scarlet cloth, hanging about him like mouldering tapestry. A small oblong room, quite dark, lay before us; it was soon lighted, however, by our conductor. A high railing of iron, also of an oblong form, surrounded a table covered with scarlet cloth, on which lay an immense sword and its scabbard, two sceptres, a large, square, scarlet cushion ornamented with golden tassels, and above all the crown of Scotland. All the due explanations were cried out by our conductor, on whose face the reflection of all the red articles was so powerfully displayed just now that it looked like a large tomato, quite as glittering, but of a very different flavor, I assure thee. We looked at all till I was tired; not long did this take, for it had not one thousandth portion of the beauties I had seen from the parapet. We left the Castle intending to proceed to the stone quarries three miles distant, but the wind was now so fierce, and the dust so troubled my eyes, that the jaunt was put off till another day. I paid young Kidd three guineas for his picture. Have just had some bread and butter and will go to bed.

March 23. Young Kidd breakfasted with me, and no sooner had he gone than I set to and packed up. I felt very low-spirited; the same wind keeps blowing, and I am now anxious to be off to Mr. Selby's Newcastle, and my dear Green Bank. My head was so full of all manner of thoughts that I thought it was Saturday, instead of Friday, and at five o'clock I dressed in a great hurry and went to Mr. Henry Witham's with all possible activity. My Lucy, I was not expected till to-morrow! Mr. Witham was not at home, and his lady tried to induce me to remain and dine with her and her lovely daughter; but I declined, and marched home as much ashamed of my blunder as a fox who has lost his tail in a trap. Once before I made a sad blunder; I promised to dine at three different houses the same day, and when it came I discovered my error, and wrote an apology to all, and went to none.

Twizel House, Belford — Northumberland, April 10, 1827. Probably since ten years I have not been so long without recording my deeds or my thoughts; and even now I feel by no means inclined to write, and for no particular reason. From Friday the 23d of March till the 5th of April my time was busily employed, copying some of my drawings, from five in the morning till seven at night. I dined out rarely, as I found the time used by this encroached too much on that needed by my ardent desire to improve myself in oil and in perspective, which I wished to study with close attention. Every day brought me packets of letters of introduction, and I called here and there to make my adieux. I went often in the evening to Mr. Lizars'; I felt the parting with him and his wife and sister would be hard, and together we attended meetings of the different societies. The last night I went to the Royal Society. Sir Wm. Hamilton[1] read a paper *against* phrenology, which would seem to quite destroy the theory of Mr. Combe. I left many things in the care of my landlady, as well as several pictures, and at six o'clock on the morning of April 5, left Edinburgh, where I hope to go again. The weather was delightful. We passed Dunbar and Berwick, our road near the sea most of the time, and at half-past four, the coach stopped opposite the lodge of Twizel House. I left my baggage in the care of the woman at the lodge, and proceeded through some small woods towards the house, which I saw after a few minutes, — a fine house, commanding an extensive view of the country, the German Ocean, and Bamborough Castle. I ascended the great staircase with pleasure, for I knew that here was congeniality of feeling. Hearing the family were

[1] One of the greatest metaphysicians of modern times. Born at Glasgow 1788, died in Edinburgh, 1856.

out and would not return for two hours, I asked to be shown to the library, and told my name. The man said not a word, went off, and about ten minutes after, whilst I was reading the preface of William Roscoe to his "Leo X.," returned and said his master would be with me in a moment. I understood all this. Mr. Selby came in, in hunting-dress, and we shook hands as hunters do. He took me at once out in his grounds, where Mrs. Selby, his three daughters, and Captain Mitford his brother-in-law were all engaged transplanting trees, and I felt at home at once. When we returned to the house Mr. Selby conducted me to his *laboratory*, where guns, birds, etc., were everywhere. I offered to make a drawing and Captain Mitford went off to shoot a Chaffinch. We had supper, after which the eagerness of the young ladies made me open my box of drawings; later we had music, and the evening passed delightfully. I thought much of home I assure thee, and of Green Bank also, and then of my first sight of thee at Fatland, and went to bed thanking God for the happy moments he has granted us. The next morning I felt afraid my early habits would create some disturbance in the repose of the family, and was trying to make good my outing at five, and thought I had already done so, when to my surprise and consternation the opening of the hall door made such a noise as I doubted not must have been heard over the whole establishment; notwithstanding, I issued into the country fresh air, and heard all around me the Black-birds, Thrushes, and Larks at their morning songs. I walked, or rather ran about, like a bird just escaped from a cage; plucked flowers, sought for nests, watched the fishes, and came back to draw. All went well; although the *shooting season* (as the English please to call it) was long since over, we took frequent walks with guns, and a few individuals were the sufferers from my anxiety to see their bills, and eyes, and feathers; and many a mile did I race over the moors to get them. More or less company came daily to see my drawings, and I finished a drawing for Mr. Selby of three birds, a Lapwing for Mrs. Selby, who drew fully as well as I did, and who is now imitating my style, and to whom I have given some lessons. Also I finished a small picture in oil for the charming elder daughter Louise; the others are Jane and Fanny. So much at home did we become that the children came about me as freely as if I had long known them; I was delighted at this, for to me to have familiar intercourse with children, the most interesting of beings, is one of my greatest enjoyments, and my time here was as happy as at Green Bank; I can say no more. The estate is well situated, highly ornamented, stocked with an immensity of game of the country, and trout abound in the little rivulets that tumble from rock to rock towards the northern ocean. To-morrow I leave this with Captain Mitford for his country seat.

Mitford Castle, near Morpeth, Northumberland, April 11, 1827. I rose as early as usual, and not to disturb my kind friends, I marched down the staircase in my stockings, as I often do where the family are not quite such early risers; instead of opening the hall door I sat down in the study, and outlined a Lapwing, in an extremely difficult position, for my friend Selby, and did not go on my walk until the servants made their appearance, and then I pushed off to the garden and the woods to collect violets. I felt quite happy, the fragrance of the air seemed equal to that of the little blue flowers which I gathered. We breakfasted, and at ten o'clock I bid farewell to Mrs. Selby; good, amiable lady, how often she repeated her invitation to me to come and spend a goodly time with them. Mr. Selby and the children walked down to the lodge with the captain and me, and having reached the place too early we walked about the woods awhile. The parting moment came at last, all too soon, our baggage was put on the top of the "Dart," an opposition coach, and away we rolled. My good companion Captain Mitford kept my spirits in better plight than they would otherwise have been, by his animated conversation about game, fishing, America, etc., and after a ride of about twelve miles we entered the small village of Alnwick, commanded by the fine castle of the Duke of Northumberland. Having to change horses and wait two hours, we took a walk, and visited the interior of that ancient mass of buildings, the whole being deserted at present, the Duke absent. I saw the armory, the dungeons, the place for racking prisoners, but the grotesque figures of stone standing in all sorts of attitudes, defensive and *offensive*, all round the top of the turrets and bastions, struck me most. They looked as if about to move, or to take great leaps to the ground, to cut our throats. This castle covers five acres of ground, is elevated, and therefore in every direction are good views of the country. From it I saw the cross put up in memory of King Malcolm killed by Hammond. At two precisely (for in England and Scotland coaches start with great punctuality) we were again *en route*. We passed over the Aln River, a very pretty little streamlet, and reached Felton, where we changed horses. The whole extent of country we passed this day was destitute of woods, and looked to me very barren. We saw little game; about five we arrived within two miles of Morpeth, where the captain and I alighted; we walked to a pretty little vale and the ruins of the old castle lay before us, still doomed to moulder more, and walking on reached the confluence of two small, pretty streams from which originated the name of my friend's ancestors, *Meetingford*. We reached the house, and having heard of his brother's indisposition, the captain and I entered quietly, and I was presented to the owner of the hall. I saw before me a thin, pale, emaciated being who begged I would go to him, as he could not rise. I shook his withered hand and received his kind welcome. During the evening I had ample opportunity to observe how clever and scientific he was, and regretted the more his frail body. He was extremely anxious to see my drawings, and he examined them more closely than I can ever remember any one to have done before, and was so well acquainted with good drawing that I felt afraid to turn them over for his inspection. After looking at probably a hundred without saying a single word, he exclaimed suddenly: "They are truly beautiful; our King ought to purchase them, they are too good to belong to a *single* individual." We talked much on subjects of natural history, and he told me that he made it a rule that not a gun was ever fired during the breeding season on any part of his beautiful estate; he delighted to see the charming creatures enjoy life and pleasure without any annoyance. Rooks, Jackdaws, Wood-Pigeons, and Starlings were flying in hundreds about the ruined castle. We sat up till after twelve, when hot water and spirits were produced, after which we said good-night; but I needed nothing to make me sleep, for in five minutes after I lay down I was — I know not where.

April 12. I am now at last where the famous Bewick produced his handsome and valuable work on the birds of England. It is a dirty-looking place, this Newcastle, and I do not know if it will prove at all pleasant. This morning early the captain and myself took a good ramble about Mitford Hall grounds; saw the rookery, the ruins of the castle, and walked some way along the little river front. We breakfasted about ten with his brother, who wished to see my drawings by daylight. Afterwards my baggage was taken to Morpeth, and the captain and I walked thither about twelve. Our way was along a pretty little stream called the Wansbeck, but the weather changed and the rain assured me that none of the persons we expected to see in the village would come, on this account, and I was not mistaken. At half-past four I mounted the coach for this place, and not an object of interest presented itself in the journey of thirteen miles.

Newcastle-upon-Tyne, April 13. At ten o'clock I left the inn, having had a very indifferent breakfast, served on dirty plates ; therefore I would not recommend the " Rose and Crown," or the hostess, to any friend of mine. Yet my bed was quite comfortable, and my sleep agreeably disturbed about one hour before day by some delightful music on the bugle. I often, even before this, have had a wish to be a performer on this instrument, so sure I am that our grand forests and rivers would re-echo its sonorous sounds with fine effect. I passed through many streets, but what a shabby appearance this Newcastle-upon-Tyne has, after a residence of nearly six months in the beautiful city of Edinburgh. All seems dark and smoky, indeed I conceive myself once more in Manchester. The cries of fish, milk, and vegetables, were all different, and I looked in vain for the rosy cheeks of the Highlanders. I had letters to the members of the Johnson family, given me by Captain Mitford, and therefore went to St. James Square, where I delivered them, and was at once received by a tall, fine-looking young gentleman, who asked me if I had breakfasted. On being answered in the affirmative, he requested me to excuse him till he had finished his, and I sat opposite the fire thinking about the curious pilgrimage I had now before me. Will the result repay the exertions? Alas! it is quite impossible for me to say, but that I shall carry the plan out in all its parts is certain unless life departs, and then I must hope that our Victor will fall into my place and accomplish my desires, with John's help to draw the birds, which he already does well. Mr. Edward Johnson soon re-entered, bringing with him Mr. John Adamson, secretary to the Literary and Philosophical Society of this place. I presented the letter for him from Mr. Selby, but I saw at once that he knew me by name. Soon after he very kindly aided me to find suitable lodgings, which I did in Collingwood Street. We then walked to Mr. Bewick's, the engraver, son of the famous man, and happily met him. He is a curious-looking man; his head and shoulders are both broad, but his keen, penetrating eyes proved that Nature had stamped him for some use in this world. I gave him the letters I had for him, and appointed a time to call on his father. I again suffered myself to be imposed upon when I paid my bill at the inn on removing to my lodgings, and thought of Gil Blas of Santillane. Five persons called to see my drawings this afternoon, and I received a note from Mr. Bewick inviting me to tea at six; so I shall see and talk with the wonderful man. I call him wonderful because I am sincerely of the opinion that his work on wood is superior to anything ever attempted in ornithology. It is now near eleven at night. Robert Bewick (the son) called for me about six, and we proceeded to his father's house. On our way I saw an ancient church with a remarkably beautiful *Lanterne* at top, St. Nicholas' Church I was told, then we passed over the Tyne, on a fine strong bridge of stone, with several arches, I think six or seven. This is distant from the sea, and I must say that the Tyne *here* is the only stream I have yet seen since my landing resembling at all a river. It is about as large as Bayou Sara opposite the Beech Woods, when full. I saw some of the boats used in carrying coals down the stream; they are almost of oval shape, and are managed with long, sweeping oars, and steerers much like our flat-boats on the Ohio. My companion did not talk much; he is more an acting man than a talker, and I did not dislike him for that. After ascending a long road or lane, we arrived at Bewick's dwelling, and I was taken at once to where he was at work, and saw the man himself. He came to me and welcomed me with a hearty shake of the hand, and took off for a moment his half-clean cotton night-cap tinged with the smoke of the place. He is tall, stout, has a very large head, and his eyes are further apart than those of any man I remember just now. A complete Englishman, full of life and energy though now seventy-four, very witty and clever, better acquainted with America than most of his countrymen, and an honor to England. Having shown me the work he was at, a small vignette cut on a block of box-wood not more than three by two inches, representing a dog frightened during the night by false appearances of men formed by curious roots and branches of trees, rocks, etc., he took me upstairs and introduced me to his three daughters — all tall, and two of them with extremely fine figures; they were desirous to make my visit an agreeable one and most certainly succeeded. I met there a Mr. Goud, and saw from his pencil a perfect portrait of Thomas Bewick, a miniature, full-length, in oil, highly finished, well drawn and composed. The old gentleman and I stuck to each other; he talked of my drawings, and I of his wood-cuts, till we liked each other very much. Now and then he would take off his cotton cap, but the moment he became animated with the conversation the cap was on, yet almost off, for he had stuck it on as if by magic. His eyes sparkled, his face was very expressive, and I enjoyed him much more, I am sure, than he supposed. He had heard of my drawings and promised to call early to-morrow morning with his daughters and some friends. I did not forget dear John's wish to possess a copy of his work on quadrupeds, and having asked where I could procure one, he answered "Here." After coffee and tea had been served, young Bewick, to please me, brought a bagpipe of a new construction, called a "Durham," and played simple, nice Scotch and English airs with peculiar taste; the instrument sounded like a hautboy. Soon after ten the company broke up, and we walked into Newcastle. The streets were desolate, and their crookedness and narrowness made me feel the more the beauty of fair Edinburgh.

April 14. The weather is now becoming tolerable and spring is approaching. The Swallows glide past my windows, and the Larks are heard across the Tyne. Thomas Bewick, his whole family, and about a hundred others have kept me busy exhibiting drawings. Mr. Bewick expressed himself as perfectly astounded at the boldness of my undertaking. I am to dine with him to-morrow, Mr. Adamson to-day, and Mr. Johnson on Wednesday if I do not go on to York that day.

April 15. Mr. Adamson called for me at church time, and we proceeded a short distance and entered St. Nicholas' church. He ordered an officer to take me to what he called *the mansion house* and I was led along the aisles to a place enclosed by an iron railing and showed a seat. In looking about me I saw a large organ over the door I had entered, and in front of this were seated many children, the lasses in white, the lads in blue. An immense painting of the Lord's Supper filled the end opposite the entrance, and the large Gothic windows were brilliant with highly colored glass. A few minutes passed, when a long train of office bearers and the magistrates of the town, headed by the mayor, came in procession and entered *the mansion house* also; a gentleman at my elbow rose and bowed to these and I followed his example; I discovered then that I was seated in the most honorable place. The service and sermon were long and tedious; often to myself I said, "Why is not Sydney Smith here?" Being in church I sat patiently, but I must say I thought the priest uncommonly stupid. Home to luncheon and afterwards went to Heath, the painter,[1] who with his wife received me with extreme kindness. He showed me many sketches, a number of which were humorous. He likes Newcastle better than Edinburgh, and I would not give an hour at Edinburgh, especially were I with friend Lizars, his wife, and sister, for a year here. So

[1] Possibly Charles Heath, engraver, 1784–1848.

much for difference of taste.—I have just returned from old Bewick's. We had a great deal of conversation, all tending towards Natural History; other guests came in as the evening fell, and politics and religion were touched upon. Whilst this was going on old Bewick sat silent chewing his tobacco; the son, too, remained quiet, but the eldest daughter, who sat next to me, was very interesting, and to my surprise resembles my kind friend Hannah Rathbone so much, that I frequently felt as if Miss Hannah, with her black eyes and slender figure, were beside me. I was invited to breakfast to-morrow at eight with Mr. Bewick to see the old gentleman at work.

April 16. I breakfasted with old Bewick this morning quite *sans cérémonie*, and then the old man set to work to show me how simple it was to *cut wood!* But cutting wood as he did is no joke; he did it with as much ease as I can feather a bird; he made all his tools, which are delicate and very beautiful, and his artist shop was clean and attractive. Later I went with Mr. Plummer, the officiating American consul at this place, to the court-rooms, and Merchant Coffee House, also to a new fish market, small and of a half-moon form, contiguous to the river, that I have forgotten to say is as dirty and muddy as an alligator hole. The coal boats were moving down by hundreds, with only one oar and a steerer, to each of which I saw three men. We then went to the Literary and Philosophical Society rooms; the library is a fine, large room with many books—the museum small, but in neat order, and well supplied with British specimens. Since then I have been showing my drawings to at least two hundred persons who called at my lodgings. I was especially struck with a young lady who came with her brother. I saw from my window a groom walking three fine horses to and fro, and almost immediately the lady and gentleman entered, whip in hand, and spurred like fighting-cocks; the lady, with a beaver and black silk neckerchief, came in first and alone, holding up with both hands her voluminous blue riding-habit, and with a *ton* very unbecoming her fine eyes and sweet face. She bowed carelessly, and said: "Compliments, sir;" and perceiving how much value she put on herself, I gave her the best seat in the room. For some time she sat without a word; when her brother began to put questions, however, she did also, and so fast and so searchingly that I thought them *Envoies Extraordinaires* from either Temminck or Cuvier. Mr. Adamson, who sat by all the time, praised me, when they had gone, for my patience, and took me home to dine with him *en famille.* A person (a glazier, I suppose), after seeing about a hundred pictures, asked me if I did not want glass and frames for them. How I wish I was in America's dark woods, admiring God's works in all their beautiful ways.

April 17. Whilst I was lying awake this morning waiting for it to get light, I presently recollected I was in Newcastle-upon-Tyne, and recalled the name of Smollett, no mean man, by the bye, and remembered his eulogium of the extraordinary fine view he obtained when travelling on foot from London to this place, looking up the Tyne from Isbet Hill, and I said, "If Smollett admired the prospect, I can too," and leaped from my bed as a hare from his form on newly ploughed ground at the sound of the sportsman's bugle, or the sight of the swift greyhound. I ran downstairs, out-of-doors, and over the Tyne, as if indeed a pack of jackals had been after me. Two miles is nothing to me, and I ascended the hill where poor Isbet, deluded by a wretched woman, for her sake robbed the mail, and afterwards suffered death on a gibbet; and saw — the sea! Far and wide it extended; the Tyne led to it, with its many boats with their coaly burdens. Up the river the view was indeed enchanting; the undulating meadows sloped gently to the water's edge on either side, and the Larks that sprang up before me, welcoming the sun's rise, animated my thoughts so much that I felt tears trickling down my cheeks as I gave praise to the God who gave life to all these in a day. There was a dew on the ground, the bees were gathering honey from the tiniest flowerets, and here and there the Blackbird so shy sought for a fibrous root to entwine his solid nest of clay. Lapwings, like butterflies of a larger size, passed wheeling and tumbling over me through the air, and had not the dense smoke from a thousand engines disturbed the peaceful harmony of Nature, I might have been there still, longing for my Lucy to partake of the pleasure with me. But the smoke recalled me to my work, and I turned towards Newcastle. So are all transient pleasures followed by sorrows, except those emanating from the adoration of the Supreme Being. It was still far from breakfast time; I recrossed the Tyne and ascended the east bank for a couple of miles before returning to my lodgings. The morning afterward was spent as usual. I mean, holding up drawings to the company that came in good numbers. *Morning* here is the time from ten to five, and I am told that in London it sometimes lengthens to eight of the evening as we term it. Among these visitors was a Mr. Donkin, who remained alone with me when the others had left, and we had some conversation; he is an advocate, or, as I would call it, a chancellor. He asked me to take a bachelor's dinner with him at five; I accepted, and he then proposed we should drive out and see a house he was building two miles in the country. I again found myself among the rolling hills, and we soon reached his place. I found a beautiful, low house of stone, erected in the simplest style imaginable, but so well arranged and so convenient that I felt satisfied he was a man of taste as well as wealth. Garden, grounds, all was in perfect harmony, and the distant views up and down the river, the fine woods and castle, all came in place, — not to satiate the eye, but to induce it to search for further beauties. On returning to town Mr. Donkin showed me the old mansion where poor Charles the First was delivered up to be beheaded. He could have escaped through a conduit to the river, where a boat was waiting, but the conduit was all darkness and his heart failed him. Now I should say that he had no heart, and was very unfit for a king. At Mr. Donkin's house I was presented to his partners, and we had a good dinner; the conversation ran much on politics, and they supported the King and Mr. Canning. I left early, as I had promised to take a cup of tea with old Bewick. The old gentleman was seated as usual with his night-cap on, and his tobacco pouch in one hand ready to open; his countenance beamed with pleasure as I shook hands with him. "I could not bear the idea of your going off without telling you in written words what I think of your 'Birds of America;' here it is in black and white, and make whatever use you may of it, if it be of use at all," he said, and put an unsealed letter in my hand. We chatted away on natural-history subjects, and he would now and then exclaim: "Oh that I was young[1] again! I would go to America. What a country it will be." "It is now, Mr. Bewick," I would retort, and then we went on. The young ladies enjoyed the sight and remarked that for years their father had not had such a flow of spirits.

April 19. This morning I paid a visit of farewell to Mr. Bewick and his family; as we parted he held my hand closely and repeated three times, "God preserve you." I looked at him in such a manner that I am sure he understood I could not speak. I walked slowly down the hilly lane, and thought of the intrinsic value of this man to the world, and compared him with Sir Walter Scott. The latter will be forever the most eminent in station, being undoubtedly the most learned and most brilliant of the two; but Thomas Bewick is a son of Nature. Nature

[1] Thomas Bewick was at this time nearly seventy-four. He died Nov. 8, 1828, being then past seventy-five.

alone has reared him under her peaceful care, and he in gratitude of heart has copied one department of her works that must stand unrivalled forever; I say "forever" because imitators have only a share of real merit, compared with inventors, and Thomas Bewick is an inventor, and *the first wood-cutter in the world!* These words, "first wood-cutter" would, I dare say, raise the ire of many of our hearty squatters, who, no doubt, on hearing me express myself so strongly, would take the axe, and fell down an enormous tree whilst talking about it; but the moment I would explain to them that each of their chips would produce under his chisel a mass of beauties, the good fellows would respect him quite as much as I do. My room was filled all day with people to see my works and *me*, whom some one had said resembled in physiognomy Napoleon of France. Strange simile this, but I care not whom I resemble, if it be only in looks, if my heart preserves the love of the truth.

Saturday, April 21. I am tired out holding up drawings, I may say, all day; but have been rewarded by an addition of five subscribers to my work. Am off to-morrow to York. God bless thee, my Lucy.

York, Sunday, April 22, 1827. Left Newcastle at eight; the weather cold and disagreeable, still I preferred a seat on top to view the country. Passed through Durham, a pretty little town with a handsome castle and cathedral, planted on an elevated peninsula formed by a turn of the river Wear, and may be seen for many miles. It is a rolling country, and the river wound about among the hills; we crossed it three times on stone bridges. Darlington, where we changed horses, is a neat, small place, supported by a set of very industrious Quakers; much table linen is manufactured here. As we approached York the woods became richer and handsomer, and trees were dispersed all over the country; it looked once more like England, and the hedges reminded me of those about "Green Bank." They were larger and less trimmed than in Scotland. I saw York Minster six or seven miles before reaching the town, that is entered by old gates. The streets are disgustingly crooked and narrow, and crossed like the burrows of a rabbit-warren. I was put down at the Black Swan. Though the coach was full, not a word had been spoken except an occasional oath at the weather, which was indeed very cold; and I, with all the other passengers, went at once to the fires. Anxious to find lodgings *not* at the Black Swan, I went to Rev. Wm. Turner, son of a gentleman I had met at Newcastle, for information. His father had prepared him for my visit at my request, and I was soon installed at Mrs. Pulleyn's in Blake Street. My present landlady's weight, in ratio with that of her husband, is as one pound avoirdupois to one ounce apothecary! She looks like a round of beef, he like a farthing candle. Oh that I were in Louisiana, strolling about the woods, looking in the gigantic poplars for new birds and new flowers!

April 23, Monday. The weather looked more like approaching winter than spring; indeed snow fell at short intervals, and it rained, and was extremely cold and misty. Nothwithstanding the disagreeable temperature, I have walked a good deal. I delivered my letters as early as propriety would allow, but found no one in; at least I was told so, for beyond that I cannot say with any degree of accuracy I fear. The Rev. Mr. Turner called with the curator of the Museum, to whom I showed some drawings. After my dinner, eaten *solus*, I went out again; the Minster is undoubtedly the finest piece of ancient architecture I have seen since I was in France, if my recollection serves me. I walked round and round it for a long time, examining its height, form, composition, and details, until my neck ached. The details are wonderful indeed, — all cut of the same stone that forms the mass outwardly. Leaving it and going without caring about my course, I found myself in front of an ancient castle,[1] standing on a mound,

[1] Probably St. Mary's Abbey.

covered with dark ivy, fissured by time and menacing its neighborhood with an appearance of all tumbling down at no remote period. I turned east and came to a pretty little stream called the Ouse, over which I threw several pebbles by way of exercise. On the west bank I found a fine walk, planted with the only trees of size I have seen in this country; it extended about half a mile. Looking up the stream a bridge of fine stone is seen, and on the opposite shores many steam mills were in operation. I followed down this mighty stream till the road gave out, and, the grass being very wet and the rain falling heavily, I returned to my rooms. York is much cleaner than Newcastle, and I remarked more Quakers; but alas! how far both these towns are below fair Edinburgh. The houses here are low, covered with tiles, and sombre-looking. No birds have I seen except Jackdaws and Rooks. To my surprise my host waited upon me at supper; when he enters my room I think of Scroggins' ghost. I have spent my evening reading "Blackwood's Magazine."

April 24. How doleful has this day been to me! It pleased to rain, and to snow, and to blow cold all day. I called on Mr. Phillips, the curator of the Museum, and he assured me that the society was too poor to purchase my work. I spent the evening by invitation at the Rev. Wm. Turner's in company with four other gentlemen. Politics and emancipation were the chief topics of conversation. How much more good would the English do by revising their own intricate laws, and improving the condition of their poor, than by troubling themselves and their distant friends with what does not concern them. I feel nearly determined to push off to-morrow, and yet it would not do; I may be wrong, and to-morrow may be fairer to me in every way; but this "hope deferred" is a very fatiguing science to study. I could never make up my mind to live and die in England whilst the sweet-scented jessamine and the magnolias flourish so purely in my native land, and the air vibrates with the songs of the sweet birds.

April 25. I went out of the house pretty soon this morning; it was cold and blowing a strong breeze. I pushed towards the river with an idea of following it downwards two hours by my watch, but as I walked along I saw a large flock of Starlings, at a time when I thought all birds were paired, and watched their motions for some time, and thereby drew the following conclusion, namely: that the bird commonly called the Meadow Lark with us is more nearly related to the Starling of this country than to any other bird. I was particularly surprised that a low note, resembling the noise made by a wheel not well greased, was precisely the same in both, that the style of their walk and gait was also precisely alike, and that in *short* flights the movement of the wings had the same tremulous action before they alighted. Later I had visitors to see my pictures, possibly fifty or more. It has rained and snowed to-day, and I feel as dull as a Martin surprised by the weather. It will be strange if York gives me no subscribers, when I had eight at Newcastle. Mr. P—— called and told me it would be well for me to call personally on the nobility and gentry in the neighborhood and take some drawings with me. I thanked him, but told him that my standing in society did not admit of such conduct, and that although there were lords in England, we of American blood think ourselves their equals. He laughed, and said I was not as much of a Frenchman as I looked.

April 26. I have just returned from a long walk out of town, on the road toward Newcastle. The evening was calm, and the sunset clear. At such an hour how often have I walked with my Lucy along the banks of the Schuylkill, Perkiomen Creek, the Ohio River, or through the fragrant woods of Louisiana; how often have we stopped short to admire the works of the Creator; how often have we been delighted at hearing the musical notes of the timid

Wood Thrush, that appeared to give her farewell melody to the disappearing day! We have looked at the glittering fire-fly, heard the Whip-poor-will, and seen the vigilant Owl preparing to search field and forest! Here the scene was not quite so pleasing, though its charms brought youth and happiness to my recollection. One or two Warblers perched on the eglantine, almost blooming, and gave their little powers full vent. The shrill notes of Thrushes (not ours) came from afar, and many Rooks with loaded bills were making fast their way towards the nests that contained their nearly half-grown offspring. The cattle were treading heavily towards their pens, and the sheep gathered to the lee of each protecting hedge. To-day have I had a great number of visitors, and three subscribers.

April 27. A long walk early, and then many visitors, Mr. Vernon [1] among them, who subscribed for my work. All sorts of people come. If Matthews the comic were now and then to present himself at my levees, how he would act the scenes over. I am quite worn out; I think sometimes my poor arms will give up their functions before I secure five hundred subscribers.

Saturday, 28th. During my early walk along the Ouse I saw a large butterfly, quite new to me, and attempted to procure it with a stroke of my cane; but as I whirled it round, off went the scabbard into the river, more than half across, and I stood with a naked small sword as if waiting for a duel. I would have swam out for it, but that there were other pedestrians; so a man in a boat brought it to me for sixpence. I have had a great deal of company, and five subscribers. Mr. Wright took me all over the Minster, and also on the roof. We had a good spy-glass, and I had an astonishing view of the spacious vales that surround the tile-covered city of York. I could easily follow the old walls of defence. It made me giddy to look directly down, as a great height is always unpleasant to me.

[1] Mr. Vernon was the president of the Philosophical Society of York.

Now I have packed up, paid an enormous bill to my landlady. I expect to be at Leeds to-morrow.

Leeds, Sunday, April 28. The town of Leeds is much superior to anything I have seen since Edinburgh, and I have been walking till I feel quite exhausted. I breakfasted in York at five this morning; the coach did not start till six, so I took my refreshing walk along the Ouse. The weather was extremely pleasant; I rode outside, but the scenery was little varied, almost uniformly level, well cultivated, but poor as to soil. I saw some "game" as every bird is called here. I was amused to see the great interest which was excited by a covey of Partridges. What would be said to a gang of Wild Turkeys, — several hundred trotting along a sand-bar of the Upper Mississippi? I reached Leeds at half-past nine, distant from York, I believe, twenty-six miles. I found lodgings at once at 39 Albion Street, and then started with my letters.

April 30. Were I to conclude from first appearances as to the amount of success I may expect here, compared with York, by the difference of attention paid me at both places so soon after my arrival, I should certainly expect much more here; for no sooner was breakfast over than Mr. Atkinson called, to be followed by Mr. George and many others, among them a good ornithologist,[1] — not a *closet naturalist*, but a real true-blue, who goes out at night and watches Owls and Night-jars and Water-fowl to some purpose, and who knows more about these things than any other man I have met in Europe. This evening I took a long walk by a small stream, and as soon as out of sight undressed and took a dive smack across the creek; the water was so extremely cold that I performed the same feat back again and dressed in a hurry; my flesh was already quite purple. Following the stream I found some gentlemen catching minnows with as much anxiety as if large trout, playing the little things with beautiful lines and wheels.

[1] Mr. John Backhouse.

Parallel to this stream is a canal; the adjacent country is rolling, with a number of fine country-seats. I wish I had some one to go to in the evenings like friend Lizars.

May 1, 1827. This is the day on which last year I left my Lucy and my boys with intention to sail for Europe. How uncertain my hopes at that time were as to the final results of my voyage, — about to leave a country where most of my life had been spent devoted to the study of Nature, to enter one wholly unknown to me, without a friend, nay, not an acquaintance in it. Until I reached Edinburgh I despaired of success; the publication of a work of enormous expense, and the length of time it must necessarily take; to accomplish the whole has been sufficient to keep my spirits low, I assure thee. Now I feel like beginning a New Year. My work is about to be known, I have made a number of valuable and kind friends, I have been received by men of science on friendly terms, and now I have a hope of success if I continue to be honest, industrious, and consistent. My pecuniary means are slender, but I hope to keep afloat, for my tastes are simple; if only I can succeed in rendering thee and our sons happy, not a moment of sorrow or discomfort shall I regret.

May 2. Mr. George called very early, and said that his colleague, the Secretary of the Literary and Philosophical Society, would call and subscribe, and he has done so. I think I must tell thee how every one stares when they read on the first engraving that I present for their inspection this name: "The Bonaparte Fly-catcher," — the very bird I was anxious to name the "Rathbone Fly-catcher," in honor of my excellent friend "Lady" Rathbone, but who refused to accept this little mark of my gratitude. I afterwards meant to call it after thee, but did not, because the world is so strangely composed just now that I feared it would be thought childish; so I concluded to call it after my friend Charles Bonaparte. Every one is struck by the name, so explanations take place, and the good people of England will know him as a great naturalist, and my friend. I intend to name, one after another, every one of my new birds, either for some naturalist deserving this honor, or through a wish to return my thanks for kindness rendered me. Many persons have called, quite a large party at one time, led by Lady B——. I am sorry to say I find it generally more difficult to please this class of persons than others, and I feel in consequence more reserved in their presence, I can scarcely say why. I walked out this evening to see Kirkstall Abbey, or better say the ruins of that ancient edifice. It is about three miles out of Leeds and is worthy the attention of every traveller. It is situated on the banks of the little river Ayre, the same I bathed in, and is extremely romantic in its appearance, covered with ivy, and having sizable trees about and amongst its walls. The entrance is defended by a board on which is painted: "Whoever enters these ruins, or damages them in the least, will be prosecuted with all the rigor of the law." I did not transgress, and soon became very cautious of my steps, for immediately after, a second board assured every one that spring-guns and steel-traps are about the gardens. However, no entreaty having been expressed to prevent me from sketching the whole, I did so on the back of one of my cards for thee. From that spot I heard a Cuckoo cry, for I do not, like the English, call it singing. I attempted to approach the bird, but in vain; I believe I might be more successful in holding a large Alligator by the tail. Many people speak in raptures of the sweet voice of the Cuckoo, and the same people tell me in cold blood that we have no birds that can sing in America. I wish they had a chance to judge of the powers of the Mock-bird, the Red Thrush, the Cat-bird, the Oriole, the Indigo Bunting, and even the Whip-poor-will. What would they say of a half-million of Robins about to take their departure for the North, making our woods fairly tremble with melodious harmony? But these pleasures are not to be enjoyed in manufacturing towns like Leeds and Manchester; neither can any one praise a bird who sings by tuition, like a pupil of Mozart, as a few Linnets and Starlings do, and that no doubt are here taken as the foundation stone of the singing powers allotted to European birds generally. Well, is not this a long digression for thee? I dare say thou art fatigued enough at it, and so am I.

May 3. Until two o'clock this day I had only one visitor, Mr. John Marshall, a member of Parliament to whom I had a letter; he told me he knew nothing at all about birds, but most generously subscribed, because, he told me, it was such a work as every one ought to possess, and to encourage enterprise. This evening I dined with the Messrs. Davy, my old friends of Mill Grove; the father, who for many months has not left his bed-chamber, desired to see me. We had not met since 1810, but he looked as fresh as when I last saw him, and is undoubtedly the handsomest and noblest-looking man I have ever seen in my life, excepting the Marquis de Dupont de Nemours. I have at Leeds only five subscribers, — poor indeed compared with the little town of York.

May 5. I breakfasted with young Mr. Davy, who after conducted me to Mr. Marshall's mills. We crossed the Ayre in a ferry boat for a half-penny each, and on the west bank stood the great works. The first thing to see was the great engine, 150 horse-power, a stupendous structure, and so beautiful in all its parts that no one could, I conceive, stand and look at it without praising the ingenuity of man. Twenty-five hundred persons of all ages and both sexes are here, yet nothing is heard but the *burr* of machinery. All is wonderfully arranged; a good head indeed must be at the commander's post in such a vast establishment.

Manchester, May 6, 1827. My journey was uneventful and through the rain. I reached Mr. Bentley's soon after noon, and we were both glad to meet.

May 7. The rooms of the Natural History Society were offered to me, to show my work, but hearing accidentally that the Royal Institution of Manchester was holding an exhibition at the Messrs. Jackson's and thinking that place better suited to me, I saw these gentlemen and was soon installed there. I have had five subscribers. I searched for lodgings everywhere, but in vain, and was debating what to do, when Dr. Harlan's friend, Mr. E. W. Sergeant, met me, and insisted on my spending my time under his roof. He would take no refusal, so I accepted. How much kindness do I meet with everywhere. I have had much running about and calling on different people, and at ten o'clock this evening was still at Mr. Bentley's, not knowing where Mr. Sergeant resided. Mr. Surr was so kind as to come with me in search of the gentleman; we found him at home and he gave me his groom to go for my portmanteau. Of course I returned to Mr. Bentley's again, and he returned with me to see me safely lodged. Mr. Sergeant insisted on his coming in; we had coffee, and sat some time conversing; it is now past two of the morning.

May 8. I saw Mr. Gregg and the fair Helen of Quarry Bank this morning; they met me with great friendship. I have saved myself much trouble here by exhibiting no drawings, only the numbers of my work now ready. Mr. Sergeant has purchased my drawing of the Doves for twenty pounds.

May 13, Sunday. My time has been so completely occupied during each day procuring subscribers, and all my evenings at the house of one or another of my friends and acquaintances that my hours have been late, and I have bidden thee good-night without writing it down.[1] Manchester has most certainly retrieved its character, for

[1] Nearly every entry in all the journals begins and ends with a morning greeting, and an affectionate good-night. These have been omitted with occasional exceptions.

I have had eighteen subscribers in *one week*, which is more than anywhere else.

Liverpool, Monday, May 14. I breakfasted with my good friend Bentley, and left in his care my box containing 250 drawings, to be forwarded by the "caravan," — the name given to covered coaches. I cannot tell how extremely kind Mr. Sergeant has been to me during all my stay. He exerted himself to procure subscribers as if the work had been his own, and made my time at his house as pleasant as I could desire. I was seated on top of the coach at ten o'clock, and at three was put down safely at Dale St. I went immediately to the Institution, where I found Mr. Munro. I did not like to go to Green Bank abruptly, therefore shall spend the night where I am, but sent word to the Rathbones I was here. I have called on Dr. Chorley and family, and Dr. Traill; found all well and as kind as ever. At six Mr. Wm. Rathbone came, and gave me good tidings of the whole family; I wait impatiently for the morrow, to see friends all so dear.

May 19, Saturday night. I leave this to-morrow morning for London, a little anxious to go there, as I have oftentimes desired to be in sight of St. Paul's Church. I have not been able to write because I felt great pleasure in letting my good friends the Rathbones know what I had done since I was here last; so the book has been in the fair hands of my friend Hannah. "Lady" Rathbone and Miss Hannah are not at Green Bank, but at Woodcroft, and there we met. While I waited in the library how different were my thoughts from those I felt on my first entry into Liverpool. As I thought, I watched the well-shaped Wagtails peaceably searching for food within a few paces of me. The door opened, and I met my good, kind friends, the same as ever, full of friendship, benevolence, and candor. I spent most of the morning with them, and left my book, as I said, with them. *Thy* book, I should have written, for it is solely for thee. I was driven into Liverpool by Mr. Rd. Rathbone, with his mother and Miss Hannah, and met Mr. Chorley by appointment, that we might make the respectful visits I owed. First to Edward Roscoe's, but saw only his charming wife; then to William Roscoe's. The venerable man had just returned from a walk, and in an instant our hands were locked. He asked me many questions about my publication, praised the engraving and the coloring. He has much changed. Time's violent influence has rendered his cheeks less rosy, his eye-brows more bushy, forced his fine eyes more deeply in their sockets, made his frame more bent, his walk weaker; but his voice had all its purity, his language all its brilliancy. I then went to the Botanic Gardens, where all was rich and beautiful; the season allows it. Then to Alexander Gordon's and Mr. Hodgson. Both out, and no card in my pocket. *Just like me.* I found the intelligent Swiss[1] in his office, and his "Ah, Audubon! Comment va?" was all-sufficient. I left him to go to Mr. Rathbone's, where I have spent every night except the last. As usual I escaped every morning at four for my walk and to write letters. I have not done much work since here, but I have enjoyed that which I have long desired, the society of my dear friends the Rathbones. Whilst writing this, I have often wished I could take in the whole at one glance, as I do a picture; this need has frequently made me think that writing a good book must be much more difficult than to paint a good picture. To my great joy, Mr. Bentley is going with me to London. With a heavy heart I said adieu to these dear Rathbones, and will proceed to London lower in spirits than I was in Edinburgh the first three days.

Shrewsbury, May 20. After all sorts of difficulties with the coach, which left one hour and a half late, we reached Chester at eleven, and were detained an hour. I therefore took a walk under the piazzas that go all through the

[1] Mr. Melly.

town. Where a street has to be crossed we went down some steps, crossed the street and re-ascended a few steps again. Overhead are placed the second stories of every house; the whole was very new and singular to me. These avenues are clean, but rather low; my hat touched the top once or twice, and I want an inch and a half of six feet, English measure. At last we proceeded; passed the village of Wrexham, and shortly after through another village, much smaller, but the sweetest, neatest, and pleasantest spot I have seen in all my travels in this country. It was composed of small, detached cottages of simple appearance, divided by gardens sufficiently large for each house, supplied with many kinds of vegetables and fruit trees, luxuriant with bloom, while round the doors and windows, and clambering over the roofs, were creeping plants and vines covered with flowers of different hues. At one spot were small beds of variegated tulips, the sweet-scented lilies at another, the hedges looked snowy white, and everywhere, in gentle curves, abundance of honeysuckle. This village was on a gentle declivity from which, far over the Mersey, rising grounds were seen, and the ascending smoke of Liverpool also. I could not learn the name of this little terrestrial paradise, and must wait for a map to tell me. We dined in a hurry at Eastham, and after passing through a narrow slip in Wales, and seeing what I would thus far call the most improved and handsomest part of England, we are now at Shrewsbury for five hours. Mr. Bentley and I had some bread and butter and pushed out to see the town, and soon found ourselves on the bank of the Severn, a pretty little stream about sixty yards wide. Many men and boys were doing what they called fishing, but I only saw two sprats in one of the boys' hats during the whole walk. Some one told us that up the river we should find a place called the "Quarry" with beautiful trees, and there we proceeded. About a dozen men, too awkward to be sailors, were rowing a long, narrow, pleasure boat, while one in the bow gave us fine music with the bugle. We soon reached the Quarry, and found ourselves under tall, luxuriant, handsome trees forming broad avenues, following the course of the river, extremely agreeable. Indeed, being a woodsman, I think this the finest sight I have seen in England. How the Severn winds round the town, in the form of a horse-shoe! About the centre of this horse-shoe, another avenue, still more beautiful, is planted, going gently up the hill towards the town. I enjoyed this walk more than I can tell thee, and when I thought of the disappointment I had felt at five hours delay at Shrewsbury, and the pleasure I now felt, I repeated for the more than one thousand and first time, "Certainly all is for the best in this world, except our own sins."

LONDON, *May 21, 1827.* I should begin this page perhaps with a great exclamation mark, and express much pleasure, but I have not the wish to do either; to me London is just like the mouth of an immense monster, guarded by millions of sharp-edged teeth, from which if I escape unhurt it must be called a miracle. I have many times longed to see London, and now I am here I feel a desire beyond words to be in my beloved woods. The latter part of the journey I spent closely wrapped in both coat and cloak, for we left Shrewsbury at ten, and the night was chilly; my companions were Mr. Bentley and two Italians, one of whom continually sang, and very well, while the other wished for daylight. In this way we continued till two of the morning, and it was then cold. From twelve until four I was so sleepy I could scarcely hold up my head, and I suffered much for the want of my regular allowance of sleep which I take between these hours; it is not much, yet I greatly missed it. We breakfasted at Birmingham at five, where the worst stuff bearing the name of coffee that I ever tasted was brought to us. I say *tasted*, for I could do no more. The country constantly improved in beauty; on we drove through Stratford-on-Avon, Woodstock, and Oxford. A cleaner and more interesting city I never saw; three thousand students are here at present. It was ten o'clock when we entered the turnpike gate that is designated as the line of demarcation of London, but for many miles I thought the road forming a town of itself. We followed Oxford Street its whole length, and then turning about a few times came to the Bull and Mouth tavern where we stay the night.

May 23. Although two full days have been spent in London, not a word have I written; my heart would not bear me up sufficiently. Monday was positively a day of gloom to me. After breakfast Mr. Bentley took a walk with me through the *City*, he leading, and I following as if an ox to the slaughter. Finally we looked for and found lodgings, at 55 Great Russell Street, to which we at once removed, and again I issued forth, noting nothing but the great dome of St. Paul's Cathedral. I delivered several letters and was well received by all at home. With Mr. Children [1] I went in the evening to the Linnaean Society and exhibited my first number. All those present pronounced my work *unrivalled*, and warmly wished me success.

Sunday, May 28. Ever since my last date I have been delivering letters, and attending the meetings of different societies. One evening was spent at the Royal Society, where, as in all Royal Societies, I heard a dull, heavy lecture. Yesterday my first call was on Sir Thos. Lawrence; it was half-past eight, as I was assured later would not do. I gave my name, and in a moment the servant returned and led me to him. I was a little surprised to see him dressed as for the whole day. He rose and shook hands with me the moment I pronounced my good friend Sully's name. While he read deliberately the two letters I had brought, I examined his face; it did not exhibit the

[1] John George Children, 1777–1852, English physicist and naturalist, at this time secretary of the Royal Society.

look of genius that one is always expecting to meet with in a man of his superior talents; he looked pale and pensive. He wished much to see my drawings, and appointed Thursday at eight of the morning, when, knowing the value of his time, I retired. Several persons came to see me or my drawings, among others Mr. Gallatin, the American minister. I went to Covent Garden Theatre with Mr. Bentley in the evening, as he had an admittance ticket. The theatre opens at six, and orders are not good after seven. I saw Madame Vestris; she sings middling well, but not so well in my opinion as Miss Neville in Edinburgh. The four brothers Hermann I admired very much; their voices sounded like four flutes.

May 29. I have been about indeed like a post-boy, taking letters everywhere. In the evening I went to the Athenæum at the corner of Waterloo Place, expecting to meet Sir Thomas Lawrence and other gentlemen; but I was assured that about eleven or half-past was the fashionable time for these gentlemen to assemble; so I returned to my rooms, being worn out; for I must have walked forty miles on these hard pavements, from Idol Lane to Grosvenor Square, and across in many different directions, all equally far apart.

Tuesday, May 30. At twelve o'clock I proceeded with some of my drawings to see Mr. Gallatin, our *Envoy extraordinaire.* He has the ease and charm of manner of a perfect gentleman, and addressed me in French. Seated by his side we soon travelled (in conversation) to America; he detests the English, and spoke in no measured terms of London as the most disagreeable place in Europe. While we were talking Mrs. and Miss Gallatin came in, and the topic was changed, and my drawings were exhibited. The ladies knew every plant, and Mr. Gallatin nearly every bird. I found at home that new suit of clothes that my friend Basil Hall insisted upon my procuring. I looked this remarkable black dress well over, put it on, and thus attired like a mournful Raven, went to dine at Mr. Children's. On my return I found a note from Lord Stanley, asking me to put his name down as a subscriber; this pleased me exceedingly, as I consider Lord Stanley a man eminently versed in *true* and *real* ornithological pursuits. Of course my spirits are better; how little does alter a man. A trifle raises him, a little later another casts him down. Mr. Bentley has come in and tells me three poor fellows were hanged at Newgate this morning for stealing sheep. My God! how awful are the laws of this land, to take a human life for the theft of a miserable sheep.

June 1. As I was walking, not caring whither, I suddenly met a face well known to me; I stopped and warmly greeted young Kidd of Edinburgh. His surprise was as great as mine, for he did not know where I had been since I left Edinburgh. Together we visited the exhibition at the British gallery. Ah! what good work is here, but most of the painters of these beautiful pictures are no longer on this earth, and who is there to keep up their standing? I was invited to dine with Sir Robert Inglis,[1] and took a seat in the Clapham coach to reach his place. The Epsom races are in full activity about sixteen miles distant, and innumerable coaches, men on horseback, barouches, foot passengers, filled the road, all classes from the *beau monde* to the beggar intent on seeing men run the chance of breaking their necks on horses going like the wind, as well as losing or gaining pence, shillings, or guineas by the thousand. Clapham is distant from London five miles, and Sir Robert invited me to see the grounds while he dressed, as he came in almost as I did. How different from noisy London! I opened a door and found myself on a circular lawn so beautifully ornamented that I was tempted to exclaim, "How beautiful are Thy works, O God!" I walked through avenues of foreign trees and shrubs, amongst which were tulip-trees, larches,

[1] Robert Inglis, 1786–1855, of the East India Company.

and cypresses from America. Many birds were here, some searching for food, while others gave vent to their happy feelings in harmonious concerts. The house itself was covered with vines, the front a mass of blooming roses exuberant with perfume. What a delightful feast I had in this peaceful spot! At dinner there were several other guests, among them the widow of Sir Thomas Stanford Raffles, governor of Java, a most superior woman, and her conversation with Dr. Horsfield was deeply interesting. The doctor is a great zoölogist, and has published a fine work on the birds of Java. It was a true *family* dinner, and therefore I enjoyed it; Sir Robert is at the head of the business of the Carnatic association of India.

Friday, June 2. At half-past seven I reached Sir Thomas Lawrence, and found him writing letters. He received me kindly, and at once examined some of my drawings, repeating frequently, "Very clever, indeed!" From such a man these words mean much. During breakfast, which was simple enough and *sans cérémonie*, he asked me many questions about America and about my work. After leaving him I met Mr. Vigors[1] by appointment, who said everything possible to encourage me, and told me I would be elected as a foreign member to the Athenæum. Young Kidd called to see me, and I asked him to come and paint in my room; his youth, simplicity, and cleverness have attached me to him very much.

June 18. Is it not strange I should suffer whole weeks to pass without writing down what happens to me? But I have felt too dull, and too harassed. On Thursday morning I received a long letter from Mr. Lizars, informing me that his colorers had struck work, and everything was at a stand-still; he requested me to try to find some persons here who would engage in that portion of the business, and he would do his best to bring all right again. This

[1] Nicholas Aylward Vigors, 1787–1840, naturalist, First Secretary of the Zoölogical Society of London.

was quite a shock to my nerves; but I had an appointment at Lord Spencer's and another with Mr. Ponton; my thoughts cooled, I concluded to keep my appointments. On my return I found a note from Mr. Vigors telling me Charles Bonaparte was in town. I walked as quickly as possible to his lodgings, but he was absent. I wrote him a note and came back to my lodgings, and very shortly was told that the Prince of Musignano was below, and in a moment I held him by the hand. We were pleased to meet each other on this distant shore. His fine head was not altered, his mustachios, his bearded chin, his keen eye, all was the same. He wished to see my drawings, and I, for the first time since I had been in London, had pleasure in showing them. Charles at once subscribed, and I felt really proud of this. Other gentlemen came in, but the moment the whole were gone my thoughts returned to the colorers, and my steps carried me in search of some; and this for three days I have been doing. I have been about the suburbs and dirtier parts of London, and more misery and poverty cannot exist without absolute starvation. By chance I entered a print shop, and the owner gave me the name of a man to whom I went, and who has engaged to color more cheaply than it is done in Edinburgh, and young Kidd has taken a letter from me to Mr. Lizars telling him to send me twenty-five copies.

June 19. I paid a visit to Sir Thomas Lawrence this morning and after waiting a short time in his gallery he came to me and invited me into his painting-room. I had a fair opportunity of looking at some of his unfinished work. The piece before me represented a fat man sitting in an arm-chair, not only correctly outlined but beautifully sketched in black chalk, somewhat in the style of Raphael's cartoons. I cannot well conceive the advantage of all that trouble, as Sir Thomas paints in opaque color, and not as I do on asphaltum grounds, as I believe the old masters did, showing a glaze under the colors, instead of over, which I am convinced can be but of short duration. His colors were ground, and his enormous palette of white wood well set; a large table was literally covered with all sorts of brushes, and the room filled with unfinished pictures, some of which appeared of very old standing. I now had the pleasure of seeing this great artist at work, which I had long desired to do. I went five times to see Mr. Havell the colorer, but he was out of town. I am full of anxiety and greatly depressed. Oh! how sick I am of London.

June 21. I received a letter from Mr. Lizars that was far from allaying my troubles. I was so struck with the tenure of it that I cannot help thinking now that he does not wish to continue my work. I have painted a great deal to-day and called on Charles Bonaparte.

June 22. I was particularly invited to dine at the Royal Society Club with Charles Bonaparte, but great dinners always so frighten me that I gave over the thought and dined peaceably at home. This evening Charles B. called with some gentlemen, among whom were Messrs. Vigors, Children, Featherstonehaugh, and Lord Clifton. My portfolios were opened before this set of learned men, and they saw many birds they had not dreamed of. Charles offered to name them for me, and I felt happy that he should; and with a pencil he actually christened upwards of fifty, urging me to publish them at once in manuscript at the Zoölogical Society. These gentlemen dropped off one by one, leaving only Charles and Mr. Vigors. Oh that *our* knowledge could be arranged into a solid mass. I am sure the best ornithological publication of the birds of my beloved country might then be published. I cannot tell you how surprised I was when at Charles's lodgings to hear his man-servant call him "your Royal Highness." I thought this ridiculous in the extreme, and I cannot conceive how good Charles can bear it; though probably he *does* bear it because he *is* good Charles. I have no painting to do to-morrow morning, or going to bed at two would not do. I was up at three this morning, and finished the third picture since in London.

June 28. I have no longer the wish to write my days. I am quite wearied of everything in London; my work does not proceed, and I am dispirited.

July 2. I am yet so completely out of spirits that in vain have I several times opened my book, held the pen, and tried to write. I am too dull, too mournful. I have finished another picture of Rabbits; that is all my consolation. I wish I was out of London.

Leeds, September 30, 1827. I arrived here this day, just five months since my first visit to the place, but it is three long months since I tarnished one of thy cheeks, my dear book. I am quite ashamed of it, for I have had several incidents well deserving to be related even in my poor humble style, — a style much resembling my *paintings in oil.* Now, nevertheless, I will in as quick a manner as possible recapitulate the principal facts.

First. I removed the publication of my work from Edinburgh to London, from the hands of Mr. Lizars into those of Robert Havell, No. 79 Newman St., because the difficulty of finding colorers made it come too slowly, and also because I have it done better and cheaper in London. I have painted much and visited little; I hate as much as ever large companies. I have removed to Great Russell St., number 95, to a Mrs. W——'s, an intelligent widow, with eleven children, and but little cash.

Second. The King!! My dear Book! it was presented to him by Sir Walter Waller, Bart., K. C. H., at the request of my most excellent friend J. P. Children, of the British Museum. His Majesty was pleased to call it fine, permitted me to publish it under his particular patronage, approbation, and protection, became a subscriber on the usual terms, not as kings generally do, but as a gentleman, and my friends all spoke as if a mountain of sovereigns had dropped in an ample purse at once, and for me. The Duchess of Clarence also subscribed. I attended to my business closely, but my agents neither attended to it nor to my orders to them; and at last, nearly at bay for means to carry on so heavy a business, I decided to make a sortie for the purpose of collecting my dues, and to augment my subscribers, and for that reason left London this day fortnight past for Manchester, where I was received by my friends *à bras ouverts*. I lived and lodged at friend Sergeant's, collected all my money, had an accession of nine subscribers, found a box of beautiful bird-skins sent Bentley by my dear boy Johnny,[1] left in good spirits, and here I am at Leeds. On my journey hither in the coach a young sportsman going from London to York was my companion; he was about to join a shooting expedition, and had two dogs with him in a basket on top of the coach. We spoke of game, fish, and such topics, and presently he said a work on ornithology was being published in London by an American (he told me later he took me for a Frenchman) named Audubon, and spoke of my industry and regretted he had not seen them, as his sisters had, and spoke in raptures of them, etc. I could not of course permit this, so told him my name, when he at once shook hands, and our conversation continued even more easily than before. I am in the same lodgings as formerly. My landlady was talking with a meagre-looking child, who told a sad story of want, which my good landlady confirmed. I never saw greater pleasure than sparkled in that child's face as I gave her a few pieces of silver for her mother. I never thought it necessary to be rich to help those poorer than ourselves; I have considered it a duty to God, and to grow poorer in so doing is a blessing to me. I told the good landlady to send for one of the child's brothers, who was out of work, to do my

[1] Then a boy not fifteen, who was at Bayou Sara with his mother.

errands for me. I took a walk and listened with pleasure to the song of the little Robin.

October 1. I called at the Philosophical Hall and at the Public Library, but I am again told that Leeds, though wealthy, has no taste; nevertheless I hope to establish an agency here.

October 3. I visited the museum of a Mr. Calvert, a man who, like myself, by dint of industry and perseverance is now the possessor of the finest collection I have seen in England, with the exception of the one at Manchester. I received a letter from Mr. Havell only one day old; wonderful activity this in the post-office department. I have been reading good Bewick's book on quadrupeds. I have had no success in Leeds, and to-morrow go to York.

York, October 5. Mr. Barclay, my agent here, I soon found had done almost nothing, had not indeed delivered all the numbers. I urged him to do better, and went to the Society Hall, where I discovered that the number which had been forwarded from Edinburgh after I had left there was miserably poor, scarcely colored at all. I felt quite ashamed of it, although Mr. Wright thought it good; but I sent it at once to Havell for proper treatment. Being then too late to pay calls, I borrowed a volume of Gil Blas, and have been reading.

October 6. No luck to-day, my Lucy. I am, one would think, generally either before or after the proper time. I am told that last week, when the Duke of Wellington was here, would have been the better moment. I shall have the same song given me at Newcastle, I dare foretell. I have again been reading Gil Blas; how replete I always find it of good lessons.

October 8. I walked this morning with Mr. Barclay to the house of Mr. F——, a mile out of town, to ascertain if he had received the first number. His house was expressly built for Queen Elizabeth, who, I was told, had never been in it after all. It resembles an old church, the whole front being of long, narrow windows. The inside is composed of large rooms, highly decorated with ancient pictures of the F—— family. The gardens are also of ancient appearance; there were many box-trees cut in the shape of hats, men, birds, etc. I was assured the number had not been received, so I suppose it never was sent. On our return Mr. Barclay showed me an asylum built by Quakers for the benefit of lunatics, and so contrived with gardens, pleasure-grounds, and such other modes of recreation, that in consequence of these pleasant means of occupying themselves many had recovered.

October 9. How often I thought during these visits of poor Alexander Wilson. When travelling as I am now, to procure subscribers, he as well as myself was received with rude coldness, and sometimes with that arrogance which belongs to *parvenus.*

October 11. It has been pouring down rain during all last night and this day, and looks as if it would not cease for some time; it is, however, not such distressing falls of water as we have in Louisiana; it carries not every object off with the storm; the banks of the rivers do not fall in with a crash, with hundreds of acres of forest along with them; no houses are seen floating on the streams with cattle, game, and the productions of the husbandman. No, it rains as if Nature was in a state of despondency, and I am myself very dull; I have been reading Stanley's Tales.

October 12. This morning I walked along the Ouse; the water had risen several feet and was quite muddy. I had the pleasure of seeing a little green Kingfisher perched close to me for a few minutes; but the instant his quick eye espied me, he dashed off with a shrill squeak, almost touching the water. I must say I longed for a gun to have stopped him, as I never saw one fresh killed. I saw several men fishing with a large scoop-net, fixed to a long pole. The fisherman laid the net gently on the water, and with a good degree of force he sank it, meantime drawing it along the bottom and grassy banks towards him. The fish, intent on feeding, attempted to escape, and threw themselves into the net and were hauled ashore. This was the first successful way of fishing I have seen in England. Some pikes of eight or ten pounds were taken, and I saw some eels. I have set my heart on having two hundred subscribers on my list by the first of May next; should I succeed I shall feel well satisfied, and able to have thee and our sons all together. Thou seest that castles are still building on hopeful foundations only; but he who does not try anything cannot obtain his ends.

October 15, Newcastle. Yesterday I took the coach and found myself here after an uneventful journey, the route being now known to me, and came to my former lodgings, where I was followed almost immediately by the Marquis of Londonderry, who subscribed at once. Then I called upon friend Adamson, who before I could speak invited me to dinner every day that I was disengaged. He advised me to have a notice in the papers of my being here for a few days, so I went to the *Tyne Mercury;* saw Mr. Donkin, who invited me to breakfast with him to-morrow at half-past seven, *quite my hour.*

October 17. During the day Mr. Wingate, an excellent practical ornithologist, came to see me, and we had much conversation which interested me greatly. Also came the mayor, who invited me to dine with him publicly to-morrow. I have writen to Mr. Selby to ask if he will be at Alnwick Castle on Friday, as if so I will meet him there, and try to find some subscribers. Several persons have asked me how I came to part with Mr. Lizars, and I have felt glad to be able to say that it was at his desire, and that we continue esteemed friends. I have been pleased to find since I left London that all my friends cry against my painting in oil; it proves to me the real taste of good William Rathbone; and *now I do declare to thee* that I will not spoil any more canvas, but will draw in my usual old, untaught way, which is what God meant me to do.

October 18. This morning I paid a visit to old Mr. Bewick. I found the good gentleman as usual at work, but he looked much better, as the cotton cap had been discarded for a fur one. He was in good spirits, and we met like old friends. I could not spend as much time with him as I wished, but saw sufficient of him and his family to assure me they were well and happy. I met Mr. Adamson, who went with me to dine at the Mansion House. We were received in a large room, furnished in the ancient style, panelled with oak all round, and very sombre. The company all arrived, we marched in couples to dinner and I was seated in the centre, the mayor at one end, the high sheriff at the other; we were seventy-two in number. As my bad luck would have it, I was toasted by John Clayton, Esq.; he made a speech, and *I*, poor fellow, was obliged to return the compliment, which I did, as usual, most awkwardly and covered with perspiration. Miserable stupidity that never will leave me! I had thousands of questions to answer about the poor aborigines. It was dark when I left, and at my room was a kind letter from Mr. Selby, inviting me to meet him at Alnwick to-morrow.

Twizel House, October 19. I arrived at Alnwick about eleven this morning, found the little village quite in a bustle, and Mr. Selby at the court. How glad I was to see him again I cannot say, but I well know I feel the pleasure yet, though twelve hours have elapsed. Again I dined with the gentlemen of the Bar, fourteen in number. A great ball takes place at Alnwick Castle this night, but Mr. Selby took me in his carriage and has brought me to his family, — a thousand times more agreeable to me than the motley crowd at the Castle. I met again Captain Mitford, most cordial to me always. To my regret many of my subscribers have not yet received the third number, not even Mr. Selby. I cannot understand this apparent neglect on the part of Mr. Lizars.

Sunday, October 21. Although it has been raining and blowing without mercy these two days, I have spent my time most agreeably. The sweet children showed their first attachment to me and scarce left me a moment during their pleasure hours, which were too short for us all. Mrs. Selby, who was away with her sick brother, returned yesterday. Confined to the house, reading, music, and painting were our means of enjoyment. Both this morning and this evening Mr. Selby read prayers and a chapter in the Bible to the whole household, the storm being so severe.

Edinburgh, October 22. I am again in the beautiful Edinburgh; I reached it this afternoon, cold, uncomfortable and in low spirits. Early as it was when I left this morning, Mrs. Selby and her lovely daughter came down to bid me good-bye, and whenever I leave those who show me such pure kindness, and especially such friends as these dear Selbys, it is an absolute pain to me. I think that as I grow older my attachment augments for those who are kind to me; perhaps not a day passes without I visit in thought those mansions where I have been so hospitably received, the inmates of which I recall with every sense of gratitude; the family Rathbone *always first*, the Selbys next, in London Mr. Children, in Manchester the Greggs and Bentleys and my good friend Sergeant, at Leeds Mr. Atkinson, at Newcastle dear old Bewick, Mr. Adamson, and the Rev. William Turner, and here Mr. Lizars and too many to enumerate; but I must go back to Liverpool to name John Chorley, to whom I feel warmly attached. It rained during my whole journey here, and I saw the German Ocean agitated, foaming and dark in the distance, scarce able to discern the line of the horizon. I send my expense account to you, to give Victor an idea of what the cost of travelling will be when he takes charge of my business here, whilst I am procuring fresh specimens. I intend next year *positively* to keep a cash account with myself and others, — a thing I have never yet done.

October 23. I visited Mr. Lizars first, and found him as usual at work; he received me well, and asked me to dine with him. I was sorry to learn that Lady Ellen Hall and W. H. Williams had withdrawn their subscriptions, therefore I must exert myself the more.

October 27. Anxious to appoint an agent at Edinburgh, I sent for Mr. Daniel Lizars the bookseller, and made him an offer which he has accepted; I urged him not to lose a moment in forwarding the numbers which have been lying too long at his brother's; many small matters have had to be arranged, but now I believe all is settled. W. H. Lizars saw the plates of No. 3, and admired them much; called his workmen, and observed to them that the London artists beat them completely. He brought his account, and I paid him in full. I think he regrets now that he decided to give my work up; for I was glad to hear him say that should I think well to intrust him with a portion of it, it should be done as well as Havell's, and the plates delivered in London at the same price. If he can fall twenty-seven pounds in the engraving of each number, and do them in superior style to his previous work, how enormous must his profits have been; good lesson this for me in the time to come, though I must remember Havell is more reasonable owing to what has passed between us in our business arrangements, and the fact that he owes so much to me.[1] I have made many calls, and been kindly welcomed at every house. The "Courant" and the "Scotchman" have honored me with fine encomiums on my work.

[1] When found by Audubon the Havells were in extreme poverty. He provided everything for them, and his publication made them comparatively wealthy.

The weather has been intolerable, raining and blowing constantly.

October 31. Mr. W. H. Lizars has dampened my spirits a good deal by assuring me that I would not find Scotland so ready at paying for my work as England, and positively advised me not to seek for more subscribers either here or at Glasgow. It is true, six of my first subscribers have abandoned the work without even giving me a reason; so my mind has wavered. If I go to Glasgow and can only obtain names that in the course of a few months will be withdrawn, I am only increasing expenses and losing time, and of neither time nor money have I too great a portion; but when I know that Glasgow is a place of wealth, and has many persons of culture, I decide to go.

November 2. I called on Professor Wilson this morning who welcomed me heartily, and offered to write something about my work in the journal called "Blackwood"; he made me many questions, and asked me to breakfast to-morrow, and promised me some letters for Glasgow.

November 3. My breakfast with the Professor was very agreeable. His fine daughter headed the table, and two sons were with us. The more I look at Wilson, the more I admire his originalities, — a man not equal to Walter Scott, it is true, but in many ways nearly approaching him; as free from the detestable stiffness of ceremonies as I am when I can help myself, no cravat, no waistcoat, but a fine *frill* of his own profuse beard, his hair flowing uncontrolled, and in his speech dashing at once at the object in view, without circumlocution; with a countenance beaming with intellect, and eyes that would do justice to the *Bird of Washington.* He gives me comfort, by being comfortable himself. With such a man I can talk for a whole day, and could listen for years.

Glasgow, November 4. At eleven I entered the coach for my ride of forty-two miles; three inside passengers besides myself made the entire journey without having uttered a single word; we all sat like so many owls of different species, as if afraid of one another, and on the *qui vive*, all as dull as the barren country I travelled this day. A few glimpses of dwarflike yellow pines here and there seemed to wish to break the dreariness of this portion of Scotland, but the attempt was in vain, and I sat watching the crows that flew under the dark sky foretelling winter's approach. I arrived here too late to see any portion of the town, for when the coach stopped at the Black Bull all was so dark that I could only see it was a fine, broad, long street.

November 8. I am off to-morrow morning, and perhaps forever will say farewell to Glasgow. I have been here *four* days and have obtained *one* subscriber. One subscriber in a city of 150,000 souls, rich, handsome, and with much learning. Think of 1400 pupils in one college! Glasgow is a fine city; the Clyde here is a small stream crossed by three bridges. The shipping consists of about a hundred brigs and schooners, but I counted eighteen steam vessels, black, ugly things as ever were built. One sees few carriages, but *thousands* of carts.

Edinburgh, November 9. In my old lodgings, after a journey back from the "City of the West" which was agreeable enough, all the passengers being men of intellect and social natures.

November 10. I left this house this morning an hour and a half before day, and pushed off for the sea-shore, or, as it is called, The Firth. It was calm and rather cold, but I enjoyed it, and reached Professor Jameson's a few minutes before breakfast. I was introduced to the "Lord of Ireland," an extremely intelligent person and an enthusiast in zoölogical researches; he had been a great traveller, and his conversation was highly interesting. In the afternoon I went to the summit of Arthur's Seat; the day was then beautiful and the extensive view cheered my spirits.

November 13. I arrived at Twizel Hall at half-past four in good time for dinner, having travelled nearly eighty miles quite alone in the coach, not the Mail but the Union. Sir William Jardine met me on my arrival. I assure thee it was a pleasure to spend two days here, — shooting while it was fair, and painting when rainy. In one of our walks I shot five Pheasants, one Hare, one Rabbit, and one Partridge; gladly would I remain here longer, but my work demands me elsewhere.

York, November 18. I have been here five hours. The day was so-so, and my companions in the coach of the dormouse order; eighty-two miles and no conversation is to me dreadful. Moreover our coachman, having in sight a coach called the "High-Flyer," felt impelled to keep up with that vehicle, and so lashed the horses that we kept close to it all the while. Each time we changed our animals I saw them quite exhausted, panting for breath, and covered with sweat and the traces of the blows they had received; I assure thee my heart ached. How such conduct agrees with the ideas of humanity I constantly hear discussed, I leave thee to judge.

Liverpool, November 22. I left Manchester at four this morning; it was very dark, and bitterly cold, but my travelling companions were pleasant, so the time passed quite quickly. At a small village about half-way here, three felons and a man to guard them mounted the coach, bound to Botany Bay. These poor wretches were chained to each other by the legs, had scarcely a rag on, and those they wore so dirty that no one could have helped feeling deep pity for them, case-hardened in vice as they seemed to be. They had some money, for they drank ale and brandy wherever we stopped. Though cold, the sun rose in full splendor, but the fickleness of the weather in this country is wonderful; before reaching here it snowed, rained, and cleared up again. On arriving I went at once to the Royal Institution, and on my way met William

Rathbone. I recognized him as far as I could see him, but could easily have passed him unnoticed, as, shivering with cold, I was wrapped up in my large cloak. Glad was I to hold him once more by the hand, and to learn that all my friends were well. I have seen Dr. Traill, John Chorley, and many others who were kind to me when I was here before. All welcomed me warmly.

November 22. This day after my arrival I rose before day and walked to Green Bank. When half my walk was over the sun rose, and my pleasure increased every moment that brought me nearer to my generous, kind "Lady" Rathbone and her sweet daughter, Miss Hannah. When I reached the house all was yet silent within, and I rambled over the frozen grass, watching the birds that are always about the place, enjoying full peace and security. The same Black Thrush (probably) that I have often heard before was perched on a fir-tree announcing the beauty of this winter morning in his melodious voice; the little Robins flitted about, making towards those windows that they knew would soon be opened to them. How I admired every portion of the work of God. I entered the hot-house and breathed the fragrance of each flower, yet sighed at the sight of some that I recognized as offsprings of my own beloved country. Henry Chorley, who had been spending the night at Green Bank, now espied me from his window, so I went in and soon was greeted by that best of friends, "Lady" Rathbone. After breakfast Miss Hannah opened the window and her favorite little Robin hopped about the carpet, quite at home. I returned to Liverpool with Mr. B.[1] Rathbone, who, much against my wishes, for I can do better work now, bought my picture of the Hawk pouncing on the Partridges.

November 26. Visited Dr. Traill, to consult with him on the best method of procuring subscribers, and we have decided that I am to call on Mr. W. W. Currie, the pres-

[1] Benson Rathbone.

ident of the Athenæum, to obtain his leave to show my work in the Reading Room, and for me to have notes of invitation printed and sent to each member, for them to come and inspect the work as far as it goes. I called on Mr. Currie and obtained his permission at once, so the matter is *en train*.

November 30. I have spent the day at Woodcroft with Richard Rathbone. Mrs. Rathbone wishes me to teach her how to paint in oils. Now is it not too bad that I cannot do so, for want of talent? My birds in *water-colors* have plumage and soft colors, but in oils — alas! I walked into town with Richard Rathbone, who rode his horse. I kept by his side all the way, the horse walking. I do not rely as much on my activity as I did twenty years ago, but I still think I could kill any horse in England in twenty days, taking the travel over rough and level grounds. This might be looked upon as a boast by many, but, I am quite satisfied, not by those who have seen me travel at the rate of five miles an hour all day. Once indeed I recollect going from Louisville to Shippingport [1] in fourteen minutes, with as much ease as if I had been on skates.

December 3. This morning I made sketches of all the parts of the Platypus [2] for William Gregg, who is to deliver a lecture on this curious animal. To-day and yesterday have been rainy, dismal indeed; very dismal is an English December. I am working very hard, writing constantly. The greater part of this day was spent at the Athenæum; many visitors, but no subscribers.

December 4. Again at the library and had one subscriber. A letter from Charles Bonaparte tells me he has decided not to reside in America, but in Florence; this I much regret. I have been reading the "Travels of the

[1] The distance between these places is about two miles.

[2] The Duck-billed Platypus, *Ornithorynchus paradoxus* of Australia. — E. C.

Marquis de Chastelleux" in our country, which contains very valuable and correct facts.

December 10. Mr. Atherton, a relation of friend Selby's, took breakfast with me, and then conducted me to see a very beautiful bird (alive) of the Eagle kind, from the Andes.[1] It is quite unknown to me; about the size of the Bird of Washington, much shorter in the wings, larger talons and longer claws, with erected feathers, in the form of a fan, on the head. The bill was dark blue, the crest yellow, upper part of the body dark brown; so was the whole head and neck, as well as the tail and vent, but the belly and breast were white. I soon perceived that it was a young bird; its cry resembled that of almost every Eagle, but was weaker in sound on account of its tender age, not exceeding ten months. Were I to give it a name, it would be the *Imperial Crowned Eagle.* It was fed on raw beef, and occasionally a live fowl by way of a treat to the by-standers, who, it seems, always take much pleasure in cruel acts. The moment I saw this magnificent bird I wished to own it, to send it as a present to the Zoölogical Gardens. I received a letter from Thomas Sully telling me in the most frank and generous manner that I have been severely handled in one of the Philadelphia newspapers. The editor calls all I said in my papers read before the different societies in Edinburgh "a pack of lies." Friend Sully is most heartily indignant, but with me my motto is: "*Le temps découvrira la vérité.*" It is, however, hard that a poor man like me, who has been so devotedly intent on bringing forth facts of curious force, should be brought before the world as a liar by a man who doubtless knows little of the inhabitants of the forests on the Schuylkill, much less of those elsewhere. It is both unjust and ungenerous, but I forgive him. I shall keep up a good heart, trust to my God, attend to my work with industry and care, and in time outlive these trifles.

1 The Andean Eagle is undoubtedly the Harpy, *Thrasaëtos harpyia.*— E. C.

December 13. I went this evening to hear the Tyrolese Singers, three brothers and their sister. They were all dressed in the costume of their country, but when they sang I saw no more; I know not how to express my feelings. I was in an instant transported into some wild glen from which arose high mountain crags, which threw back the melodious echoes. The wild, clear, harmonious music so entered into my being that for a time I was not sure that what I heard was a reality. Imagine the warbling of strong-throated Thrushes, united with the bugle-horn, a flute, and a hautboy, in full unison. I could have listened all night.

December 14, 1827. By the advice of our consul, Mr. Maury, I have presented a copy of my work to the President of the United States, and another to the House of Congress through Henry Clay.

December 16, Sunday. I went to the service at my favorite church, the one at the Blind Asylum; the anthems were so exquisitely sung that I felt, as all persons ought to do when at church, full of fervent devotion.

December 18. It was with great regret that I found my friend Wm. Roscoe very unwell. This noble man has had a paralytic attack; his mind is fully sensible of the decay of his body, and he meets this painful trial with patience and almost contentment. This only can be the case with those who in their past life have been upright and virtuous. I finished drawing a little Wren for my good friend Hannah, as well as artificial light would allow.

December 20. I have done nothing to-day; I have had that sort of laziness that occasionally feeds upon my senses unawares; it is a kind of constitutional disease with me from time to time, as if to give my body necessary rest, and enable me to recommence with fresh vigor and alacrity whatever undertaking I have in hand. When it has passed, however, I always reproach myself that I have lost a day. I went to the theatre with John Chorley to see "The Hypocrite;" it is stolen from Molière's famous "Tartuffe," — cut and sliced to suit the English market. I finished my evening by reading the Life of Tasso.

December 24. The whole town appears to be engaged in purchasing eatables for to-morrow. I saw some people carrying large nosegays of holly ornamented with flowers in imitation of white roses, carnations, and others, cut out of turnips and carrots; but I heard not a single gun fire, no fireworks going on anywhere, — a very different time to what we have in Louisiana. I spent my evening with Dr. Rutter looking at his valuable collection of prints of the men of the Revolution. Poor Charette,[1] whom I saw shot on the Place de Viarme at Nantes, was peculiarly good, as were General Moreau, Napoleon, when Consul, and many others; and Dr. Rutter knew their lives well.

December 25. At midnight I was awakened by Dr. Munroe, who came with a bottle of that smoky Scotch whiskey which I can never like, and who insisted on my taking a glass with him in honor of the day. Christmas in my country is very different indeed from what I have seen here. With us it is a general merry-making, a day of joy. Our lads have guns, and fire almost all night, and dance all day and the next night. Invitations are sent to all friends and acquaintances, and the time passes more gayly than I can describe. Here, *families* only join together, they go to church together, eat a very good dinner together, I dare say; but all is dull — silent — mournful. As to myself, I took a walk and dined with Mr. Munroe and family, and spent a quiet evening with John Chorley. This is my Christmas day for 1827.

December 28. Immediately after breakfast the box came containing the fifth number, and three full sets for my new subscribers here. The work pleased me quite.

[1] François Athanase de Charette, a leader of the Vendéans against the French Republic; executed at Nantes, on May 12, 1797.

December 29. This morning I walked to "Lady" Rathbone's with my fifth number. It is quite impossible to approach Green Bank, when the weather is at all fair, without enjoying the song of some birds; for, Lucy, that sweet place is sacred, and all the feathered tribe in perfect safety. A Redwing particularly delighted me to-day; I found something of the note of our famous Mock-bird in his melody.

January 1, 1828, Manchester. How many times since daylight reached my eyes, I have wished thee, my Lucy, our sons, and our friends, a year of comfort, of peace and enjoyment, I cannot tell, for the day is to me always one on which to pray for those we love. Now, my Lucy, when I wished thee a happy New Year this morning I emptied my snuff box, locked up the box in my trunk, and will take *no more.* The habit within a few weeks has grown upon me, so farewell to it; it is a useless and not very clean habit, besides being an expensive one. Snuff! farewell to thee. Thou knowest, Lucy, well that when I will *I will.* I came here straight to friend Sergeant's; I need not say I was welcomed; and Bentley soon came in to spend the evening with us.

London, January 5, 1828. At six last evening I was in the coach with three companions; I slept well after we stopped for supper at nine o'clock, but not long enough. I cannot sleep in the morning, and was awake four long hours before day. The moon, that had shone brightly, sunk in the west as day dawned, the frost appeared thickly strewn over the earth, and not a cloud was in sight. I saw a few flocks of Partridges on their roost, which thou knowest well is on the ground, with their heads all turned to east, from which a gentle waft of air was felt; the cattle were lying here and there; a few large flocks of Starlings were all that interested me. The dawn was clear, but before we left Northampton it rained, snowed, and blew as if the elements had gone mad; strange country, to be sure. The three gentlemen in the coach with me suggested cards, and asked me to take a hand; of course I said yes, but only on condition that they did not play for money, a thing I have never done. They agreed very courteously, though expressing their surprise, and we played whist all day, till I was weary. I know little about cards, and never play unless obliged to by circumstances; I feel no pleasure in the game, and long for other occupation. Twenty-four hours after leaving Manchester, we stopped at the Angel Inn, Islington Road. I missed my snuff all day; whenever my hands went into my pockets in search of my box, and I discovered the strength of habit, thus acting without thought, I blessed myself that my mind was stronger than my body. I am again in London, but not dejected and low of spirits and disheartened as I was when I came in May last; no, indeed! I have now *friends* in London, and hope to keep them.

95 Great Russell St., January 6. I took a famous walk before day, up to Primrose Hill, and was back before anyone in the house was up. I have spent the whole day going over my drawings, and decided on the twenty-five that are to form the numbers for 1828. The new birds I have named as follows: Children,[1] Vigors,[2] Temminck, Cuvier.[3] Havell came and saw the drawings; it gave him an idea of the work to be performed between now and next January.

January 8. I have ordered one set of my birds to be colored by Havell *himself*, for Congress, and the numbers already out will soon be *en route*. My frame maker came in, and the poor man took it for granted that I was *an artist*, but, dear me! what a mistake; I can draw, but I shall never paint well. The weather is extremely dull and

1 Children's Warbler. Plate xxxv.

2 Vigors' Warbler. Plate xxx.

3 Cuvier's Regulus. Plate lv. No bird was named after Temminck by Audubon.

gloomy; during the morning the light was of a deep yellow cast.

January 9. Had a long letter from John Chorley, and after some talk with my good friend J. G. Children, have decided to write nothing more except the biographies of my birds. It takes too much time to write to this one and that one, to assure them that what I have written is *fact*. When Nature as it is found in my beloved America is better understood, these things will be known generally, and when I have been dead twenty years, more or less, my statements will be accepted everywhere; till then they may wait.[1] I have a violent cough and sore throat that renders me heavy and stupid; twenty-five years ago I would not have paid it the least attention; now I am told that at my age and in this climate (which, God knows, is indeed a very bad one), I may have trouble if I do not take some remedy. I walked out at four this morning, but the air was thick and I did not enjoy it.

January 10. I am going to surprise thee. I had a dentist inspect my teeth, as they ached; he thought it was the effect of my cold, as all are quite perfect and I have never lost one. My throat continuing very sore, I remained in my rooms, and have had Havell, Robert Sully, and Mr. Children for companions.

January 14. I feel now much better, after several feverish days, but have not moved from the house; every one of my friends show me much kindness.

January 17. A long morning with Havell settling accounts; it is difficult work for a man like me to see that I am neither cheating nor cheated. All is paid for 1827, and I am well ahead in funds. Had I made such regular settle-

[1] This decision was made in consequence of various newspaper and personal attacks, which, then as now, came largely from people who knew nothing of the matter under consideration. It was a decision, however, never altered except in so far as regards the Episodes published in the "Ornithological Biography."

ments all my life, I should never have been as poor a man as I have been; but on the other hand I should never have published the "Birds of America." America! my country! Oh, to be there!

January 18. Spent the morning with Dr. Lambert and Mr. Don,[1] the famous botanist; we talked much of the plants and trees of America and of Mr. Nuttall[2] while opening and arranging a great parcel of dried plants from the Indies. This afternoon I took a cab and with my portfolio went to Mr. Children's. I cannot, he tells me, take my portfolio on my shoulder in London as I would in New York, or even *tenacious* Philadelphia.

January 20. Oh! how dull I feel; how long am I to be confined in this immense jail? In London, amidst all the pleasures, I feel unhappy and dull; the days are heavy, the nights worse. Shall I ever again see and enjoy the vast forests in their calm purity, the beauties of America? I wish myself anywhere but in London. *Why* do I dislike London? Is it because the constant evidence of the contrast between the rich and the poor is a torment to me, or is it because of its size and crowd? I know not, but I long for sights and sounds of a different nature. Young Green came to ask me to go with him to see Regent's Park, and we went accordingly, I rather an indifferent companion, I fear, till we reached the bridge that crosses the waters there, where I looked in vain for water-fowl. Failing to find any I raised my eyes towards the peaceful new moon, and to my astonishment saw a large flock of Wild Ducks passing over me; after a few minutes a second flock passed, which I showed my young friend. Two flocks of Wild Ducks, of upwards of twenty each! Wonderful indeed! I thought of the many I have seen when bent

[1] David Don, Scottish botanist, 1800–1840; at this time Librarian of Linnæan Society.

[2] Thomas Nuttall, botanist and ornithologist; born in England 1786, died at St. Helen's, England, September 10, 1859.

on studying their habits, and grew more homesick than ever.

January 21. Notwithstanding this constant darkness of mood, my business must be attended to; therefore soon after dawn I joined Havell and for many hours superintended his coloring of the plates for Congress. While I am not a colorist, and Havell is a very superior one, I *know* the birds; would to God I was among them. From here I went to find a bookseller named Wright, but I passed the place twice because I looked too high for his sign; the same occurs to young hunters, who, when first they tread the woods in search of a Deer, keep looking high, and far in the distance, and so pass many a one of these cunning animals, that, squatted in a parcel of dry brush-wood, sees his enemy quite well, and suffers him to pass without bouncing from his couch. The same instinct that leads me through woods struck me in the Haymarket, and now I found Mr. Wright. Our interview over, I made for Piccadilly, the weather as mild as summer, and the crowd innumerable. Piccadilly was filled with carriages of all sorts, men on horseback, and people everywhere; what a bustle!

January 22. I was so comfortless last night that I scarcely closed my eyes, and at last dressed and walked off in the dark to Regent's Park, led there because *there* are some objects in the shape of trees, the grass is green, and from time to time the sweet notes of a Blackbird strike my ear and revive my poor heart, as it carries my mind to the woods around thee, my Lucy. As daylight came a flock of Starlings swept over my head, and I watched their motions on the green turf where they had alighted, until I thought it time to return to breakfast, and I entered my lodgings quite ready for my usual bowl of bread and milk, which I still keep to for my morning meal; how often have I partaken of it in simple cabins, much more to my taste than all the pomp of London. Drawing all day long.

January 23. How delighted and pleased I have been this day at the receiving of thy letter of the 1st of November last. My Lucy, thou art so good to me, and thy advices are so substantial, that, rest assured, I will follow them closely.

January 24. To my delight friend Bentley appeared this evening. I was glad I could give him a room while he is in London. He brought news of some fresh subscribers, and a letter from the Rev. D—— to ask to be excused from continuing the work. Query: how many amongst my now long list of subscribers will continue the work throughout?

January 25. I usually leave the house two hours before day for a long walk; this morning it was again to Regent's Park; this gives me a long day for my work. After breakfast Bentley and I paid a long visit to Mr. Leadbeater, the great stuffer of birds. He was very cordial, and showed us many beautiful and rare specimens; but they were all *stuffed*, and I cannot bear them, no matter how well mounted they may be. I received to-day a perpetual ticket of admission to Mr. Cross's exhibition of quadrupeds, live birds, etc., which pleased me very much, for there I can look upon Nature, even if confined in iron cages. Bentley made me a present of a curiosity,—a "double penny" containing a single one, a half-penny within that, a farthing in that, and a silver penny within all. Now, my Lucy, who could have thought to make a thing like that?

January 26. Of course my early walk. After breakfast, Bentley being desirous to see Regent's Park, I accompanied him thither and we walked all round it; I think it is rather more than a mile in diameter. We saw a squadron of horse, and as I am fond of military manœuvres, and as the horses were all handsome, with full tails, well mounted and managed, it was a fine sight, and we both admired it. We then went to Mr. Cross, and I had the honor of riding on a very fine and gentle elephant; I say "honor," because the immense animal was so well trained and so obedient as to be an example to many human beings who are neither. The Duchess of A—— came in while I was there, — a large, very fat, red-faced woman, but with a sweet voice, who departed in a coach drawn by four horses with two riders, and two footmen behind; almost as much attendance as when she was a queen on the boards of —— theatre, thirty years ago.

January 28. I received a letter from D. Lizars to-day announcing to me the loss of four subscribers; but these things do not damp my spirits half so much as the smoke of London. I am as dull as a beetle.

January 31. I have been in my room most of this day, and very dull in this dark town.

February 1, 1828. Another Journal! It has now twenty-six brothers; [1] some are of French manufacture, some from Gilpin's "Mills on the Brandywine," some from other parts of America, but you are positively a Londoner. I bought you yesterday from a man across the street for fourteen shillings; and what I write in you is for my wife, Lucy Audubon, a matchless woman, and for my two Kentucky lads, whom I do fervently long to press to my heart again.

It has rained all day. Bentley and I paid a visit to the great anatomist, Dr. J. Brookes,[2] to see his collection of skeletons of divers objects. He received us with extreme kindness. I saw in his yard some few rare birds. He was called away on sudden and important business before we saw his museum, so we are to go on Monday. Mr. Cross, of the Exeter Exchange, had invited Bentley and me to dinner with his quadrupeds and bipeds, and at three o'clock we took a coach, for the rain was too heavy for Bentley, and drove to the Menagerie. Mr. Cross by no means

[1] Of all the twenty-six only three are known to be in existence; the other volumes now extant are all of later date.

[2] Joshua Brookes, 1761–1833, anatomist and surgeon.

deserves his name, for he is a pleasant man, and we dined with his wife and himself and the keepers of the BEASTS (name given by *men* to quadrupeds). None of the company were very polished, but all behaved with propriety and good humor, and I liked it on many accounts. Mr. Cross conversed very entertainingly. Bentley had two tickets for Drury Lane Theatre. It was "The Critic" again; immediately after, as if in spite of that good lesson, "The Haunted Inn" was performed, and the two gentlemen called *Matthews* and *Litton* so annoyed me with their low wit that I often thought that, could Shakespeare or Garrick be raised from their peaceful places of rest, tears of sorrow would have run down their cheeks to see how abused their darling theatre was this night. Bentley was more fortunate than I, he went to sleep. At my rooms I found a little circular piece of ivory with my name, followed by "and friends," and a letter stating it was a perpetual ticket of admission to the Zoölogical Gardens. This was sent at the request of Mr. Brookes.

February 2. Bentley and I went to the Gardens of the Zoölogical Society, which are at the opposite end of Regent's Park from my lodgings. The Gardens are quite in a state of infancy; I have seen more curiosities in a swamp in America in one morning than is collected here since eighteen months; all, however, is well planned, clean, and what specimens they have are fine and in good condition. As we were leaving I heard my name called, and turning saw Mr. Vigors with a companion to whom he introduced me; it was the famous Captain Sabine,[1] a tall, thin man, who at once asked me if among the Eagles they had, any were the young of the White-headed Eagle, or as he called the bird, the *Falco leucocephalus.* Strange that such great men should ask a woodsman questions like that,

[1] Captain (Sir) Edward Sabine accompanied Parry's expedition to the Arctic regions,—a mathematician, traveller, and Fellow of the Royal Society, 1819. Born in Dublin, 1788, died in Richmond, 1883.

which I thought could be solved by either of them at a glance. I answered in the affirmative, for I have seen enough of them to know.

February 4. I made a present to Bentley of the first number of my work, and some loose prints for his brothers. Then we went to Mr. Brookes, the surgeon, and saw his immense and wonderful collection of anatomical subjects. The man has spent about the same number of years at this work as I have at my own, and now offers it for sale at £10,000. I then called on Vigors and told him I wished to name my new bird in No. 6 after him, and he expressed himself well pleased. This evening I took my portfolio to Soho Square and entered the rooms of the Linnæan Society, where I found I was the first arrival. I examined the various specimens till others came in. The meeting was called to order, and I was shortly after elected a member; my drawings were examined, and more than one told me it was a sad thing they were so little known in London.

February 7. Havell brought me the sets he owed me for 1827, and I paid him in full. Either through him or Mr. Lizars I have met with a loss of nearly £100, for I am charged for fifty numbers more than can be accounted for by my agents or myself. This seems strange always to me, that people cannot be honest, but I must bring myself to believe many are not, from my own experiences. My evening was spent in Bruton Street, at the Zoölogical Society rooms, where Lord Stanley accompanied me, with Lord Auckland and good old General Hardwicke, and my portfolio was again opened and my work discussed.

February 10. This morning I took one of my drawings from my portfolio and began to copy it, and intend to finish it in better style. It is the White-headed Eagle which I drew on the Mississippi some years ago, feeding on a Wild Goose; now I shall make it breakfast on a Catfish, the drawing of which is also with me, with the marks of the talons of another Eagle, which I disturbed on the banks of that same river, driving him from his prey. I worked from seven this morning till dark.

February 11. Precisely the same as yesterday, neither cross nor dull, therefore, but perfectly happy.

February 12. Still hard at it, and this evening the objects on my paper look more like a bird and a fish than like a windmill, as they have done. Three more days and the drawing will be finished if I have no interruptions.

February 14. No drawing to-day; no, indeed! At nine this morning I was at the house of friend Hays, No. 21 Queen Street, to meet the Secretary of the Colonial Department. Mr. Hays showed me a superb figure of a Hercules in brass, found in France by a peasant while ploughing, and for which £300 has been refused.

February 16. Yesterday I worked at my drawing all day, and began this morning at seven, and worked till half-past four, only ceasing my work to take a glass of milk brought me by my landlady. I have looked carefully at the effect and the finishing. Ah! my Lucy, that I could paint in oils as I can in my own style! How proud I should be, and what handsome pictures I should soon have on hand.

February 24. I heard to-day of the death of Mrs. Gregg of Quarry Bank. I was grieved to know that kind lady, who had showed me much hospitality, should have died; I have hesitated to write to her son-in-law, Mr. Rathbone, fearing to disturb the solemnity of his sorrow. At the Linnæan Society this evening, my friend Selby's work lay on the table by mine, and very unfair comparisons were drawn between the two; I am quite sure that had he had the same opportunities that my curious life has granted me, his work would have been far superior to mine; I supported him to the best of my power. The fact is, *I* think, that no man yet has done anything in the way of illustrating the birds of England comparable to his great work; then besides, he is an excellent man, devoted to his science, and if he has committed slight errors, it becomes men of science not to dwell upon these to the exclusion of all else. I was to-day elected an original member of the Zoölogical Society. I also learned that it was Sir Thomas Lawrence who prevented the British Museum from subscribing to my work; he considered the drawing so-so, and the engraving and coloring bad; when I remember how he praised these same drawings *in my presence*, I wonder — that is all.

February 25. A most gloomy day; had I no work what a miserable life I should lead in London. I receive constantly many invitations, but all is so formal, so ceremonious, I care not to go. Thy piano sailed to-day; with a favorable voyage it may reach New Orleans in sixty days. I have read the Grand Turk's proclamation and sighed at the awful thought of a war all over Europe; but there, thou knowest I am no politician. A fine young man, Mr. J. F. Ward, a bird-stuffer to the King, came to me this afternoon to study some of the positions of my birds. I told him I would lend him anything I had.

February 28. To-day I called by appointment on the Earl of Kinnoul, a small man, with a face like the caricature of an owl; he said he had sent for me to tell me all my birds *were alike*, and he considered my work a swindle. He may really think this, his knowledge is probably small; but it is not the custom to send for a gentleman to abuse him in one's own house. I heard his words, bowed, and without speaking, left the rudest man I have met in this land; but he is only thirty, and let us hope may yet learn how to behave to a perfect stranger under his roof.

February 29. A man entered my room this afternoon, and said: "Sir, I have some prisoners to deliver to you from the town of York." "Prisoners!" I exclaimed, "why, who are they?" The good man produced a very small cage, and I saw two sweet little Wood Larks, full of vivacity, and as shy as prisoners in custody. Their eyes sparkled with fear, their little bodies were agitated, the motions of their breasts showed how their hearts palpitated; their plumage was shabby, but they were Wood Larks, and I saw them with a pleasure bordering on frenzy. Wood Larks! The very word carried me from this land into woods indeed. These sweet birds were sent to me from York, by my friend John Backhouse, an ornithologist of real merit, and with them came a cake of bread made of a peculiar mixture, for their food. I so admired the dear captives that for a while I had a strong desire to open their prison, and suffer them to soar over London towards the woodlands dearest to them; and yet the selfishness belonging to man alone made me long to keep them. Ah! man! *what a brute thou art!* — so often senseless of those sweetest feelings that ought to ornament our species, if indeed we are the "lords of creation."

Cambridge, March 3. I arrived at this famous University town at half-past four this afternoon, after a tedious ride of eight and a half hours from London, in a heavy coach in which I entered at the White Horse, Fetter Lane, and I am now at the Blue Boar, and blue enough am I. But never mind, I was up *truly early*, took a good walk in Regent's Park, and was back before any one in the house was up. Sully took breakfast with me, and took charge of my Larks, and saw me off. I thought we never would get rid of London, it took just one hour to get clear of the city. What a place! Yet many persons live there solely because they like it. At last the refreshing country air filled my lungs; I saw with pleasure many tender flowers peeping out of the earth, anxious to welcome the approaching spring. The driver held confidences with every grog shop between London and Cambridge, and his purple face gave powerful evidences that malt liquor is more enticing to him than water. The country is flat, but it was country, and I saw a few lambs gambolling by their timorous dams, a few Rooks digging the new-ploughed ground for worms, a few Finches on the budding hedges. On entering Cambridge I was struck with its cleanliness, the regular shape of the colleges, and the number of students with floating mantles, flat caps, and long tassels of silk, hanging sideways. I had a letter for a lodging house where I expected to stay, but no numbers are affixed to any doors in Cambridge. I do not know if it is so in order to teach the students to better remember things, but I found it very inconvenient; I hunted and searched in vain, and as the students in their gay moods have been in the habit of destroying all the door-bells, I had to knock loudly at any door where I wished to make inquiries, but not finding the good lady to whom my letter was addressed, I am still at the inn.

March 4. One of my travelling-companions, Mr. ——, an architect, offered to show me some of the Colleges, and put me in the way of delivering some of my letters; so we walked through the different courts of Trinity, and I was amazed at the exquisite arrangement of the buildings, and when we arrived at the walks I was still more pleased. I saw beautiful grass-plats, fine trees, around which the evergreen, dark, creeping ivy, was entwined, and heard among the birds that enlivened these the shrill notes of the Variegated Woodpecker, quite enchanting. As I passed under these trees I tried to recollect how many illustrious learned men have studied within the compass of their shade. A little confined, but pure streamlet, called the Cam, moved slowly on, and the air was delicious. We went to St. John's, where my companion was engaged in some work, and here I left him, and continued on my way alone, to deliver my letters. I called on the Rev. H. Greenwood, Professor Sedgwick,[1] and Professor Whewell;[2] all were most kind, as were the Rev.

[1] Adam Sedgwick, geologist. 1785–1873.

[2] William Whewell, 1795–1866, Professor of Moral Philosophy, Mineralogy, and other sciences.

Thos. Catton, Mr. G. A. Brown, Mr. George Heath, and Professor Henslow,[1] and I have made several engagements to dine, etc.

March 5. Since I left Edinburgh, I have not had a day as brilliant as this in point of being surrounded by learned men. This morning I took a long walk among the Colleges, and watched many birds; while thus employed, a well dressed man handed me a card on which was written in *English*, "The bearer desires to meet with some one who speaks either French, Italian, or Spanish." I spoke to him in Spanish and French, both of which he knew well. He showed me a certificate from the consul of Sweden, at Leith, which affirmed his story, that he with three sailors had been shipwrecked, and now wished to return to the Continent, but they had only a few shillings, and none of them spoke English. I gave him a sovereign, just as I saw Professor Sedgwick approaching; he came to my room to see my birds, but could only give me a short time as he had a lecture to deliver. I returned to my rooms, and just as I was finishing lunch the Vice-Chancellor made his appearance, — a small old man, with hair as white as snow, dressed in a flowing gown, with two little bits of white muslin in lieu of cravat. He remained with me upwards of two hours; he admired my work, and promised to do all he could. I was delighted with his conversation; he is a man of wide knowledge, and it seemed to me of sound judgment. Professor Henslow invited me to dine on Friday, and just as I finished my note of acceptance, came in with three gentlemen. At four I went to Mr. Greenwood's to dine; as I entered I saw with dismay upwards of thirty gentlemen; I was introduced to one after another, and then we went to the "Hall," where dinner was set. This hall resembled the interior of a Gothic church; a short prayer was said, and we sat down to a sumptuous dinner.

[1] John Stevens Henslow, botanist, 1796–1861.

Eating was not precisely my object, it seldom is; I looked first at the *convives.* A hundred students sat apart from our table, and the "Fellows," twelve in number, with twenty guests constituted our "mess." The dinner, as I said, was excellent, and I thought these learned "Fellows" must have read, among other studies, Dr. Kitchener on the "Art of Cookery." The students gradually left in parcels, as vultures leave a carcass; we remained. A fine gilt or gold tankard, containing a very strong sort of nectar, was handed to me; I handed it, after tasting, to the next, and so it went round. Now a young man came, and as we rose, he read a short prayer from a small board (such as butchers use to kill flies with). We then went to the room where we had assembled, and conversation at once began; perhaps the wines went the rounds for an hour, then tea and coffee, after which the table was cleared, and I was requested to open my portfolio. I am proud *now* to show them, and I saw with pleasure these gentlemen admired them. I turned over twenty-five, but before I had finished received the subscription of the Librarian for the University, and the assurance of the Secretary of the Philosophical Society that they would take it. It was late before I was allowed to come away.

Thursday, March 6. A cold snowy day; I went to the library of the University and the Philosophical Society rooms, and dined again in "Hall," with Professor Sedgwick. There were four hundred students, and forty "Fellows;" quite a different scene from Corpus College. Each one devoured his meal in a hurry; in less than half an hour grace was read again by *two* students, and Professor Whewell took me to his own rooms with some eight or ten others. My book was inspected as a matter of courtesy. Professor Sedgwick was gay, full of wit and cleverness; the conversation was very animated, and I enjoyed it much. Oh! my Lucy, that I also had received a university education! I listened and admired for a long time, when suddenly Professor Whewell began asking me questions about the woods, the birds, the aborigines of America. The more I rove about, the more I find how little known the interior of America is; we sat till late. No subscriber to-day, but I must not despair; nothing can be done without patience and industry, and, thank God, I have both.

March 7. The frost was so severe last night that the ground was white when I took my walk; I saw ice an eighth of an inch thick. As most of the fruit trees are in blossom, the gardeners will suffer this year. Inclement though it was, the birds were courting, and some, such as Jackdaws and Rooks, forming nests. After breakfast I went to the library, having received a permit, and looked at three volumes of Le Vaillant's "Birds of Africa," which contain very bad figures. I was called from here to show my work to the son of Lord Fitzwilliam, who came with his tutor, Mr. Upton. The latter informed me the young nobleman wished to own the book. I showed my drawings, and he, being full of the ardor of youth, asked where he should write his name. I gave him my list; his youth, his good looks, his courtesy, his refinement attracted me much, and made me wish his name should stand by that of some good friend. There was no room by Mrs. Rathbone's, so I asked that he write immediately above the Countess of Morton, and he wrote in a beautiful hand, which I wish I could equal, "Hon. W. C. Wentworth Fitzwilliam." He is a charming young man, and I wish him *bon voyage* through life. On returning to my lodgings this evening, my landlord asked me to join him in what he called "a glass of home-brewed." I accepted, not to hurt his feelings, a thing I consider almost criminal; but it is muddy-looking stuff, not to my taste.

Saturday, 8th. The weather bad, but my eyes and ears were greeted by more birds than I have seen yet in this country. I dined at the Vice-Chancellor's, and found myself among men of deep research, learning, and knowledge, — mild in expressions, kind in attentions, and under whom I fervently wished it had been my lot to have received such an education as they possess.

Sunday, March 9. Cambridge on a Sunday is a place where I would suppose the basest mind must relax, for the time being, from the error of denying the existence of a Supreme Being; all is calm — silent — solemn — almost sublime. The beautiful bells fill the air with melody, and the heart with a wish for prayer. I went to church with Mr. Whewell at Great St. Mary's, and heard an impressive sermon on Hope from Mr. Henslow. After that I went to admire Nature, as the day was beautifully inviting. Professor Heath of King's College wished me to see his splendid chapel, and with a ticket of admission I resorted there at three. We had simple hymns and prayers, the former softly accompanied by the notes of an immense organ, standing nearly in the centre of that astonishing building; the chanters were all young boys in white surplices. I walked with Mr. Heath to Mr. Whewell's, and with him went to Trinity Chapel. The charm that had held me all day was augmented many fold as I entered an immense interior where were upward of four hundred collegians in their white robes. The small wax tapers, the shadowy distances, the slow footfalls of those still entering, threw my imagination into disorder. A kind of chilliness almost as of fear came to me, my lips quivered, my heart throbbed, I fell on my knees and prayed to be helped and comforted. I shall remember this sensation forever, my Lucy. When at Liverpool, I always go to the church for the blind; did I reside at Cambridge, I would be found each Sunday at Trinity Chapel.

March 12. I was introduced to Judge ——, on his way to court, — a monstrously ugly old man, with a wig that might make a capital bed for an Osage Indian during the whole of a cold winter on the Arkansas River.

London, March 15. The scene is quite changed, or better say returned, for I am again in London. I found my little Larks as lively as ever, but judge of my pleasure when I found three letters from thee and Victor and Johnny, dated Nov. 10, Dec. 19, and Jan. 20. What comfort would it be to see thee. Havell tells me a hundred sets of No. 6 are in hand for coloring. Mr. David Lyon called to see my work, and said it had been recommended to him by Sir Thos. Lawrence. This seems strange after what I heard before, but like all other men Sir Thomas has probably his enemies, and falsehoods have been told about him.

March 20. Called on Havell and saw the plate of the Parroquets nearly finished; I think it is a beautiful piece of work. My landlady received a notice that if she did not pay her rent to-morrow an officer would be put in possession. I perceived she was in distress when I came in, and asking her trouble gave her what assistance I could by writing a cheque for £20, which she has promised to repay. This evening I went to Covent Garden to see "Othello;" I had an excellent seat. I saw Kean, Young, and Kemble; the play was terrifyingly well performed.

Saturday, March 20. To-day I was with friend Sergeant most of the time; this evening have paid Havell in full, and now, thank God, feel free to leave noisy, smoky London.

Oxford, March 24. I am now in Oxford *the clean*, and in comfortable lodgings. I arrived at four o'clock, shrunk to about one half my usual size by the coldness of the weather, having ridden on top of the coach, facing the northern blast, that caused a severe frost last night, and has, doubtless, nipped much fruit in the bud. As I travelled I saw Windsor Castle about two miles distant, and also witnessed the turning out of a Stag from a cart, before probably a hundred hounds and as many huntsmen. A curious land, and a curious custom, to catch an animal, and set it free merely to catch again. We crossed the Thames twice, near its head; it does not look like the Ohio, I assure thee; a Sand-hill Crane could easily wade across it without damping its feathers.

March 25. My feet are positively sore battering the pavement; I have walked from one house and College to another all day, but have a new subscriber, and one not likely to die soon, the Anatomical School, through Dr. Kidd.[1] He and I ran after each other all day like the Red-headed Woodpeckers in the spring. I took a walk along two little streams, bearing of course the appellation of rivers, the Isis and the Charwell; the former freezes I am told at the bottom, never at the top. Oxford seems larger than Cambridge, but is not on the whole so pleasing to me. I do not think the walks as fine, there are fewer trees, and the population is more mixed. I have had some visitors, and lunched with Dr. Williams, who subscribed for the Radcliffe Library, whither we both went to inspect the first number. When I saw it, it drew a sigh from my heart. Ah! Mr. Lizars! was this the way to use a man who paid you so amply and so punctually? I rolled it up and took it away with me, for it was hardly colored at all, and have sent a fair new set of five numbers. I dined at the Vice-Chancellor's at six; his niece, Miss Jenkins, did the honors of the table most gracefully. There were ten gentlemen and four ladies, and when the latter left, the conversation became more general. I was spoken to about Wilson and C. Bonaparte, and could heartily praise both.

March 27. Breakfasted with Mr. Hawkins, Provost of Oriel College, and went immediately after with him to

[1] Dr. John Kidd, 1775–1851, Professor of Chemistry and Medicine at Oxford.

the Dean of Trinity. The large salon was filled with ladies and gentlemen engaged with my work; my drawings followed, and I showed them, but, oh, Lucy, how tired I am of doing this. The Dean has, I think, the finest family of daughters I have ever seen; eight blooming, interesting young ladies; from here to Dr. Kidd, where was another room full of company to see my drawings. Among my visitors was Dr. Ed. Burton,[1] who invited me to breakfast to-morrow.

March 28. Never since I was at the delightful Green Bank, or at Twizel House have I had so agreeable a breakfast as I enjoyed this morning. I was shown into a neat parlor giving on a garden, and was greeted by a very beautiful and gracious woman; this was Mrs. Burton. Dr. Burton came in through the window from the garden; in a moment we were at table and I felt at once at home, as if with my good friend "Lady" Rathbone. Dr. and Mrs. Burton have an astonishing collection of letters, portraits, etc., and I was asked to write my name and the date of my birth as well as the present date. The former, I could not do, except approximately, and Mrs. Burton was greatly amused that I should not know; what I *do* know is that I am no longer a young man. A letter from Mr. Hawkins told me Dr. Buckland[2] was expected to-morrow, and I was asked to meet him at dinner at his own house by Mrs. Buckland. I dined with the Provost of Oriel and nine other gentlemen, among them the son of the renowned Mr. Wilberforce.

March 29. To-morrow, probably, I leave here, and much disappointed. There are here twenty-two colleges intended to promote science in all its branches; I have brought here samples of a work acknowledged to be at least good, and not one of the colleges has subscribed. I have been most hospitably treated, but with so little en-

[1] Edward Burton, D.D., 1794–1836, Professor of Divinity at Oxford.

[2] William Buckland, D.D., 1784–1856, geologist.

couragement for my work there is no reason for me to remain.

London, March 30. Left Oxford at eleven this morning, the weather still intensely cold. We had a guard dressed in red with sizable buttons, a good artist on the bugle, who played in very good style, especially fugues and anthems, which were harmonious but not cheerful. I saw a poor man and his wife trudging *barefoot* this weather, a sight which drew the rings of my purse asunder. Almost as soon as I reached my lodgings a gentleman, Mr. Loudon,[1] called to ask me to write zoölogical papers for his journal. I declined, for I will never write anything to call down upon me a second volley of abuse. I can only write *facts*, and when I write those the Philadelphians call me a liar.

April 1, 1828. I have the honor to be a Fellow of the Linnæan Society of London, quite fresh from the mint, for the news reached me when the election was not much more than over. Mr. Vigors tells me Baron Cuvier is to be here this week. I had some agreeable time with a gentleman from Ceylon, Bennett[2] by name, who has a handsome collection of fish from that place.

April 2. Called on Mr. Children, and together we walked to Mr. Havell's, where he saw the drawings for No. 7. How slowly my immense work progresses; yet it goes on apace, and may God grant me life to see it accomplished and finished. Then, indeed, will I have left a landmark of my existence.

April 3. I have had many corrections to make to my Prospectus, which have taken much time. I also examined many of my drawings, which I thought had suffered exceedingly from the damp; this quite frightened me. What a misfortune it would be if they should be spoiled,

[1] John Claudius Loudon, 1783–1843, writer on horticulture and arboriculture. In 1828–1836, editor of the "Magazine of Natural History."

[2] Edward Turner Bennett, 1797–1836, zoölogist.

for few men would attempt the severe task I have run through, I think. And as to me, alas! I am growing old, and although my spirits are as active as ever, my body declines, and perhaps I never could renew them all. I shall watch them carefully. Indeed, should I find it necessary, I will remove them to Edinburgh or Paris, where the atmosphere is less dangerous.

April 6. I have not written a word for three days, because, in truth, I have little to mention. Whenever I am in this London all is alike indifferent to me, and I in turn indifferent. Ah! my love, on a day like this in America I could stroll in magnificent woods, I could listen to sounds fresh and pure, I could look at a *blue* sky. Mr. Loudon called and said he was anxious to have a review of my work in his magazine, and would write to Mr. Wm. Swainson,[1] a naturalist and friend of Dr. Traill's, to do so. He again begged me to write an article for him, for which he would pay eight guineas; but no, I will write no more for publication except, as has been urged, to accompany my own pictures.

April 10. I have now only one set on hand; I had fifteen when I went to Cambridge. I hope soon to hear from Liverpool; the silence of a friend sometimes terrifies me; I dread to learn that my venerable, good "Lady" Rathbone is ill.

April 14. I cannot conceive why, but my spirits have been much too low for my own comfort. I thought strongly of returning to America; such a long absence from thee is dreadful. I sometimes fear we shall never meet again *in this world.* I called on Havell, who showed me the White-headed Eagle, a splendid plate indeed, and nearly finished.

April 17. I did but little yesterday, I was quite unwell; in the afternoon I walked to Bruton St. and saw

[1] William Swainson, naturalist and writer. Born in England 1789, emigrated in 1841 to New Zealand, where he died 1855.

Mr. Vigors, who assisted me in the nomenclature of the Hawk for Lord Stanley. This afternoon I received a letter from Mr. Wm. Swainson, inviting me to go to spend a day with him. My work continues to be well received, and as I have a tolerable list of subscribers I hope it will continue to improve.

April 21. The same feelings still exist this year that I felt last, during my whole stay in London. I hate it, yes, I cordially hate London, and yet cannot escape from it. I neither can write my journal when here, nor draw well, and if I walk to the fields around, the very voice of the sweet birds I hear has no longer any charm for me, the pleasure being too much mingled with the idea that in another hour all will again be bustle, filth, and smoke. Last Friday, when about to answer Mr. Swainson's letter, I suddenly thought that it would be best for me to go to see him at once. The weather was shocking; a dog would scarce have turned out to hunt the finest of game. I dined at two, and went to a coach office, when, after waiting a long time, the coachman assured me that unless I had been to Mr. Swainson's before, it would be madness to go that day, as his house lay off from the main road fully five miles, and it was a difficult place to find; moreover, the country, he said, was *swimming*. This is the first advice I have ever had from a coachman to stop me from paying my fare; I thanked him, and returned home, and wrote to Mr. Swainson; then walked twice round Kensington Gardens, most dull and melancholy. Ah! cannot I return to America?

April 24. I have been so harassed in mind and body, since ten days, that I am glad to feel partially relieved at last. All the colorers abandoned the work because I found *one* of their number was doing miserable daubing, and wished him dismissed unless he improved; but now they are all replaced.

May 1. Mr. Swainson has published a review of my work in Mr. Loudon's magazine, and how he has raised my talents. Would that I could do as well as he says I do; then indeed would my pencil be eager to portray the delicate and elegant contours of the feathered tribe, the softness of their plumage, and their gay movements. Alas, now I must remain in London overlooking engravers, colorers, and agents. Yet when I close my eyes I hear the birds warbling, nay, every sound; the shriek of the Falcon, the coy Doves cooing; the whistling note of the Grackle seems to fill my ear, again I am in the cornfield amidst millions of these birds, and then, transported afar, I must tread lightly and with care, to avoid the venomous Rattler. I sent the first proof of the White-headed Eagle to the Marquis of Landsdowne; he being the president of the Zoölogical Society, I thought it courteous to do so.

Sunday, May 4. Immediately after breakfast I went out with George Woodley, and walked to the pretty village called Hampstead. The rain that fell last night seemed only sufficient to revive nature's productions; the trees were lightly covered with foliage of a tender hue; the hawthorns dispersed along the thickets had opened their fragrant cups, the rich meadows showed promise of a fair crop. Here and there a shy Blackbird's note burst clearly, yet softly, while the modest Blackcap skipped across our way. I enjoyed it all, but only transiently; I felt as if I must return to the grand beauties of the Western World, so strong is the attachment impressed in man for his own country. I have been summing up the pros and cons respecting a voyage to America, with an absence of twelve months. The difficulties are many, but I am determined to arrange for it, if possible. I should like to renew about fifty of my drawings; I am sure that now I could make better compositions, and select better plants than when I drew merely for amusement, and without the thought of ever bringing them to public view. To effect this wish of mine, I must find a true, devoted friend who will superintend my work and see to its delivery — this is no trifle in itself. Then I must arrange for the regular payments of twelve months' work, and *that* is no trifle; but when I consider the difficulties I have surmounted, the privations of all sorts that I have borne, the many hairbreadth escapes I have had, the times I have been near sinking under the weight of the enterprise — ah! such difficulties as even poor Wilson never experienced — what reasons have I now to suppose, or to make me think for a moment, that the omnipotent God who gave me a heart to endure and overcome all these difficulties, will abandon me now. No! my faith is the same — my desires are of a pure kind; I only wish to enjoy more of Him by admiring His works still more than I have ever done before. He will grant me life, He will support me in my journeys, and enable me to meet thee again in America.

May 6. I walked early round the Regent's Park, and there purchased four beautiful little Redpolls from a sailor, put them in my pocket, and, when arrived at home, having examined them to satisfy myself of their identity with the one found in our country, I gave them all liberty to go. What pleasure they must have felt rising, and going off over London; and I felt pleasure too, to know they had the freedom I so earnestly desired.

May 10. I received a long letter from Charles Bonaparte, and perceived it had been dipped in vinegar to prevent it from introducing the plague from Italy to England.

June 2. I was at Mr. Swainson's from May 28 till yesterday, and my visit was of the most agreeable nature. Mr. and Mrs. Swainson have a charming home at Tittenhanger Green, near St. Albans. Mrs. Swainson plays well on the piano, is amiable and kind; Mr. Swainson a superior man indeed; and their children blooming with health and full of spirit. Such talks on birds we have had together. Why, Lucy, thou wouldst think that birds were all that we cared for in this world, but thou knowest this is not so. Whilst there I began a drawing for Mrs. Swainson, and showed Mr. Swainson how to put up birds in my style, which delighted him.

August 9. More than two months have passed since I have opened my journal — not through idleness, but because, on the contrary, I have been too busy with my plates, and in superintending the coloring of them, and with painting. I wished again to try painting in oil, and set to with close attention, day after day, and have now before me eight pictures begun, but not one entirely finished. I have a great desire to exhibit some of these in this wonderful London. One of these pictures is from my sketch of an Eagle pouncing on a Lamb,[1] dost thou remember it? They are on the top of a dreary mountain; the sky is dark and stormy, and I am sure the positions of the bird and his prey are wholly correct. My drawing is good, but the picture at present shows great coldness and want of strength. Another is a copy of the very group of Black Cocks, or Grouse, for which Mr. Gally paid me £100, and I copy it with his permission; if it is better than his, and I think it will be, he must exchange, for assuredly he should own the superior picture. The others are smaller and less important. With the exception of such exercise as has been necessary, and my journeys (often several times a day) to Havell's, I have not left my room, and have labored as if not to be painting was a heinous crime. I have been at work from four every morning till dark; I have kept up my large correspondence, my publication goes on well and regularly, and this very day seventy sets have been distributed; yet

[1] This picture is still in the family, being owned by one of the granddaughters.

the number of my subscribers has not increased; on the contrary, I have lost some.

I have met a Mr. Parker, whom I once knew in Natchez; he asked me to permit him to paint my portrait as a woodsman, and though it is very tiresome to me, I have agreed to his request. The return of Captain Basil Hall to England has rather surprised me; he called on me at once; he had seen our dear Victor, Mr. Sully, Dr. Harlan, and many of my friends, to whom I had given him letters, for which he thanked me heartily. He has seen much of the United States, but says he is too true an Englishman to like things there. Time will show his ideas more fully, as he told me he should publish his voyage, journeys, and a number of anecdotes.

August 10. My usual long walk before breakfast, after which meal Mr. Parker took my first sitting, which consisted merely of the outlines of the head; this was a job of more than three hours, much to my disgust. We then went for a walk and turned into the Zoölogical Gardens, where we remained over an hour. I remarked two large and beautiful Beavers, seated with the tail as usual under the body, their forelegs hanging like those of a Squirrel.

August 13. I wrote to Mr. Swainson asking if he could not accompany me to France, where he said he wished to go when we were talking together at Tittenhanger.

August 19. My absence from this dusty place has prevented my writing daily, but I can easily sum up. Thursday afternoon on returning from Havell's, I found Mr. Swainson just arrived. He had come to take me to Tittenhanger Green, where the pure air, the notes of the birds, the company of his wife and children, revived my drooping spirits. How very kind this was of him, especially when I reflect on what a short time I have known him. We procured some powder and shot, and seated ourselves in the coach for the journey. Just as we were leaving London and its smoke, a man begged I would take a paper bag from him, containing a Carrier Pigeon, and turn it out about five miles off. The poor bird could have been put in no better hands, I am sure; when I opened the bag and launched it in the air, I wished from my heart I had its powers of flight; I would have ventured across the ocean to Louisiana. At Tittenhanger Mrs. Swainson and her darling boy came to meet us, and we walked slowly to the house; its happy cheer had great influence on my feelings. Our evening was spent in looking over Levaillant's[1] work. We discovered, to the great satisfaction of my friend, two species of Chatterers, discovered by the famous traveller in Africa; until now our American species stood by itself, in the mind of the naturalist. My time afterwards was spent in shooting, painting, reading, talking, and examining specimens. But, my Lucy, the most agreeable part of all this is that we three have decided to go to Paris about the first of September, from there probably to Brussels, Rotterdam, and possibly Amsterdam.

August 20. Messrs. Children and Gray[2] of the British Museum called to see me this afternoon, and we talked much of that establishment. I was surprised when Mr. Gray told me £200 per annum was all that was allowed for the purchase of natural curiosities. We were joined by Captain Basil Hall. I now feel more and more convinced that he has not remained in America long enough, and that his judgment of things there must be only superficial. Since these gentlemen left I have written to Charles Bonaparte a long letter, part of which I copy for thee: "My *Sylvia roscoe*, is, I assure you, a distinct species from Vieillot's; my *Turdus aquaticus* is very different from Wilson's Water Thrush, as you will see when both birds are published. Mine never reaches further south than Savannah, its habits are quite different.

[1] François Levaillant, born at Paramaribo, 1753; died in France, 1824.
[2] John Edward Gray, 1800–1875, zoölogist.

Troglodytes bewickii is a new and rather a rare species, found only in the lowlands of the Mississippi and Louisiana. I have killed five or six specimens, and it differs greatly from *Troglodytes ludovicianus;* I wish I had a specimen to send you. I particularly thank you for your observations, and I hope that you will criticise my work at all points, as a good friend should do, for how am I to improve if not instructed by men of superior talents? I cannot determine at present about '*Stanleii,*' because I never have seen the *Falco* you mention. My bird is surely another found in the south and north, but a very rare species in all my travels; when you see the two figures, size of life, then you will be able to judge and to inform me. My journey to the mouth of the Columbia is always uppermost in my mind, and I look to my return from that country to this as the most brilliant portion of my life, as I am confident many new birds and plants must be there, yet unknown to man. You are extremely kind to speak so favorably of my work, and to compare it with your own; it would be more worthy of that comparison, perhaps, if I had had the advantages of a classical education; all I deserve, I think, is the degree of encouragement due to my exertions and perseverance in figuring *exactly* the different birds, and the truth respecting their habits, which will appear in my text. However, I accept all your kind sayings as coming from a friend, and one himself devoted to that beautiful department of science, Ornithology." My subscribers are yet far from enough to pay my expenses, and my purse suffers severely for the want of greater patronage. The Zoölogical Gardens improve daily; they are now building winter quarters for the animals there. The specimens of skins from all parts of the world which are presented there are wonderful, but they have no place for them.

August 25. I have had the pleasure of a long letter from our Victor, dated July 20; this letter has reached me more rapidly than any since I have been in England. I am becoming impatient to start for Paris. I do not expect much benefit by this trip, but I shall be glad to see what may be done. Mr. Parker has nearly finished my portrait, which he considers a good one, and *so do I.*[1] He has concluded to go to Paris with us, so we shall be quite a party. Mr. Vigors wrote asking me to write some papers for the "Zoölogical Journal," but I have refused him as all others. No *money* can pay for abuse. This afternoon I had a visit from a Mr. Kirkpatrick, who bought my picture of the Bantams.

August 29. I packed up my clothes early this morning and had my trunk weighed, as only forty pounds are allowed to each person. I also put my effects to rights, and was ready to start for anywhere by seven.

August 30. While Mr. Swainson was sitting with me, old Bewick and his daughters called on me. Good old man! how glad I was to see him again. It was, he said, fifty-one years since he had been in London, which is no more congenial to him than to me. He is now seventy-eight, and sees to engrave as well as when he was twenty years of age.

DOVER, *September 1, 1828.* Now, my dear book, prepare yourself for a good scratching with my pen, for I have entered on a journey that I hope will be interesting. I had breakfast at six with Mr. Parker; we were soon joined by Mr. and Mrs. Swainson and proceeded to the office in Piccadilly, where we took our seats in the coach. At the "Golden Cross" in Charing Cross we took up the rest of our cargo. Bless me! what a medley! A little, ill-looking Frenchman — who fastened a gilt balancing-pole *under* the coach, and put his wife and little daughter on top, — four men all foreigners, and a tall, rather good-looking demoiselle, with a bonnet not wanting in height or breadth or bows of blue ribbon, so stiff they must have been

[1] No trace of this portrait can be found.

starched. She took her seat on top of the coach and soared aloft, like a Frigate Pelican over the seas. We started at eight and were soon out of London. The pure air of the country animated my spirits, and all were gay. We passed over Black Heath, through Hartford and Canterbury, the first a poor, dirty-looking place, the latter quite the contrary. The majestic cathedral rose above every other object, like one of God's monuments made to teach us His glory. The country more hilly, on an average, than any part of this island I have yet seen, but the land very poor. We saw the Thames several times, and the sea at a great distance. The river Medway, which we crossed at Rochester, is influenced by the tides as far as that town. About six miles from this little seaport we suddenly saw Dover Castle, which with the sea and the undulating landscape made a pretty picture. As soon as we arrived we all went to see the cliffs that rise almost perpendicularly along the shore, the walks crowded with persons come to see the regatta to-morrow.

Paris, September 4. I arrived here this morning at seven o'clock, and I assure thee, my Lucy, that I and all my companions were pleased to get rid of the diligence, and the shocking dust that tormented us during our whole journey. We left Dover at one, on Tuesday, 2d; the wind blew sharply, and I felt that before long the sea would have evil effects on me, as it always has. We proceeded towards Calais at a good rate, going along the shores of England until opposite the French port, for which we then made direct, and landed after three and a half hours' beating against wind and water. As soon as we landed we left our luggage and passports with a Commissionaire, and went to dine at Hôtel Robart, where we had been recommended. Our still sickly bodies were glad to rest, and there our passports were returned to us. I was much tickled to read that my complexion was *copper red;* as the Monsieur at the office had never seen me, I suppose the word American suggested that all the natives of our country were aborigines. We then entered the diligence, a vehicle ugly and clumsy in the extreme, but tolerably comfortable unless over-crowded, and it travelled from six to seven miles an hour, drawn generally by five horses, two next the coach, and three abreast before those; the driver rides on the near wheel-horse dressed precisely like the monkeys in shows of animals. Calais is a decaying fortified town; the ditches are partly filled with earth, and I cannot tell why there should exist at this time a drawbridge. As we proceeded it did not take much time to see already many differences between France and England. I will draw no parallel between these countries, I will merely tell thee what I saw. The country is poorly cultivated, although the land is good. No divisions exist to the eye, no cleanly trimmed hedges, no gates, no fences; all appeared to me like one of the old abandoned cotton plantations of the South. I remarked that there were more and taller trees than in England, and nearly the whole road was planted like the avenue to a gentleman's house. The road itself was better than I had expected, being broad, partly macadamized, and partly paved with square stones; I found it much alike during the whole journey. Night coming on we lost the means of observation for a time, and stopped soon after dark for refreshment, and had some excellent coffee. I assure thee, Lucy, that coffee in France is certainly better than anywhere else. We passed through St. Omer, and a little farther on saw the lights of the fires from an encampment of twelve thousand soldiers. Breakfast was had at another small village, where we were sadly annoyed by beggars. The country seems *very poor;* the cottages of the peasants are wretched mud huts. We passed through the Departments of Artois and Picardy, the country giving now and then agreeable views. We dined at Amiens, where the cathedral externally is magnificent. After travelling all night again, we found ourselves within forty miles of Paris, and now saw patches of vineyards and found fruit of all kinds cheap, abundant, and good. We were put down at the Messagerie Royale rue des Victoires, and I found to my sorrow that my plates were not among the luggage; so I did what I could about it, and we went to lodgings to which we had been recommended, with M. Percez. Mrs. Swainson's brother, Mr. Parkes, came to see us at once, and we all went to the Jardin des Plantes, or Jardin du Roi, which fronts on a very bad bridge, built in great haste in the days of Napoleon, then called Le pont d'Austerlitz, but now Le pont Ste. Geneviève. I thought the gardens well laid out, large, handsome, but not everywhere well kept. We saw everything, then walked to the entrance of the famous Musée; it was closed, but we knocked and asked for Baron Cuvier.[1] He was in, but, we were told, too busy to be seen. Being determined to look at the Great Man, we waited, knocked again, and with a certain degree of *firmness* sent our names. The messenger returned, bowed, and led the way upstairs, where in a minute Monsieur le Baron, like an excellent good man, came to us. He had heard much of my friend Swainson and greeted him as he deserves to be greeted; he was polite and kind to me, though my name had never made its way to his ears. I looked at him, and here follows the result: age about sixty-five; size corpulent, five feet five, English measure; head large; face wrinkled and brownish; eyes gray, brilliant and sparkling; nose aquiline, large and red; mouth large, with good lips; teeth few, blunted by age, excepting one on the lower jaw, measuring nearly three-quarters of an inch square. Thus, my Lucy, have I described Cuvier almost as if a *new species of man*. He has invited us to dine with him next Saturday at six, and as I hope to have

[1] George Chrétien Léopold Frédéric Dagobert Cuvier, Baron, 1769–1832; statesman, author, philosopher, and one of the greatest naturalists of modern times.

many opportunities of seeing him I will write more as I become acquainted with him. After dinner Mr. Parker and I went roving anywhere and everywhere, but as it grew dark, and Paris is very badly lighted, little can I say, more than that we saw the famous Palais Royal, and walked along each of its four avenues. The place was crowded, and filled with small shops, themselves filled with all sorts of bagatelles.

September 5. After breakfast, which was late but good, consisting of grapes, figs, sardines, and *French* coffee, Swainson and I proceeded to Les Jardins des Plantes, by the side of the famous river Seine, which here, Lucy, is not so large as the Bayou Sara, where I have often watched the Alligators while bathing. Walking in Paris is disagreeable in the extreme; the streets are paved, but with scarcely a sidewalk, and a large gutter filled with dirty black water runs through the centre of each, and the people go about without any kind of order, in the centre, or near the houses; the carriages, carts, etc., do the same, and I have wondered that so few accidents take place. We saw a very ugly bridge of iron called the Pont Neuf, and the splendid statue of Henri Quatre. We were, however, more attracted by the sight of the immense numbers of birds offered for sale along the quays, and some were rare specimens. A woman took us into her house and showed us some hundreds from Bengal and Senegal, and I assure thee that we were surprised. We proceeded to our appointment with Baron Cuvier, who gave us tickets for the Musée, and promised all we could wish. At the Musée M. Valenciennes[1] was equally kind. Having a letter for M. Geoffroy de St. Hilaire,[2] we went to his house in the Jardins, and with him we were particularly pleased. He proved to me that he understood the difference in the ideas of the French and English perfectly. He repeated the

[1] Achille Valenciennes, born 1794, French naturalist.

[2] Étienne Geoffroy de St. Hilaire, 1772–1844, French naturalist.

words of Cuvier and assured us my work had not been heard of in France. He promised to take us to the Académie des Sciences on Monday next. I left Swainson at work in the Musée, and went to the Louvre. There, entering the first open door, I was shown into the public part of the King's *Appartement*, a thing I have never been able to accomplish in England. I saw the room where the grand councils are held, and many paintings illustrating the horrors of the French Revolution. Then to the galleries of painting and sculpture, where I found Parker, and saw a number of artists copying in oil the best pictures. This evening we went to the Théâtre Français, where I saw the finest drop curtain I have yet beheld, and a fine tragedy, Fiésque, which I enjoyed much.

September 6. The strange things one sees in this town would make a mountain of volumes if closely related; but I have not time, and can only speak to thee of a few. After our breakfast of figs and bread and butter, Swainson and I went down the Boulevard to the Jardins Royaux. These boulevards are planted with trees to shade them, and are filled with shops containing more objects of luxury and of necessity than can well be imagined. The boulevard we took is a grand promenade, and the seat of great bargains. I mean to say that a person unacquainted with the ways of the French *petit marchand* may be cheated here, with better grace, probably, than anywhere else in the world; but one used to their tricks may buy cheap and good articles. In the afternoon we went again to the Louvre, and admired the paintings in the splendid gallery, and lunched on chicken, a bottle of good wine, vegetables and bread, for thirty-five sous each. Evening coming on, we proceeded, after dressing, to Baron Cuvier's house to dine. We were announced by a servant in livery, and received by the Baron, who presented us to his only remaining daughter, — a small, well-made, good-looking lady, with sparkling black eyes, and extremely amiable. As I seldom go anywhere without meeting some one who has met me, I found among the guests a Fellow of the Linnæan Society, who knew me well. The Baroness now came in — a good-looking, motherly lady, and the company, amounting to sixteen, went to dinner. The Baroness led the way with a gentleman, and the Baron took in his daughter, but made friend Swainson and me precede them; Swainson sat next mademoiselle, who, fortunately for him, speaks excellent English. I was opposite to her, by the side of the Baron. There was not the show of opulence at this dinner that is seen in the same rank of life in England, no, not by far, but it was a good dinner, served *à la française*. All seemed happy, and went on with more simplicity than in London. The dinner finished, the Baroness rose, and we all followed her into the library. I liked this much; I cannot bear the *drinking matches* of wine at the English tables. We had coffee, and the company increased rapidly; amongst them all I knew only Captain Parry, M. de Condolleot (?), and Mr. Lesson,[1] just returned from a voyage round the world. Cuvier stuck to us, and we talked ornithology; he asked me the price of my work, and I gave him a prospectus. The company filled the room, it grew late, and we left well satisfied with the introductory step among *les savans français*.

Sunday, September 7. The traveller who visits France without seeing a fête, such as I have seen this day at St. Cloud, leaves the country unacquainted with that species of knowledge best adapted to show the manners of a people. St. Cloud is a handsome town on the Seine, about five miles below Paris, built in horseshoe form on the undulating hills of this part of the country. These hills are covered with woods, through which villas, cottages, and chateaux emerge, and give life to the scene. On the west side of the village, and on its greatest elevation, stands the

[1] René Primevère Lesson, a French naturalist and author, born at Rochefort, 1794, died 1849.

Palace of the Kings, the Emperors, and the people. I say the people, because they are allowed to see the interior every day. With Parker, I took a cab directly after breakfast to the *barrière des bons hommes*, and walked the remaining distance, say three miles. We had the Seine in view most of the way, and crossed it on a fine iron bridge, one end of which forms the entrance to St. Cloud, in front of which the river winds. We reached the gates of the palace, and found they were not opened till twelve o'clock; but a sergeant offered to show us the King's garden, — an offer we accepted with pleasure. The entrance is by an avenue of fine trees, their tops meeting over our heads, and presenting, through the vista they made, a frame for a beautiful landscape. We passed several pieces of water, the peaceful abode of numerous fish, basking on the surface; swans also held their concave wings unfurled to the light breeze — orange trees of fair size held their golden fruit pendent — flowers of every hue covered the borders, and a hundred statues embellished all with their well-modelled forms. So unmolested are the birds that a Green Woodpecker suffered my inspection as if in the woods of our dear, dear America. At the right time we found ourselves in the King's antechamber, and then passed through half a dozen rooms glittering with richest ornaments, painted ceilings, large pictures, and lighted by immense windows; all, however, too fine for my taste, and we were annoyed by the *gens d'armes* watching us as if we were thieves. It was near two o'clock when we left, the weather beautiful, and heat such as is usually felt in Baltimore about this season. The population of Paris appeared now to flock to St. Cloud; the road was filled with conveyances of all sorts, and in the principal walk before the Palace were hundreds of *petits marchands*, opening and arranging their wares. Music began in different quarters, groups lay on the grass, enjoying their repasts; every one seemed joyous and happy. One thing surprised me: we were at St. Cloud ten hours, — they told us fifty thousand (?) were there, and I saw only three women of noticeable beauty; yet these short brunettes are animated and apparently thoughtless, and sing and dance as if no shadow could ever come over them. At four o'clock all was in full vigor; the sounds of horns and bugles drew us towards a place where we saw on a platform a party of musicians, three of whom were Flemish women, and so handsome that they were surrounded by crowds. We passed through a sort of turnstile, and in a few minutes an equestrian performance began, in which the riders showed great skill, jugglers followed with other shows, and then we left; the same show in London would have cost three shillings; here, a franc. We saw people shooting at a target with a crossbow. When the marksman was successful in hitting the centre, a spring was touched, and an inflated silken goldfish, as large as a barrel, rose fifty yards in the air, — a pretty sight, I assure thee; the fins of gauze moved with the breeze, he plunged and rose and turned about, almost as a real fish would do in his element. Shows of everything were there; such a medley — such crowds — such seeming pleasure in all around us, I never remarked anywhere but in France. No word of contention did I hear; all was peace and joy, and when we left not a disturbance had taken place. We had an excellent dinner, with a bottle of Chablis, for three francs each, and returning to the place we had left, found all the fountains were playing, and dancing was universal; the musicians were good and numerous, but I was surprised to remark very few fine dancers. The woods, which were illuminated, looked extremely beautiful; the people constantly crossing and re-crossing them made the lights appear and disappear, reminding me of fireflies in our own woods in a summer night. As we passed out of the gates, we perceived as many persons coming as going, and were told the merriment would last till day. With difficulty we secured two seats in a cart, and returned to Paris along a road with a double line of vehicles of all sorts going both ways. Every few rods were guards on foot, and *gens d'armes* on horseback, to see that all went well; and we at last reached our hotel, tired and dusty, but pleased with all we had seen, and at having had such an opportunity to see, to compare, and to judge of the habits of a people so widely different from either Americans or English.

September 8. We went to pay our respects to Baron Cuvier and Geoffroy St. Hilaire;[1] we saw only the first, who told us to be at the Académie Royale des Sciences in an hour. I had *hired* a portfolio, and took my work. As soon as we entered, Baron Cuvier very politely came to us, ordered a porter to put my book on a table, and gave me a seat of honor. The séance was opened by a tedious lecture on the vision of the Mole; then Cuvier arose, announcing my friend Swainson and me and spoke of my work; it was shown and admired as usual, and Cuvier requested to review it for the "Mémoires of the Academy." Poor Audubon! here thou art, a simple woodsman, among a crowd of talented men, yet kindly received by all — so are the works of God as shown in His birds loved by them. I left my book, that the librarian might show it to all who wished to see it.

September 9. Went to the Jardin du Roi, where I met young Geoffroy, who took me to a man who stuffs birds for the Prince d'Essling, who, I was told, had a copy of my work, but after much talk could not make out whether it was Wilson's, Selby's, or mine. I am to call on him tomorrow. I took a great walk round the Boulevards, looking around me and thinking how curious my life has been, and how wonderful my present situation is. I took Mrs. Swainson to the Louvre, and as we were about to pass one of the gates of the Tuileries, the sentinel stopped us, saying no one could pass with a *fur cap;* so we went to another

[1] Isidore Geoffroy St. Hilaire, 1805–1861, zoölogist.

gate, where no such challenge was given, and reached the Grand Gallery. Here amongst the Raphaels, Correggios, Titians, Davids, and thousands of others, we feasted our eyes and enlarged our knowledge. Taking Mrs. Swainson home, I then made for L'Institut de France by appointment, and gave my prospectus to the secretary of the library. Young Geoffroy, an aimable and learned young man, paid me every attention, and gave me a room for Swainson and myself to write in and for the inspection of specimens. How very different from the public societies in England, where instead of being bowed to, you have to bow to every one. Now, my Lucy, I have certainly run the gauntlet of England and Paris, and may feel proud of two things, that I am considered the first ornithological painter, and the first practical naturalist of America; may God grant me life to accomplish my serious and gigantic work.

September 10. Breakfast over, I made for the Boulevards to present the letters from good friends Rathbone and Melly. I saw Mr. B——, the banker, who read the letter I gave him, and was most polite, but as to ornithology, all he knew about it was that large feathers were called *quills*, and were useful in posting ledgers. From there to the Jardin du Roi, where I called on Monsieur L. C. Kiener, bird stuffer to the Prince of Massena (or Essling), [1] who wished me to call on the Prince with him at two, the Prince being too ill to leave the house. Mr. and Mrs. Swainson were to go with me to see the collection he had made, of many curious and beautiful things, and when we reached the house we were shown at once to the museum, which surpasses in magnificence and number of rare specimens of birds, shells, and books, all I have yet seen. This for a while, when I was told the Prince would receive me. I took my *pamphlet* in my arms and entered a fine room, where he was lying on a sofa; he rose at once,

[1] Son of André, Prince d'Essling and Duc de Rivoli, one of the marshals of Napoleon.

bowed, and presented his beautiful wife. As soon as I had untied my portfolio, and a print was seen, both exclaimed, "Ah! c'est bien beau!" I was asked if I did not know Charles Bonaparte, and when I said yes, they again both exclaimed, "Ah! c'est lui, the gentleman of whom we have heard so much, the man of the woods, who has made so many and such wonderful drawings." The Prince regretted very much there were so few persons in France able to subscribe to such a work, and said I must not expect more than six or eight names in Paris. He named all whom he and his lady knew, and then said it would give him pleasure to add his name to my list; he wrote it himself, next under that of the Duke of Rutland. This prince, son of the famous marshal, is about thirty years of age, apparently delicate, pale, slender, and yet good-looking, entirely devoted to Natural History; his wife a beautiful young woman, not more than twenty, extremely graceful and polite. They both complimented me on the purity of my French, and wished me all success. My room at the hotel being very cramped, I have taken one at L'Hôtel de France, large, clean, and comfortable, for which I pay twenty-five sous a day. We are within gun-shot of Les Jardins des Tuileries. The *retraite* is just now beating. This means that a few drummers go through the streets at eight o'clock in the evening, beating their drums, to give notice to all soldiers to make for their quarters.

September 12. I went early to Rue Richelieu to see the librarian of the King, Mr. Van Praët, a small, white-haired gentleman, who assured me in the politest manner imaginable that it was out of the question to subscribe for such a work; he, however, gave me a card of introduction to M. Barbier, a second librarian, belonging to the King's private library at the Louvre. On my way I posted my letters for London; the inland postage of a single letter from Paris to London is twenty-four sous, and the mail for London leaves four days in the week. M. Barbier was out, but when I saw him later he advised me to write to the Baron de la Bouillerie, intendant of the King's household. So go my days. — This evening we went to the Italian Opera; it was not open when we arrived, so we put ourselves in the line of people desirous to enter, and at seven followed regularly, with no pushing or crowding (so different from England), as the arrangements are so perfect. We received our tickets, the change was counted at leisure, and we were shown into the pit, which contains three divisions; that nearest the orchestra contains the most expensive seats. The theatre is much less in extent than either Drury Lane or Covent Garden, but is handsome, and splendidly decorated and lighted. The orchestra contains more than double the number of musicians, and when the music began, not another sound was heard, all was silence and attention. Never having been at the opera since my youth, the music astounded me. The opera was Semiramis, and well executed, but I was not much pleased with it; it was too clamorous, a harmonious storm, and I would have preferred something more tranquil. I remarked that persons who left their seats intending to return laid on their seats a hat, glove, or card, which was quite sufficient to keep the place for them. In London what a treat for the thieves, who are everywhere. I walked home; the pure atmosphere of Paris, the clear sky, the temperature, almost like that of America, make me light-hearted indeed, yet would that I were again in the far distant, peaceful retreats of my happiest days. Europe might whistle for me; I, like a free bird, would sing, "Never — no, never, will I leave America."

September 13. I had to take my portfolio to Baron Cuvier, and I went first to Geoffroy de St. Hilaire, who liked it much, and retracted his first opinion of the work being too large. Monsieur Dumesnil, a first-rate engraver, came to see me, sent by Prince de Massena, and we talked of the work, which he told me honestly could not be published in France *to be delivered in England* as cheaply as if the work were done in London, and probably not so well. This has ended with me all thoughts of ever removing it from Havell's hands, unless he should discontinue the present excellent state of its execution. Copper is dearer here than in England, and good colorers much scarcer. I saw Cuvier, who invited us to spend the evening, and then returned to the Pont des Arts to look for bird-skins. I found none, but purchased an engraved portrait of Cuvier, and another of "Phidias and the Thorn." I have just returned with Swainson from Baron Cuvier's, who gives public receptions to scientific men every Saturday. My book was on the table; Cuvier received me with special kindness, and put me at my ease. Mademoiselle Cuvier I found remarkably agreeable, as also Monsieur de Condillot. The first very willingly said he would sit to Parker for his portrait, and the other told me that if I went to Italy, I must make his house my home. My work was seen by many, and Cuvier pronounced it the finest of its kind in existence.

September 14, Sunday. Versailles, where we have spent our day, is truly a magnificent place; how long since I have been here, and how many changes in my life since those days! We first saw the orangerie, of about two hundred trees, that to Frenchmen who have never left Paris look well, but to me far from it, being martyrized by the hand of man, who has clipped them into stiff ovals. One is 407 years old. They produce no golden fruit, as their boxes are far too small to supply sufficient nourishment, and their fragrant blossoms are plucked to make orange-flower water. From this spot the woods, the hunting-grounds of the King, are seen circling the gardens, and are (we are told) filled with all kinds of game. The King's apartments, through which we afterwards went, are too full of gilding for my eyes, and I frequently resorted to the large windows to glance at the green trees. Amongst the paintings I admired most little Virginia and Paul standing under a palm-tree with their mothers; Paul inviting the lovely child to cross a brook. In the stables are a hundred beautiful horses, the choice of Arabia, Australasia, Normandy, Limousin, etc., each the model of his race, with fiery eyes, legs sinewy and slender, tails to the ground, and manes never curtailed. Among them still remain several that have borne the great Napoleon. From here we walked again through woods and gardens; thus, my Lucy, once more have I been at Versailles, and much have I enjoyed it.

September 15. France, my dearest friend, is indeed poor! This day I have attended at the Royal Academy of Sciences, and had all my plates spread over the different large tables, and they were viewed by about one hundred persons. "Beau! bien beau!" issued from every mouth, but, "Quel ouvrage!" "Quel prix!" as well. I said that I had thirty subscribers at Manchester; they seemed surprised, but acknowledged that England, the little isle of England, alone was able to support poor Audubon. Poor France! thy fine climate, thy rich vineyards, and the wishes of the learned avail nothing; thou art a destitute beggar, and not the powerful friend thou wast represented to be. Now I see plainly how happy, or lucky, or prudent I was, not to follow friend Melly's enthusiastic love of country. Had I come first to France my work never would have had even a beginning; it would have perished like a flower in October. It happened that a gentleman who saw me at Versailles yesterday remembered my face, and spoke to me; he is the under secretary of this famous society, and he wrote for me a note to be presented to the Minister of the Interior, who has, I am told, the power to subscribe to anything, and for as many copies of any work as the farmers of France can well pay for through the enormous levies imposed on them. Cuvier, St. Hilaire, and many others spoke to me most kindly. I had been to Cuvier in the morning to talk with him and Parker about the portrait the latter is to paint, and I believe I will describe Cuvier's house to thee. The footman asked us to follow him upstairs, and in the first room we caught a glimpse of a slight figure dressed all in black, that glided across the floor like a sylph; it was Mlle. Cuvier, not quite ready to see gentlemen: off she flew like a Dove before Falcons. We followed our man, who continually turned, saying, "This way, gentlemen." Eight rooms we passed filled with books, and each with a recessed bed, and at last reached a sort of laboratory, the *sanctum sanctorum* of Cuvier; there was nothing in it but books and skeletons of animals, reptiles, etc. Our conductor, surprised, bid us sit down, and left us to seek the Baron. My eyes were fully employed, and I contemplated in imagination the extent of the great man's knowledge. His books were in great disorder, and I concluded that he read and studied them, and owned them for other purposes than for show. Our man returned and led us back through the same avenue of bed-chambers, lined with books instead of satin, and we were conducted through the kitchen to another laboratory, where the Baron was found. Politeness in great men is shown differently from the same quality in fashionable society: a smile suffices to show you are welcome, without many words, and the work in hand is continued as if you were one of the family. Ah! how I delight in this! and how pleased I was to be thus welcomed by this learned man. Cuvier was looking at a small lizard in a tiny vial filled with spirit. I see now his sparkling eye half closed, as if quizzing its qualities, and as he put it down he wrote its name on a label. He made an appointment with Mr. Parker, and went on quizzing lizards. Being desirous of seeing a gambling house, young Geoffroy took me to one in the Palais Royal, a very notorious one, containing several roulette tables, and there we saw a little of the tactics of the gentlemen of the trade. The play, however, was not on this occasion high. The *banquiers*, or head thieves, better call them, are lank and pale, their countenances as unmoved as their hearts. From here we went to the establishment of Franconi, where I saw wonderful feats of horsemanship.

September 17. There is absolutely nothing to be done here to advance my subscription list, and at two o'clock I went with Swainson to a *marchand naturaliste* to see some drawings of birds of which I had heard. They were not as well drawn as mine, but much better painted.

September 18. I went to install Parker at Baron Cuvier's. He had his canvas, etc., all ready and we arrived at half-past nine, too early quite. At ten, having spent our time in the apartment of the Giraffe, Parker went in to take a second breakfast, and I to converse with Mlle. Cuvier. The Baron came in, and after a few minutes to arrange about the light, sat down in a comfortable armchair, quite ready. Great men as well as great women have their share of vanity, and I soon discovered that the Baron thinks himself a fine-looking man. His daughter seemed to know this, and remarked more than once that her father's under lip was swelled more than usual, and she added that the line of his nose was extremely fine. I passed my fingers over mine, and, lo! I thought just the same. I see the Baron now, quite as plainly as I did this morning; an old green surtout about him, a neck-cloth, that might well surround his body if unfolded, loosely tied about his chin, and his silver locks like those of a man more bent on studying books than on visiting barbers. His fine eyes shot fire from under his bushy eyebrows, and he smiled as he conversed with me. Mlle. Cuvier, asked to read to us, and opening a book, read in a clear, well accentuated manner a comic play, well arranged to amuse us for a time, for sitting for a portrait is certainly a great bore. The Baroness joined us; I thought her looks not those of a happy person, and her melancholy affected me. The Baron soon said he was fatigued, rose and went out, but soon returned, and I advised Parker not to keep him too long. The time was adjourned to Sunday next. In Connecticut this would be thought horrible, in England it would be difficult to effect it, and in Paris it is considered the best day for such things. Again I went to the Louvre, and this evening went with young Geoffroy to the celebrated Frascati. This house is a handsome hôtel, and we were introduced by two servants in fine livery into a large wainscoted room, where a roulette table was at work. Now none but *gentlemen* gamble here. We saw, and saw only! In another room *rouge et noir* was going on, and the double as well as the single Napoleons easily changed hands, yet all was smiling and serene. Some wealthy personage drew gold in handsful from his pockets, laid it on a favorite spot, and lost it calmly, more than once. Ladies also resort to this house, and good order is always preserved; without a white cravat, shoes instead of boots, etc., no one is admitted. I soon became tired of watching this and we left.

September 19. Friend Swainson requested me to go with him this morning to complete a purchase of skins, and this accomplished I called on M. Milbert, to whom I had a letter from my old friend Le Sueur,[1] but he was absent. I now went to the Jardin du Roi, and at the library saw the so-called fine drawings of Mr. H——. Lucy, they were just such drawings as our boy Johnny made before I left home, stiff and dry as a well-seasoned fiddle-stick. The weather and the sky are most charming. This evening M. Cainard, whom I have met several times, asked me to play billiards with him, but the want of practice was such that I felt as if I never had played before. Where is the time gone when I was considered one of the best of players? To-morrow I will try to see M. Redouté.[2]

[1] Charles Alexandre Le Sueur, French naturalist. 1778–1846.

[2] Pierre Joseph Redouté, French painter of flowers. 1759–1840.

September 20. I had the pleasure of seeing old Redouté this morning, the flower-painter *par excellence.* After reading Le Sueur's note to him, dated five years ago, he looked at me fixedly, and said, "Well, sir, I am truly glad to become acquainted with you," and without further ceremony showed me his best works. His flowers are grouped with peculiar taste, well drawn and precise in the outlines, and colored with a pure brilliancy that depicts nature incomparably better than I ever saw it before. Old Redouté dislikes all that is not *nature alone;* he cannot bear either the drawings of stuffed birds or of quadrupeds, and evinced a strong desire to see a work wherein nature was delineated in an animated manner. He said that as he dined every Friday at the Duke of Orleans', he would take my work there next week, and procure his subscription, if not also that of the Duchess, and requested me to give him a prospectus. I looked over hundreds of his drawings, and found out that he sold them well; he showed me some worth two hundred and fifty guineas. On my way to the Comte de Lasterie, I met the under secretary of the King's private library, who told me that the Baron de la Bouillerie had given orders to have my work inspected and if approved of to subscribe to it. I reached the Comte de Lasterie's house, found him half dressed, very dirty, and not very civil. He was at breakfast with several gentlemen, and told me to call again, which I will take into *consideration.* I must not forget that in crossing the city this morning I passed through the flower market, a beautiful exhibition to me at all times. This market is abundantly supplied twice a week with exotics and flowers of all sorts, which are sold at a cheap rate.

September 21. The weather is still beautiful, and Parker and I took the omnibus at the Pont des Arts, which vehicle, being Sunday, was crowded. I left Parker to make a second sitting with Cuvier, and went to the Jardin du Roi, already filled with pleasure-seekers. I took a seat beside a venerable old soldier, and entered into conversation with him. Soldier during more than thirty years, he had much to relate. The Moscow campaign was spoken of, and I heard from the lips of this veteran the sufferings to which Napoleon's armies had been exposed. He had been taken prisoner, sent to the interior for two years, fed on musty bread by the Cossacks, who forced them to march all day. He had lost his toes and one ear by the frost, and sighed, as he said, "And to lose the campaign after all this!" I offered him a franc, and to my surprise he refused it, saying he had his pension, and was well fed. The garden was now crowded, children were scrambling for horse-chestnuts, which were beginning to fall, ladies playing battledore and shuttlecock, venders of fruit and lemonade were calling their wares, and I was interested and amused by all. Now to Baron Cuvier again. I found him sitting in his arm-chair; a gentleman was translating the dedication of Linné (Linnæus) to him, as he was anxious that the Latin should not be misconstrued; he often looked in some book or other, and I dare say often entirely forgot Parker, who notwithstanding has laid in a good likeness. The Baron wishes me to be at the Institute to-morrow at half-past one.

September 22. I was at the Institute at half-past one — no Baron there. I sat opposite the clock and counted minutes one after another; the clock ticked on as if I did not exist; I began the counting of the numerous volumes around me, and as my eyes reached the centre of the hall they rested on the statue of Voltaire; he too had his share of troubles. Savants entered one after another; many bowed to me, and passed to their seats. My thoughts journeyed to America; I passed from the Missouri to the Roanoke, to the Hudson, to the Great Lakes — then floated down the gentle Ohio, and met the swift Mississippi which would carry me to thee. The clock vibrated in my ears, it struck two, and I saw again that I was in an immense library, where the number of savants continually increased, but no Cuvier; I tried to read, but could not; now it was half-past two; I was asked several times if I was waiting for the Baron, and was advised to go to his house, but like a sentinel true to his post I sat firm and waited. All at once I heard his voice, and saw him advancing, very warm and apparently fatigued. He met me with many apologies, and said, "Come with me;" and we walked along, he explaining all the time why he had been late, while his hand drove a pencil with great rapidity, and he told me that he was actually *now* writing the report on my work!! I thought of La Fontaine's fable of the Turtle and the Hare; I was surprised that so great a man should leave till the last moment the writing of a report to every word of which the forty critics of France would lend an attentive ear. For being on such an eminence he has to take more care of his actions than a common individual, to prevent his fall, being surrounded, as all great men are more or less, by envy and malice. My enormous book lay before him, and I shifted as swift as lightning the different plates that he had marked for examination. His pencil moved as constantly and as rapidly. He turned and returned the sheets of his manuscript with amazing accuracy, and noted as quickly as he saw, *and he saw all.* We were both wet with perspiration. It wanted but a few minutes of three when we went off to the Council room, Cuvier still writing, and bowing to every one he met. I left him, and was glad to get into the pure air. At my lodgings I found a card asking me to go to the Messageries Royales, and I went at once, thinking perhaps it was my numbers from London; but no such thing. My name was asked, and I was told that orders had been received to remit me ten francs, the coach having charged me for a seat better than the one I had had. This is indeed honesty. When I asked the gentleman how he had found out my lodgings, he smiled, and answered that he knew every stranger in Paris that had arrived for the last three months, through his line of employees, and that any police-officer was able to say how I spent my time.

September 23. The great Gérard, the pupil of my old master, David, has written saying he wishes to see my work, and myself also, and I have promised to go to-morrow evening at nine. To-day I have been to the King's library, a fine suite of twelve rooms, filled with elegant and most valuable copies of all the finest works. I should suppose that a hundred thousand volumes are contained here, as well as portfolios filled with valuable originals of the first masters. The King seldom reads, but he shoots well. Napoleon read, or was read to, constantly, and hardly knew how to hold a gun. I was surprised when I spoke of Charles Bonaparte to notice that no response was made, and the conversation was abruptly turned from ornithologists to engraving. I have now been nearly three weeks in Paris and have *two* subscribers — almost as bad as Glasgow. I am curious to see the Baron's report, and should like to have it in his own handwriting. This is hardly possible; he seldom writes, Mlle. Cuvier does his writing for him.

September 24. To have seen me trot about from pillar to post, across this great town, from back of the Palais Royal to the Jardin du Luxembourg, in search of M. Le Médecin Bertrand and a copy of Cuvier's report, would have amused any one, and yet I did it with great activity. Such frailty does exist in man, all of whom are by nature avaricious of praise. Three times did I go in vain to each place, *i. e.*, to the house in the Rue d'Enfans, and the Globe Office, three miles asunder. Fatigue at last brought me to bay, and I gave up the chase. I proceeded to the King's library. My work had had the honor to have been inspected by the Committee, who had passed a favorable judgment on its merits. I was informed that should the King subscribe, I must leave in

France a man authorized by act of attorney to receive my dues, without which I might never have a sol. The librarian, a perfect gentleman, told me this in friendship, and would have added (had he dared) that Kings are rarely expected to pay. I, however, cut the matter short, knowing within myself that, should I not receive my money, I was quite able to keep the work. In the evening I dressed to go to M. Gérard's with M. Valenciennes; but he did not come, so there must have been some mistake — probably mine.

September 25. Went with Swainson to the Panthéon, to see if the interior corresponds with the magnificence of the exterior; it is fine, but still unfinished. All, or almost all, the public edifices of Paris far surpass those of London. Then to see Cuvier, who was sitting for his portrait, while the Baroness was reading to him the life of Garrick. He had known Mrs. Garrick, and his observations were interesting. The likeness is good, and Cuvier is much pleased with it; he gave me a note for M. Vallery the King's librarian. Parker had received a note from M. Valenciennes, saying he had forgot my address, and had spent the evening going from place to place searching for me, and requested I would go with him to Gérard next Thursday. Did he forget to question the all-knowing police, or did the gentleman at the Messageries exaggerate?

September 26. I spent some time in the Louvre examining *very closely* the most celebrated pictures of animals, birds, fruits, and flowers. Afterwards we all went to the French Opera, or, as it is called here, L'École de Musique Royale. The play was "La Muette," a wonderful piece, and the whole arrangement of the performance still more so. There were at one time two hundred persons on the stage. The scenery was the finest I have ever beheld, — at the last, Mount Vesuvius in full and terrific eruption; the lava seemed absolutely to roll in a burning stream down the sides of the volcano, and the stones which were apparently cast up from the earth added to the grand representation. The whole house resounded with the most vociferous applause, and we enjoyed our evening, I assure thee.

September 27. Found old Redouté at his painting. The size of my portfolio surprised him, and when I opened the work, he examined it most carefully, and spoke highly of it, and wished he could afford it. I proposed, at last, that we should exchange works, to which he agreed gladly, and gave me at once nine numbers of his "Belles fleurs" and promised to send "Les Roses." Now, my Lucy, this will be a grand treat for thee, fond of flowers as thou art; when thou seest these, thy eyes will feast on the finest thou canst imagine. From here to the Globe office, where I saw the *rédacteur,* who was glad to have me correct the proof sheets as regarded the technical names. I did so, and he gave me, to my delight, the original copy of Cuvier himself. It is a great eulogium certainly, but not so feelingly written as the one by Swainson, nevertheless it will give the French an idea of my work.

September 28. I have lived many years, and have only seen one horse race. Perhaps I should not have seen that, which took place to-day at the Champ de Mars, had I not gone out of curiosity with M. Vallery. The Champ de Mars is on the south side of the Seine, about one and one half miles below Paris; we passed through Les Jardins des Tuileries, followed the river, and crossed the Pont de Jéna opposite the entrance to l'École Militaire, situated at the farther end of the oval that forms the Champ de Mars. This is a fine area, and perfectly level, surrounded by a levee of earth, of which I should suppose the material was taken from the plain on which the course is formed. Arriving early, we walked round it; saw with pleasure the trees that shaded the walks; the booths erected for the royal family, the prefect, the gentry, and the *canaille,* varying greatly in elegance, as you may suppose.

Chairs and benches were to be hired in abundance, and we each took one. At one o'clock squadrons of *gens d'armes* and whole regiments of infantry made their appearance from different points, and in a few minutes the whole ground was well protected. The King was expected, but I saw nothing of him, nor, indeed, of any of the royal family, and cannot even assert that they came. At two every seat was filled, and several hundreds of men on horseback had taken the centre of the plain divided from the race track by a line of ropes. The horses for the course made their appearance, — long-legged, slender-bodied, necks straight, light of foot, and fiery-eyed. They were soon mounted, and started, but I saw none that I considered swift; not one could have run half as fast as a buck in our woods. Five different sets were run, one after another, but I must say I paid much greater attention to a Mameluke on a dark Arab steed, which with wonderful ease leaped over the ground like a Squirrel; going at times like the wind, then, being suddenly checked by his rider, almost sat on his haunches, wheeled on his hind legs, and cut all sorts of mad tricks at a word from his skilful master. I would rather see *him* again than all the races in the world; horse racing, like gambling, can only amuse people who have nothing better to attend to; however, I have seen a race!

September 30. I saw Constant, the great engraver, Rue Percie, No. 12; he was at work, and I thought he worked well. I told him the purpose of my visit, and he dropped his work at once to see mine. How he stared! how often he exclaimed, "Oh, mon Dieu, quel ouvrage!" I showed him all, and he began calculating, but did so, far too largely for me, and we concluded no bargain. Old Redouté visited me and brought me a letter from the Duc d'Orléans, whom I was to call upon at one o'clock. Now, dearest friend, as I do not see Dukes every day I will give thee a circumstantial account of my visit. The Palais of the Duc d'Orléans is actually the entrance of the Palais-Royal, where we often go in the evening, and is watched by many a sentinel. On the right, I saw a large, fat, red-coated man through the ground window, whom I supposed the porter of his Royal Highness. I entered and took off my fur cap, and went on in an unconcerned way towards the stairs, when he stopped me, and asked my wishes. I told him I had an engagement with his master at one, and gave him my card to take up. He said Monseigneur was not in (a downright lie), but that I might go to the antechamber. I ordered the fat fellow to have my portfolio taken upstairs, and proceeded to mount the finest staircase my feet have ever trod. The stairs parted at bottom in rounding form of about twenty-four feet in breadth, to meet on the second floor, on a landing lighted by a skylight, which permitted me to see the beauties of the surrounding walls, and on this landing opened three doors, two of which I tried in vain to open. The third, however, gave way, and I found myself in the antechamber, with about twelve servants, who all rose and stood, until I had seated myself on a soft, red-velvet-covered bench. Not a word was said to me, and I gazed at all of them with a strange sensation of awkwardness mingled with my original pride. This room had bare walls, and a floor of black and white square marble flags. A man I call a sergeant d'armes, not knowing whether I am right or wrong, wore a sword fastened to a belt of embroidered silk, very wide; and he alone retained his hat. In a few minutes a tall, thin gentleman made his entrance from another direction from that by which I had come. The servants were again all up in a moment, the sergeant took off his hat, and the gentleman disappeared as if he had not seen me, though I had risen and bowed. A few minutes elapsed, when the same thing occurred again. Not knowing how long this might continue, I accosted the sergeant, told him I came at the request of the Duke, and wished to see him. A profound bow was the answer, and I was conducted to another room, where several gentlemen were seated writing. I let one of them know my errand, and in a moment was shown into an immense and superbly furnished apartment, and my book was ordered to be brought up. In this room I bowed to two gentlemen whom I knew to be members of the Légion d'Honneur, and walked about admiring the fine marble statues and the paintings. A gentleman soon came to me, and asked if perchance my name was Audubon? I bowed, and he replied: "Bless me, we thought that you had gone and left your portfolio; my uncle has been waiting for you twenty minutes; pray, sir, follow me." We passed through a file of bowing domestics, and a door being opened I saw the Duke coming towards me, to whom I was introduced by the nephew. Lucy, Kentucky, Tennessee, and Alabama have furnished the finest men in the world, as regards physical beauty; I have also seen many a noble-looking Osage chief; but I do not recollect a finer-looking man, in form, deportment, and manners, than this Duc d'Orléans. He had my book brought up, and helped me to untie the strings and arrange the table, and began by saying that he felt a great pleasure in subscribing to the work of an American, for that he had been most kindly treated in the United States, and should never forget it. The portfolio was at last opened, and when I held up the plate of the Baltimore Orioles, with a nest swinging amongst the tender twigs of the yellow poplar, he said: "This surpasses all I have seen, and I am not astonished now at the eulogiums of M. Redouté." He spoke partly English, and partly French; spoke much of America, of Pittsburgh, the Ohio, New Orleans, the Mississippi, steamboats, etc., etc., and added: "You are a great nation, a wonderful nation."

The Duke promised me to write to the Emperor of Austria, King of Sweden, and other crowned heads, and asked me to write to-day to the Minister of the Interior. I remained talking with him more than an hour; I showed him my list of English subscribers, many of whom he knew. I asked him for his own signature; he took my list and with a smile wrote, in very large and legible characters, "Le Duc d'Orléans." I now felt to remain longer would be an intrusion, and thanking him respectfully I bowed, shook hands with him, and retired. He wished to keep the set I had shown him, but it was soiled, and to such a good man a good set must go. At the door I asked the fat porter if he would tell me again his master was out. He tried in vain to blush.

October 1. Received to-day the note from the Minister of the Interior asking me to call to-morrow at two. At eight in the evening I was ready for M. Valenciennes to call for me to go with him to Gérard. I waited till ten, when my gentleman came, and off we went; what a time to pay a visit! But I was told Gérard[1] keeps late hours, rarely goes to bed before two, but is up and at work by ten or eleven. When I entered I found the rooms filled with both sexes, and my name being announced, a small, well-formed man came to me, took my hand, and said, "Welcome, Brother in Arts." I liked this much, and was gratified to have the ice broken so easily. Gérard was all curiosity to see my drawings, and old Redouté, who was present, spoke so highly of them before the book was opened, that I feared to discover Gérard's disappointment. The book opened accidentally at the plate of the Parrots, and Gérard, taking it up without speaking, looked at it, I assure thee, with as keen an eye as my own, for several minutes; put it down, took up the one of the Mocking-Birds, and, offering me his hand, said: "Mr. Audubon, you are the king of ornithological painters; we are all children in France and in Europe. Who would have expected such things from the woods of America?" My

[1] François Gérard, born at Rome 1770, died 1837; the best French portrait painter of his time, distinguished also for historical pictures.

heart thrilled with pride at his words. Are not we of America men? Have we not the same nerves, sinews, and mental faculties which other nations possess? By Washington! we have, and may God grant us the peaceable use of them forever. I received compliments from all around me; Gérard spoke of nothing but my work, and requested some prospectuses for Italy. He repeated what Baron Cuvier had said in the morning, and hoped that the Minister would order a good, round set of copies for the Government. I closed the book, and rambled around the rooms which were all ornamented with superb prints, mostly of Gérard's own paintings. The ladies were all engaged at cards, and money did not appear to be scarce in this portion of Paris.

October 2. Well, my Lucy, this day found me, about two o'clock, in contemplation of a picture by Gérard in the salon of the Minister of the Interior. Very different, is it not, from looking up a large decaying tree, watching the movements of a Woodpecker? I was one of several who were waiting, but only one person was there when I arrived, who entered into conversation with me, — a most agreeable man and the King's physician, possessed of fine address and much learning, being also a good botanist. Half an hour elapsed, when the physician was called; he was absent only a few minutes, and returning bowed to me and smiled as my name was called. I found the Minister a man about my own age, apparently worn out with business; he wore a long, loose, gray surtout, and said, "Well, sir, I am glad to see you; where is your great work?" I had the portfolio brought in, and the plates were exhibited. "Really, monsieur, it is a very fine thing;" and after some questions and a little conversation he asked me to write to him again, and put my terms in writing, and he would reply as soon as possible. He looked at me very fixedly, but so courteously I did not mind it. I tied up my portfolio and soon departed, having taken as much of the time of M. de Marignac as I felt I could do at this hour.

October 4. Went with Swainson to the Jardin du Roi to interpret for him, and afterwards spent some time with Geoffroy de St. Hilaire, hearing from him some curious facts respecting the habits and conformation of the Mole. He gave me a ticket to the distribution of the Grand Prix at the Institut. I then ascended four of the longest staircases I know, to reach the cabinet of M. Pascale, the director of the expenses of S. A. R. the Duc d'Orléans. What order was here! Different bookcases contained the papers belonging to the forests — horses — furniture — fine arts — libraries — fisheries — personal expenses, and so on. M. Pascale took out M. Redouté's letter, and I perceived the day of subscription, number of plates per annum, all, was noted on the margin. M. Pascale sent me to the private apartments of the Duchesse. Judge of my astonishment when I found this house connected with the Palais-Royal. I went through a long train of corridors, and reached the cabinet of M. Goutard. He took my name and heard my request and promised to make an appointment for me through M. Redouté, who is the drawing-master of the daughters of the Duchesse. With Parker I went to see the distribution of prizes at L'Institut Français. The entrance was crowded, and, as in France pushing and scrambling to get forward is out of the question, and very properly so, I think, we reached the amphitheatre when it was already well filled with a brilliant assemblage, but secured places where all could be seen. The members dress in black trimmed with rich green laces. The youths aspiring to rewards were seated round a table, facing the audience. The reports read, the prizes were given, those thus favored receiving a crown of laurel with either a gold or silver medal. We remained here from two till five.

Sunday, October 5. After a wonderful service at Notre Dame I wandered through Les Jardins des Plantes, and on to Cuvier's, who had promised me a letter to some one who would, he thought, subscribe to my book; but with his usual procrastination it was not ready, and he said he would write it to-morrow. Oh, cursed to-morrow! Do men forget, or do they not know how swiftly time moves on?

October 6. Scarce anything to write. No letter yet from the Minister of the Interior, and I fear he too is a "To-morrow man." I went to Cuvier for his letter; when he saw me he laughed, and told me to sit down and see his specimens for a little while; he was surrounded by reptiles of all sorts, arranging and labelling them. In half an hour he rose and wrote the letter for me to the Duke of Levis, but it was too late to deliver it to-day.

October 7. While with M. Lesson to-day, he spoke of a Monsieur d'Orbigny[1] of La Rochelle; and on my making some inquiries I discovered he was the friend of my early days, my intimate companion during my last voyage from France to America; that he was still fond of natural history, and had the management of the Musée at La Rochelle. His son Charles, now twenty-one, I had held in my arms many times, and as M. Lesson said he was in Paris, I went at once to find him; he was out, but shortly after I had a note from him saying he would call to-morrow morning.

October 8. This morning I had the great pleasure of receiving my god-son Charles d'Orbigny. Oh! what past times were brought to my mind. He told me he had often heard of me from his father, and appeared delighted to meet me. He, too, like the rest of his family, is a naturalist, and I showed him my work with unusual pleasure. His father was the most intimate friend I have ever had, except thee, my Lucy, and my father. I think I must have asked a dozen times to-day if no letter had come for me. Oh, Ministers! what patience you do teach artists!

[1] Charles d'Orbigny, son of Audubon's early friend, M. le docteur d'Orbigny.

October 11. This afternoon, as I was despairing about the ministers, I received a note from Vicomte Siméon,[1] desiring I should call on Monday. I may then finish with these high dignitaries. I saw the King and royal family get out of their carriages at the Tuileries; bless us! what a show! Carriages fairly glittering — eight horses in each, and two hundred hussars and outriders. A fine band of music announced their arrival. Dined at Baron Cuvier's, who subscribed to my work; he being the father of all naturalists, I felt great pleasure at this. I left at eleven, the streets dark and greasy, and made for the shortest way to my hotel, which, as Paris is a small town compared to London, I found no difficulty in doing. I am astonished to see how early all the shops close here.

October 13. At twelve o'clock I was seated in the antechamber of the Vicomte Siméon; when the sergeant perceived me he came to me and said that M. Siméon desired me to have the first interview. I followed him and saw a man of ordinary stature, about forty, fresh-looking, and so used to the courtesy of the great world that before I had opened my lips he had paid me a very handsome compliment, which I have forgot. The size of my work astonished him, as it does every one who sees it for the first time. He told me that the work had been under discussion, and that he advised me to see Baron de la Brouillerie and Baron Vacher, the secretary of the Dauphin. I told him I wished to return to England to superintend my work there, and he promised I should have the decision to-morrow (hated word!) or the next day. I thought him kind and complaisant. He gave the signal for my departure by bowing, and I lifted my book, as if made of feathers, and passed out with swiftness and alacrity. I ordered the cab at once to the Tuileries, and after some trouble found the Cabinet of the Baron de Vacher; there, Lucy, I really waited like a Blue Heron

[1] **Count Joseph Jérôme Siméon, French Minister of State. 1781–1846.**

on the edge of a deep lake, the bottom of which the bird cannot find, nor even know whether it may turn out to be good fishing. Many had their turns before me, but I had my interview. The Baron, a fine young man about twenty-eight, promised me to do all he could, but that his master was allowed so much (how much I do not know), and his expenses swallowed all.

October 14. Accompanied Parker while he was painting Redouté's portrait, and during the outlining of that fine head I was looking over the original drawings of the great man; never have I seen drawings more beautifully wrought up, and so true to nature. The washy, slack, imperfect messes of the British artists are *nothing* in comparison. I remained here three hours, which I enjoyed much.

October 15. Not a word from the minister, and the time goes faster than I like, I assure thee. Could the minister know how painful it is for an individual like me to wait nearly a month for a decision that might just as well have been concluded in one minute, I am sure things would be different.

October 18. I have seen two ministers this day, but from both had only promises. But this day has considerably altered my ideas of ministers. I have had a fair opportunity of seeing how much trouble they have, and how necessary it is to be patient with them. I arrived at Baron de la Brouillerie's at half-past eleven. A soldier took my portfolio, that weighs nearly a hundred pounds, and showed me the entrance to a magnificent antechamber. Four gentlemen and a lady were there, and after they had been admitted and dismissed, my name was called. The Baron is about sixty years old; tall, thin, not handsome, red in the face, and stiff in his manners. I opened my book, of which he said he had read much in the papers, and asked me why I had not applied to him before. I told him I had written some weeks ago. This he had forgot, but now remembered, somewhat to his embarrassment. He examined every sheet very closely, said he would speak to the King, and I must send him a written and exact memorandum of everything. He expressed surprise the Duc d'Orléans had taken only one copy. I walked from here to Vicomte Siméon. It was his audience day, and in the antechamber twenty-six were already waiting. My seat was close to the door of his cabinet, and I could not help hearing some words during my penance, which lasted one hour and a half. The Vicomte received every one with the same words, "Monsieur (or Madame), j'ai l'honneur de vous saluer;" and when each retired, "Monsieur, je suis votre très humble serviteur." Conceive, my Lucy, the situation of this unfortunate being, in his cabinet since eleven, repeating these sentences to upwards of one hundred persons, answering questions on as many different subjects. What brains he must have, and — how long can he keep them? As soon as I entered he said: "Your business is being attended to, and I give you *my word* you shall have your answer on Tuesday. Have you seen Barons Vacher and La Brouillerie?" I told him I had, and he wished me success as I retired.

October 19. About twelve walked to the plains d'Issy to see the review of the troops by the King in person. It is about eight miles from that portion of Paris where I was, and I walked it with extreme swiftness, say five and a half miles per hour. The plain is on the south bank of the Seine, and almost level. Some thousands of soldiers were already ranged in long lines, handsomely dressed, and armed as if about to be in action. I made for the top of a high wall, which I reached at the risk of breaking my neck, and there, like an Eagle on a rock, I surveyed all around me. The carriage of the Duc d'Orléans came first at full gallop, all the men in crimson liveries, and the music struck up like the thunder of war. Then the

King, all his men in white liveries, came driving at full speed, and followed by other grandees. The King and these gentry descended from their carriages and mounted fine horses, which were in readiness for them; they were immediately surrounded by a brilliant staff, and the review began, the Duchesses d'Orléans and de Berry having now arrived in open carriages; from my perch I saw all. The Swiss troops began, and the manœuvres were finely gone through; three times I was within twenty-five yards of the King and his staff, and, as a Kentuckian would say, "could have closed his eye with a rifle bullet." He is a man of small stature, pale, not at all handsome, and rode so bent over his horse that his appearance was neither kingly nor prepossessing. He wore a three-cornered hat, trimmed with white feathers, and had a broad blue sash from the left shoulder under his right arm. The Duc d'Orléans looked uncommonly well in a hussar uniform, and is a fine rider; he sat his horse like a Turk. The staff was too gaudy; I like not so much gold and silver. None of the ladies were connections of Venus, except most distantly; few Frenchwomen are handsome. The review over, the King and his train rode off. I saw a lady in a carriage point at me on the wall; she doubtless took me for a large black Crow. The music was uncommonly fine, especially that by the band belonging to the Cuirassiers, which was largely composed of trumpets of various kinds, and aroused my warlike feelings. The King and staff being now posted at some little distance, a new movement began, the cannon roared, the horses galloped madly, the men were enveloped in clouds of dust and smoke; this was a sham battle. No place of retreat was here, no cover of dark woods, no deep swamp; there would have been no escape here. This was no battle of New Orleans, nor Tippecanoe. I came down from my perch, leaving behind me about thirty thousand idlers like myself, and the soldiers, who must have been hot and dusty enough.

October 20. Nothing to do, and tired of sight-seeing. Four subscriptions in seven weeks. Slow work indeed. I took a long walk, and watched the Stock Pigeons or Cushats in the trees of Le Jardin des Tuileries, where they roost in considerable numbers, arriving about sunset. They settle at first on the highest trees, and driest, naked branches, then gradually lower themselves, approach the trunks of the trees, and thickest parts, remain for the night, leave at day-break, and fly northerly. Blackbirds do the same, and are always extremely noisy before dark; a few Rooks are seen, and two or three Magpies. In the Jardin, and in the walks of the Palais-Royal, the common Sparrow is prodigiously plenty, very tame, fed by ladies and children, killed or missed with blow-guns by mischievous boys. The Mountain Finch passes in scattered numbers over Paris at this season, going northerly, and is caught in nets. Now, my love, wouldst thou not believe me once more in the woods, hard at it? Alas! I wish I was; what precious time I am wasting in Europe.

October 21. Redouté told me the young Duchesse d'Orléans had subscribed, and I would receive a letter to that effect. Cuvier sent me one hundred printed copies of his *Procès verbal.*

October 22. The second day of promise is over, and not a word from either of the ministers. Now, do those good gentlemen expect me to remain in Paris all my life? They are mistaken. Saturday I pack; on Tuesday morning farewell to Paris. Redouté sent me three volumes of his beautiful roses, which thou wilt so enjoy, and a compliment which is beyond all truth, so I will not repeat it.

October 26. I received a letter from Baron de la Brouillerie announcing that the King had subscribed to my work for his private library. I was visited by the secretary of the Duc d'Orléans, who sat with me some time, a clever and entertaining man with whom I felt quite at ease. He told me that I might now expect the subscriptions of most of the royal family, because none of them liked to be outdone or surpassed by any of the others.[1] Good God! what a spirit is this; what a world we live in! I also received a M. Pitois, who came to look at my book, with a view to becoming my agent here; Baron Cuvier recommended him strongly, and I have concluded a bargain with him. He thinks he can procure a good number of names. His manners are plain, and I hope he will prove an honest man. He had hardly gone, when I received a letter from M. Siméon, telling me the Minister of the Interior would take six copies for various French towns and universities, and he regretted it was not twelve. So did I, but I am well contented. I have now thirteen subscribers in Paris; I have been here two months, and have expended forty pounds. My adieux will now be made, and I shall be *en route* for London before long.

London, November 4. I travelled from Paris to Boulogne with two nuns, that might as well be struck off the calendar of animated beings. They stirred not, they spoke not, they saw not; they replied neither by word nor gesture to the few remarks I made. In the woods of America I have never been in such silence; for in the most retired places I have had the gentle murmuring streamlet, or the sound of the Woodpecker tapping, or the sweet melodious strains of that lovely recluse, my greatest favorite, the Wood Thrush. The great poverty of the country struck me everywhere; the peasantry are beggarly and ignorant, few know the name of the *Département* in which they live; their hovels are dirty and uncomfortable, and appear wretched indeed after Paris. In Paris alone can the refinements of society, education, and the fine arts be found. To Paris, or to the large cities, the country gentleman must go, or have nothing; how unlike the beautiful country homes of the English. I doubt not

[1] The words of the secretary were fully verified within a few months.

the "New Monthly" would cry out: "Here is Audubon again, in all his extravagance." This may be true, but I write as I think I see, and that is enough to render me contented with my words. The passage from Calais was short, and I was free from my usual seasickness, and London was soon reached, where I have been busy with many letters, many friends, and my work. I have presented a copy of my birds to the Linnæan Society, and sold a little picture for ten guineas. And now I must to work on the pictures that have been ordered in France.

November 7. To-day is of some account, as Mr. Havell has taken the drawings that are to form the eleventh number of my work. It will be the first number for the year 1829. I have as yet had no answer from the Linnæan Society, but thou knowest how impatient my poor nature always is.

November 10. I have been painting as much as the short days will allow, but it is very hard for me to do so, as my Southern constitution suffers so keenly from the cold that I am freezing on the side farthest from the fire at this very instant. I have finished the two pictures for the Duc d'Orléans; that of the Grouse I regret much to part with, without a copy; however, I may at some future time group another still more naturally.

November 15. We have had such dismal fog in this London that I could scarcely see to write at twelve o'clock; however, I did write nearly all day. It has been extremely cold besides, and in the streets in the middle of the day I saw men carrying torches, so dark it was.

November 17. I anticipated this day sending all my copies for Paris, but am sadly disappointed. One of the colorers employed brought a number so shamefully done that I would not think of forwarding it. It has gone to be washed, hot pressed, and done over again. Depend upon it, my work will not fail for the want of my own very particular attention.

December 23. After so long neglecting thee, my dear book, it would be difficult to enter a connected account of my time, but I will trace the prominent parts of the lapse. Painting every day, and I may well add constantly, has been the main occupation. I have (what I call) finished my two large pictures of the Eagle and the Lamb, and the Dog and the Pheasants, and now, as usual, can scarce bear to look at either. My friends the Swainsons have often been to see me, and good Bentley came and lived with me for a month as a brother would. I parted from him yesterday with pain and regret. Several artists have called upon me, and have given me *false praises,* as I have heard afterwards, and I hope they will keep aloof. It is charity to speak the truth to a man who knows the poverty of his talents and wishes to improve; it is villanous to mislead him, by praising him to his face, and laughing at his work as they go down the stairs of his house. I have, however, applied to one whom I *know* to be candid, and who has promised to see them, and to give his opinion with truth and simplicity; this is no other, my Lucy, than the president of the Royal Academy, Sir Thomas Lawrence. The steady work and want of exercise has reduced me almost to a skeleton; I have not allowed myself the time even to go to the Zoölogical Gardens.

December 26. I dined yesterday (another Christmas day away from my dear country) at a Mr. Goddard's; our company was formed of Americans, principally sea-captains. During my absence Sir Thomas Lawrence came to see my paintings, which were shown to him by Mr. Havell, who reported as follows. On seeing the Eagle and Lamb he said, "That is a fine picture." He examined it closely, and was shown that of the Pheasants, which I call "*Sauve qui peut.*" He approached it, looked at it sideways, up and down, and put his face close to the canvas, had it moved from one situation to two others in different lights, but gave no opinion. The Otter came next, and he said that the "animal" was very fine, and told Havell he would come again to see them in a few days. I paid him my respects the next morning, and thought him kinder than usual. He said he would certainly come to make a choice for me of one to be exhibited at Somerset House, and would speak to the Council about it.

. . . .

The remaining three months before Audubon sailed for America, April 1, 1829, were passed in preparations for his absence from his book, and many pages of his fine, close writing are filled with memoranda for Mr. Havell, Mr. J. G. Children, and Mr. Pitois. Audubon writes: "I have made up my mind to go to America, and with much labor and some trouble have made ready. My business is as well arranged for as possible; I have given the agency of my work to my excellent friend Children, of the British Museum, who kindly offered to see to it during my absence. I have collected some money, paid all my debts, and taken my passage in the packet-ship 'Columbia,' Captain Delano. I chose the ship on account of her name, and paid thirty-pounds for my passage. I am about to leave this smoky city for Portsmouth, and shall sail on April 1." The voyage was uneventful, and America was reached on May 1. Almost immediately began the search for new birds, and those not delineated already, for the continuation and completion of the "Birds of America."

EAGLE AND LAMB.

PAINTED BY AUDUBON, LONDON, 1828. IN THE POSSESSION OF THE FAMILY.

THE LABRADOR JOURNAL

1833

INTRODUCTION

THE Labrador trip, long contemplated, was made with the usual object, that of procuring birds and making the drawings of them for the continuation of the "Birds of America," the publication of which was being carried on by the Havells, under the supervision of Victor, the elder son, who was in London at this time. To him Audubon writes from Eastport, Maine, under date of May 31, 1833: —

"We are on the eve of our departure for the coast of Labrador. Our party consists of young Dr. George Shattuck of Boston, Thomas Lincoln of Dennysville, William Ingalls, son of Dr. Ingalls of Boston, Joseph Coolidge, John, and myself. I have chartered a schooner called the 'Ripley,' commanded by Captain Emery, who was at school with my friend Lincoln; he is reputed to be a gentleman, as well as a good sailor. Coolidge, too, has been bred to the sea, and is a fine, active youth of twenty-one. The schooner is a new vessel, only a year old, of 106 tons, for which we pay three hundred and fifty dollars per month for the entire use of the vessel with the men, but we supply ourselves with provisions.[1] The hold of the vessel has been floored, and our great table solidly fixed in a tolerably good light under the main hatch; it is my intention to draw whenever possible, and that will be many hours, for the daylight is with us nearly all the time in those latitudes, and the fishermen say you can do with little sleep, the air is so pure. I have been working hard at the birds from the Grand Menan, as well as John, who is overcoming his habit of sleeping late, as I call him every morning at four, and we have famous long days. We are well provided as to clothes, and strange figures indeed do we cut in our dresses, I promise you: fishermen's boots, the soles of which are all nailed to enable us to keep our footing on the sea-weeds, trousers of *fearnought* so coarse that our legs look like bears' legs, oiled jackets and over-trousers for rainy weather, and round, white, wool hats with a piece of oil cloth dangling on our shoulders to prevent the rain from running down our necks. A coarse bag is strapped on the back to carry provisions on inland journeys, with our guns and hunting-knives; you can form an idea of us from this. Edward Harris is not to be with us; this I regret more than I can say. This day seven vessels sailed for the fishing-grounds, some of them not more than thirty tons' burden, for these hardy fishermen

[1] These terms were not, however, held to by the owners of the vessel, and the provisioning was left also to them, the whole outlay being about $1500 for the entire trip.

care not in what they go; but *I do*, and, indeed, such a boat would be too small for us."

The 1st of June was the day appointed for the start, but various delays occurred which retarded this until the 6th, when the journal which follows tells its own tale.

Of all the members of the party Mr. Joseph Coolidge, now (1897) living in San Francisco, is the sole survivor.

M. R. A.

AUDUBON.

From the portrait by George P. A. Healy, London, 1838. Now in the possession of the Boston Society of Natural History.

THE LABRADOR JOURNAL

1833

Eastport, Maine, June 4. Our vessel is being prepared for our reception and departure, and we have concluded to hire two extra sailors and a lad; the latter to be a kind of major-domo, to clean our guns, etc., search for nests, and assist in skinning birds. Whilst rambling in the woods this morning, I found a Crow's nest, with five young, yet small. As I ascended the tree, the parents came to their offspring crying loudly, and with such perseverance that in less than fifteen minutes upwards of fifty pairs of these birds had joined in their vociferations; yet when first the parents began to cry I would have supposed them the only pair in the neighborhood.

Wednesday, June 5. This afternoon, when I had concluded that everything relating to the charter of the "Ripley" was arranged, some difficulty arose between myself and Mr. Buck, which nearly put a stop to our having his vessel. Pressed, however, as I was, by the lateness of the season, I gave way and suffered myself to be imposed upon as usual, with a full knowledge that I was so. The charter was signed, and we hoped to have sailed, but to-morrow is now the day appointed. Our promised Hampton boat is not come.

Thursday, June 6. We left the wharf of Eastport about one o'clock P. M. Every one of the male population came to see the show, just as if no schooner the size of the

"Ripley" had ever gone from this mighty port to Labrador. Our numerous friends came with the throng, and we all shook hands as if never to meet again. The batteries of the garrison, and the cannon of the revenue cutter, saluted us, each firing four loud, oft-echoing reports. Captain Coolidge accompanied us, and indeed was our pilot, until we had passed Lubec. The wind was light and ahead, and yet with the assistance of the tide we drifted twenty-five miles, down to Little River, during the night, and on rising on the morning of June 7 we were at anchor near some ugly rocks, the sight of which was not pleasing to our good captain.

June 7. The whole morning was spent trying to enter Little River, but in vain; the men were unable to tow us in. We landed for a few minutes, and shot a Hermit Thrush, but the appearance of a breeze brought us back, and we attempted to put to sea. Our position now became rather dangerous, as we were drawn by the current nearly upon the rocks; but the wind rose at last, and we cleared for sea. At three o'clock it became suddenly so foggy that we could not see the bowsprit. The night was spent in direful apprehensions of ill luck; at midnight a smart squall decided in our favor, and when day broke on the morning of June 8 the wind was from the northeast, blowing fresh, and we were dancing on the waters, all shockingly sea-sick, crossing that worst of all dreadful bays, the Bay of Fundy. We passed between the Seal Islands and the Mud Islands; in the latter *Procellaria wilsonii*, the Stormy Petrel, breeds abundantly; their nests are dug out of the sand in an oblique direction to the depth of two, or two and a half feet. At the bottom of these holes, and on the sand, the birds deposit their pure white eggs. The holes are perforated, not in the banks like the Bank Swallow, but are like rat holes over the whole of the islands. On Seal Islands *Larus argentatus*, the Herring Gull, breeds as abundantly as on Grand Menan, but altogether *on trees*. As we passed Cape Sable, so called on account of its being truly a sand-point of some caved-in elevation, we saw a wrecked ship with many small crafts about it. I saw there *Uria troile*, the Foolish Guillemot, and some Gannets. The sea was dreadful, and scarcely one of us was able to eat or drink this day. We came up with the schooner "Caledonia," from Boston for Labrador; her captain wished to keep in our company, and we were pretty much together all night and also on Sunday.

June 9. We now had a splendid breeze, but a horrid sea, and were scarce able to keep our feet, or sleep. The "Caledonia" was very near to us for some time, but when the breeze increased to a gale, and both vessels had to reef, we showed ourselves superior in point of sailing. So good was our run that on the next morning, June 10, we found ourselves not more than thirty miles from Cape Canseau, ordinarily called Cape Cancer. The wind was so fair for proceeding directly to Labrador that our captain spoke of doing so, provided it suited my views; but, anxious as I am not to suffer any opportunity to escape of doing all I can to fulfil my engagements, I desired that we should pass through what is called "The Gut of Canseau," and we came into the harbor of that name[1] at three of the afternoon. Here we found twenty vessels, all bound to Labrador, and, of course, all fishermen. We had been in view of the southeastern coast of Nova Scotia all day, a dreary, poor, and inhospitable-looking country. As we dropped our anchor we had a snowfall, and the sky had an appearance such as I never before recollect having seen. Going on shore we found not a tree in blossom, though the low plants near the ground were all in bloom; I saw azaleas, white and blue violets, etc., and in some situations the grass really looked well. The Robins were in full song; one nest of that bird was found; the White-

1 Now commonly spelled Canso — not Canseau.

throated Sparrow and Savannah Finch were also in full song. The *Fringilla nivalis*[1] was seen, and we were told that *Tetrao canadensis*[2] was very abundant, but saw none. About a dozen houses form this settlement; there was no Custom House officer, and not an individual who could give an answer of any value to our many questions. We returned on board and supped on a fine codfish. The remainder of our day was spent in catching lobsters, of which we procured forty. They were secured simply by striking them in shallow water with a gaff-hook. It snowed and rained at intervals, and to my surprise we did not observe a single seabird.

June 11. *Larus marinus* (the Great Black-backed Gull) is so superior both in strength and courage to Fulmars, *Lestris*, or even Gannets, to say nothing of Gulls of all sorts, that at its approach they all give way, and until it has quite satiated itself, none venture to approach the precious morsel on which it is feeding. In this respect, it is as the Eagle to the Vultures or Carrion Crows. I omitted saying that last night, before we retired to rest, after much cold, snow, rain, and hail, the frogs were piping in all the pools on the shore, and we all could hear them clearly, from the deck of the "Ripley." The weather to-day is beautiful, the wind fair, and when I reached the deck at four A. M. we were under way in the wake of the whole of the fleet which last evening graced the Harbor of Canseau, but which now gave life to the grand bay across which all were gliding under easy pressure of sail. The land locked us in, the water was smooth, the sky pure, and the thermometer was only 46°, quite cold; indeed, it was more grateful to see the sunshine whilst on deck this morning, and to feel its warmth, than I can recollect before at this season. After sailing for twenty-one miles, and passing one after another every vessel of the fleet, we entered the

[1] *Plectrophenax nivalis*, the Snow Bunting. — E. C.

[2] *Canachites canadensis*, the Canada Grouse. —E. C.

Gut of Canseau, so named by the Spanish on account of the innumerable Wild Geese which, in years long past and forgotten, resorted to this famed passage. The land rises on each side in the form of an amphitheatre, and on the Nova Scotia side, to a considerable height. Many *appearances* of dwellings exist, but the country is too poor for comfort; the timber is small, and the land, very stony. Here and there a small patch of ploughed land, planted, or to be planted, with potatoes, was all we could see evincing cultivation. Near one house we saw a few apple-trees, yet without leaves. The general appearance of this passage reminded me of some parts of the Hudson River, and accompanied as we were by thirty smaller vessels, the time passed agreeably. Vegetation about as forward as at Eastport; saw a Chimney Swallow, heard some Blue Jays, saw some Indians in a bark canoe, passed Cape Porcupine, a high, rounding hill, and Cape George, after which we entered the Gulf of St. Lawrence. From this place, on the 20th of May last year, the sea was a complete sheet of ice as far as a spy-glass could inform. As we advanced, running parallel with the western coast of Cape Breton Island, the country looked well, at the distance we were from it; the large, undulating hills were scattered with many hamlets, and here and there a bit of cultivated land was seen. It being calm when we reached Jestico Island, distant from Cape Breton about three miles, we left the vessel and made for it. On landing we found it covered with well grown grass sprinkled everywhere with the blossoms of the wild strawberry; the sun shone bright, and the weather was quite pleasant. Robins, Savannah Finches, Song Sparrows, Tawny Thrushes, and the American Redstart were found. The Spotted Sand-piper, *Totanus macularius*, was breeding in the grass, and flew slowly with the common tremor of their wings, uttering their "wheet-wheet-wheet" note, to invite me to follow them. A Raven had a nest and three young in it, one standing near it, the old birds not seen. *Uria troile*[1] and *U. grylle*[2] were breeding in the rocks, and John saw several *Ardea herodias*[3] flying in pairs, also a pair of Red-breasted Mergansers that had glutted themselves with fish so that they were obliged to disgorge before they could fly off. Amongst the plants the wild gooseberry, nearly the size of a green pea, was plentiful, and the black currant, I think of a different species from the one found in Maine. The wind rose and we returned on board. John and the sailors almost killed a Seal with their oars.

June 12. At four this morning we were in sight of the Magdalene Islands, or, as they are called on the chart, Amherst Islands; they appeared to be distant about twenty miles. The weather was dull and quite calm, and I thought the prospect of reaching these isles this day very doubtful, and returned to my berth sadly disappointed. After breakfast a thick fog covered the horizon on our bow, the islands disappeared from sight, and the wind rose sluggishly, and dead ahead. Several brigs and ships loaded with lumber out from Miramichi came near us, beating their way towards the Atlantic. We are still in a great degree landlocked by Cape Breton Island, the highlands of which look dreary and forbidding; it is now nine A. M., and we are at anchor in four fathoms of water, and within a quarter of a mile of an island, one of the general group; for our pilot, who has been here for ten successive years, informs us that all these islands are connected by dry sand-bars, without any other ship channel between them than the one which we have taken, and which is called Entrée Bay, formed by Entrée Island and a long, sandy, projecting reef connected with the main island. This latter measures forty-eight miles in length, by an average of about three in breadth; Entrée Island contains about fifteen hundred acres of land, such as it is, of a red, rough, sandy formation, the northwest side constantly falling into the sea, and ex-

[1] Foolish Guillemot. [2] Black Guillemot. [3] Great Blue Heron.

hibiting a very interesting sight. Guillemots were seen seated upright along the projecting shelvings in regular order, resembling so many sentinels on the look-out. Many Gannets also were seen about the extreme point of this island. On Amherst Island we saw many houses, a small church, and on the highest land a large cross, indicating the Catholic tendency of the inhabitants. Several small schooners lay in the little harbor called Pleasant Bay, and we intend to pay them an early visit to-morrow. The wind is so cold that it feels to us all like the middle of December at Boston.

Magdalene Islands, June 13. This day week we were at Eastport, and I am sure not one of our party thought of being here this day. At four this morning we were seated at breakfast around our great drawing-table; the thermometer was at 44°; we blew our fingers and drank our coffee, feeling as if in the very heart of winter, and when we landed I felt so chilled that it would have been quite out of the question to use my hands for any delicate work. We landed between two great bluffs, that looked down upon us with apparent anger, the resort of many a Black Guillemot and noble Raven, and following a tortuous path, suddenly came plump upon one of God's best finished jewels, a woman. She saw us first, for women are always keenest in sight and sympathy, in perseverance and patience, in fortitude, and love, and sorrow, and faith, and, for aught I know, much more. At the instant that my eyes espied her, she was in full run towards her cottage, holding to her bosom a fine babe, simply covered with a very short shirt, the very appearance of which set me shivering. The woman was dressed in coarse French homespun, a close white cotton cap which entirely surrounded her face tied under her chin, and I thought her the wildest-looking woman, both in form and face, I had seen for many a day. At a venture, I addressed her in French, and it answered well, for she responded in a wonderful jargon, about one third of which I understood, and abandoned the rest to a better linguist, should one ever come to the island. She was a plain, good woman, I doubt not, and the wife of an industrious fisherman. We walked through the woods, and followed the *road* to the church. Who would have thought that on these wild islands, among these impoverished people, we should have found a church; that we should have been suddenly confronted with a handsome, youthful, vigorous, black-haired, black-bearded fellow, in a soutane as black as the Raven's wedding-dress, and with a heart as light as a bird on the wing? Yet we met with both church and priest, and our ears were saluted by the sound of a bell which measures one foot by nine and a half inches in diameter, and weighs thirty pounds; and this bell may be heard a full quarter of a mile. It is a festival day, *La Petite Fête de Dieu.* The chapel was illuminated at six o'clock, and the inhabitants, even from a distance, passed in; among them were many old women, who, staff in hand, had trudged along the country road. Their backs were bent by age and toil, their eyes dimmed by time; they crossed their hands upon their breasts, and knelt before the sacred images in the church with so much simplicity and apparent truth of heart that I could not help exclaiming, "This is indeed religion!" The priest, Père Brunet, is originally from Quebec. These islands belong, or are attached, to Lower Canada; he, however, is under the orders of the Bishop of Halifax. He is a shrewd-looking fellow, and, if I mistake not, has a dash of the devil in him. He told me there were no reptiles on the island, but this was an error; for, while rambling about, Tom Lincoln, Ingalls, and John saw a snake, and I heard Frogs a-piping. He also told me that Black and Red Foxes, and the changeable Hare, with Rats lately imported, were the only quadrupeds to be found, except cows, horses, and mules, of which some had been brought over many years ago, and which had multiplied, but to no great extent. The land, he assured us, was poor in every respect, — soil, woods, game; that the Seal fisheries had been less productive these last years than formerly. On these islands, about a dozen in number, live one hundred and sixty families, all of whom make their livelihood by the Cod, Herring, and Mackerel fisheries. One or two vessels from Quebec come yearly to collect this produce of the ocean. Not a bird to be found larger than a Robin, but certainly thousands of those. Père Brunet said he lived the life of a recluse, and invited us to accompany him to the house where he boarded, and take a glass of good French wine. During our ramble on the island we found the temperature quite agreeable; indeed, in some situations the sun was pleasant and warm. Strawberry blossoms were under our feet at every step, and here and there the grass looked well. I was surprised to find the woods (by woods I mean land covered with any sort of trees, from the noblest magnolia down to dwarf cedars) rich in Warblers, Thrushes, Finches, Buntings, etc. The Fox-tailed Sparrow breeds here, the Siskin also. The Hermit and Tawny Thrushes crossed our path every few yards, the Black-capped Warbler flashed over the pools, the Winter Wren abounded everywhere. Among the water-birds we found the Great Tern (*Sterna hirundo*) very abundant, and shot four of them on the sand-ridges. The Piping Plover breeds here — shot two males and one female; so plaintive is the note of this interesting species that I feel great aversion to killing them. These birds certainly are the swiftest of foot of any water-birds which I know, of their size. We found many land-snails, and collected some fine specimens of gypsum. This afternoon, being informed that across the bay where we are anchored we might, perhaps, purchase some Black Fox skins, we went there, and found Messieurs Muncey keen fellows; they asked £5 for Black Fox and $1.50 for Red. No purchase on our part. Being told that Geese, Brents, Mergansers, etc., breed eighteen miles from here, at the eastern extremity of these islands, we go off there to-morrow in boats. Saw Bank Swallows and House Swallows. The woods altogether small evergreens, extremely scrubby, almost impenetrable, and swampy beneath. At seven this evening the thermometer is at 52°. This morning it was 44°. After our return to the "Ripley," our captain, John, Tom Lincoln, and Coolidge went off to the cliffs opposite our anchorage, in search of Black Guillemots' eggs. This was found to be quite an undertaking; these birds, instead of having to *jump* or *hop* from one place to another on the rocks, to find a spot suitable to deposit their spotted egg, as has been stated, are on the contrary excellent walkers, at least upon the rocks, and they can fly from the water to the very entrance of the holes in the fissures, where the egg is laid. Sometimes this egg is deposited not more than eight or ten feet above high-water mark, at other times the fissure in the rock which has been chosen stands at an elevation of a hundred feet or more. The egg is laid on the bare rock without any preparation, but when the formation is sandy, a certain scoop is indicated on the surface. In one instance, I found two feathers with the egg; this egg is about the size of a hen's, and looks extravagantly large, splashed with black or deep umber, apparently at random, the markings larger and more frequent towards the great end. At the barking of a dog from any place where these birds breed, they immediately fly towards the animal, and will pass within a few feet of the observer, as if in defiance. At other times they leave the nest and fall in the water, diving to an extraordinary distance before they rise again. John shot a Gannet on the wing; the flesh was black and unpleasant. The Piping Plover, when missed by the shot, rises almost perpendicularly, and passes sometimes out of sight; this is, I am convinced by the many opportunities I have had to witness the occurrence, a habit of the species. These islands are well watered by large springs, and rivulets intersect the country in many directions. We saw large flocks of Velvet Ducks feeding close to the shores; these did not appear to be in pairs. The Gannet dives quite under the water after its prey, and when empty of food rises easily off the water.

June 14, off the Gannett Rocks. We rose at two o'clock with a view to proceed to the eastern extremity of these islands in search of certain ponds, wherein, so we were told, Wild Geese and Ducks of different kinds are in the habit of resorting annually to breed. Our informer added that formerly Brents bred there in abundance, but that since the erection of several buildings owned by Nova Scotians, and in the immediate vicinity of these ponds or lakes, the birds have become gradually very shy, and most of them now proceed farther north. Some of these lakes are several miles in circumference, with shallow, sandy bottoms; most of them are fresh water, the shores thickly overgrown with rank sedges and grasses, and on the surface are many water-lilies. It is among these that the wild fowl, when hid from the sight of man, deposit their eggs. Our way to these ponds would have been through a long and narrow bay, formed by what seamen call sea-walls. In this place these walls are entirely of light-colored sand, and form connecting points from one island to another, thus uniting nearly the whole archipelago. Our journey was abandoned just as we were about to start, in consequence of the wind changing, and being fair for our passage to Labrador, the ultimatum of our desires. Our anchor was raised, and we bid adieu to the Magdalenes. Our pilot, a Mr. Godwin from Nova Scotia, put the vessel towards what he called "The Bird Rocks," where he told us that Gannets (*Sula bassana*) bred in great numbers. For several days past we have met with an increased number of Gannets, and as we sailed this morning we observed long and numerous files, all flying in the direction of the rocks. Their flight now was low above the water, forming easy undulations, flapping thirty or forty times, and sailing about the same distance; these were all returning from fishing, and were gorged with food for their mates or young. About ten a speck rose on the horizon, which I was told was the Rock; we sailed well, the breeze increased fast, and we neared this object apace. At eleven I could distinguish its top plainly from the deck, and thought it covered with snow to the depth of several feet; this appearance existed on every portion of the flat, projecting shelves. Godwin said, with the coolness of a man who had visited this Rock for ten successive seasons, that what we saw was not snow — but Gannets! I rubbed my eyes, took my spy-glass, and in an instant the strangest picture stood before me. They were birds we saw, — a mass of birds of such a size as I never before cast my eyes on. The whole of my party stood astounded and amazed, and all came to the conclusion that such a sight was of itself sufficient to invite any one to come across the Gulf to view it at this season. The nearer we approached, the greater our surprise at the enormous number of these birds, all calmly seated on their eggs or newly hatched brood, their heads all turned to windward, and towards us. The air above for a hundred yards, and for some distance around the whole rock, was filled with Gannets on the wing, which from our position made it appear as if a heavy fall of snow was directly above us. Our pilot told us the wind was too high to permit us to land, and I felt sadly grieved at this unwelcome news. Anxious as we all were, we decided to make the attempt; our whale-boat was overboard, the pilot, two sailors, Tom Lincoln, and John pushed off with guns and clubs. Our vessel was brought to, but at that instant the wind increased, and heavy rain began to fall. Our boat neared the rock, and went to the lee of it, and was absent nearly an hour, but could not land. The air was filled with Gannets, but no difference could we perceive on the surface of the rock. The birds, which we now could distinctly see, sat almost touching each other and in regular lines, seated on their nests quite unconcerned. The discharge of the guns had no effect on those that were not touched by the shot, for the noise of the Gulls, Guillemots, etc., deadened the sound of the gun; but where the shot took effect, the birds scrambled and flew off in such multitudes, and in such confusion, that whilst some eight or ten were falling into the water either dead or wounded, others pushed off their eggs, and these fell into the sea by hundreds in all directions. The sea now becoming very rough, the boat was obliged to return, with some birds and some eggs; but the crew had not climbed the rock, a great disappointment to me. Godwin tells me the top of the rock is about a quarter of a mile wide, north and south, and a little narrower east and west; its elevation above the sea between three and four hundred feet. The sea beats round it with great violence, except after long calms, and it is extremely difficult to land upon it, and much more so to climb to the top of it, which is a platform; it is only on the southeast shore that a landing can be made, and the moment a boat touches, it must be hauled up on the rocks. The whole surface is perfectly covered with nests, placed about two feet apart, in such regular order that you may look through the lines as you would look through those of a planted patch of sweet potatoes or cabbages. The fishermen who kill these birds, to get their flesh for codfish bait, ascend in parties of six or eight, armed with clubs; sometimes, indeed, the party comprises the crews of several vessels. As they reach the top, the birds, alarmed, rise with a noise like thunder, and fly off in such hurried, fearful confusion as to throw each other down, often falling on each other till there is a bank of them many feet high. The men strike them down and kill them until fatigued or satisfied. Five hundred and forty have been thus murdered in one hour by six men. The birds are skinned with little care, and the flesh cut off in chunks; it will keep fresh about a fortnight. The nests are made by scratching down a few inches, and the edges surrounded with sea-weeds. The eggs are pure white, and as large as those of a Goose. By the 20th of May the rock is already covered with birds and eggs; about the 20th of June they begin to hatch. So great is the destruction of these birds annually that their flesh supplies the bait for upwards of forty fishing-boats, which lie close to the Byron Island each season. When the young are hatched they are black, and for a fortnight or more the skin looks like that of the dog-fish. They become gradually downy and white, and when two months old look much like young lambs. Even while shooting at these birds, hundreds passed us carrying great masses of weeds to their nests. The birds were thick above our heads, and I shot at one to judge of the effect of the report of the gun; it had none. A great number of Kittiwake Gulls breed on this rock, with thousands of Foolish Guillemots. The Kittiwake makes its nest of eel-weeds, several inches in thickness, and in places too small for a Gannet or a Guillemot to place itself; in some instances these nests projected some inches over the edge of the rock. We could not see any of their eggs. The breeze was now so stiff that the waves ran high; so much so that the boat was perched on the comb of the wave one minute, the next in the trough. John steered, and he told me afterwards he was nearly exhausted. The boat was very cleverly hauled on deck by a single effort. The stench from the rock is insufferable, as it is covered with the remains of putrid fish, rotten eggs, and dead birds, old and young. No man who has not seen what we have this day can form the least idea of the impression the sight made on our minds. By dark it blew a gale and we are now most of us rather shaky; rain is falling in torrents, and the sailors are reefing. I forgot to say that when a man walks towards the Gannets, they will now and then stand still, merely opening and shutting their bills; the Gulls remained on their nests with more confidence than the Guillemots, all of which flew as we approached. The feathering of the Gannet is curious, differing from that of most other birds, inasmuch as each feather is concave, and divided in its contour from the next. Under the roof of the mouth and attached to the upper mandible, are two fleshy appendages like two small wattles.

June 15. All our party except Coolidge were deadly sick. The thermometer was down to 43°, and every sailor complained of the cold. It has rained almost all day. I felt so very sick this morning that I removed from my berth to a hammock, where I soon felt rather more easy. We lay to all this time, and at daylight were in sight of the Island of Anticosti, distant about twenty miles; but the fog soon after became so thick that nothing could be observed. At about two we saw the sun, the wind hauled dead ahead, and we ran under one sail only.

June 16, Sunday. The weather clear, beautiful, and much warmer; but it was calm, so we fished for cod, of which we caught a good many; most of them contained crabs of a curious sort, and some were filled with shrimps. One cod measured three feet six and a half inches, and weighed twenty-one pounds. Found two curious insects fastened to the skin of a cod, which we saved. At about six o'clock the wind sprang up fair, and we made all sail for Labrador.

June 17. I was on deck at three this morning; the sun, although not above the horizon, indicated to the mariner at the helm one of those doubtful days the result of which seldom can be truly ascertained until sunset. The sea was literally covered with Foolish Guillemots, playing in the very spray of the bow of our vessel, plunging under it, as if in fun, and rising like spirits close under our rudder. The breeze was favorable, although we were hauled to the wind within a point or so. The helmsman said he saw land from aloft, but the captain pronounced his assertion must be a mistake, by true calculation. We breakfasted on the best of fresh codfish, and I never relished a breakfast more. I looked on our landing on the coast of Labrador as a matter of great importance. My thoughts were filled, not with airy castles, but with expectations of the new knowledge of birds and quadrupeds which I hoped to acquire. The "Ripley" ploughed the deep, and proceeded swiftly on her way; she always sails well, but I thought that now as the land was expected to appear every moment, she fairly skipped over the waters. At five o'clock the cry of land rang in our ears, and my heart bounded with joy; so much for anticipation. We sailed on, and in less than an hour the land was in full sight from the deck. We approached, and saw, as we supposed, many sails, and felt delighted at having hit the point in view so very closely; but, after all, the sails proved to be large snow-banks. We proceeded, however, the wind being so very favorable that we could either luff or bear away. The air was now filled with Velvet Ducks; *millions* of these birds were flying from the northwest towards the southeast. The Foolish Guillemots and the *Alca torda*[1] were in immense numbers, flying in long files a few yards above the water, with rather undulating motions, and passing within good gunshot of the vessel, and now and then rounding to us, as if about to alight on the very deck. We now saw a schooner at anchor, and the country looked well at this distance, and as we neared the shore the thermometer, which had been standing at 44°, now rose up to nearly 60°; yet the appearance of the great snow-drifts was forbidding. The shores appeared to be margined with a broad and handsome sand-beach; our imaginations now

[1] Razor-billed Auk.

saw Bears, Wolves, and Devils of all sorts scampering away on the rugged shore. When we reached the schooner we saw beyond some thirty fishing-boats, fishing for cod, and to our great pleasure found Captain Billings of Eastport standing in the bow of his vessel; he bid us welcome, and we saw the codfish thrown on his deck by thousands. We were now opposite to the mouth of the Natasquan River, where the Hudson's Bay Company have a fishing establishment, but where no American vessels are allowed to come in. The shore was lined with bark-covered huts, and some vessels were within the bight, or long point of land which pushes out from the extreme eastern side of the entrance of the river. We went on to an American Harbor, four or five miles distant to the westward, and after a while came to anchor in a small bay, perfectly secure from any winds. And now we are positively on the Labrador coast, latitude 50° and a little more, — farther north than I ever was before. But what a country! When we landed and passed the beach, we sank nearly up to our knees in mosses of various sorts, producing as we moved through them a curious sensation. These mosses, which at a distance look like hard rocks, are, under foot, like a velvet cushion. We scrambled about, and with anxiety stretched our necks and looked over the country far and near, but not a square foot of *earth* could we see. A poor, rugged, miserable country; the trees like so many mops of wiry composition, and where the soil is not rocky it is boggy up to a man's waist. We searched and searched; but, after all, only shot an adult Pigeon-Hawk, a summer-plumage Tell-tale Godwit, and an *Alca torda.* We visited all the islands about the harbor; they were all rocky, nothing but rocks. The *Larus marinus* was sailing magnificently all about us. The Great Tern was plunging after shrimps in every pool, and we found four eggs of the *Totanus macularius;*[1] the nest was situ-

[1] Spotted Sandpiper, now *Actitis macularia.* — E. C.

ated under a rock in the grass, and made of a quantity of dried grass, forming a very decided nest, at least much more so than in our Middle States, where the species breed so very abundantly. Wild Geese were seen by our party, and these birds also breed here; we saw Loons and Eider Ducks, *Anas obscura*[1] and the *Fuligula* [*Œdemia*] *americana.*[2] We came to our anchorage at twenty minutes past twelve. Tom Lincoln and John heard a Ptarmigan. Toads were abundant. We saw some rare plants, which we preserved, and butterflies and small bees were among the flowers which we gathered. We also saw Red-breasted Mergansers. The male and female Eider Ducks separate as soon as the latter begin to lay; after this they are seen flying in large flocks, each sex separately. We found a dead Basking Shark, six and a half feet long; this fish had been wounded by a harpoon and ran ashore, or was washed there by the waves. At Eastport fish of this kind have been killed thirty feet long.

June 18. I remained on board all day, drawing; our boats went off to some islands eight or ten miles distant, after birds and eggs, but the day, although very beautiful, did not prove valuable to us, as some eggers from Halifax had robbed the places ere the boats arrived. We, however, procured about a dozen of *Alca torda, Uria troile*, a female Eider Duck, a male Surf Duck, and a Sandpiper, or *Tringa*, — which, I cannot ascertain, although the *least*[3] I ever saw, not the *Pusilla* of Bonaparte's Synopsis. Many nests of the Eider Duck were seen, some at the edge of the woods, placed under the rampant boughs of the fir-trees, which in this latitude grow only a few inches above the surface of the ground, and to find the nest, these boughs had to be raised. The nests were scooped a few inches deep in the mossy, rotten substance

[1] Dusky Duck. [2] Scoter Duck.

[3] The Least or Wilson's Sandpiper, *Tringa* (*Actodromas*) *minutilla.* — E. C.

that forms here what must be called earth; the eggs are deposited on a bed of down and covered with the same material; and so warm are these nests that, although not a parent bird was seen near them, the eggs were quite warm to the touch, and the chicks in some actually hatching in the absence of the mother. Some of the nests had the eggs uncovered; six eggs was the greatest number found in a nest. The nests found on grassy islands are fashioned in the same manner, and generally placed at the foot of a large tussock of grass. Two female Ducks had about twelve young on the water, and these they protected by flapping about the water in such a way as to raise a spray, whilst the little ones dove off in various directions. Flocks of thirty to forty males were on the wing without a single female among them. The young birds procured were about one week old, of a dark mouse-color, thickly covered with a soft and warm down, and their feet appeared to be more perfect, for their age, than any other portion, because more necessary to secure their safety, and to enable them to procure food. John found many nests of the *Larus marinus*, of which he brought both eggs and young. The nest of this fine bird is made of mosses and grasses, raised on the solid rock, and handsomely formed within; a few feathers are in this lining. Three eggs, large, hard-shelled, with ground color of dirty yellowish, splashed and spotted with dark umber and black. The young, although small, were away from the nest a few feet, placing themselves to the lee of the nearest sheltering rock. They did not attempt to escape, but when taken uttered a cry not unlike that of a young chicken under the same circumstances. The parents were so shy and so wary that none could be shot. At the approach of the boats to the rocks where they breed, a few standing as sentinels gave the alarm, and the whole rose immediately in the air to a great elevation. On another rock, not far distant, a number of Gulls of the same size, white, and with the same hoarse note, were to be seen, but they had no nests; these, I am inclined to think (at present) the bird called *Larus argentatus* (Herring Gull), which is simply the immature bird of *Larus marinus.*[1] I am the more led to believe this because, knowing the tyrannical disposition of the *L. marinus*, I am sure they would not suffer a species almost as powerful as themselves in their immediate neighborhood. They fly altogether, but the white ones do not alight on the rocks where the *Marinus* has its nests. John watched their motion and their cry very closely, and gave me this information. Two eggs of a Tern,[2] resembling the Cayenne Tern, were found in a nest on the rocks, made of moss also, but the birds, although the eggs were nearly ready to hatch, kept out of gunshot. These eggs measured one and a half inches in length, very oval, whitish, spotted and dotted irregularly with brown and black all over. The cry of those Terns which *I* saw this afternoon resembles that of the Cayenne Tern that I met with in the Floridas, and I could see a large orange bill, but could not discern the black feet. Many nests of the Great Tern (*Sterna hirundo*) were found—two eggs in each, laid on the short grass scratched out, but no nest. One *Tringa pusilla* [*minutilla*], the smallest I ever saw, was procured; these small gentry are puzzles indeed; I do not mean to say in nature, but in Charles's[3] Synopsis. We went ashore this afternoon and made a Bear trap with a gun, baited with heads and entrails of codfish, Bruin having been seen within a few hundred yards of where the lure now lies in wait. It is truly interesting to see the activity of the cod-fishermen about us, but I will write of this when I know more of their filthy business.

[1] A mistake, which Audubon later corrected. The Herring Gull is of course quite distinct from the Black-backed. The former is of the variety called by me *Larus argentatus smithsonianus*, as it differs in some respects from the common Herring Gull of Europe.—E. C.

[2] Perhaps Forster's Tern, *Sterna forsteri.*—E. C.

[3] Charles Lucien Bonaparte.

June 19. Drawing as much as the disagreeable motion of the vessel would allow me to do; and although at anchor and in a good harbor, I could scarcely steady my pencil, the wind being high from southwest. At three A. M. I had all the young men up, and they left by four for some islands where the *Larus marinus* breeds. The captain went up the little Natasquan River. When John returned he brought eight *Alca torda* and four of their eggs *identified;* these eggs measure three inches in length, one and seven-eighths in breadth, dirty-white ground, broadly splashed with deep brown and black, more so towards the greater end. This *Alca* feeds on fish of a small size, flies swiftly with a quick beat of the wings, rounding to and fro at the distance of fifty or more yards, exhibiting, as it turns, the pure white of its lower parts, or the jet black of its upper. These birds sit on the nest in an almost upright position; they are shy and wary, diving into the water, or taking flight at the least appearance of danger; if wounded slightly they dive, and we generally lost them, but if unable to do this, they throw themselves on their back and defend themselves fiercely, biting severely whoever attempts to seize them. They run over and about the rocks with ease, and not awkwardly, as some have stated. The flesh of this bird when stewed in a particular manner is good eating, much better than would be expected from birds of its class and species. The *Larus argentatus* breeds on the same islands, and we found many eggs; the nests were all on the rocks, made of moss and grasses, and rather neat inwardly. The Arctic Tern was found breeding abundantly; we took some of their eggs; there were two in each nest, one and a quarter inches long, five-eighths broad, rather sharp at the little end. The ground is light olive, splashed with dark umber irregularly, and more largely at the greater end; these were deposited two or three on the rocks, wherever a little grass grew, no nest of any kind apparent. In habits this bird resembles the *S. hirundo*, and has nearly the same harsh note; it feeds principally on shrimps, which abound in these waters. Five young *L. marinus* were brought alive, small and beautifully spotted yet over the head and back, somewhat like a Leopard; they walked well about the deck, and managed to pick up the food given them; their cry was a "hac, hac, hac, wheet, wheet, wheet." Frequently, when one was about to swallow a piece of flesh, a brother or sister would jump at it, tug, and finally deprive its relative of the morsel in an instant. John assured me that the old birds were too shy to be approached at all. John shot a fine male of the Scoter Duck, which is scarce here. Saw some Wild Geese (*Anser canadensis*), which breed here, though they have not yet formed their nests. The Red-breasted Merganser (*Mergus serrator*) breeds also here, but is extremely shy and wary, flying off as far as they can see us, which to me in this wonderfully wild country is surprising; indeed, thus far all the sea-fowl are much wilder than those of the Floridas. Twenty nests of a species of Cormorant,[1] not yet ascertained, were found on a small detached, rocky island; these were built of sticks, sea-weeds, and grasses, on the naked rock, and about two feet high, as filthy as those of their relations the Floridians.[2] Three eggs were found in one nest, which is the complement, but not a bird could be shot — too shy and vigilant. This afternoon the captain and I walked to the Little Natasquan River, and proceeded up it about four miles to the falls or rapids — a small river, dark, irony waters, sandy shores, and impenetrable woods along these, except here and there is a small space overgrown with short wiry grass unfit for cattle; a thing of little consequence, as no

[1] No doubt the common species, *Phalacrocorax carbo*, as Audubon afterward identified it. See beyond, date of June 30. — E. C.

[2] That is, the species which Audubon named the Florida Cormorant, *Phalacrocorax floridanus*, now known to be a small southern form of the Double-crested Cormorant, *P. dilophus*. — E. C.

cattle are to be found here. Returning this evening the tide had so fallen that we waded a mile and a half to an island close to our anchorage; the sailors were obliged to haul the boat that distance in a few inches of water. We have removed the "Ripley" closer in shore, where I hope she will be steady enough for my work to-morrow.

June 20. Thermometer 60° at noon. Calm and beautiful. Drew all day, and finished two *Uria troile.* I rose at two this morning, for we have scarcely any darkness now; about four a man came from Captain Billings to accompany some of our party to Partridge Bay on a shooting excursion. John and his party went off by land, or rather by rock and moss, to some ponds three or four miles from the sea; they returned at four this afternoon, and brought only one Scoter Duck, male; saw four, but could not discover the nests, although they breed here; saw also about twenty Wild Geese, one pair Red-necked Divers, one *Anas fusca,* one Three-toed Woodpecker, and Tell-tale Godwits. The ponds, although several miles long, and of good proportion and depth, had no fish in them that could be discovered, and on the beach no shells nor grasses; the margins are reddish sand. A few toads were seen, which John described as "pale-looking and poor." The country a barren rock as far as the eye extended; mosses more than a foot deep on the average, of different varieties but principally the white kind, hard and crisp. Saw not a quadruped. Our Bear trap was discharged, but we could not find the animal for want of a dog. An Eider Duck's nest was found fully one hundred yards from the water, unsheltered on the rocks, with five eggs and clean down. In no instance, though I have tried with all my powers, have I approached nearer than eight or ten yards of the sitting birds; they fly at the least appearance of danger. We concluded that the absence of fish in these ponds was on account of their freezing solidly every winter, when fish must die. Captain Billings paid me a visit, and very generously offered to change our whale-boat for a large one, and his pilot boat for ours; the industry of this man is extraordinary. The specimen of *Uria troile* drawn with a white line round the eye[1] was a female; the one without this line was a young bird. I have drawn seventeen and a half hours this day, and my poor head aches badly enough. One of Captain Billings' mates told me of the *Procellarias* breeding in great numbers in and about Mount Desert Island rocks, in the months of June and July; there they deposit their one white egg in the deepest fissures of the rocks, and sit upon it only during the night. When approached whilst on the egg, they open their wings and bill, and offer to defend themselves from the approach of intruders. The Eider Ducks are seen leaving the islands on which they breed, at daybreak every fair morning, in congregated flocks of males or females separately, and proceed to certain fishing grounds where the water is only a few fathoms deep, and remain till towards evening, when the females sit on their eggs for the night, and the males group on the rocks by themselves. This valuable bird is extremely abundant here; we find their nests without any effort every time we go out. So sonorous is the song of the Fox-colored Sparrow that I can hear it for hours, most distinctly, from the cabin where I am drawing, and yet it is distant more than a quarter of a mile. This bird is in this country what the Towhee Bunting is in the Middle States.

June 22. I drew all day at an adult Gannet which we brought from the great rock of which I have spoken; it was still in good order. Many eggs of the Arctic Tern were collected to-day, two or three in a nest; these birds are as shy here as all others, and the moment John and

[1] This is the so-called Bridled Guillemot, *Uria ringvia.* The white mark is not characteristic of sex, age, or season. The bird is not specifically distinct from *Uria troile.* — E. C.

Coolidge landed, or indeed approached the islands on which they breed, they all rose in the air, passed high overhead, screaming and scolding all the time the young men were on the land. When one is shot the rest plunge towards it, and can then be easily shot. Sometimes when wounded in the body, they sail off to extraordinary distances, and are lost. The same is the case with the *Larus marinus*. When our captain returned he brought about a dozen female Eider Ducks, a great number of their eggs, and a bag of down; also a fine Wild Goose, but nothing new for the pencil. In one nest of the Eider ten eggs were found; this is the most we have seen as yet in any one nest. The female draws the down from her abdomen as far towards her breast as her bill will allow her to do, but the *feathers* are not pulled, and on examination of several specimens I found these well and regularly planted, and cleaned from their original down, as a forest of trees is cleared of its undergrowth. In this state the female is still well clothed, and little or no difference can be seen in the plumage unless examined. These birds have now nearly all hatched in this latitude, but we are told that we shall over-reach them in that, and meet with nests and eggs as we go northeast until August. So abundant were the nests of these birds on the islands of Partridge Bay, about forty miles west of this place, that a boat load of their eggs might have been collected if they had been fresh; they are then excellent eating. Our captain called on a half-breed Indian in the employ of the Northeast Fur and Fish Co., living with his squaw and two daughters. A potato patch of about an acre was planted in *sand*, for not a foot of *soil* is there to be found hereabouts. The man told him his potatoes grew well and were good, ripening in a few weeks, which he called the summer. The mosquitoes and black gnats are bad enough on shore. I heard a Wood Pewee. The Wild Goose is an excellent diver, and when with its young uses many beautiful stratagems to save its brood, and elude the hunter. They will dive and lead their young under the surface of the water, and always in a contrary direction to the one expected; thus if you row a boat after one it will dive under it, and now and then remain under it several minutes, when the hunter with outstretched neck, is looking, all in vain, in the distance for the *stupid Goose!* Every time I read or hear of a stupid animal in a wild state, I cannot help wishing that the stupid animal who speaks thus, was half as wise as the brute he despises, so that he might be able to thank his Maker for what knowledge he may possess. I found many small flowers open this day, where none appeared last evening. All vegetable life here is of the pygmy order, and so ephemeral that it shoots out of the tangled mass of ages, blooms, fructifies, and dies, in a few weeks. We ascertained to-day that a party of four men from Halifax took last spring nearly forty thousand eggs, which they sold at Halifax and other towns at twenty-five cents per dozen, making over $800; this was done in about two months. Last year upwards of twenty sail were engaged in "egging;" so some idea may be formed of the birds that are destroyed in this rascally way. The eggers destroy all the eggs that are sat upon, to force the birds to lay again, and by robbing them regularly, they lay till nature is exhausted, and few young are raised. In less than half a century these wonderful nurseries will be entirely destroyed, unless some kind government will interfere to stop the shameful destruction.

June 22. It was very rainy, and thermometer 54°. After breakfast dressed in my oilskins and went with the captain in the whale-boat to the settlement at the entrance of the true Natasquan, five miles east. On our way we saw numerous Seals; these rise to the surface of the water, erect the head to the full length of the neck, snuff the air, and you also, and sink back to avoid any further acquaintance with man. We saw a great number of Gulls of various kinds, but mostly *L. marinus* and *L. tridactylus;* these were on the extreme points of sand-bars, but could not be approached, and certainly the more numerous they are, the more wild and wary. On entering the river we saw several nets set across a portion of the stream for the purpose of catching salmon; these seines were fastened in the stream about sixty yards from either shore, supported by buoys; the net is fastened to the shore by stakes that hold it perpendicular to the water; the fish enter these, and entangle themselves until removed by the fishermen. On going to a house on the shore, we found it a tolerably good cabin, floored, containing a good stove, a chimney, and an oven at the bottom of this, like the ovens of the French peasants, three beds, and a table whereon the breakfast of the family was served. This consisted of coffee in large bowls, good bread, and fried salmon. Three Labrador dogs came and sniffed about us, and then returned under the table whence they had issued, with no appearance of anger. Two men, two women, and a babe formed the group, which I addressed in French. They were French Canadians and had been here several years, winter and summer, and are agents for the Fur and Fish Co., who give them food, clothes, and about $80 per annum. They have a cow and an ox, about an acre of potatoes planted in sand, seven feet of snow in winter, and two-thirds less salmon than was caught here ten years since. Then three hundred barrels was a fair season; now one hundred is the maximum; this is because they will catch the fish both ascending and descending the river. During winter the men hunt Foxes, Martens, and Sables, and kill some Bear of the black kind, but neither Deer nor other game is to be found without going a great distance in the interior, where Reindeer are now and then procured. One species of Grouse and one of Ptarmigan, the latter white at all seasons; the former I suppose to be the Willow Grouse. The men would neither sell nor give us a single salmon, saying that so strict were their orders that, should they sell *one*, the place might be taken from them. If this should prove the case everywhere, I shall not purchase many for my friends. The furs which they collect are sent off to Quebec at the first opening of the waters in spring, and not a skin of any sort was here for us to look at. We met here two large boats containing about twenty Montagnais Indians, old and young, men and women. They carried canoes lashed to the sides, like whale-ships, for the Seal fishery. The men were stout and good-looking, spoke tolerable French, the skin redder than any Indians I have ever seen, and more *clear;* the women appeared cleaner than usual, their hair braided and hanging down, jet black, but short. All were dressed in European costume except the feet, on which coarse moccasins of sealskin took the place of shoes. I made a bargain with them for some Grouse, and three young men were despatched at once. On leaving the harbor this morning we saw a black man-of-war-like looking vessel entering it with the French flag; she anchored near us, and on our return we were told it was the Quebec cutter. I wrote a note to the officer commanding, enclosing my card, and requesting an interview. The commander replied he would receive me in two hours. His name was Captain Bayfield, the vessel the "Gulnare." The sailor who had taken my note was asked if I had procured many birds, and how far I intended to proceed. After dinner, which consisted of hashed Eider Ducks, which were very good, the females always being fat when sitting, I cut off my three weeks' beard, put on clean linen, and with my credentials in my pocket went to the "Gulnare." I was received politely, and after talking on deck for a while, was invited into the cabin, and was introduced to the doctor, who appeared to be a man of talents, a student of botany and conchology. Thus men of the same tastes meet everywhere, yet surely I did not expect to meet a naturalist on the Labrador coast. The vessel is on a surveying cruise, and we are likely to be in company the whole summer. The first lieutenant studies ornithology and collects. After a while I gave my letter from the Duke of Sussex to the captain, who read and returned it without comment. As I was leaving, the rain poured down, and I was invited to remain, but declined; the captain promised to do anything for me in his power. Saw many Siskins, but cannot get a shot at one.

June 23. It was our intention to have left this morning for another harbor, about fifty miles east, but the wind being dead ahead we are here still. I have drawn all day, at the background of the Gannets. John and party went off about six miles, and returned with half a dozen Guillemots, and ten or twelve dozen eggs. Coolidge brought in Arctic Terns and *L. marinus;* two young of the latter about three weeks old, having the same voice and notes as the old ones. When on board they ran about the deck, and fed themselves with pieces of fish thrown to them. These young Gulls, as well as young Herons of every kind, sit on the tarsus when fatigued, with their feet extended before them in a very awkward-looking position, but one which to them is no doubt comfortable. Shattuck and I took a walk over the dreary hills about noon; the sun shone pleasantly, and we found several flowers in full bloom, amongst which the *Kalmia glauca,* a beautiful small species, was noticeable. The captain and surgeon from the "Gulnare" called and invited me to dine with them to-morrow. This evening we have been visiting the Montagnais Indians' camp, half a mile from us, and found them skinning Seals, and preparing the flesh for use. Saw a robe the size of a good blanket made of seal-skins tanned so soft and beautiful, with the hair on, that it was as pliant as a kid glove; they would not sell it. The chief of the party proves to be well informed, and speaks French so as to be understood. He is a fine-looking fellow of about forty; has a good-looking wife and fine babe. His brother is also married, and has several sons from fourteen to twenty years old. When we landed the men came to us, and after the first salutations, to my astonishment offered us some excellent rum. The women were all seated apart outside of the camp, engaged in closing up sundry packages of provisions and accoutrements. We entered a tent, and seated ourselves round a cheerful fire, the smoke of which escaped through the summit of the apartment, and over the fire two kettles boiled. I put many questions to the chief and his brother, and gained this information. The country from here to the first settlement of the Hudson's Bay Co. is as barren and rocky as that about us. Very large lakes of great depth are met with about two hundred miles from this seashore; these lakes abound in very large trout, carp, and white fish, and many mussels, unfit to eat, which they describe as black outside and purple within, and are no doubt unios. Not a bush is to be met with, and the Indians who now and then go across are obliged to carry their tent poles with them, as well as their canoes; they burn moss for fuel. So tedious is the travelling said to be that not more than ten miles on an average per day can be made, and when the journey is made in two months it is considered a good one. Wolves and Black Bear are frequent, no Deer, and not many Caribous; not a bird of any kind except Wild Geese and Brent about the lakes, where they breed in perfect peace. When the journey is undertaken in the winter, which is very seldom the case, it is performed on snow-shoes, and no canoes are taken. Fur animals are scarce, yet some few Beavers and Otters are caught, a few Martens and Sables, and some Foxes and Lynx, but every year diminishes their numbers. The Fur Company may be called the exterminating medium of these wild and almost uninhabitable climes, where cupidity and the love of gold can alone induce man to reside for a while. Where can I go now, and visit nature undisturbed? The *Turdus migratorius*[1] must be the hardiest of the whole genus. I hear it at this moment, eight o'clock at night, singing most joyously its "Good-night!" and "All 's well!" to the equally hardy Labradorians. The common Crow and the Raven are also here, but the Magdalene Islands appear to be the last outpost of the Warblers, for here the Black-poll Warbler, the only one we see, is scarce. The White-throated and the White-crowned Sparrows are the only tolerably abundant land birds. The Indians brought in no Grouse. A fine adult specimen of the *Larus marinus* killed this day has already changed full half of its primary feathers next the body; this bird had two young ones, and was shot as it dove through the air towards John, who was near the nest; this is the first instance we have seen of so much attachment being shown to the progeny with danger at hand. Two male Eider Ducks were shot and found very much advanced in the moult. No doubt exists in my mind that male birds are much in advance of female in their moults; this is very slow, and indeed is not completed until late in winter, after which the brilliancy of the bills and the richness of the coloring of the legs and feet only improve as they depart from the south for the north.

June 24. Drawing most of this day, no birds procured, but some few plants. I dined on board the "Gulnare" at five o'clock, and was obliged to shave and dress — quite a bore on the coast of Labrador, believe me. I found the captain, surgeon, and three officers formed our party; the conversation ranged from botany to politics, from the Established Church of England to the hatching of eggs by steam. I saw the maps being made of this coast, and

[1] *Merula migratoria*, the American Robin.

was struck with the great accuracy of the shape of our present harbor, which I now know full well. I returned to our vessel at ten, and am longing to be farther north; but the wind is so contrary it would be a loss of time to attempt it now. The weather is growing warmer, and mosquitoes are abundant and hungry. Coolidge shot a White-crowned Sparrow, a male, while in the act of carrying some materials to build a nest with; so they must breed here.

June 25. Made a drawing of the Arctic Tern, of which a great number breed here. I am of Temminck's opinion that the upper plumage of this species is much darker than that of *S. hirundo.* The young men, who are always ready for sport, caught a hundred codfish in half an hour, and *somewhere* secured three fine salmon, one of which we sent to the "Gulnare" with some cod. Our harbor is called "American Harbor," and also "Little Natasquan;" it is in latitude 50° 12′ north, longitude 23° east of Quebec and 61° 53 west of Greenwich. The waters of all the streams which we have seen are of a rusty color, probably on account of the decomposed mosses, which appear to be quite of a peaty nature. The rivers appear to be formed by the drainage of swamps, fed apparently by rain and the melting snows, and in time of freshets the sand is sifted out, and carried to the mouth of every stream, where sand-bars are consequently met with. Below the mouth of each stream proves to be the best station for cod-fishing, as there the fish accumulate to feed on the fry which runs into the river to deposit spawn, and which they follow to sea after this, as soon as the fry make off from the rivers to deep water. It is to be remarked that so shy of strangers are the agents of the Fur and Fish Company that they will evade all questions respecting the interior of the country, and indeed will willingly tell you such untruths as at once disgust and shock you. All this through the fear that strangers should attempt to settle here, and divide with them the profits which they enjoy. Bank Swallows in sight this moment, with the weather thick, foggy, and an east wind; where are these delicate pilgrims bound? The Black-poll Warbler is more abundant, and forever singing, if the noise it makes can be called a song; it resembles the clicking of small pebbles together five or six times, and is renewed every few minutes.

June 26. We have been waiting five days for wind, and so has the "Gulnare." The fishing fleet of six or seven sails has made out to beat four miles to other fishing grounds. It has rained nearly all day, but we have all been on shore, to be beaten back by the rain and the mosquitoes. John brought a female White-crowned Sparrow; the black and white of the head was as pure as in the male, which is not common. It rains hard, and is now calm. God send us a fair wind to-morrow morning, and morning here is about half-past two.

June 27. It rained quite hard when I awoke this morning; the fog was so thick the very shores of our harbor, not distant more than a hundred yards, were enveloped in gloom. After breakfast we went ashore; the weather cleared up and the wind blew fresh. We rambled about the brushwoods till dinner time, shot two Canada Jays, one old and one young, the former much darker than those of Maine; the young one was full fledged, but had no white about its head; the whole of the body and head was of a deep, very deep blue. It must have been about three weeks old, and the egg from which it was hatched must have been laid about the 10th of May, when the thermometer was below the freezing-point. We shot also a Ruby-crowned Wren;[1] no person who has not heard it would believe that the song of this bird is louder, stronger, and far more melodious than that of the Canary

[1] Kinglet, *Regulus calendula.*—E. C.

bird. It sang for a long time ere it was shot, and perched on the tops of the tallest fir-trees removing from one to another as we approached. So strange, so beautiful was that song that I pronounced the musician, ere it was shot, a new species of Warbler. John shot it; it fell to the ground, and though the six of us looked for it we could not find it, and went elsewhere; in the course of the afternoon we passed by the spot again, and John found it and gave it to me. We shot a new species of Finch, which I have named *Fringilla lincolnii;* it is allied to the Swamp Sparrow in general appearance, but is considerably smaller, and may be known at once from all others thus far described, by the light buff streak which runs from the base of the lower mandible, until it melts into the duller buff of the breast, and by the bright ash-streak over the eye. The note of this bird attracted me at once; it was loud and sonorous; the bird flew low and forward, perching on the firs, very shy, and cunningly eluding our pursuit; we, however, shot three, but lost one. I shall draw it to-morrow.[1]

June 28. The weather shocking — rainy, foggy, dark and cold. I began drawing at daylight, and finished one of my new Finches and outlined another. At noon the wind suddenly changed and blew hard from the northwest, with heavy rain, and such a swell that I was almost sea-sick, and had to abandon drawing. We dined, and immediately afterward the wind came round to southwest; all was bustle with us and with the "Gulnare," for we both were preparing our sails and raising our anchors ere proceeding to sea. *We* sailed, and managed so well that we cleared the outer cape east of our harbor, and went out to sea in good style. The "Gulnare" was not so fortunate; she attempted to beat out in vain, and returned to

[1] An interesting note of this new species figured in B. of Am., folio pl. 193, and described in Orn. Biogr. ii., 1834, p. 539. It is now known as *Melospiza lincolni.* — E. C.

her anchorage. The sea was so high in consequence of the late gales that we all took to our berths, and I am only now able to write.

June 29. At three this morning we were off the land about fifteen miles, and about fifty from American Harbor. Wind favorable, but light; at about ten it freshened. We neared the shore, but as before our would-be pilot could not recognize the land, and our captain had to search for the harbor where we now are, himself. We passed near an island covered with Foolish Guillemots, and came to, for the purpose of landing; we did so through a heavy surf, and found two eggers just landed, and running over the rocks for eggs. We did the same, and soon collected about a hundred. These men told me they visited every island in the vicinity every day, and that, in consequence they had fresh eggs every day. They had collected eight hundred dozen, and expect to get two thousand dozen. The number of broken eggs created a fetid smell on this island, scarcely to be borne. The *L. marinus* were here in hundreds, and destroying the eggs of the Guillemots by thousands. From this island we went to another, and there found the *Mormon arcticus*[1] breeding in great numbers. We caught many in their burrows, killed some, and collected some of the eggs. On this island their burrows were dug in the light black loam formed of decayed moss, three to six feet deep, yet not more than about a foot under the surface. The burrows ran in all directions, and in some instances connected; the end of the burrow is rounded, and there is the pure white egg. Those caught at the holes bit most furiously and scratched shockingly with the inner claw, making a mournful noise all the time. The whole island was perforated with their burrows. No young were yet hatched, and the eggers do not collect these eggs, finding them indifferent. They say the same of the eggs of the *Alca*

[1] The Common Puffin, now called *Fratercula arctica.*—E. C.

torda, which they call "Tinkers."[1] The *Mormon*, they call "Sea Parrots." Each species seems to have its own island except the *Alca torda*, which admits the Guillemots. As we advanced, we passed by a rock literally covered with Cormorants, of what species I know not yet; their effluvia could be perceived more than a mile off. We made the fine anchorage where we now are about four o'clock. We found some difficulty in entering on account of our pilot being an ignorant ass; *twice* did we see the rocks under our vessel. The appearance of the country around is quite different from that near American Harbor; nothing in view here as far as eye can reach, but bare, high, rugged rocks, grand indeed, but not a shrub a foot above the ground. The moss is shorter and more compact, the flowers are fewer, and every plant more diminutive. No matter which way you glance, the prospect is cold and forbidding; deep banks of snow appear here and there, and yet I have found the Shore Lark (*Alauda alpestris*[2]) in beautiful summer plumage. I found the nest of the Brown Lark (*Anthus spinoletta*[3]) with five eggs in it; the nest was planted at the foot of a rock, buried in dark mould, and beautifully made of fine grass, well and neatly worked in circularly, without any hair or other lining. We shot a White-crowned Sparrow, two Savannah Finches, and saw more, and a Red-bellied Nuthatch; this last bird must have been blown here accidentally, as not a bush is there for it to alight upon. I found the tail of an unknown Owl, and a dead Snow-bird which from its appearance must have died from cold and famine. John brought a young Cormorant alive from the nest, but I cannot ascertain its species without the adult, which we hope to secure to-morrow. At dusk the "Gul-

[1] This is the usual sailors' name of the Razor-billed Auk in Labrador and Newfoundland, and was the only one heard by me in Labrador in 1860 (see Proc. Acad Nat. Sci., 1861, p. 249). — E. C.

[2] Now *Otocorys alpestris.* — E. C.

[3] Now *Anthus pennsylvanicus.* — E. C.

VICTOR GIFFORD AUDUBON.

FROM THE MINIATURE BY F. CRUIKSHANK, 1838.

nare" passed us. All my young men are engaged in skinning the *Mormon arcticus.*

June 30. I have drawn three birds this day since eight o'clock, one *Fringilla lincolnii,* one Ruby-crowned Wren, and a male White-winged Crossbill. Found a nest of the Savannah Finch with two eggs; it was planted in the moss, and covered by a rampant branch; it was made of fine grass, neither hair nor feathers in its composition. Shot the *L. marinus* in fine order, all with the wings extending nearly two inches beyond the tail, and all in the same state of moult, merely showing in the middle primaries. These birds suck other birds' eggs like Crows, Jays, and Ravens. Shot six *Phalacrocorax carbo*[1] in full plumage, species well ascertained by their white throat; found abundance of their eggs and young.

July 1. The weather was so cold that it was painful for me to draw almost the whole day, yet I have drawn a White-winged Crossbill[2] and a *Mormon arcticus.* We have had three of these latter on board, alive, these three days past; it is amusing to see them running about the cabin and the hold with a surprising quickness, watching our motions, and particularly our eyes. A Pigeon Hawk's[3] nest was found to-day; it was on the top of a fir-tree about ten feet high, made of sticks and lined with moss, and as large as a Crow's nest; it contained two

[1] Common Cormorant. See note on page 370.

[2] *Loxia leucoptera.*

[3] *Le petit caporal, Falco temerarius,* AUD. Ornith. Biog. i., 1831, p. 381, pl. 85. *Falco columbarius,* AUD. Ornith. Biog. i., 1831, p. 466, pl. 92; v., 1838, p. 368. Synopsis, 1839, p. 16. B. Amer. 8vo, ed. 1., 1840, p. 88, pl. 21. *Falco auduboni,* BLACKWALL, Zoöl. Researches, 1834. — E. C.

In vol. v., p. 368, Audubon says: "The bird represented in the last mentioned plate, and described under the name of *Falco temerarius,* was merely a beautiful adult of the Pigeon Hawk, *F. columbarius.* The great inferiority in size of the individual represented as *F. temararius* was the cause of my mistaking it for a distinct species, and I have pleasure in stating that the Prince of Musignano [Charles Bonaparte] was the first person who pointed out my error to me soon after the publication of my first volume."

Bonaparte alludes to this in his edition of Wilson, vol. iii. p. 252.

birds just hatched, and three eggs, which the young inside had just cracked. The parent birds were anxious about their newly born ones, and flew close to us. The little ones were pure white, soft and downy. We found also three young of the *Charadrius semipalmatus,*[1] and several old ones; these birds breed on the margin of a small lake among the low grasses. Traces have been seen of Hares or Rabbits, and one island is perforated throughout its shallow substratum of moss by a species of Rat, but in such burrows search for them is vain. The "Gulnare" came in this evening; our captain brought her in as pilot. We have had an almost complete eclipse of the moon this evening at half-past seven. The air very chilly.

July 2. A beautiful day for Labrador. Drew another *M. arcticus.* Went on shore, and was most pleased with what I saw. The country, so wild and grand, is of itself enough to interest any one in its wonderful dreariness. Its mossy, gray-clothed rocks, heaped and thrown together as if by chance, in the most fantastical groups imaginable, huge masses hanging on minor ones as if about to roll themselves down from their doubtful-looking situations, into the depths of the sea beneath. Bays without end, sprinkled with rocky islands of all shapes and sizes, where in every fissure a Guillemot, a Cormorant, or some other wild bird retreats to secure its egg, and raise its young, or save itself from the hunter's pursuit. The peculiar cast of the sky, which never seems to be certain, butterflies flitting over snow-banks, probing beautiful dwarf flowerets of many hues pushing their tender stems from the thick bed of moss which everywhere covers the granite rocks. Then the morasses, wherein you plunge up to your knees, or the walking over the stubborn, dwarfish shrubbery, making one think that as he goes he treads down the *forests* of Labrador. The unex-

[1] American Ring Plover, now known as *Ægialitis semipalmata.* — E. C.

pected Bunting, or perhaps Sylvia, which perchance, and indeed as if by chance alone, you now and then see flying before you, or hear singing from the creeping plants on the ground. The beautiful fresh-water lakes, on the rugged crests of greatly elevated islands, wherein the Red and Black-necked Divers swim as proudly as swans do in other latitudes, and where the fish appear to have been cast as strayed beings from the surplus food of the ocean. All — all is wonderfully grand, wild — aye, and terrific. And yet how beautiful it is now, when one sees the wild bee, moving from one flower to another in search of food, which doubtless is as sweet to it, as the essence of the magnolia is to those of favored Louisiana. The little Ring Plover rearing its delicate and tender young, the Eider Duck swimming man-of-war-like amid her floating brood, like the guardship of a most valuable convoy; the White-crowned Bunting's sonorous note reaching the ear ever and anon; the crowds of sea-birds in search of places wherein to repose or to feed — how beautiful is all this in this wonderful rocky desert at this season, the beginning of July, compared with the horrid blasts of winter which here predominate by the will of God, when every rock is rendered smooth with snows so deep that every step the traveller takes is as if entering into his grave; for even should he escape an avalanche, his eye dreads to search the horizon, for full well does he know that snow — snow — is all that can be seen. I watched the Ring Plover for some time; the parents were so intent on saving their young that they both lay on the rocks as if shot, quivering their wings and dragging their bodies as if quite disabled. We left them and their young to the care of the Creator. I would not have shot one of the old ones, or taken one of the young for any consideration, and I was glad my young men were as forbearing. The *L. marinus* is extremely abundant here; they are forever harassing every other bird, sucking their eggs, and devouring their young; they take here the place of Eagles and Hawks; not an Eagle have we seen yet, and only two or three small Hawks, and one small Owl; yet what a harvest they would have here, were there trees for them to rest upon.

July 3. We had a regular stiff gale from the eastward the whole day, accompanied with rain and cold weather, and the water so rough that I could not go ashore to get plants to draw. This afternoon, however, the wind and waves abated, and we landed for a short time. The view from the topmost rock overlooking the agitated sea was grand; the small islets were covered with the angry foam. Thank God! we were not at sea. I had the pleasure of coming immediately upon a Cormorant's nest, that lay in a declivity not more than four or five yards below me; the mother bird was on her nest with three young; I was unobserved by her for some minutes, and was delighted to see how kindly attentive she was to her dear brood; suddenly her keen eye saw me, and she flew off as if to dive in the sea.

July 4. At four this morning I sent Tom Lincoln on shore after four plants and a Cormorant's nest for me to draw. The nest was literally *pasted* to the rock's edge, so thick was the decomposed, putrid matter below it, and to which the upper part of the nest was attached. It was formed of such sticks as the country affords, sea-moss and other garbage, and weighed over fifteen pounds. I have drawn all day, and have finished the plate of the *Fringilla lincolnii*, to which I have put three plants of the country, all new to me and probably never before figured; to us they are very fitting for the purpose, as Lincoln gathered them. Our party divided as usual into three bands: John and Lincoln off after Divers; Coolidge, Shattuck, and Ingalls to the main land, and our captain and four men to a pond after fish, which they will catch with a seine. Captain Bayfield sent us a quarter of mutton, a rarity, I will venture to say, on this coast even on the Fourth of July. John and Lincoln returned with a Red-necked Diver, or Scapegrace, Coolidge and party with the nest and two eggs of the *Colymbus glacialis.*[1] This nest was found on the margin of a pond, and was made of short grasses, weeds, etc.; well fashioned and fifteen inches in diameter. After dinner John and I went on shore to release a *Uria grylle* that we had confined in the fissure of a rock; the poor thing was sadly weak, but will soon recover from this trial of ours.

July 5. John and Lincoln returned at sunset with a Red-necked Diver, and one egg of that bird; they also found *Uria grylle,* whose pebbled nests were placed beneath large rolling stones on the earth, and not in fissures; Lincoln thought them a different species, but John did not. They brought some curious Eels, and an Arctic Tern, and saw the tracks of Deer and Caribou, also Otter paths from one pond to another. They saw several Loons and *tolled* them by running towards them hallooing and waving a handkerchief, at which sight and cry the Loon immediately swam towards them, until within twenty yards. This "tolling" is curious and wonderful. Many other species of water-fowl are deceived by these manœuvres, but none so completely as the Loon. Coolidge's party was fortunate enough to kill a pair of Ptarmigans, and to secure seven of the young birds, hatched yesterday at furthest. They met with these on the dreary, mossy tops of the hills, over which we tread daily in search of knowledge. This is the species of Grouse of which we heard so much at Dennysville last autumn, and glad I am that it is a resident bird with us. The *Larus marinus* was observed trying to catch the young of the Eiders. I drew from four o'clock this morning till three this after-

[1] Great Northern Diver or Loon, now called *Urinator,* or *Gavia, imber.* The other Diver above mentioned as the "Scapegrace" is *U., or G., lumme* —E. C.

noon; finished a figure of the *Colymbus septentrionalis.*[1] Feeling the want of exercise, went off with the captain a few miles, to a large rough island. To tread over the spongy moss of Labrador is a task beyond conception until tried; at every step the foot sinks in a deep, soft cushion which closes over it, and it requires a good deal of exertion to pull it up again. Where this moss happens to be over a marsh, then you sink a couple of feet deep every step you take; to reach a bare rock is delightful, and quite a relief. This afternoon I thought the country looked more terrifyingly wild than ever; the dark clouds, casting their shadows on the stupendous masses of rugged rock, lead the imagination into regions impossible to describe. The Scoter Ducks, of which I have seen many this day, were partially moulted, and could fly only a short distance, and must be either barren or the young bachelors, as I find *parents* in full plumage, convincing me that these former moult earlier than the breeding Ducks. I have observed this strange fact so often now that I shall say no more about it; I have found it in nearly all the species of the birds here. I do not know of any writer on the history of birds having observed this curious fact before. I have now my hands full of work, and go to bed delighted that to-morrow I shall draw a Ptarmigan which I can swear to, as being a United States species. I am much fatigued and wet to the very skin, but, oh! we found the nest of a Peregrine Falcon on a tremendous cliff, with a young one about a week old, quite white with down; the parents flew fiercely at our eyes.

July 6. By dint of hard work and rising at three, I have drawn a *Colymbus septentrionalis* and a young one, and nearly finished a Ptarmigan; this afternoon, however, at half-past five, my fingers could no longer hold my pencil, and I was forced to abandon my work and go

[1] Red-throated Diver, now *Urinator*, or *Gavia, lumme.*—E. C.

ashore for exercise. The fact is that I am growing old too fast; alas! I feel it — and yet work I will, and may God grant me life to see the last plate of my mammoth work finished. I have heard the Brown Lark (*Anthus spinoletta*) sing many a time this day, both on the wing and whilst sitting on the ground. When on the wing it sings while flying very irregularly in zigzags, up and down, etc.; when on a rock (which it prefers) it stands erect, and sings, I think, more clearly. John found the nest of a White-crowned Bunting with five eggs; he was creeping through some low bushes after a Red-necked Diver, and accidentally coming upon it, startled the female, which made much noise and complaint. The nest was like the one Lincoln found placed in the moss, under a low bough, and formed of beautiful moss outwardly, dried, fine grass next inside, and exquisitely lined with fibrous roots of a rich yellow color; the eggs are light greenish, slightly sprinkled with reddish-brown, in size about the same as eggs of the Song Sparrow. This *Fringilla*[1] is the most abundant in this part of Labrador. We have seen two Swamp Sparrows only. We have found two nests of the Peregrine Falcon, placed high on rocky declivities. Coolidge and party shot two Oyster Catchers; these are becoming plentiful. Lieutenant Bowen of the "Gulnare" brought me a Peregrine Falcon, and two young of the *Alca torda*, the first hatched we have seen, and only two or three days old.

July 7. Drawing all day; finished the female Grouse and five young, and prepared the male bird. The captain, John, and Lincoln, went off this afternoon with a view to camp on a bay about ten miles distant. Soon after, we had a change of weather, and, for a wonder, bright lightning and something like summer clouds. When fatigued with drawing I went on shore for exercise, and saw many pretty flowers, amongst them a flowering Sea-pea, quite rich in

[1] The White-crowned and White-throated Sparrows are now placed in the genus *Zonotrichia*. — E. C.

color. Dr. Kelly from the "Gulnare" went with me. Captain Bayfield and Lieutenant Bowen went off this morning on a three weeks' expedition in open boats, but with tents and more comforts than I have ever enjoyed in hunting excursions. The mosquitoes quite as numerous as in Louisiana.

July 8. Rainy, dirty weather, wind east. Was at work at half-past three, but disagreeable indeed is my situation during bad weather. The rain falls on my drawing-paper, despite all I can do, and even the fog collects and falls in large drops from the rigging on my table; now and then I am obliged to close my skylight, and then may be said to work almost in darkness. Notwithstanding, I finished my cock Ptarmigan, and three more young, and now consider it a handsome large plate. John and party returned, cold, wet, and hungry. Shot nothing, camp disagreeable, and nothing to relate but that they heard a Wolf, and found an island with thousands of the *Mormon arcticus* breeding on it. To-morrow I shall draw the beautiful *Colymbus glacialis* in most perfect plumage.

July 9. The wind east, of course disagreeable; wet and foggy besides. The most wonderful climate in the world. Cold as it is, mosquitoes in profusion, plants blooming by millions, and at every step you tread on such as would be looked upon with pleasure in more temperate climes. I wish I were a better botanist, that I might describe them as I do birds. Dr. Wm. Kelly has given me the list of such plants as he has observed on the coast as far as Macatine Island. I have drawn all day at the Loon, a most difficult bird to imitate. For my part, I cannot help smiling at the presumption of some of our authors, who modestly assert that their figures are "up to nature." May God forgive them, and teach me to *copy* His works; glad and happy shall I then be. Lincoln and Shattuck brought some fresh-water shells from a large pond inland; they saw a large bird which they took for an Owl, but which they could not approach; they also caught a frog, but lost it out of their game bag.

July 10. Could I describe one of these dismal gales which blow ever and anon over this desolate country, it would in all probability be of interest to one unacquainted with the inclemency of the climate. Nowhere else is the power of the northeast gale, which blows every week on the coast of Labrador, so keenly felt as here. I cannot describe it; all I can say is that whilst we are in as fine and safe a harbor as could be wished for, and completely land-locked all round, so strong does the wind blow, and so great its influence on our vessel, that her motion will not allow me to draw, and indeed once this day forced me to my berth, as well as some others of our party. One would imagine all the powers of Boreas had been put to work to give us a true idea of what his energies can produce, even in so snug a harbor. What is felt outside I cannot imagine, but greatly fear that few vessels could ride safely before these horrid blasts, that now and then seem strong enough to rend the very rocks asunder. The rain is driven in sheets which seem scarcely to fall on sea or land; I can hardly call it rain, it is rather a mass of water, so thick that all objects at any distance from us are lost to sight every three or four minutes, and the waters comb up and beat about us in our rock-bound harbor as a newly caged bird does against its imprisoning walls. The Great Black-backed Gull alone is seen floating through the storm, screaming loudly and mournfully as it seeks its prey; not another bird is to be seen abroad; the Cormorants are all settled in the rocks close to us, the Guillemots are deep in the fissures, every Eider Duck lays under the lee of some point, her brood snugly beneath her opened wings, the Loon and the Diver have crawled among the rankest weeds, and are patiently waiting for a return of fair weather, the Grouse is quite hid under the creeping willow, the Great Gray Owl is perched on the southern declivity of some stupendous rock, and the gale continues as if it would never stop. On rambling about the shores of the numerous bays and inlets of this coast, you cannot but observe immense beds of round stone of all sizes, some of very large dimensions rolled side by side and piled one upon another many deep, cast there by some great force of nature. I have seen many such places, and never without astonishment and awe. If those great boulders are brought from the bottom of the sea, and cast hundreds of yards on shore, this will give some idea of what a gale on the coast of Labrador can be, and what the force of the waves. I tried to finish my drawing of the Loon, but in vain; I covered my paper to protect it from the rain, with the exception only of the few inches where I wished to work, and yet that small space was not spared by the drops that fell from the rigging on my table; there is no window, and the only light is admitted through hatches.

July 11. The gale, or hurricane, or whatever else the weather of yesterday was, subsided about midnight, and at sunrise this morning it was quite calm, and the horizon fiery red. It soon became cloudy, and the wind has been all round the compass. I wished to go a hundred miles farther north, but the captain says I must be contented here, so I shall proceed with my drawings. I began a Cormorant and two young, having sent John and Lincoln for them before three this morning; and they procured them in less than half an hour. Many of the young are nearly as large as their parents, and yet have scarcely a feather, but are covered with woolly down, of a sooty black. The excursions brought in nothing new. The Shore Lark has become abundant, but the nest remains still unknown. A tail feather of the Red-tailed Hawk, young, was found; therefore that species exists here. We are the more surprised that not a Hawk nor an Owl is seen, as we find hundreds of sea-birds devoured, the wings only remaining.

July 12. At this very moment it is blowing another gale from the east, and it has been raining hard ever since the middle of the day. Of course it has been very difficult to draw, but I have finished the Cormorant. John and Lincoln brought in nothing new, except the nest and ten eggs of a Red-breasted Merganser. The nest was placed near the edge of a very small fresh-water pond, under the creeping branches of one of this country's fir-trees, the top of which would be about a foot above ground; it is like the Eider's nest, but smaller and better fashioned, of weeds and mosses, and warmly lined with down. The eggs are dirty yellow, very smooth shelled, and look like hen's-eggs, only rather stouter. John lay in wait for the parent over two hours, but though he saw her glide off the nest, she was too wary to return. I saw a Black-backed Gull plunge on a Crab as big as my two fists, in about two feet of water, seize it and haul it ashore, where it ate it while I watched it; I could see the Crab torn piece by piece, till the shell and legs alone remained. The Gull then flew in a direct line towards her nest, distant about a mile, probably to disgorge her food in favor of her young. Our two young Gulls, which we now have had for nearly a month, act just as Vultures would. We throw them a dead Duck or even a dead Gull, and they tear it to pieces, drinking the blood and swallowing the flesh, each constantly trying to rob the other of the piece of flesh which he has torn from the carcass. They do not drink water, but frequently wash the blood off their bills by plunging them in water, and then violently shaking their heads. They are now half fledged.

July 13. When I rose this morning at half-past three, the wind was northeast, and but little of it. The weather was cloudy and looked bad, as it always does here after a storm. I thought I would spend the day on board the "Gulnare," and draw at the ground of my Grouse, which I had promised to Dr. Kelly. However, at seven the wind was west, and we immediately prepared to leave our fine harbor. By eight we passed the "Gulnare," bid her officers and crew farewell, beat out of the narrow passage beautifully, and proceeded to sea with the hope of reaching the harbor of Little Macatine, distant forty-three miles; but ere the middle of the day it became calm, then rain, then the wind to the east again, and all were sea-sick as much as ever. I saw a *Lestris* [1] near the vessel, but of what kind I could not tell, — it flew like a Pigeon Hawk, alighting on the water like a Gull, and fed on some codfish liver which was thrown overboard for it, — and some *Thalassidroma*,[2] but none came within shot, and the sea was too rough to go after them. About a dozen common Crossbills, and as many Redpolls (*Fringilla* [*Acanthis*] *linaria*) came and perched on our top-yards, but I would not have them shot, and none were caught. Our young men have been fishing to pass the time, and have caught a number of cod.

July 14. The wind blew cold and sharp from the north-east this morning, and we found ourselves within twenty miles of "Little Macatine," the sea beating heavily on our bows, as we beat to the windward, tack after tack. At noon it was quite calm, and the wished-for island in sight, but our captain despairs of reaching it to-day. It looks high and horribly rugged, the highest land we have yet seen. At four o'clock, being about a mile and a half distant, we took the green boat, and went off. As we approached, I was surprised to see how small some Ducks looked which flew between us and the rocks, so stupendously high were the rough shores under which our little bark moved along. We doubled the cape and came to the entrance of the Little Macatine harbor, but so small did it appear to me that I doubted if it was the harbor; the shores were terribly wild, fearfully high and rugged, and nothing was heard but the croaking of a pair of Ravens and their half-grown brood, mingling with the roar of the surf against the rocky

[1] Jager. [2] Petrels, most probably *Cymochorea leucorrhoa*. — E. C.

ledges which projected everywhere, and sent the angry waters foaming into the air. The wind now freshened, the "Ripley's" sails swelled, and she was gently propelled through the water and came within sight of the harbor, on the rocks of which we stood waiting for her, when all of a sudden she veered, and we saw her topsails hauled in and bent in a moment; we thought she must have seen a sunken rock, and had thus wheeled to avoid it, but soon saw her coming up again and learned that it was merely because she had nearly passed the entrance of the harbor ere aware of it. Our harbor is the very representation of the bottom of a large bowl, in the centre of which our vessel is now safely at anchor, surrounded by rocks fully a thousand feet high, and the wildest-looking place I ever was in. After supper we all went ashore; some scampered up the steepest hills next to us, but John, Shattuck, and myself went up the harbor, and after climbing to the top of a mountain (for I cannot call it a hill) went down a steep incline, up another hill, and so on till we reached the crest of the island, and surveyed all beneath us. Nothing but rocks — barren rocks — wild as the wildest of the Apennines everywhere; the moss only a few inches deep, and the soil or decomposed matter beneath it so moist that, wherever there was an incline, the whole slipped from under our feet like an avalanche, and down we slid for feet or yards. The labor was excessive; at the bottom of each dividing ravine the scrub bushes intercepted our way for twenty or thirty paces, over which we had to scramble with great exertion, and on our return we slid down fifty feet or more into an unknown pit of moss and mire, more or less deep. We started a female Black-cap Warbler from her nest, and I found it with four eggs, placed in the fork of a bush about three feet from the ground; a beautiful little mansion, and I will describe it to-morrow. I am wet through, and find the mosquitoes as troublesome as in the Floridas.

July 15. Our fine weather of yesterday was lost sometime in the night. As every one was keen to go off and see the country, we breakfasted at three o'clock this morning. The weather dubious, wind east. Two boats with the young men moved off in different directions. I sat to finishing the ground of my Grouse, and by nine had to shift my quarters, as it rained hard. By ten John and Lincoln had returned; these two always go together, being the strongest and most active, as well as the most experienced shots, though Coolidge and Ingalls are not far behind them in this. They brought a Red-necked Diver and one egg of that bird; the nest was placed on the edge of a very small pond, not more than ten square yards. Our harbor had many *Larus zonorhynchus*[1] (Common Gull); the captain shot one. I have never seen them so abundant as here. Their flight is graceful and elevated; when they descend for food the legs and feet generally drop below the body. They appear to know gunshot distance with wonderful precision, and it is seldom indeed that one comes near enough to be secured. They alight on the water with great delicacy, and swim beautifully. Coolidge's party brought a nest of the White-crowned Bunting (*Fringilla leucophyrs*) and three specimens of the bird, also two *Charadrius semipalmatus.* They found an island with many nests of the *Phalacrocorax dilophus*,[2] but only one egg, and thought the nests were old and abandoned. One of the young Ravens from the nest flew off at the sight of one of our men, and fell into the water; it was caught and brought to me; it was nearly fledged. I trimmed one of its wings, and turned it loose on the deck, but in attempting to rejoin its mother, who called most loudly from on high on the wing, the young one walked to the end of the bowsprit, jumped into the water, and was drowned; and soon after I saw the poor mother chased by a Peregrine

[1] Now *L. delawarensis,* also called Ring-billed Gull. — E. C.

[2] Double-crested Cormorant.

Falcon with great fury; she made for her nest, and when the Falcon saw her alight on the margin of her ledge, it flew off. I never thought that such a Hawk could chase with effect so large and so powerful a bird as the Raven. Some of our men who have been eggers and fishermen have seen these Ravens here every season for the last eight or nine years.

July 16. Another day of dirty weather, and all obliged to remain on board the greater portion of the time. I managed to draw at my Grouse and put in some handsome wild peas, Labrador tea-plant, and also one other plant, unknown to me. This afternoon the young men went off, and the result has been three White-crowned Buntings, and a female Black-capped Warbler. Our captain did much better for me, for in less than an hour he returned on board with thirty fine codfish, some of which we relished well at our supper. This evening the fog is so thick that we cannot see the summit of the rocks around us. The harbor has been full of Gulls the whole day. The captain brought me what he called an Esquimau codfish, which perhaps has never been described, and we have *spirited* him. We found a new species of floweret of the genus *Silene*,[1] but unknown to us. We have now lost four days in succession.

July 17. The mosquitoes so annoyed me last night that I did not even close my eyes. I tried the deck of the vessel, and though the fog was as thick as fine rain, these insects attacked me by thousands, and I returned below, where I continued fighting them till daylight, when I had a roaring fire made and got rid of them. The fog has been as thick as ever, and rain has fallen heavily, though the wind is southwest. I have drawn five eggs of land-birds: that of *Falco columbarius*,[2] *Fringilla leucophyrs*,[3] *Anthus spinoletta*,[4] *Sylvia striata*,[5] and *Fringilla savanna*.[6] I

[1] The Catchfly. [2] Pigeon Hawk. [3] White-crowned Sparrow.
[4] Brown Titlark. [5] Black-poll Warbler. [6] Savannah Finch.

also outlined in the mountainous hills near our vessel, as a background to my Willow Grouse. John and Coolidge with their companions brought in several specimens, but nothing new. Coolidge brought two young of the Red-necked Diver, which he caught *at the bottom* of a small pond by putting his gun rod on them, — the little things diving most admirably, and going about the bottom with as much apparent ease as fishes would. The captain and I went to an island where the *Phalacrocorax dilophus*[1] were abundant; thousands of young of all sizes, from just hatched to nearly full-grown, all opening their bills and squawking most vociferously; the noise was shocking and the stench intolerable. No doubt exists with us now that the Shore Lark breeds here; we meet with them very frequently. A beautiful species of violet was found, and I have transplanted several for Lucy, but it is doubtful if they will survive the voyage.

July 18. We all, with the exception of the cook, left the "Ripley" in three boats immediately after our early breakfast, and went to the main land, distant some five miles. The fog was thick enough, but the wind promised fair weather, and we have had it. As soon as we landed the captain and I went off over a large extent of marsh ground, the first we have yet met with in this country; the earth was wet, our feet sank far in the soil, and walking was extremely irksome. In crossing what is here called a wood, we found a nest of *Parus hudsonicus*[2] containing four young, able to fly; we procured the parents also, and I shall have the pleasure of drawing them to-morrow; this bird has never been figured that I know. Their *manners* resemble those of the Black-headed Titmouse, or Chickadee, and their notes are fully as strong, and clamorous, and constant as those of either of our own species. Few birds do I know that possess more active powers. The nest was dug by the bird out of a dead and

[1] Double-crested Cormorant. [2] Hudson's Bay Titmouse.

rotten stump, about five feet from the ground; the aperture, one and a quarter inches in diameter, was as round as if made by a small Woodpecker, or a Flying-squirrel. The hole inside was four by six inches; at the bottom a bed of chips was found, but the nest itself resembled a purse formed of the most beautiful and softest hair imaginable, — of Sables, Ermines, Martens, Hares, etc.; a warmer and snugger apartment no bird could desire, even in this cold country. On leaving the wood we shot a Spruce Partridge leading her young. On seeing us she ruffled her feathers like a barnyard hen, and rounded within a few feet of us to defend her brood; her very looks claimed our forbearance and clemency, but the enthusiastic desire to study nature prompted me to destroy her, and she was shot, and her brood secured in a few moments; the young very pretty and able to fly. This bird was so very gray that she might almost have been pronounced a different species from those at Dennysville, Me., last autumn; but this difference is occasioned by its being born so much farther north; the difference is no greater than in *Tetrao umbellus* [1] in Maine, and the same bird in western Pennsylvania. We crossed a savannah of many miles in extent; in many places the soil appeared to wave under us, and we expected at each step to go through the superficial moss carpet up to our middles in the mire; so wet and so spongy was it that I think I never labored harder in a walk of the same extent. In travelling through this quagmire we met with a small grove of good-sized, fine white-birch trees, and a few pines full forty feet high, quite a novelty to us at this juncture. On returning to our boats the trudging through the great bog was so fatiguing that we frequently lay down to rest; our sinews became cramped, and for my part, more than once I thought I should give up from weariness. One man killed a *Falco columbarius*, in the finest plumage I have ever seen. I

[1] The Ruffed Grouse, *Bonasa umbellus.* — E. C.

heard the delightful song of the Ruby-crowned Wren again and again; what would I give to find the nest of this *northern Humming-Bird?* We found the Fox-colored Sparrow in full song, and had our captain been up to birds' ways, he would have found its nest; for one started from his feet, and doubtless from the eggs, as she fluttered off with drooping wings, and led him away from the spot, which could not again be found. John and Co. found an island with upwards of two hundred nests of the *Larus canus,*[1] all with eggs, but not a young one hatched. The nests were placed on the bare rock; formed of seaweed, about six inches in diameter within, and a foot without; some were much thicker and larger than others; in many instances only a foot apart, in others a greater distance was found. The eggs are much smaller than those of *Larus marinus.* The eggs of the Cayenne Tern,[2]

[1] Common Gull. This record raises an interesting question, which can hardly be settled satisfactorily. *Larus canus,* the common Gull of Europe, is given by various authors in Audubon's time, besides himself, as a bird of the Atlantic coast of North America, from Labrador southward. But it is not known as such to ornithologists of the present day. The American Ornithologists' Union catalogues *L. canus* as merely a straggler in North America, with the query, "accidental in Labrador?" In his Notes on the Ornithology of Labrador, in Proc. Acad. Nat. Sci., Phila. 1861, p. 246, Dr. Coues gives *L. delawarensis,* the Ring-billed Gull, three specimens of which he procured at Henley Harbor, Aug. 21, 1860. These were birds of the year, and one of them, afterward sent to England, was identified by Mr. Howard Saunders as *L. canus* (P. Z. S. 1877, p. 178; Cat. B. Brit. Mus., xxv. 1896, p. 281). This would seem to bear out Audubon's Journal; but the "Common American Gull" of his published works is the one he calls *L. zonorhynchus* (*i. e., L. delawarensis*), and on p. 155 of the Birds of Am., 8vo ed., he gives the very incident here narrated in his Journal, as pertaining to the latter species. The probabilities are that, notwithstanding Dr. Coues' finding of the supposed *L. canus* in Labrador, the whole Audubonian record really belongs to *L. delawarensis.* — E. C.

[2] This appears to be an error, reflected in all of Audubon's published works. The Cayenne Tern of Audubon, as described and figured by him, is *Sterna regia,* which has never been known to occur in Labrador. Audubon never knew the Caspian Tern, *S. tschegrava,* and it is believed that this is the species which he saw in Labrador, and mistook for the Cayenne Tern — as he might easily do. See Coues, Birds of the Northwest, 1874, p. 669, where the case is noted. — E. C.

were also found, and a single pair of those remarkable birds, which could not be approached. Two Ptarmigans were killed; these birds have no whirring of the wings, even when surprised; they flew at the gunners in defence of the young, and one was killed with a gun-rod. The instant they perceive they are observed, when at a distance, they squat or lie flat on the moss, when it is almost impossible to see them unless right under your feet. From the top of a high rock I had fine view of the most extensive and the dreariest wilderness I have ever beheld. It chilled the heart to gaze on these barren lands of Labrador. Indeed I now dread every change of harbor, sò horribly rugged and dangerous is the whole coast and country, especially to the inexperienced man either of sea or land. The mosquitoes, many species of horse-fly, small bees, and black gnats filled the air; the frogs croaked; and yet the thermometer was not high, not above 55°. This is one of the wonders of this extraordinary country. We have returned to our vessel, wet, shivering with cold, tired, and very hungry. During our absence the cook caught some fine lobsters; but fourteen men, each with a gun, six of which were double-barrelled, searched all day for game, and have not averaged two birds apiece, nineteen being all that were shot to-day. We all conclude that no one man could provide food for himself without extreme difficulty. Some animal was seen at a great distance, so far indeed that we could not tell whether it was a Wolf or a Caribou.

July 19. So cold, rainy, and foggy has this day been that no one went out shooting, and only a ramble on shore was taken by way of escaping the motion of the vessel, which pitched very disagreeably, the wind blowing almost directly in our harbor; and I would not recommend this anchorage to a *painter naturalist*, as Charles Bonaparte calls me. I have drawn two *Parus hudsonicus*, and this evening went on shore with the captain for exercise, and enough have I had. We climbed the rocks and. followed from one to another, crossing fissures, holding to the moss hand and foot and with difficulty, for about a mile, when suddenly we came upon the deserted mansion of a Labrador sealer. It looked snug outside, and we entered it. It was formed of short slabs, all very well greased with seal oil; an oven without a pipe, a salt-box hung on a wooden peg, a three-legged stool, and a wooden box of a bedstead, with a flour-barrel containing some hundreds of seine-floats, and an old Seal seine, completed the list of goods and chattels. Three small windows, with four panes of glass each, were still in pretty good order, and so was the low door, which moved on wooden hinges, for which the maker has received no patent, I 'll be bound. This cabin made of hewn logs, brought from the main, was well put together, about twelve feet square, well roofed with bark of birch and spruce, thatched with moss, and every aperture rendered air-tight with oakum. But it was deserted and abandoned; the Seals are all caught, and the sealers have nought to do here now-a-days. We found a pile of good hard wood close to this abode, which we will have removed on board our vessel to-morrow. I discovered that this cabin had been the abode of two French Canadians; first, because their almanac, written with chalk on one of the logs, was in French; and next, the writing was in two very different styles. As we returned to our vessel I paused several times to contemplate the raging waves breaking on the stubborn, precipitous rocks beneath us, and thought how dreadful they would prove to any one who should be wrecked on so inhospitable a shore. No vessel, the captain assured me, could stand the sea we gazed upon at that moment, and I fully believed him, for the surge dashed forty feet or more high against the precipitous rocks. The Ravens flew above us, and a few Gulls beat to windward by dint of superior sailing; the horizon was hid by fog, so thick there, and on the crest of the island, that it looked like dense smoke. Though I wore thick mittens and very heavy clothing, I felt chilly with the cold. John's violin notes carry my thoughts far, far from Labrador, I assure thee.

July 20. Labrador deserves credit for *one* fine day! To-day has been calm, warm, and actually such a day as one might expect in the Middle States about the month of May. I drew from half-past three till ten this morning. The young men went off early, and the captain and myself went to the island next to us, but saw few birds: a Brown Lark, some Gulls, and the two White-crowned Buntings. In some small bays which we passed we found the stones thrown up by the sea in immense numbers, and of enormous size. These stones I now think are probably brought on shore in the masses of ice during the winter storms. These icebergs, then melting and breaking up, leave these enormous pebble-shaped stones, from ten to one hundred feet deep. When I returned to my drawing the captain went fishing, and caught thirty-seven cod in less than an hour. The wind rose towards evening, and the boats did not get in till nine o'clock, and much anxiety did I feel about them. Coolidge is an excellent sailor, and John too, for that matter, but very venturesome; and Lincoln equally so. The chase, as usual, poor; two Canadian Grouse in moult, — these do moult earlier than the Willow Grouse,[1] — some White-throated Sparrows, Yellow-rump Warblers, the Green Black-cap Flycatcher, the small Wood Pewee (?). I think this a new species, but cannot swear to it.[2] The

[1] Or Willow Ptarmigan, *Lagopus albus* — the same that Audubon has already spoken of procuring and drawing; but this is the first mention he makes which enables us to judge which of two species occurring in Labrador he had. The other is the Rock Grouse, or Ptarmigan, *L. rupestris.* — E. C.

[2] This is the bird which Audubon afterward identified with *Tyrannula richardsonii* of Swainson, Fn., Bor.-Am., ii., 1831, p. 146, pl. 46, lower fig., and published under the name of the Short-legged Pewee or Pewit Fly-catcher, *Muscicapa phœbe*, in Orn. Biogr., v. p. 299, pl. 434; B. Am., 8vo ed., i. p. 219, pl. 61. The species is now well known as the Western Wood Pewee, *Contopus richardsoni;* but it has never since Audubon's time been authenticated as a bird of Labrador. Audubon was of course perfectly familiar

young of the Tawny Thrush were seen with the mother, almost full-grown. All the party are very tired, especially Ingalls, who was swamped up to his arm-pits and was pulled out by his two companions; tired as they are, they have yet energy to eat tremendously.

July 21. I write now from a harbor which has no name, for we have mistaken it for the right one, which lies two miles east of this; but it matters little, for the coast of Labrador is all alike comfortless, cold and foggy, yet grand. We left Little Macatine at five this morning, with a stiff southwest breeze, and by ten our anchor was dropped here. We passed Captain Bayfield and his two boats engaged in the survey of the coast. We have been on shore; no birds but about a hundred Eider Ducks and Red-breasted Mergansers in the inner bay, with their broods all affrighted as our boats approached. Returning on board, found Captain Bayfield and his lieutenants, who remained to dine with us. They were short of provisions, and we gave them a barrel of ship-bread, and seventy pounds of beef. I presented the captain with a ham, with which he went off to their camp on some rocks not far distant. This evening we paid him a visit; he and his men are encamped in great comfort. The tea-things were yet arranged on the iron-bound bed, the trunks served as seats, and the sail-cloth clothes-bags as pillows. The moss was covered with a large tarred cloth, and neither wind nor damp was admitted. I gazed on the camp with much pleasure, and it was a great enjoyment to be with men of education and refined manners, such as are these officers of the Royal Navy; it was indeed a treat. We talked of the country where we were, of the beings best fitted to live and prosper here, not only of our species, but of all species,

with the common Wood Pewee, *Contopus virens*, and with the Pewit Flycatcher, *Sayornis phœbe*. We can hardly imagine him mistaken regarding the identity of either of these familiar birds; yet there is something about this Labrador record of supposed *C. richardsoni* which has never been satisfactorily explained. — E. C.

and also of the enormous destruction of everything here, except the rocks; the aborigines themselves melting away before the encroachments of the white man, who looks without pity upon the decrease of the devoted Indian, from whom he rifles home, food, clothing, and life. For as the Deer, the Caribou, and all other game is killed for the dollar which its skin brings in, the Indian must search in vain over the devastated country for that on which he is accustomed to feed, till, worn out by sorrow, despair, and want, he either goes far from his early haunts to others, which in time will be similarly invaded, or he lies on the rocky seashore and dies. We are often told rum kills the Indian ; I think not; it is oftener the want of food, the loss of hope as he loses sight of all that was once abundant, before the white man intruded on his land and killed off the wild quadrupeds and birds with which he has fed and clothed himself since his creation. Nature herself seems perishing. Labrador must shortly be depeopled, not only of aboriginal man, but of all else having life, owing to man's cupidity. When no more fish, no more game, no more birds exist on her hills, along her coasts, and in her rivers, then she will be abandoned and deserted like a worn-out field.

July 22. At six this morning, Captain Bayfield and Lieutenant Bowen came alongside in their respective boats to bid us farewell, being bound westward to the "Gulnare." We embarked in three boats and proceeded to examine a small harbor about a mile east, where we found a whaling schooner of fifty-five tons from Cape Gaspé in New Brunswick. When we reached it we found the men employed at boiling blubber in what, to me, resembled sugar boilers. The blubber lay heaped on the shore in chunks of six to twenty pounds, and looked filthy enough. The captain, or owner, of the vessel appeared to be a good, sensible man of that class, and cut off for me some strips of the skin of the whale from under the throat, with large and curious barnacles attached to it. They had struck four whales, of which three had sunk and were lost; this, I was told, was a very rare occurrence. We found at this place a French Canadian, a Seal-catcher, who gave me the following information. This portion of Labrador is free to any one to settle on, and he and another man had erected a small cabin, have Seal-nets, and traps to catch Foxes, and guns to shoot Bears and Wolves. They carry their quarry to Quebec, receive fifty cents per gallon for Seal oil, and from three to five guineas for Black and Silver-Fox skins, and other furs in proportion. From November till spring they kill Seals in great numbers. Two thousand five hundred were killed by seventeen men in three days; this great feat was done with short sticks, each Seal being killed with a single blow on the snout, while resting on the edges of the field ice. The Seals are carried to the camp on sledges drawn by Esquimaux dogs, that are so well trained that on reaching home they push the Seals off the sledge with their noses, and return to the hunters with despatch. (Remember, my Lucy, this is hearsay.) At other times the Seals are driven into nets one after another, until the poor animals become so hampered and confined that, the gun being used, they are easily and quickly despatched. He showed me a spot within a few yards of his cabin where, last winter, he caught six Silver-gray Foxes; these had gone to Quebec with his partner, who was daily expected. Bears and Caribous abound during winter, as well as Wolves, Hares, and Porcupines. The Hare (I suppose the Northern one) is brown at this season, and white in winter; the Wolves are mostly of a dun color, very ferocious and daring. A pack of about thirty followed a man to his cabin, and have more than once killed his dogs at his very door. I was the more surprised at this, as the dogs he had were as large as any Wolves I have ever seen. These dogs are extremely tractable; so much so that, when harnessed to a sledge, the leader starts at the word of command, and the whole pack gallops off swiftly enough to convey a man sixty miles in the course of seven or eight hours. They howl like Wolves, and are not at all like our common dogs. They were extremely gentle, came to us, jumped on us, and caressed us, as if we were old acquaintances. They do not take to the water, and are only fitted for drawing sledges and chasing Caribou. They are the only dogs which at all equal the Caribou in speed. As soon as winter's storms and thick ice close the harbors and the spaces between the mainland and the islands, the Caribous are seen moving in great gangs, first to the islands, where, the snow being more likely to be drifted, the animal finds places where the snow has blown away, and he can more easily reach the moss, which at this season is its only food. As the season increases in severity, the Caribous follow a due northwestern direction, and gradually reach a comparatively milder climate; but nevertheless, on their return in March and April, which return is as regular as the migration of birds, they are so poor and emaciated that the white man himself takes pity on them, and does not kill them. (Merciful beings, who spare life when the flesh is off the bones, and no market for the bones is at hand.) The Otter is tolerably abundant; these are principally trapped at the foot of the waterfalls to which they resort, these places being the latest to freeze, and the first to thaw. The Marten and the Sable are caught, but are by no means abundant, and every winter makes a deep impression on beast as well as on man. These Frenchmen receive their supplies from Quebec, where they send their furs and oil. At this time, which the man here calls "the idle time," he lolls about his cabin, lies in the sunshine like a Seal, eats, drinks, and sleeps his life away, careless of all the world, and the world, no doubt, careless of him. His dogs are his only companions until his partner's return, who, for all I know, is not himself better company than a dog. They have placed their very small cabin in a delightful situation, under the protection of an island, on the southwestern side of the main shore, where I was surprised to find the atmosphere quite warm, and the vegetation actually rank; for I saw plants with leaves fully a foot in breadth, and grasses three feet high. The birds had observed the natural advantages of this little paradise, for here we found the musical Winter Wren in full song, the first time in Labrador, the White-crowned Sparrow, or Bunting, singing melodiously from every bush, the Fox-tail Sparrow, the Black-cap Warbler, the Shore Lark nesting, but too cunning for us; the White-throated Sparrow and a Peregrine Falcon, besides about half a dozen of Lincoln's Finch. This afternoon the wind has been blowing a tremendous gale; our anchors have dragged with sixty fathoms of chain out. Yet one of the whaler's boats came to us with six men, who wished to see my drawings, and I gratified them willingly; they, in return, have promised to let me see a whale before cut up, if they should catch one ere we leave this place for Bras d'Or. Crows are not abundant here; the Ravens equal them in number, and Peregrine Falcons are more numerous. The horse-flies are so bad that they drove our young men on board.

July 23. We visited to-day the Seal establishment of a Scotchman, Samuel Robertson, situated on what he calls Sparr Point, about six miles east of our anchorage. He received us politely, addressed me by name, and told me that he had received intimation of my being on a vessel bound to this country, through the English and Canadian newspapers. This man has resided here twenty years, married a Labrador lady, daughter of a Monsieur Chevalier of Bras d'Or, a good-looking woman, and has six children. His house is comfortable, and in a little garden he raises a few potatoes, turnips, and other vegetables. He appears to be lord of these parts and quite contented with his lot. He told me his profits last year amounted to £600. He will not trade with the Indians, of whom we saw about twenty, of the Montagnais tribes, and employs only white serving-men. His Seal-oil tubs were full, and he was then engaged in loading two schooners for Quebec with that article. I bought from him the skin of a Cross Fox for three dollars. He complained of the American fishermen very much, told us they often acted as badly as pirates towards the Indians, the white settlers, and the eggers, all of whom have been more than once obliged to retaliate, when bloody encounters have been the result. He assured me he had seen a fisherman's crew kill thousands of Guillemots in the course of a day, pluck the feathers from the breasts, and throw the bodies into the sea. He also told me that during mild winters his little harbor is covered with pure white Gulls (the Silvery), but that all leave at the first appearance of spring. The travelling here is effected altogether on the snow-covered ice, by means of sledges and Esquimaux dogs, of which Mr. Robertson keeps a famous pack. With them, at the rate of about six miles an hour, he proceeds to Bras d'Or seventy-five miles, with his wife and six children, in one sledge drawn by ten dogs. Fifteen miles north of this place, he says, begins a lake represented by the Indians as four hundred miles long by one hundred broad. This sea-like lake is at times as rough as the ocean in a storm; it abounds with Wild Geese, and the water-fowl breed on its margins by millions. We have had a fine day, but very windy; Mr. R. says this July has been a remarkable one for rough weather. The Caribou flies have driven the hunters on board; Tom Lincoln, who is especially attacked by them, was actually covered with blood, and looked as if he had had a gouging fight with some rough Kentuckians. Mr. R.'s newspapers tell of the ravages of cholera in the south and west, of the indisposition of General Jackson at the Tremont House, Boston, etc.; thus even here the news circulates now and then. The mosquitoes trouble me so much that in driving them away I bespatter my paper with ink, as thou seest, God bless thee! Good-night.

July 24. The *Charadrius semipalmatus* breeds on the tops or sides of the high hills, and amid the moss of this country. I have not found the nest, but have been so very near the spot where it undoubtedly was, that the female has moved before me, trailing her wings and spreading her tail to draw me away; uttering a plaintive note, the purpose of which I easily conceive. The Shore Lark has served us the same way; that nest must also be placed amid the deep mosses, over which these beautiful birds run as nimbly as can be imagined. They have the power of giving two notes, so very different from each other that a person not seeing the bird would be inclined to believe that two birds of different species were at hand. Often after these notes comes a sweet trill; all these I have thought were in intimation of danger, and with the wish to induce the sitting mate to lie quiet and silent. Tom Lincoln, John, and I went on shore after two Bears, which I heard distinctly, but they eluded our pursuit by swimming from an island to the main land. Coolidge's party went to the Murre Rocks, where the Guillemots breed, and brought about fifteen hundred eggs. Shattuck killed two Gannets with a stick; they could have done the same with thousands of Guillemots when they landed; the birds scrambled off in such a hurried, confused, and frightened manner as to render them what Charles Bonaparte calls *stupid*, and they were so terrified they could scarcely take to wing. The island was literally covered with eggs, dung, and feathers, and smelt so shockingly that Ingalls and Coolidge were quite sick. Coolidge killed a White-winged Crossbill on these Murre rocks; for several weeks we have seen these birds pass over us, but have found none anywhere on shore. We have had a beautiful day, and would have sailed for Bras

JOHN WOODHOUSE AUDUBON.

FROM THE MINIATURE BY F. CRUIKSHANK, 1838.

d'Or, but our anchor stuck into a rock, and just as we might have sailed, a heavy fog came on, so here we are.

July 26. I did not write last night because we were at sea and the motion was too disagreeable, and my mind was as troubled as the ocean. We left Baie de Portage before five in the morning, with a good breeze, intending to come to at Chevalier's settlement, forty-seven miles; but after sailing thirty, the wind failed us, it rained and blew, with a tremendous sea which almost shook the masts out of our good vessel, and about eight we were abreast of Bonne Espérance; but as our pilot knew as much of this harbor as he did of the others, which means *nothing at all,* our captain thought prudent to stand off and proceed to Bras d'Or. The coast we have followed is like that we have hitherto seen, crowded with islands of all sizes and forms, against which the raging waves break in a frightful manner. We saw few birds, with the exception of Gannets, which were soaring about us most of the day feeding on capelings, of which there were myriads. I had three *Uria troile* thrown overboard alive to observe their actions. Two fluttered on top of the water for twenty yards or so, then dove, and did not rise again for fully a hundred yards from the vessel. The third went in head-foremost, like a man diving, and swam *under the surface* so smoothly and so rapidly that it looked like a fish with wings. At daylight we found ourselves at the mouth of Bras d'Or harbor, where we are snugly moored. Our pilot not knowing a foot of the ground, we hoisted our ensign, and Captain Billings came to us in his Hampton boat and piloted us in. Bras d'Or is the grand rendezvous of almost all the fishermen that resort to this coast for codfish. We found here a flotilla of about one hundred and fifty sail, principally fore-and-aft schooners, a few pickaxes, etc., mostly from Halifax and the eastern portions of the United States. There was a life and stir about this harbor which surprised us after so many weeks of wilderness and loneliness — the boats moving to and fro, going after fish, and returning loaded to the gunwales, others with seines, others with capelings for bait. A hundred or more were anchored out about a mile from us, hauling the poor codfish by thousands; hundreds of men engaged at cleaning and salting, their low jokes and songs resembling those of the Billingsgate gentry. On entering the port I observed a large flock of small Gulls, which species I could not ascertain, also *Lestris* of two species, one small and one large. As soon as breakfast was over, the young men went ashore to visit Mr. Jones, the owner of the Seal-fishing establishment here. He received them well — a rough, brown Nova Scotia man, the lord of this portion of Labrador — and he gave John and the others a good deal of information. Four or five species of Grouse, the Velvet Duck, the *Anas glacialis*,[1] and *Fuligula histrionica*,[2] the Wild Goose, and others breed in the swampy deserts at the head waters of the rivers, and around the edges of the lakes and ponds which everywhere abound. He also knew of my coming. John and Coolidge joined parties and brought me eight Red-polls, *Fringilla linaria*, old and young, which I will draw to-morrow. Query, is it the same which is found in Europe? Their note resembles that of the Siskin; their flight that of the Siskin and Linnet combined. The young were as large as the old, and could fly a mile at a stretch; they resort to low bushes along the edges of ponds and brooks; the hunters saw more than they shot. They brought also Savannah Finches, and White-crowned Sparrows. They saw a fine female *Tetrao canadensis*, not quite so gray as the last; the young flew well and alighted on trees and bushes, and John would not allow any of them to be shot, they were so trusting. They saw a Willow Grouse, which at sight of them, though at some distance, flew off and flew far; on

[1] *Harelda hiemalis*, the Old Squaw or Long-Tailed Duck. — E. C.

[2] *Histrionicus histrionicus*, the Harlequin Duck. —E. C.

being started again, flew again to a great distance with a loud, cackling note, but no whirr of the wings. They were within three hundred yards of an Eagle, which, from its dark color and enormous size and extent of wings, they took to be a female Washington Eagle.[1] I have made many inquiries, but every one tells me Eagles are most rare. It sailed away over the hills slowly and like a Vulture. After drawing two figures of the female White-winged Crossbill, I paid a visit to the country seat of Mr. Jones.[2] The snow is still to be seen in patches on every hill around us; the borders of the water courses are edged with grasses and weeds as rank of growth as may be seen in the Middle States in like situations. I saw a small brook filled with fine trout; but what pleased me best, I found a nest of the Shore Lark; it was embedded in moss so much the color of the birds, that when these sit on it, it is next to impossible to observe them; it was buried to its full depth, about seven inches, — composed outwardly of mosses of different sorts; within, fine grass circularly arranged, and mixed with many large, soft Duck feathers. These birds breed on high table-lands, one pair to a certain district. The place where I found the nest was so arid, poor and rocky that nothing grew there. We see the high mountains of Newfoundland, the summits, at present, far above the clouds. Two weeks since, the ice filled the very harbor where we now are, and not a vessel could approach; since then the ice has sunk, and none is to be seen far or near.

July 27. It has blown a tremendous gale the whole day; fortunately I had two *Fringilla linaria* to draw. The adult male alone possesses those rich colors on the breast; the female has only the front head crimson. They

[1] The Washington Eagle, or "Bird of Washington," of Audubon's works, is based upon the young Bald Eagle, *Haliaëtus leucocephaluis.* The bird here noted may have been either this species, or the *Aquila chrysaëtus.* — E. C.

[2] See Episode "A Labrador Squatter."

resemble the Cross-bills, notwithstanding Bonaparte, Nuttall, and others to the contrary. John kept me company and skinned fourteen small birds. Mr. Jones dined with us, after which the captain and the rest of our party went off through the storm to Blanc Sablons, four miles distant. This name is turned into "Nancy Belong" by the fishermen, who certainly tell very strange tales respecting this country. Mr. Jones entertained us by his account of travelling with dogs during winter. They are harnessed, he says, with a leather collar, a belly and back band, through the upper part of which passes the line of sealskin, which is attached to the sledge, and acts for a rein as well as a trace. An odd number of dogs always form the gang, from seven up, according to the distance of the journey, or the weight of the load; each dog is estimated to draw two hundred pounds, at a rate of five or six miles an hour. The leader is always a well-broken dog, and is placed ahead of the pack with a draught-line of from six to ten fathoms' length, and the rest with gradually shorter ones, to the last, which is about eight feet from the sledge; they are not, however, coupled, as often represented in engravings, but are each attached separately, so that when in motion they are more like a flock of Partridges, all flying loosely and yet in the same course. They always travel at a gallop, no matter what the state of the country may be, and to go down-hill is both difficult and dangerous; and at times it is necessary for the driver to guide the sledge with his feet, or with a strong staff planted in the snow as the sledge proceeds; and when heavily laden, and the descent great, the dogs are often taken off, and the sledge glides down alone, the man steering with his toes, and lying flat on his face, thus descending head-foremost like boys on their sleds. The dogs are so well acquainted with the courses and places in the neighborhood, that they never fail to take their master and his sledge to their destination, even should a tremendous snow-storm occur whilst under way; and it is always safer to leave one's fate to the instinct which these fine animals possess than to trust to human judgment, for it has been proved more than once that men who have made their dogs change their course have been lost, and sometimes died, in consequence. When travellers meet, both parties come circuitously, and as slowly as possible towards each other, which gives the separate packs the opportunity of observing that their masters are acquainted, when they meet without fighting, a thing which almost always occurs if the dogs meet unexpectedly. Mr. Jones lost a son of fourteen, a few years ago, in a snow-storm, owing to the servant in whose care he was, imprudently turning the dogs from their course; the dogs obeyed the command and struck towards Hudson's Bay; when the weather cleared the servant perceived his mistake, but alas! too late; the food was exhausted, and the lad gradually sank, and died in the arms of the man.

July 28. At daylight this morning the storm had abated, and although it was almost calm, the sea was high, and the "Ripley" tossed and rolled in a way which was extremely unpleasant to me. Breakfast over, we all proceeded to Mr. Jones' establishment with a view to procuring more information, and to try to have some of his men make Esquimaux boots and garments for us. We received little information, and were told no work could be done for us; on asking if his son, a youth of about twenty-three, could be hired to guide some of us into the interior some forty miles, Mr. Jones said the boy's mother had become so fearful of accidents since the loss of the other son that he could not say without asking her permission, which she would not grant. We proceeded over the table-lands towards some ponds. I found three young Shore Larks just out of the nest, and not yet able to fly; they hopped pretty briskly over the moss, uttering a soft *peep*, to which the parent bird responded at every call. I am glad that it is in my power to make a figure of these birds in summer, winter, and young plumage. We also found the breeding-place of the *Fuligula histrionica* in the corner of a small pond in some low bushes. By another pond we found the nest of the Velvet Duck, called here the White-winged Coot; it was placed on the moss among the grass, close to the water; it contained feathers, but no down as others. The female had six young, five of which we procured. They were about a week old, and I could readily recognize the male birds; they all had the white spot under the eye. Four were killed with one shot; one went on shore and squatted in the grass, where Lincoln caught it; but I begged for its life, and we left it to the care of its mother, and of its Maker. We also found the breeding-place of *Fuligula glacialis* by a very large pond; these breed in companies and are shyer than in the States. The Pied Duck[1] breeds here on the top of the low bushes, but the season is so far advanced we have not found its nest. Mr. Jones tells me the King Duck passes here northwards in the early part of March, returning in October, flying high, and in lines like the Canada Goose. The Snow Goose is never seen here; none, indeed, but oceanic species are seen here. (I look on *Anas fusca*[2] as an oceanic species.) Mr. Jones has never been more than a mile in the interior, and knows nothing of it. There are two species of Woodpecker here, and only two, the Three-toed and the Downy. When I began writing it was calm, now it blows a hurricane, rains hard, and the sea is as high as ever.

July 29. Another horrid, stormy day. The very fishermen complain. Five or six vessels left for further east, but I wish and long to go west. The young men, except

[1] Or Labrador Duck, *Camptolæmus labradorius.* This is a notable record, considering that the species became extinct about 1875.—E. C.

[2] This is the White-winged Coot or Scoter just mentioned above, *Œdemia deglandi.*— E. C.

Coolidge, went off this morning after an early breakfast to a place called Port Eau, eighteen miles distant, to try to procure some Esquimaux dresses, particularly moccasins. I felt glad when the boat which took them across the bay returned, as it assured me they were at least on terra firma. I do not expect them till to-morrow night, and I greatly miss them. When all our party is present, music, anecdotes, and jokes, journalizing and comparing notes, make the time pass merrily; but this evening the captain is on deck, Coolidge is skinning a bird, and I am writing that which is scarcely worth recording, with a horridly bad patent pen. I have to-day drawn three young Shore Larks, *Alauda alpestris*, the first ever portrayed by man. I did wish to draw an adult male, in full summer plumage, but could not get a handsome one. In one month all these birds must leave this coast, or begin to suffer. The young of many birds are full-fledged, and scamper over the rocks; the Ducks alone seem backward, but being more hardy can stay till October, when deep snows drive them off, ready or not for their laborious journey. I saw this afternoon two, or a pair, of the *Phalaropus hyperboreus;*[1] they were swimming in a small fresh-water pond, feeding on insects, and no doubt had their nest close by, as they evinced great anxiety at my approach. I did not shoot at them, and hope to find the nest or young; but to find nests in the moss is a difficult job, for the whole country looks alike. "The Curlews are coming;" this is as much of a saying here as that about the Wild Pigeons in Kentucky. What species of Curlew, I know not yet, for none have been killed, but one of our men, who started with John and party, broke down, and was sent back; he assured me that he had seen some with bills about four inches long, and the body the size of a Wild Pigeon. The accounts given of these Curlews border on the miraculous, and I shall say nothing

[1] Brown or Northern Phalarope.

about them till I have tested the fishermen's stories.[1] It is now calm, for a wonder, but as cold as vengeance, on deck; we have a good fire in the stove, and I am roasting on one side and freezing on the other. The water of our harbor is actually coated with oil, and the bottom fairly covered with the refuse of the codfish; the very air I breathe and smell is impregnated with essence of codfish.

July 30. It was a beautiful morning when I arose, and such a thing as a beautiful morning in this mournful country almost amounts to a phenomenon. The captain and myself went off to an island and searched for an *Alauda alpestris*, and found a good number of old and young, associated, both equally wild. The young were led off with great care by the adults, and urged to squat quietly till nearly within gunshot, when at a "tweet" from the parent they took to the wing and were off. These birds are very pugnacious, and attack a rival at once, when both come to the scratch with courage and tenacity. I saw one beautiful male in full summer dress, which I secured, and have drawn, with a portion of moss. I intend to add two drawn in winter plumage. This afternoon we visited Mr. Jones and his wife, a good motherly woman, who talked well. Our young men returned from Port Eau fatigued, and, as usual, hungry; complained, as I expected, of the country, the climate, and the scarcity of birds and plants, and not a pair of moccasins to be bought; so Lincoln and Shattuck are now barefooted. They brought a *Lestris pomarinus*,[2] female, a full-grown young Raven, and some Finches. Coolidge's party had some Lesser Red-polls, several Swamp Sparrows, three

[1] The Curlew which occurs in almost incredible numbers in Labrador is the Eskimo, *Numenius borealis;* the one with the bill about four inches long, also found in that country, but less commonly, is the Hudsonian, *N. hudsonicus.* See Coues, Proc. Acad. Nat. Sci., Philada., 1861, p. 236. —E. C.

[2] Pomarine Jager, or Gull-hunter, now called *Stercorarius pomarinus.* —E. C.

small Black-cap Green Flycatchers, Black-cap Warblers, old and young, the last fully grown, a *Fringilla lincolnii*, and a Pine Grosbeak. They saw many Gulls of various species, and also an iceberg of immense size. There is at Port Eau a large fishing establishment belonging to fishermen who come annually from the Island of Jersey, and have a large store with general supplies. Ere I go to rest let me tell thee that it is now blowing a young hurricane, and the prospect for to-morrow is a bad one. A few moments ago the report of a cannon came to our ears from the sea, and it is supposed that it was from the "Gulnare." I wish she was at our side and snugly moored as we are.

July 31. Another horrid hurricane, accompanied with heavy rain. I could not go on with my drawing either in the cabin or the hold, though everything was done that could be thought of, to assist me in the attempt; not a thing to relate, as not one of us could go on shore.

August 1. Bras d'Or, Coast of Labrador.[1] I have drawn my *Lestris pomarinus*, but under difficulties; the weather has quite changed; instead of a hurricane from the east, we have had one all day from the southwest, but no rain. At noon we were visited by an iceberg, which has been drifting within three miles of us, and is now grounded at the entrance of the bay; it looks like a large man-of-war dressed in light green muslin, instead of canvas, and when the sun strikes it, it glitters with intense brilliancy. When these transient monuments of the sea happen to tumble or roll over, the fall is tremendous, and the sound produced resembles that of loud, distant thunder; these icebergs are common here all summer, being wafted south with every gale that blows; as the winds are usually easterly, the coast of Newfoundland is more free from them than that of Labrador. I have determined to

[1] A small village on the coast of Labrador, latitude 51°; *not* the Bras D'Or of Cape Breton Island.

make a last thorough search of the mountain tops, plains and ponds, and if no success ensues, to raise anchor and sail towards the United States once more; and blessed will the day be when I land on those dear shores, where all I long for in the world exists and lives, I hope. We have been on shore for an hour for exercise, but the wind blew so fiercely we are glad to return.

August 2. Noon. The thermometer has risen to 58°, but it has rained hard all day; about dinner time a very handsome schooner from Boston, the size of ours, called the "Wizard," commanded by Captain Wilcomb of Ipswich, arrived, only nine days from Boston; but to our sorrow and disappointment, not a letter or paper did she bring, but we learned with pleasure that our great cities are all healthy, and for this intelligence I thank God. The "Wizard" brought two young Italian clerks as supercargo, who are going to purchase fish; they visited us and complained bitterly of the cold and the general appearance of the country. The retrograde migration of many birds has already commenced, more especially that of the lesser species both of land and water birds.

August 3. I was suddenly awakened last night about one o'clock by the shock which our vessel received from the "Wizard," which had broken her stern chain in the gale, which at that time was raging most furiously. Our captain was up in a moment, the vessels were parted and tranquillity was restored, but to John's sorrow, and my vexation, our beautiful and most comfortable gig had been struck by the "Wizard," and her bows stove in; at daylight it rained hard and the gale continued. Lincoln went on shore and shot some birds, but nothing of importance. This afternoon we all went ashore, through a high and frightful sea which drenched us to the skin, and went to the table-lands; there we found the true Esquimau Curlew, *Numenius borealis,* so carelessly described in Bonaparte's Synopsis. This species here takes the place of the Migratory Pigeon; it has now arrived; I have seen many hundreds this afternoon, and shot seven. They fly in compact bodies, with beautiful evolutions, overlooking a great extent of country ere they make choice of a spot on which to alight; this is done wherever a certain berry, called here "Curlew berry,"[1] proves to be abundant. Here they balance themselves, call, whistle, and of common accord come to the ground, as the top of the country here must be called. They devour every berry, and if pursued squat in the manner of Partridges. A single shot starts the whole flock; off they fly, ramble overhead for a great distance ere they again alight. This rambling is caused by the scarcity of berries. This is the same bird of which three specimens were sent to me by William Oakes, of Ipswich, Mass. The iceberg has been broken into thousands of pieces by the gale.

August 4. Still raining as steadily as ever; the morning was calm, and on shore the mosquitoes were shockingly bad, though the thermometer indicates only 49°. I have been drawing at the *Numenius borealis;* I find them difficult birds to represent. The young men went on shore and brought me four more; every one of the lads observed to-day the great tendency these birds have, in squatting to elude the eye, to turn the tail towards their pursuer, and to lay the head flat. This habit is common to many of the *Tringas*, and some of the *Charadrius*. This species of Curlew, the smallest I ever saw, feeds on the berries it procures, with a rapidity equalled only by that of the Passenger Pigeon; in an instant all the ripe berries on the plant are plucked and swallowed, and the whole country is cleared of these berries as our Western woods are of the mast. In their evolutions they resemble Pigeons also, sweeping over the ground, cutting backward and forward in the most interesting manner, and now and then poising in the air like a Hawk in sight of quarry. There

[1] *Empetrum nigrum.*

is scarcely any difference in the appearance of the adult and the young. The *Alauda alpestris* of this season has now made such progress in its growth that the first moulting is so forward that the small wing-coverts and secondaries are already come, and have assumed the beautiful rosy tints of the adults in patches at these parts; a most interesting state of their plumage, probably never seen by any naturalist before. It is quite surprising to see how quickly the growth is attained of every living thing in this country, either animal or vegetable. In six weeks I have seen the eggs laid, the birds hatched, their first moult half over, their association in flocks, and preparations begun for their leaving the country. That the Creator should have commanded millions of delicate, diminutive, tender creatures to cross immense spaces of country to all appearance a thousand times more congenial to them than this, to cause them to people, as it were, this desolate land for a time, to enliven it by the songs of the sweet feathered musicians for two months at most, and by the same command induce them to abandon it almost suddenly, is as wonderful as it is beautiful. The fruits are now ripe, yet six weeks ago the whole country was a sheet of snow, the bays locked in ice, the air a constant storm. Now the grass is rich in growth, at every step flowers are met with, insects fill the air, the snow-banks are melting; now and then an appearance as of summer does exist, but in thirty days all is over; the dark northern clouds will enwrap the mountain summits; the rivulets, the ponds, the rivers, the bays themselves will begin to freeze; heavy snowfalls will cover all these shores, and nature will resume her sleeping state, nay, more than that, one of desolation and death. Wonderful! Wonderful! But this marvellous country must be left to an abler pen than mine to describe. The *Tringa maritima* [1]

[1] The Purple or Rock Sandpiper, *Tringa* (*Arquatella*) *maritima*. — E. C.

and *Tringa pusilla*[1] were both shot in numbers this day; the young are now as large as the old, and we see little flocks everywhere. We heard the "Gulnare" was at Bonne Espérance, twenty miles west of us; I wish she was here, I should much like to see her officers again.

August 5. This has been a fine day, no hurricane. I have finished two Labrador Curlews, but not the ground. A few Curlews were shot, and a Black-breasted Plover. John shot a Shore Lark that had almost completed its moult; it appears to me that northern birds come to maturity sooner than southern ones, yet the reverse is the case in our own species. Birds of the Tringa kind are constantly passing over our heads in small bodies bound westward, some of the same species which I observed in the Floridas in October. The migration of birds is perhaps much more wonderful than that of fishes, almost all of which go feeling their way along the shores and return to the very same river, creek, or even hole to deposit their spawn, as birds do to their former nest; but the latter do not *feel* their way, but launching high in air go at once and correctly too, across vast tracts of country, yet at once stopping in portions heretofore their own, and of which they know by previous experiences the comforts and advantages. We have had several arrivals of vessels, some so heavily loaded with fish that the water runs over their decks; others, in ballast, have come to purchase fish.

August 10. I now sit down to post my poor book, while a heavy gale is raging furiously around our vessel. My reason for not writing at night is that I have been drawing so constantly, often seventeen hours a day, that the weariness of my body at night has been unprecedented, by such work at least. At times I felt as if my physical powers would abandon me; my neck, my shoulders, and,

[1] Not *Ereunetes pusillus*, but the Least Sandpiper, *Tringa* (*Actodromas*) *minutilla*, which appears as *Tringa pusilla* in Audubon's works. — E. C.

more than all, my fingers, were almost useless through actual fatigue at drawing. Who would believe this? — yet nothing is more true. When at the return of dawn my spirits called me out of my berth, my body seemed to beg my mind to suffer it to rest a while longer; and as dark forced me to lay aside my brushes I immediately went to rest as if I had walked sixty-five miles that day, as I have done *a few times* in my stronger days. Yesternight, when I rose from my little seat to contemplate my work and to judge of the effect of it compared with the nature which I had been attempting to copy, it was the affair of a moment; and instead of waiting, as I always like to do, until that hazy darkness which is to me the best time to judge of the strength of light and shade, I went at once to rest as if delivered from the heaviest task I ever performed. The young men think my fatigue is added to by the fact that I often work in wet clothes, but I have done that all my life with no ill effects. No! no! it is that I am no longer young. But I thank God that I did accomplish my task; my drawings are finished to the best of my ability, the skins well prepared by John. We have been to Paroket Island to procure the young of the *Mormon àrcticus*. As we approached the breeding-place, the air was filled with these birds, and the water around absolutely covered with them, while on the rocks were thousands, like sentinels on the watch. I took a stand, loaded and shot twenty-seven times, and killed twenty-seven birds, singly and on the wing, without missing a shot; as friend Bachman would say, "Pretty fair, Old Jostle!" The young men laughed, and said the birds were so thick no one could miss if he tried; however, none of them did so well. We had more than we wanted, but the young were all too small to draw with effect. Nearly every bird I killed had a fish in its beak, closely held by the head, and the body dangling obliquely in the air. These fish were all of the kind called here *Lints*, a long slender fish now in shoals of millions. How many must the multitude of Mormons inhabiting this island destroy daily? Whilst flying they all issue a rough croak, but none dropped the fish, nor indeed did they let it go when brought to the earth. The *Larus marinus* have now almost all gone south with their young; indeed, very few Gulls of any sort are now to be seen. Whilst on the island we saw a Hawk pounce on a Puffin and carry it off. Curlews have increased in numbers, but during two fair days we had they could not be approached; indeed, they appear to be so intent on their passage south that whenever the weather permits they are seen to strike high in the air across the harbor. The gale is so severe that our anchors have dragged forty or fifty yards, but by letting out still more chain we are now safe. It blows and rains so hard that it is impossible to stand in the bow of our vessel. But this is not all, — who, *now*, will deny the existence of the Labrador Falcon?[1] Yes, my Lucy, one more new species is on the list of the "Birds of America," and may we have the comfort of seeing its beautiful figure multiplied by Havell's engraver. This bird (both male and female) was shot by John whilst on an excursion with all our party, and on the 6th inst., when I sat till after twelve o'clock that night to outline one of them to save daylight the next day to color it, as I have done hundreds of times before. John shot them on the wing, whilst they were in company with their two young ones. The birds, one would be tempted to believe, had never seen a man before, for these affectionate parents dashed towards the gunners with fierce velocity, and almost instantly died from the effects of two well-directed shots. All efforts to procure the young birds were ineffectual;

[1] This is the bird figured by Audubon as *Falco labradora* on folio pl. 196, 8vo pl. 19, but which he afterward considered to be the same as his *F. islandicus*. It is now held, however, to represent a dark variety of Gyrfalcon, known as *F. gyrfalco obsoletus*, confined to Labrador and thence southward in winter to New England and New York. — E. C.

they were full grown, and as well as could be seen, exactly resembled the dead ones. The whole group flew much like the Peregrine Falcon, which indeed resembles them much in form, but neither in size nor color. Sometimes they hover almost high in air like a small Sparrow Hawk when watching some object fit for prey on the ground, and now and then cry much like the latter, but louder in proportion with the difference of size in the two species. Several times they alighted on stakes in the sandbar at the entrance of Bras d'Or River, and stood not as Hawks generally do, uprightly, but horizontally and much like a *Lestris* or a Tern. Beneath their nest we found the remains of *Alca torda*, *Uria troile*, and *Mormon arcticus*—all of which are within their reach on an island here called Parocket Island—also the remains of Curlews and Ptarmigans. The nest was so situated that it could not be reached, only seen into. Both birds were brought to me in excellent order. No more is known of this bird, I believe.

My evening has been enlivened by the two Italians from the "Wizard," who have been singing many songs to the accompaniment of John's violin.

August 11. At sea, Gulf of St. Lawrence. We are now, seven of the evening, fully fifty miles from the coast of Labrador. We left our harbor at eleven o'clock with a fair breeze; the storm of last night had died away and everything looked promising. The boats were sent ashore for a supply of fresh water; John and Coolidge went after Curlews; the rest of the crew, assisted by that of the "Wizard," raised the anchors, and all was soon in readiness. The bottom of our vessel had been previously scraped and cleaned from the thousands of barnacles, which, with a growth of seaweeds, seemed to feed upon her as they do on the throat of a whale. The two Italians and Captain Wilcomb came on board to bid us adieu; we hoisted sail, and came out of the Labrador harbor. Seldom in my life have I left a country with as little regret as I do this; the next nearest to this was East Florida, after my excursions up the St. John's River. As we sailed away, and I saw, probably for the last time, the high rugged hills partly immersed in masses of the thick fog that usually hovers over them, and knew that now the bow of our truly fine vessel was turned towards the place where thou, my Lucy, art waiting for me, I felt rejoiced, although yet far away. Now we are sailing in full sight of the northwestern coast of Newfoundland, the mountains of which are high, with drifted snow-banks dotted over them, and cut horizontally with floating strata of fogs reaching along the land as far as the eye can see. The sea is quite smooth; at least I think so, or have become a better seaman through habit. John and Lincoln are playing airs on the violin and flute; the other young men are on deck. It is worth saying that during the two months we have been on the coast of Labrador, moving from one harbor to another, or from one rocky isle to another, only three nights have we spent at sea. Twenty-three drawings have been executed, or commenced and nearly completed. Whether this voyage will prove a fruitful one remains to be proved; but I am content, and hope the Creator will permit us to reach our country and find our friends well and happy.

August 13. Harbor of St. George, St. George's Bay, Newfoundland. We have been running, as the sailors say, till five this evening, when we anchored here. Our way here was all in sight of land along the northwest shores of Newfoundland, the highest land we have yet seen; in some places the scenery was highly picturesque and agreeable to the eye, though little more vegetation appeared than in Labrador. Last night was a boisterous one, and we were all uncomfortable. This morning we entered the mouth of St. George's Bay, about thirteen leagues broad and fully eighteen deep. A more beautiful and ample basin cannot easily be found; not an obstruction is within it. The northeast shores are high and rocky, but the southern ones are sandy, low, and flat. It took us till five o'clock to ascend it and come to our present anchorage, in sight of a small village, the only one we have seen these two months, and on a harbor wherein more than fifty line-of-battle ships could safely ride, the bottom being of clay. The village is built on an elongated point of sand, or natural sea-wall, under which we now are, and is perfectly secure from every wind but the northeast. The country as we ascended the bay became more woody and less rough. The temperature changed quite suddenly, and this afternoon the weather was so mild that it was agreeable on deck, and congenial even to a southerner like myself. We find here several small vessels engaged in the fisheries, and an old hulk from Hull, England, called "Charles Tennison"; she was lost near this on her way from Quebec to Hull some years ago. As we came up the bay, a small boat with two men approached and boarded us, assisting as pilots. They had a barrel of fine salmon, which I bought for ten dollars. As soon as our anchors touched bottom, our young men went on shore to try to purchase some fresh provisions, but returned with nothing but two bottles of milk, though the village is said to contain two hundred inhabitants. Mackerel are caught all round us, and sharks of the man-eating kind are said to be abundant just now, and are extremely troublesome to the fishers' nets. Some signs of cultivation are to be seen across the harbor, and many huts of Mic-Mac Indians *adorn* the shores. We learn the winter here is not nearly as severe as at Quebec; the latitude of this place and the low, well-guarded situation of the little village, at once account for this; yet not far off I see patches of snow remaining from last winter. Some tell us birds are abundant, others that there are none; but we shall soon ascertain which report is true. I have not slept a minute since we left Labrador. The ice here did not break up so that the bay could be navigated till the 17th of May, and I feel confident no one could enter the harbors of Labrador before the 10th of June, or possibly even later.

August 14. All ashore in search of birds, plants, shells, and all the usual *et ceteras* attached to our vocations; but we all were driven on board soon, by a severe storm of wind and rain, showing that Newfoundland has its share of bad weather. Whilst on shore we found the country quite rich compared with Labrador, all the vegetable productions being much larger, more abundant, and finer. We saw a flock of House Swallows that had bred about the little village, now on their passage southwest, and all gay and singing. I forgot to say that two days since, when about forty miles out at sea, we saw a flock of the Republican Swallow. I saw here the Blue yellow-eyed Warbler, the Fish-Hawk, several species of Sparrows, among them the Lincoln's Finch, the Canada Titmouse, Black-headed ditto, White-winged Crossbill, Pine Grosbeak, Maryland Yellow-throat, Pigeon Hawk, Hairy Woodpecker, Bank Swallow, Tell-tale Godwit, Golden-eyed Duck, Red-breasted Merganser, three Loons, — of which two were young and almost able to fly; the Spotted Sandpiper, and a flock of Tringas, the species of which could not be ascertained. We spoke to some of the native Indians to try to engage them to show us the way to the interior, where we are told the Small, or True Ptarmigan abounds, but they were too lazy even to earn money. Among the plants we found two varieties of rose, and the narrow-leaved kalmia. Few supplies can be obtained, and a couple of small clearings are all the cultivated land we have seen since we left the Magdalene Islands. On returning to our vessel, I was rowed on the roughest sea I have ever before encountered in an open boat, but our captain was at the helm and we reached the deck safely but drenched to the skin. The wind has now abated, and I hope to draw plants all day. This evening a flock of Terns, twenty or thirty with their young, travelled due south; they were very clamorous and beat against the gale most beautifully. Several Indians came on board and promised to go to-morrow after Hares.

August 15. We have had a beautiful day; this morning some Indians came alongside; they had half a Reindeer or Caribou, and a Hare which I had never seen before. We took the forty-four pounds of fresh meat and gave in exchange twenty-one of pork and thirty-three of ship-biscuit, and paid a quarter of a dollar for the Hare, which plainly shows that these Indians know full well the value of the game which they procure. I spent a portion of the day in adding a plant to my drawing of the Red-necked Diver, after which we all went on shore to the Indians' camp across the bay. We found them, as I expected, all lying down pell-mell in their wigwams. A strong mixture of blood was apparent in their skins, shape, and deportment; some indeed were nearly white, and sorry I am to say that the nearer to our own noble selves, the filthier and lazier they are; the women and children were particularly disgusting. Some of the former, from whom I purchased some rough baskets, were frightfully so. Other women had been out collecting the fruit called here "baked apple" [*Rubus chamæmorus*]. When a little roasted it tastes exactly like baked apple. The children were engaged in catching lobsters and eels, of which there are numbers in all the bays here; at Labrador, lobsters are rare. The young Indians simply waded out up to their knees, turned the eel grass over, and secured their prey. After much parley, we engaged two hunters to go as guides into the interior to procure Caribou and Hares, for which they were to receive a dollar a day each. Our men caught ninety-nine lobsters, all of good size; the shores truly abound in this valuable shell-fish. The Indians roast them in a fire of brushwood, and devour them without salt or any other *et ceteras*. The Caribous are now "in velvet," and their skins light gray, the flesh tender, but the animal poor. The average weight when in good condition, four hundred pounds. In the early part of March the Caribou leave the hills and come to the sea-shore to feed on kelp and sea-grasses cut off by the ice and cast on the shore. Groups of many hundreds may be seen thus feeding. The flesh here is held in low estimation; it tastes like poor venison. I saw to-day several pairs of Cayenne Terns on their way south; they flew high, and were very noisy. The Great Terns passed also in vast multitudes. When the weather is stormy, they skim close over the water; if fair, they rise very high and fly more at leisure. The Tell-tale Godwit is now extremely fat, extremely juicy, extremely tender, and extremely good. The *Parus hudsonicus* is very abundant; so is the Pine Grosbeak, but in a shocking state of moult. The *Kalmia angustifolia*,[1] the natives say, is an antidote for cramp and rheumatism. I was on the point of bidding thee good-night, when we all were invited to a ball[2] on shore. I am going with the rest out of curiosity.

August 16. The people seemed to enjoy themselves well at the ball, and John played the violin for them till half-past two. I returned on board before eleven, and slept soundly till the young men hailed for a boat. This morning has been spent drawing a kalmia to a bird. The young men went off with the Indians this morning, but returned this evening driven back by flies and mosquitoes. Lincoln is really in great pain. They brought a pair of Willow Grouse, old and young; the latter had no hairy feathers yet on the legs. They saw Canada Jays, Crossbills, Pine Grosbeaks, Robins, one Golden-winged Woodpecker, many Canadian Titmice, a Martin Swallow, a Kingfisher (none in Labrador) heard a Squirrel which sounded like the Red Squirrel. The country was described as being "up and down the whole

[1] Sheep laurel. [2] See Episode, "A Ball in Newfoundland."

way." The moss almost as deep as in Labrador, the morasses quite as much so; no tall wood, and no hard wood. The lads were all so fatigued that they are now sound asleep.

August 17. We would now be "ploughing the deep" had the wind been fair; but as it was not, here we still are *in statu quo.* I have drawn a curious species of alder to my White-winged Crossbill, and finished it. I had a visit from an old Frenchman who has resided on this famous island for fifty years; he assured me that no Red Indians were now to be found: the last he heard of were seen twenty-two years ago. These native Indians give no quarter to anybody; usually, after killing their foes, they cut the heads off the latter, and leave the body to the wild beasts of the country. Several flocks of Golden Plovers passed over the bay this forenoon; two *Lestris pomarina* came in this evening. Ravens abound here, but no Crows have been seen. The Great Tern is passing south by thousands, and a small flock of Canada Geese was seen. A young of the Golden-crested Wren was shot, full grown and fledged, but not a sign of yellow on the head. A *Muscicapa* (Flycatcher) was killed which probably is new; to-morrow will tell. I bought seven Newfoundland dogs for seventeen dollars; now I shall be able to fulfil my promises to friends. The American Bittern breeds here, and leaves in about two weeks hence.

August 18. At daylight the wind was fair, and though cloudy, we broke our anchorage, and at five were under way. We coasted Newfoundland till evening, when the wind blew a gale from the southwest, and a regular tempest set in. Our vessel was brought to at dusk, and we danced and kicked over the waves all evening, and will do so all night.

August 19. The storm still continues, without any sign of abating; we are still at anchor, tossed hither and thither, and withal sea-sick.

August 21. To-day the storm ceased, but the wind is still so adverse that we could make no port of Newfoundland; towards this island we steered, for none of us wished to return to Labrador. We tried to enter the Strait of Canseau, but the wind failed us; while the vessel lay becalmed we decided to try to reach Pictou in Nova Scotia and travel by land. We are now beating about towards that port and hope to reach it early to-morrow morning. The great desire we all have to see Pictou, Halifax, and the country between them and Eastport, is our inducement.

August 22. After in vain attempting to reach Pictou, we concluded, after dinner, that myself and party should be put ashore anywhere, and the "Ripley" should sail back towards the Straits of Canseau, the wind and tide being favorable. We drank a glass of wine to our wives and our friends, and our excellent little captain took us to the shore, while the vessel stood still, with all sails up, awaiting his return. We happened to land on an island called Ruy's Island, where, fortunately for us, we found some men making hay. Two of these we engaged to carry our trunks and two of the party to this place, Pictou, for two dollars — truly cheap. Our effects, or rather those we needed, were soon put up, we all shook hands most heartily with the captain — to whom we now feel really attached — said farewell to the crew, and parted, giving three hearty cheers. We were now, thanks to God, positively on the mainland of our native country, and after four days' confinement in our berths, and sick of sea-sickness, the sea and all its appurtenances, we felt so refreshed that the thought of walking nine miles seemed like nothing more than dancing a quadrille. The air felt deliciously warm, the country, compared with those we have so lately left, appeared perfectly beautiful, and the smell of the new-mown grass was the sweetest that ever existed. Even the music of the crickets was delightful to mine ears, for no such insect does either Labrador or Newfoundland afford. The voice of a Blue Jay was melody to me, and the sight of a Humming-bird quite filled my heart with delight. We were conveyed a short distance from the island to the main; Ingalls and Coolidge remained in the boat, and the rest of us took the road, along which we moved as lightly as if boys just out of school. The roads were good, or seemed to be so; the woods were all of tall timber, and the air that circulated freely was filled with perfume. Almost every plant we saw brought to mind some portion of the United States; in a word, all of us felt quite happy. Now and then, as we crossed a hill and looked back over the sea, we saw our beautiful vessel sailing freely before the wind, and as she gradually neared the horizon, she looked like a white speck, or an Eagle high in air. We wished our captain a most safe voyage to Quoddy. We arrived opposite Pictou in two hours and a half, and lay down on the grass to await the arrival of the boat, enjoying the scenery around us. A number of American vessels were in the harbor, loading with coal; the village, placed at the upper end of a fine bay, looked well, though small. Three churches rose above the rest of the buildings, all of which are of wood, and several vessels were on the stocks. The whole country appeared in a high state of cultivation, and looked well; the population is about two thousand. Our boat came, we crossed the bay, and put up at the "Royal Oak," the best house, and have had what seemed to be, after our recent fare, a most excellent supper. The very treading on a carpeted floor was quite wonderful. This evening we called on Professor McCullough, who received us very kindly, gave us a glass of wine, showed his fine collection of well-preserved birds and other things, and invited us to breakfast to-morrow at eight, when we are again to inspect his curiosities. The Professor's mansion is a quarter of a mile out of town, and looks much like a small English villa.

August 23. We had an excellent Scotch breakfast at Professor McCullough's. His whole family were present, four sons and a daughter, besides his wife and her sister. I became more pleased with the professor the more he talked. I showed a few Labrador drawings, after which we went in a body to the University, once more to examine his fine collection. I found there half a dozen specimens of birds which I longed for and said so; the Professor had the cases opened, the specimens taken out, and he offered them to me with so much apparent good will that I took them. He then asked me to look around and not to leave any object which might be of assistance in my publication; but so generous had he already proved himself that I remained mute; I saw several I would have liked to have, but I could not mention them. He offered me all his fresh-water shells, and any minerals I might choose. I took a few specimens of iron and copper. I am much surprised that this valuable collection is not purchased by the government of the Province; he offered it for £500. I think it well worth £1,000. Thou wilt say I am an enthusiast; to this I will reply — True, but there are many more in the world, particularly in Europe. On our return to the "Royal Oak" we were called on by Mr. Blanchard, the deputy consul for the United States, an agreeable man, who offered to do whatever he could for us; but the coach was almost ready, our birds were packed, our bill paid, and the coach rolled off. I walked on ahead with Mr. Blanchard for about a mile; he spoke much of England, and knew John Adamson of Newcastle and other friends there. The coach came up, and we said farewell. The wind had commenced to blow, and soon rain fell heavily; we went on smoothly, the road being as good as any in England, and broader. We passed through a fine tract of country, well wooded, well cultivated, and a wonderful relief to our eyes after the barren and desolate regions of rocks, snow, tempests, and storms. We stopped to dine at four in the afternoon at a wayside house. The rain poured down; two ladies and a gentleman — the husband of one of them — had arrived before us in an open cart, or "jersey," and I, with all the gallantry of my nature, at once offered to change vehicles with them. They accepted the exchange at once, but did not even thank us in return. Shattuck, Ingalls, and I jumped into the open cart when dinner was ended. I was seated by a very so-so Irish dame named Katy; her husband was our driver. Our exchange proved a most excellent one: the weather cleared up; we saw the country much better than we could have done in the coach. To our surprise we were suddenly passed by Professor McCullough, who said he would see us at Truro. Towards sunset we arrived in view of this pretty, scattered village, in sight of the head waters of the Bay of Fundy. What a delightful sensation at that moment ran through my frame, as I realized that I was within a few days of home! We reached the tavern, or hotel, or whatever else the house of stoppage might be called, but as only three of us could be accommodated there we went across the street to another. Professor McCullough came in and introduced us to several members of the Assembly of this Province, and I was handed several pinches of snuff by the Professor, who *loves it.* We tried in vain to obtain a conveyance for ourselves to-morrow morning instead of going by coach to-night; it could not be done. Professor McCullough then took me to the house of Samuel George Archibald, Esq., Speaker of the Assembly, who introduced me to his wife and handsome young daughter. I showed them a few drawings, and received a letter from Mr. Archibald to the Chief Justice of Halifax, and now we are waiting for the mail coach to proceed to that place. The village of Truro demands a few words. It is situated in the middle of a most beautiful valley, of great extent and well cultivated; several brooks water this valley, and empty into the Bay of Fundy, the broad expanse of which we see to the westward. The buildings, though principally of wood, are good-looking, and as cleanly as those in our pretty eastern villages, white, with green shutters. The style of the people, be it loyal or otherwise, is extremely genteel, and I was more than pleased with all those whom I saw. The coach is at the door, the cover of my trunk is gaping to receive this poor book, and therefore once more, good-night.

August 24. Wind due east, hauling to the northeast, good for the "Ripley." We are now at Halifax in Nova Scotia, but let me tell thee how and in what manner we reached it. It was eleven last night when we seated ourselves in the coach; the night was beautiful, and the moon shone brightly. We could only partially observe the country until the morning broke; but the road we can swear was hilly, and our horses lazy, or more probably very poor. After riding twenty miles, we stopped a good hour to change horses and warm ourselves. John went to sleep, but the rest of us had some supper, served by a very handsome country girl. At the call, "Coach ready!" we jumped in, and had advanced perhaps a mile and a half when the linch-pin broke, and there we were at a standstill. Ingalls took charge of the horses, and responded with great energy to the calls of the owls that came from the depths of the woods, where they were engaged either at praying to Diana or at calling to their parents, friends, and distant relations. John, Lincoln, and Shattuck, always ready for a nap, made this night no exception; Coolidge and I, not trusting altogether to Ingalls' wakefulness, kept awake and prayed to be shortly delivered from this most disagreeable of travelling experiences, detention — at all times to be avoided if possible, and certainly to be dreaded on a chilly night in this latitude. Looking up the road, the vacillating glimmer of the flame intended to assist the coachman in the recovery of the lost linch-pin was all that could be distinguished, for by this the time was what is called "wolfy." The man returned, put out the pine-knot — the linch-pin could not be found — and another quarter of an hour was spent in repairing with all sorts of odds and ends. How much longer Ingalls could, or would, have held the horses, we never asked him, as from different exclamations we heard him utter we thought it well to be silent on that subject. The day dawned fair and beautiful. I ran a mile or so ahead of the coach to warm my feet, and afterwards sat by the driver to obtain, if possible, some information about the country, which became poorer and poorer as our journey proceeded. We were all very hungry, and were told the "*stand*" stood twenty-five miles from the lost linch-pin. I asked our driver to stop wherever he thought we could procure a dozen or so of hard-boiled eggs and some coffee, or indeed anything eatable; so he drew up at a house where the owner looked us over, and said it would be quite impossible to provide a breakfast for six persons of our appearance. We passed on and soon came on the track of a tolerably large bear, *in the road*, and at last reached the breakfast ground at a house on the margin of Green Lake, a place where fish and game, in the season, abound. This lake forms part of the channel which was intended to be cut for connecting by canal the Atlantic, the Baie of Fundy, and the Gulf of St. Lawrence, at Bay Verte. Ninety thousand pounds have been expended, but the canal is not finished, and probably never will be; for we are told the government will not assist the company by which it was undertaken, and private spirit is slumbering. We had an excellent breakfast at this house, seventeen miles from Halifax; this place would be a most delightful summer residence. The road was now level, but narrow; the flag of the Halifax garrison was seen when two miles distant. Suddenly we turned short, and stopped at a gate fronting a wharf, where was a small ferry-boat. Here we were detained nearly an hour; how would this work in the States? Why did Mrs. Trollope not visit Halifax?

The number of beggarly-looking negroes and negresses would have afforded her ample scope for contemplation and description. We crossed the harbor, in which rode a sixty-four-gun flag-ship, and arrived at the house of one Mr. Paul. This was the best hotel in Halifax, yet with great difficulty we obtained *one* room with four beds, but no private parlor — which we thought necessary. With a population of eighteen thousand souls, and just now two thousand soldiers added to these, Halifax has not one good hotel, for here the attendance is miserable, and the table far from good. We have walked about to see the town, and all have aching feet and leg-bones in consequence of walking on hard ground after tramping only on the softest, deepest mosses for two months.

August 25. I rose at four and wrote to thee and Dr. Parkman;[1] Shattuck wrote to his father, and he and I took these letters to an English schooner bound to Boston. I was surprised to find every wharf gated, the gates locked and barred, and sentinels at every point. I searched everywhere for a barber; they do not here shave on Sunday; finally, by dint of begging, and assuring the man that I was utterly unacquainted with the laws of Halifax, being a stranger, my long beard was cut at last. Four of us went to church where the Bishop read and preached; the soldiers are divided up among the different churches and attend in full uniform. This afternoon we saw a military burial; this was a grand sight. The soldiers walked far apart, with arms reversed; an excellent band executed the most solemn marches and a fine anthem. I gave my letters from Boston to Mr. Tremaine, an amiable gentleman.

August 26. This day has been spent in writing letters to thyself, Nicholas Berthoud, John Bachman, and Edward Harris; to the last I have written a long letter describing all our voyage. I took the letters to the "Cordelia" packet,

[1] Dr. George Parkman, of Boston, who was murdered by Professor J. W. Webster in Boston, November 23, 1849.

which sails on Wednesday, and may reach Boston before we do. I delivered my letters to Bishop Inglis and the Chief-Justice, but were assured both were out. John and Ingalls spent their evening very agreeably with Commissary Hewitson.

August 27. Breakfast eaten and bill paid, we entered the coach at nine o'clock, which would only contain five, so though it rained one of us sat with the driver. The road between Halifax and Windsor, where we now are, is macadamized and good, over hills and through valleys, and though the distance is forty-five miles, we had only one pair of horses, which nevertheless travelled about six and a half miles an hour. Nine miles of our road lay along the Bay of Halifax, and was very pleasant. Here and there a country home came in sight. Our driver told us that a French squadron was pursued by an English fleet to the head of this bay, and the seven French vessels were compelled to strike their colors; but the French commodore or admiral sunk all his vessels, preferring this to surrendering them to the British. So deep was the water that the very tops of the masts sank far out of sight, and once only since that time, twenty years ago, have they been seen; this was on an unusually calm, clear day seven years past. We saw *en passant* the abandoned lodge of Prince Edward, who spent a million pounds on the building, grounds, etc. The whole now is in the greatest state of ruin; thirty years have gone by since it was in its splendor. On leaving the bay, we followed the Salmon River, a small rivulet of swift water, which abounds in salmon, trout, and other fish. The whole country is miserably poor, yet much cultivation is seen all the way. Much game and good fishing was to be had round the inn where we dined; the landlord said his terms were five dollars a week, and it would be a pleasant summer residence. We passed the seat of Mr. Jeffries, President of the Assembly, now Acting Governor. The house is large and the grounds in fine order. It is between two handsome fresh-water lakes; indeed, the country is covered with lakes, all of which are well supplied with trout. We saw the college and the common school, built of free-stone, both handsome buildings. We crossed the head of the St. Croix River, which rolls its impetuous waters into the Bay of Fundy. From here to Windsor the country improved rapidly and the crops looked well. Windsor is a neat, pretty village; the vast banks of plaster of Paris all about it give employment to the inhabitants and bring wealth to the place; it is shipped from here in large quantities. Our coach stopped at the best *boarding-house* here, for nowhere in the Provinces have we heard of hotels; the house was full and we were conveyed to another, where, after more than two hours' delay, we had a very indifferent supper. Meantime we walked to see the Windsor River, on the east bank of which the village is situated. The view was indeed novel; the bed of the river, nearly a mile wide and quite bare as far as eye could reach,—about ten miles. Scarcely any water to be seen, and yet the spot where we stood, sixty-five feet above the river bed, showed that at high tide this wonderful basin must be filled to the brim. Opposite to us, indeed, the country is diked in, and vessels left dry at the wharves had a strange appearance. We are told that there have been instances when vessels have slid sidewise from the top of the bank to the level of the gravelly bed of the river. The shores are covered for a hundred yards with mud of a reddish color. This conveys more the idea of a flood or great freshet than the result of tide, and I long to see the waters of the ocean advancing at the rate of four knots an hour to fill this extraordinary basin; this sight I hope to enjoy to-morrow.

August 28. I can now say that I have seen the tide waters of the Bay of Fundy rise sixty-five feet.[1] We were

[1] See Episode, "The Bay of Fundy."

seated on one of the wharves and saw the mass of water accumulating with a rapidity I cannot describe. At half-flow the water rose three feet in ten minutes, but it is even more rapid than this. A few minutes after its greatest height is attained it begins to recede, and in a few hours the whole bed of the river is again emptied. We rambled over the beautiful meadows and fields, and John shot two Marsh Hawks, one of each sex, and we saw many more. These birds here are much darker above and much deeper rufous below, than any I ever procured in the Middle States or farther south. Indeed, it may be said that the farther north I have been, the deeper in tint have I found the birds. The steamboat has just arrived, and the young men have been on board to secure our passage. No news from the States.

Eastport, Maine, August 31. We arrived here yesterday afternoon in the steamer "Maid of the Mist." We left Windsor shortly before twelve noon, and reached St. John's, New Brunswick, at two o'clock at night. Passed "Cape Blow-me-down," "Cape Split," and "Cape d'Or." We were very comfortable, as there were few passengers, but the price was sufficient for all we had, and more. We perambulated the streets of St. John's by moonlight, and when the shops opened I purchased two suits of excellent stuff for shooting garments. At the wharf, just as the steamer was about to leave, I had the great pleasure of meeting my most excellent friend Edward Harris, who gave me a letter from thee, and the first intelligence from the big world we have left for two months. Here we were kindly received by all our acquaintance; our trunks were not opened, and the new clothes paid no duties; this ought to be the case with poor students of nature all over the world. We gave up the "Ripley" to Messrs. Buck and Tinkham, took up our quarters with good Mr. Weston, and all began packing immediately.

We reached New York on Saturday morning, the 7th of September, and, thank God, found all well. Whilst at Boston I wrote several letters, one very long one to Thomas Nuttall, in which I gave him some account of the habits of water-birds with which he was unacquainted; he sent me an extremely kind letter in answer.

THE MISSOURI RIVER JOURNALS

1843

INTRODUCTION

THIS journey, which occupied within a few days of eight months, — from March 11, 1843, to November 6 of the same year, — was undertaken in the interest of the "Quadrupeds of North America," in which the three Audubons and Dr. Bachman were then deeply engaged. The journey has been only briefly touched upon in former publications, and the entire record from August 16 until the return home was lost in the back of an old secretary from the time of Audubon's return in November, 1843, until August, 1896, when two of his granddaughters found it. Mrs. Audubon states in her narrative that no record of this part of the trip was known to exist, and none of the family now living had ever seen it until the date mentioned.

Not only is the diary most valuable from the point of view of the naturalist, but also from that of the historian interested in the frontier life of those days.

M. R. A.

As the only account of the journey from New York to St. Louis which can now be found is contained in a letter to my uncle Mr. James Hall, dated St. Louis, March 29, 1843, the following extract is given:—

"The weather has been bad ever since we left Baltimore. There we encountered a snow-storm that accompanied us all the way to this very spot, and at this moment the country is whitened with this precious, semi-congealed, heavenly dew. As to ice! — I wish it were all in your ice-house when summer does come, should summer show her bright features in the year of our Lord 1843. We first encountered ice at Wheeling, and it has floated down the Ohio all around us, as well as up the Mississippi to pleasant St. Louis. And such a steamer as we have come in from Louisville here! — the very filthiest of all filthy old rat-traps I ever travelled in; and the fare worse, certainly much worse, and so scanty withal that our worthy commander could not have given us another meal had we been detained a night longer. I wrote a famous long letter to my Lucy on the subject, and as I know you will hear it, will not repeat the account of our situation on board the 'Gallant' — a pretty name, too, but alas! her name, like mine, is only a shadow, for as she struck a sawyer[1] one night we all ran like mad to make ready to leap overboard; but as God would have it, our lives and the 'Gallant,' were spared — she from sinking, and we from swimming amid rolling and crashing hard ice. THE LADIES screamed, the babies squalled, the dogs yelled, the steam roared, the captain (who, by the way, is a very gallant

[1] A fallen tree that rests on the root end at the bottom of a stream or river, and sways up or down with the current.

man) swore — not like an angel, but like the very devil — and all was confusion and uproar, just as if Miller's prophecy had actually been nigh. Luckily, we had had our *supper*, as the thing was called on board the 'Gallant,' and every man appeared to feel resolute, if not resolved to die.

"I would have given much at that moment for a picture of the whole. Our *compagnons de voyage*, about one hundred and fifty, were composed of Buckeyes, Wolverines, Suckers, Hoosiers, and gamblers, with drunkards of each and every denomination, their ladies and babies of the same nature, and specifically the dirtiest of the dirty. We had to dip the water for washing from the river in tin basins, soap ourselves all from the same cake, and wipe the one hundred and fifty with the same solitary one towel rolling over a pin, until it would have been difficult to say, even with your keen eyes, whether it was manufactured of hemp, tow, flax, or cotton. My bed had two sheets, of course, measuring seven-eighths of a yard wide; my pillow was filled with corn-shucks. Harris fared even worse than I, and our 'state-room' was evidently better fitted for the smoking of hams than the smoking of Christians. When it rained outside, it rained also within, and on one particular morning, when the snow melted on the upper deck, or roof, it was a lively scene to see each person seeking for a spot free from the many spouts overhead.

"We are at the Glasgow Hotel, and will leave it the day after to-morrow, as it is too good for our purses. We intended to have gone twenty miles in Illinois to Edwardsville, but have changed our plans, and will go northwest sixteen miles to Florissant, where we are assured game is plenty, and the living quite cheap. We do not expect to leave this till the 20th or 22d of April, and should you feel inclined to write to me, do so by return of mail, if possible, and I may get your letter before I leave this for the Yellowstone.

"The markets here abound with all the good things of the land, and of nature's creation. To give you an idea of this, read the following items: Grouse, two for a York shilling; three chickens for the same; Turkeys, wild or tame, 25 cents; flour $2.00 a barrel; butter, sixpence for the best — fresh, and really good. Beef, 3 to 4 cents; veal, the same; pork, 2 cents; venison hams, large and dried, 15 cents each; potatoes, 10 cents a bushel; Ducks, three for a shilling; Wild Geese, 10 cents each; Canvas-back Ducks, a shilling a pair; vegetables for the asking, as it were; and only think, in the midst of this abundance and cheapness, we are paying at the rate of $9.00 per week at our hotel, the Glasgow, and at the Planters we were asked $10.00.

"I have been extremely kindly received and treated by Mr. Chouteau and partners. Mr. Sire, the gentleman who will command the steamer we go in, is one of the finest-looking men I have seen for many a day, and the accounts I hear of him correspond with his noble face and general appearance."

THE MISSOURI RIVER JOURNALS

1843

I LEFT home at ten o'clock of the morning, on Saturday the 11th of March, 1843, accompanied by my son Victor. I left all well, and I trust in God for the privilege and happiness of rejoining them all some time next autumn, when I hope to return from the Yellowstone River, an expedition undertaken solely for the sake of our work on the Quadrupeds of North America. The day was cold, but the sun was shining, and after having visited a few friends in the city of New York, we departed for Philadelphia in the cars, and reached that place at eleven of the night. As I was about landing, I was touched on the shoulder by a tall, robust-looking man, whom I knew not to be a sheriff, but in fact my good friend Jediah Irish,[1] of the Great Pine Swamp. I also met my friend Edward Harris, who, with old John G. Bell,[2] Isaac Sprague, and young Lewis Squires, are to be my companions for this campaign. We all put up at Mr. Sanderson's. Sunday was spent in visits to Mr. Bowen,[3] Dr. Morton,[4] and others, and we had many calls made upon us at the hotel. On Monday morning we took the cars for Baltimore, and Victor returned home to Minniesland. The weather was rainy, blustery, cold, but we reached Baltimore in time to eat our dinner there, and we there spent the afternoon and the night.

1 See Episode "Great Pine Swamp."

2 The celebrated taxidermist. Born Sparkhill, New York, July 12, 1812, died at the same place, October, 1879.

3 J. T. Bowen, Lithographer of the Quad. of N. A.

4 Samuel G. Morton, the eminent craniologist.

I saw Gideon B. Smith and a few other friends, and on the next morning we entered the cars for Cumberland, which we reached the same evening about six. Here we had all our effects weighed, and were charged thirty dollars additional weight — a first-rate piece of robbery. We went on now by coaches, entering the gap, and ascending the Alleghanies amid a storm of snow, which kept us company for about forty hours, when we reached Wheeling, which we left on the 16th of March, and went on board the steamer, that brought us to Cincinnati all safe.

We saw much game on our way, such as Geese, Ducks, etc., but no Turkeys as in times of yore. We left for Louisville in the U. S. mail steamer, and arrived there before daylight on the 19th inst. My companions went to the Scott House, and I to William G. Bakewell's, whose home I reached before the family were up. I remained there four days, and was, of course, most kindly treated; and, indeed, during my whole stay in this city of my youth I did enjoy myself famously well, with dancing, dinner-parties, etc. We left for St. Louis on board the ever-to-be-remembered steamer "Gallant," and after having been struck by a log which did not send us to the bottom, arrived on the 28th of March.

On the 4th of April, Harris went off to Edwardsville, with the rest of my companions, and I went to Nicholas Berthoud, who began housekeeping here that day, though Eliza was not yet arrived from Pittsburgh. My time at St. Louis would have been agreeable to any one fond of company, dinners, and parties; but of these matters I am not, though I did dine at three different houses, *bon gré, mal gré.* In fact, my time was spent procuring, arranging, and superintending the necessary objects for the comfort and utility of the party attached to my undertaking. The Chouteaux supplied us with most things, and, let it be said to their honor, at little or no profit. Captain Sire took me in a light wagon to see old Mr. Chouteau one afternoon,

AUDUBON.

FROM THE PORTRAIT BY JOHN WOODHOUSE AUDUBON (ABOUT 1841).

and I found the worthy old gentleman so kind and so full of information about the countries of the Indians that I returned to him a few days afterwards, not only for the sake of the pleasure I enjoyed in his conversation, but also with the view to procure, both dead and alive, a species of Pouched Rat (*Pseudostoma bursarius*)[1] wonderfully abundant in this section of country. One day our friend Harris came back, and brought with him the prepared skins of birds and quadrupeds they had collected, and informed me that they had removed their quarters to B——'s. He left the next day, after we had made an arrangement for the party to return the Friday following, which they did. I drew four figures of Pouched Rats, and outlined two figures of *Sciurus capistratus*,[2] which is here called "Fox Squirrel."

The 25th of April at last made its appearance, the rivers were now opened, the weather was growing warm, and every object in nature proved to us that at last the singularly lingering winter of 1842 and 1843 was over. Having conveyed the whole of our effects on board the steamer, and being supplied with excellent letters, we left St. Louis at 11.30 A. M., with Mr. Sarpy on board, and a hundred and one trappers of all descriptions and nearly a dozen different nationalities, though the greater number were French Canadians, or Creoles of this State. Some were drunk, and many in that stupid mood which follows a state of nervousness produced by drinking and over-excitement. Here is the scene that took place on board the "Omega" at our departure, and what followed when the roll was called.

First the general embarkation, when the men came in

[1] Described and figured under this name by Aud. and Bach., Quad. N. Am. i., 1849, p. 332, pl. 44. This is the commonest Pocket Gopher of the Mississippi basin, now known as *Geomys bursarius*. — E. C.

[2] Aud. and Bach., Quad. N. Am. ii., 1851, p. 132, pl. 68. The plate has three figures. This is the Fox Squirrel with white nose and ears, now commonly called *Sciurus niger*, after Linnæus, 1758, as based on Catesby's Black Squirrel. *S. capistratus* is Bosc's name, bestowed in 1802. — E. C.

pushing and squeezing each other, so as to make the boards they walked upon fairly tremble. The Indians, poor souls, were more quiet, and had already seated or squatted themselves on the highest parts of the steamer, and were tranquil lookers-on. After about three quarters of an hour, the crew and all the trappers (these are called *engagés*)[1] were on board, and we at once pushed off and up the stream, thick and muddy as it was. The whole of the effects and the baggage of the *engagés* was arranged in the main cabin, and presently was seen Mr. Sarpy, book in hand, with the list before him, wherefrom he gave the names of these *attachés*. The men whose names were called nearly filled the fore part of the cabin, where stood Mr. Sarpy, our captain, and one of the clerks. All awaited orders from Mr. Sarpy. As each man was called, and answered to his name, a blanket containing the apparel for the trip was handed to him, and he was ordered at once to retire and make room for the next. The outfit, by the way, was somewhat scanty, and of indifferent quality. Four men were missing, and some appeared rather reluctant; however, the roll was ended, and one hundred and one were found. In many instances their bundles were thrown to them, and they were ordered off as if slaves. I forgot to say that as the boat pushed off from the shore, where stood a crowd of loafers, the men on board had congregated upon the hurricane deck with their rifles and guns of various sorts, all loaded, and began to fire what I should call a very disorganized sort of a salute, which lasted for something like an hour, and which has been renewed at intervals, though in a more desultory manner,

[1] The *Engagés* of the South and Southwest corresponded to the *Coureurs de Bois*, of whom Irving says, in his "Astoria," p. 36: "Originally men who had accompanied the Indians in their hunting expeditions, and made themselves acquainted with remote tracts and tribes. . . . Many became so accustomed to the Indian mode of living that they lost all relish for civilization, and identified themselves with the savages among whom they dwelt. . . . They may be said to have sprung up out of the fur trade."

at every village we have passed. However, we now find them passably good, quiet, and regularly sobered men. We have of course a motley set, even to Italians. We passed the mouth of the Missouri, and moved very slowly against the current, for it was not less than twenty minutes after four the next morning, when we reached St. Charles,[1] distant forty-two miles. Here we stopped till half-past five, when Mr. Sarpy, to whom I gave my letters home, left us in a wagon.

April 26. A rainy day, and the heat we had experienced yesterday was now all gone. We saw a Wild Goose running on the shore, and it was killed by Bell; but our captain did not stop to pick it up, and I was sorry to see the poor bird dead, uselessly. We now had found out that our berths were too thickly inhabited for us to sleep in; so I rolled myself in my blanket, lay down on deck, and slept very sound.

27th. A fine clear day, cool this morning. Cleaned our boilers last night, landing where the "Emily Christian" is sunk, for a few moments; saw a few Gray Squirrels, and an abundance of our common Partridges in flocks of fifteen to twenty, very gentle indeed. About four this afternoon we passed the mouth of the Gasconade River, a stream coming from the westward, valuable for its yellow-pine lumber. At a woodyard above us we saw a White Pelican[2] that had been captured there, and which, had it been clean, I should have bought. I saw that its legs and

[1] One of the oldest settlements in Missouri, on the left bank of the river, still known by the same name, and giving name to St. Charles County, Mo. It was once called Petite Côte, from the range of small hills at the foot of which it is situated. When Lewis and Clark were here, in May, 1804, the town had nearly 100 small wooden houses, including a chapel, and a population of about 450, chiefly of Canadian French origin. See "Lewis and Clark," Coues' ed., 1893, p. 5. — E. C.

[2] The species which Audubon described and figured as new under the name of *Pelecanus americanus:* Ornith. Biogr. iv., 1838, p. 88, pl. 311; Birds of Amer. vii., 1844, p. 20, pl. 422. This is *P. erythrorhynchus* of Gmelin, 1788, and *P. trachyrhynchus* of Latham, 1790. — E. C.

feet were red, and not yellow, as they are during autumn and winter. Marmots are quite abundant, and here they perforate their holes in the loose, sandy soil of the river banks, as well as the same soil wherever it is somewhat elevated. We do not know yet if it is *Arctomys monax*, or a new species.[1] The weather being fine, and the night clear, we ran all night and on the morning of the 28th, thermometer 69° to 78° at sunrise, we were in sight of the seat of government, Jefferson. The State House stands prominent, with a view from it up and down the stream of about ten miles; but, with the exception of the State House and the Penitentiary, Jefferson is a poor place, the land round being sterile and broken. This is *said* to be 160 or 170 miles above St. Louis.[2] We saw many Gray Squirrels this morning. Yesterday we passed under long lines of elevated shore, surmounted by stupendous rocks of limestone, with many curious holes in them, where we saw Vultures and Eagles[3] enter towards dusk Harris saw a Peregrine Falcon; the whole of these rocky shores are ornamented with a species of white cedar quite satisfactorily known to us. We took wood at several places; at one I was told that Wild Turkeys were abundant and Squirrels also, but as the squatter observed, " Game is very scarce, especially Bears." Wolves begin to be troublesome to the settlers who have sheep; they are obliged to drive the latter home, and herd them each night.

This evening the weather became cloudy and looked like rain; the weather has been very warm, the thermometer being at 78° at three this afternoon. We saw a pair of Peregrine Falcons, one of them with a bird in its

[1] No other species of Marmot than the common Woodchuck, *Arctomys monax*, is known to occur in this locality. — E. C.

[2] The actual distance of Jefferson City above the mouth of the river is given on the Missouri River Commission map as $145\frac{8}{10}$ miles. The name of the place was once Missouriopolis. — E. C.

[3] Turkey-buzzards (*Cathartes aura*) and Bald Eagles (*Haliæëtus leucocephalus*). — E. C.

talons; also a few White-fronted Geese, some Blue-winged Teal, and some Cormorants,[1] but none with the head, neck, and breast pure white, as the one I saw two days ago. The strength of the current seemed to increase; in some places our boat merely kept her own, and in one instance fell back nearly half a mile to where we had taken in wood. At about ten this evening we came into such strong water that nothing could be done against it; we laid up for the night at the lower end of a willow island, and then cleaned the boilers and took in 200 fence-rails, which the French Canadians call "perches." Now a *perche* in French means a pole; therefore this must be *patois*.

29th. We were off at five this rainy morning, and at 9 A. M. reached Booneville,[2] distant from St. Louis about 204 miles. We bought at this place an axe, a saw, three files, and some wafers; also some chickens, at one dollar a dozen. We found here some of the Santa Fé traders with whom we had crossed the Alleghanies. They were awaiting the arrival of their goods, and then would immediately start. I saw a Rabbit sitting under the shelf of a rock, and also a Gray Squirrel. It appears to me that *Sciurus macrourus*[3] of Say relishes the bottom lands in

[1] What Cormorants these were is somewhat uncertain, as more than one species answering to the indications given may be found in this locality. Probably they were *Phalacrocorax dilophus floridanus*, first described and figured by Audubon as the Florida Cormorant, *P. floridanus:* Orn. Biog. iii., 1835, p. 387, pl. 251; B. of Amer. vi., 1843, p. 430, pl. 417. The alternative identification in this case is *P. mexicanus* of Brandt. — E. C.

[2] In present Cooper County, Mo., near the mouth of Mine River. It was named for the celebrated Daniel Boone, who owned an extensive grant of land in this vicinity. Booneville followed upon the earlier settlement at Boone's Lick, or Boone's Salt Works, and in 1819 consisted of eight houses. According to the Missouri River Commission charts, the distance from the mouth of the Missouri River is 197 miles. — E. C.

[3] Say, in Long's Exped. i., 1823, p. 115, described from what is now Kansas. This is the well-known Western Fox Squirrel, *S. ludovicianus* of Custis, in Barton's Med. and Phys. Journ. ii., 1806, p. 43. It has been repeatedly described and figured under other names, as follows: *S. subauratus*,

preference to the hilly or rocky portions which alternately present themselves along these shores. On looking along the banks of the river, one cannot help observing the half-drowned young willows, and cotton trees of the same age, trembling and shaking sideways against the current; and methought, as I gazed upon them, of the danger they were in of being immersed over their very tops and thus dying, not through the influence of fire, the natural enemy of wood, but from the force of the mighty stream on the margin of which they grew, and which appeared as if in its wrath it was determined to overwhelm, and undo all that the Creator in His bountifulness had granted us to enjoy. The banks themselves, along with perhaps millions of trees, are ever tumbling, falling, and washing away from the spots where they may have stood and grown for centuries past. If this be not an awful exemplification of the real course of Nature's intention, that all should and must live and die, then, indeed, the philosophy of our learned men cannot be much relied upon!

This afternoon the steamer "John Auld" came up near us, but stopped to put off passengers. She had troops on board and a good number of travellers. We passed the *city* of Glasgow[1] without stopping there, and the blackguards on shore were so greatly disappointed that they actually fired at us with rifles; but whether with balls or not, they did us no harm, for the current proved so strong that we had to make over to the opposite side of the river.

Aud. and Bach. ii., 1851, p. 67, pl. 58; *S. rubicaudatus*, Aud. and Bach. ii., 1851, p. 30, pl. 55; *S. auduboni*, Bach. P. Z. S. 1838, p. 97 (dusky variety); Aud. and Bach. iii., 1854, p. 260, pl. 152, fig. 2; *S. occidentalis*, Aud. and Bach., Journ. Philada. Acad. viii., 1842, p. 317 (dusky variety); *S. sayii*, Aud. and Bach. ii., 1851, p. 274, pl. 89. The last is ostensibly based on the species described by Say, whose name *macroura* was preoccupied for a Ceylonese species. The Western Fox Squirrel has also been called *S. rufiventer* and *S. magnicaudatus*, both of which names appear in Harlan's Fauna Americana, 1825, p. 176 and p. 178.—E. C.

[1] Audubon underscores "city" as a bit of satire, Glasgow being at that time a mere village or hamlet.—E. C.

We did not run far; the weather was still bad, raining hard, and at ten o'clock, with wood nearly exhausted, we stopped on the west shore, and there remained all the night, cleaning boilers, etc.

Sunday 30th. This morning was cold, and it blew a gale from the north. We started, however, for a wooding-place, but the "John Auld" had the advantage of us, and took what there was; the wind increased so much that the waves were actually running pretty high down-stream, and we stopped until one o'clock. You may depend my party was not sorry for this; and as I had had no exercise since we left St. Louis, as soon as breakfast was over we started — Bell, Harris, Squires, and myself, with our guns — and had quite a frolic of it, for we killed a good deal of game, and lost some. Unfortunately we landed at a place where the water had overflowed the country between the shores and the hills, which are distant about one mile and a half. We started a couple of Deer, which Bell and I shot at, and a female Turkey flying fast; at my shot it extended its legs downwards as if badly wounded, but it sailed on, and must have fallen across the muddy waters. Bell, Harris, and myself shot running exactly twenty-eight Rabbits, *Lepus sylvaticus,* and two Bachmans, two *Sciurus macrourus* of Say, two *Arctomys monax*, and a pair of *Tetrao* [*Bonasa*] *umbellus.* The woods were alive with the Rabbits, but they were very wild; the Ground-hogs, Marmots, or *Arctomys,* were in great numbers, judging from the innumerable burrows we saw, and had the weather been calm, I have no doubt we would have seen many more. Bell wounded a Turkey hen so badly that the poor thing could not fly; but Harris frightened it, and it was off, and was lost. Harris shot an *Arctomys* without pouches, that had been forced out of its burrow by the water entering it; it stood motionless until he was within ten paces of it; when, ascertaining what it was, he retired a few yards, and shot it with No. 10 shot, and it fell dead on the spot. We found the woods filled with birds — all known, however, to us: Golden-crowned Thrush, Cerulean Warblers, Woodpeckers of various kinds, etc.; but not a Duck in the bayou, to my surprise. At one the wind lulled somewhat, and as we had taken all the fence-rails and a quantity of dry stuff of all sorts, we were ready to attempt our ascent, and did so. It was curious to see sixty or seventy men carrying logs forty or fifty feet long, some well dried and some green, on their shoulders, all of which were wanted by our captain, for some purpose or other. In a great number of instances the squatters, farmers, or planters, as they may be called, are found to abandon their dwellings or make towards higher grounds, which fortunately are here no farther off than from one to three miles. After we left, we met with the strength of the current, but with our stakes, fence-rails, and our dry wood, we made good headway. At one place we passed a couple of houses, with women and children, perfectly surrounded by the flood; these houses stood apparently on the margin of a river[1] coming in from the eastward. The whole farm was under water, and all around was the very perfection of disaster and misfortune. It appeared to us as if the men had gone to procure assistance, and I was grieved that we could not offer them any. We saw several trees falling in, and beautiful, though painful, was the sight. As they fell, the spray which rose along their whole length was exquisite; but alas! these magnificent trees had reached the day of oblivion.

A few miles above New Brunswick we stopped to take in wood, and landed three of our Indians, who, belonging to the Iowa tribe, had to travel up La Grande Rivière. The wind lulled away, and we ran all night, touching, for a few minutes, on a bar in the middle of the river.

[1] This is the stream then as now known as Grand River, which at its mouth separates Chariton from Carroll County, Mo. Here is the site of Brunswick, or New Brunswick, which Audubon presently mentions.— E. C.

May 1. This morning was a beautiful one; our run last night was about thirty miles, but as we have just begun this fine day, I will copy here the habits of the Pouched Rats, from my notes on the spot at old Mr. Chouteau's, and again at St. Louis, where I kept several alive for four or five days: —

Plantation of Pierre Chouteau, Sen., four miles west of St. Louis, April 13, 1843. I came here last evening in the company of Mr. Sarpy, for the express purpose of procuring some Pouched Rats, and as I have been fortunate enough to secure several of these strange creatures, and also to have seen and heard much connected with their habits and habitats, I write on the spot, with the wish that no recollection of facts be passed over. The present species is uncommonly abundant throughout this neighborhood, and is even found in the gardens of the city of St. Louis, upon the outskirts. They are extremely pernicious animals to the planter and to the gardener, as they devour every root, grass, or vegetable within their reach, and burrow both day and night in every direction imaginable, wherever they know their insatiable appetites can be recompensed for their labor. They bring forth from five to seven young, about the 25th of March, and these are rather large at birth. The nest, or place of deposit, is usually rounded, and about eight inches in diameter, being globular, and well lined with the hair of the female. This nest is not placed at the end of a burrow, or in any particular one of their long galleries, but oftentimes in the road that may lead to hundreds of yards distant. From immediately around the nest, however, many galleries branch off in divers directions, all tending towards such spots as are well known to the parents to afford an abundance of food. I cannot ascertain how long the young remain under the care of the mother. Having observed several freshly thrown-up mounds in Mr. Chouteau's garden, this excellent gentleman called to some negroes to bring spades, and to dig for the animals with the hope I might procure one alive. All hands went to work with alacrity, in the presence of Dr. Trudeau of St. Louis, my friends the father and son Chouteau, and myself. We observed that the "Muloë"[1] (the name given these animals by the creoles of this country) had worked in two or more opposite directions, and that the main gallery was about a foot beneath the surface of the ground, except where it had crossed the walks, when the burrow was sunk a few inches deeper. The work led the negroes across a large square and two of the walks, on one side of which we found large bunches of carnations, from which the roots had been cut off obliquely, close to the surface of the ground, thereby killing the plants. The roots measured $\frac{7}{8}$ of an inch, and immediately next to them was a rose-bush, where ended the burrow. The other side was now followed, and ended amidst the roots of a fine large peach-tree; these roots were more or less gashed and lacerated, but no animal was there, and on returning on our tracks, we found that several galleries, probably leading outside the garden, existed, and we gave up the chase.

This species throws up the earth in mounds rarely higher than twelve to fifteen inches, and these mounds are thrown up at extremely irregular distances, being at times near to each other, and elsewhere ten to twenty, or even thirty, paces apart, yet generally leading to particular spots, well covered with grapes or vegetables of different kinds. This species remains under ground during the whole winter, inactive, and probably dormant, as they never raise or work the earth at this time. The earth thrown up is as if pulverized, and as soon as the animal has finished his labors, which are for no other purpose than to convey him securely from one spot to another, he closes the aperture, which is sometimes on the top, though more usually on the side towards the sun, leaving a kind of ring

[1] From the French "Mulots," field-mice.

nearly one inch in breadth, and about the diameter of the body of the animal. Possessed of an exquisite sense of hearing and of feeling the external pressure of objects travelling on the ground, they stop their labors instantaneously on the least alarm; but if you retire from fifteen to twenty paces to the windward of the hole, and wait for a quarter of an hour or so, you see the "Gopher" (the name given to it by the Missourians — *Americans*) raising the earth with its back and shoulders, and forcing it out forward, leaving the aperture open during the process, and from which it at times issues a few steps, cuts the grasses around, with which it fills its pouches, and then retires to its hole to feed upon its spoils; or it sometimes sits up on its haunches and enjoys the sun, and it may then be shot, provided you are quick. If missed you see it no more, as it will prefer altering the course of its burrow and continuing its labors in quite a different direction. They may be caught in common steel-traps, and two of them were thus procured to-day; but they then injure the foot, the hind one. They are also not uncommonly thrown up by the plough, and one was caught in this manner. They have been known to destroy the roots of hundreds of young fruit-trees in the course of a few days and nights, and will cut roots of grown trees of the most valued kinds, such as apple, pear, peach, plum, etc. They differ greatly in their size and also in their colors, according to age, but not in the sexes. The young are usually gray, the old of a dark chestnut, glossy and shining brown, very difficult to represent in a drawing. The opinion commonly received and entertained, that these Pouched Rats fill their pouches with the earth of their burrows, and empty them when at the entrance, is, I think, quite erroneous; about a dozen which were shot in the act of raising their mounds, and killed at the very mouth of their burrows, had no earth in any of these sacs; the fore feet, teeth, nose, and the anterior portion of the head were found covered with adhesive earth, and most of them had their pouches filled either with blades of grass or roots of different sizes; and I think their being hairy rather corroborates the fact that these pouches are only used for food. In a word, they appear to me to raise the earth precisely in the manner employed by the Mole.

When travelling the tail drags on the ground, and they hobble along with their long front claws drawn underneath; at other times, they move by slow leaping movements, and can travel backwards almost as fast as forwards. When turned over they have much difficulty in replacing themselves in their natural position, and you may see them kicking with their legs and claws for a minute or two before they are right. They bite severely, and do not hesitate to make towards their enemies or assailants with open mouth, squealing like a rat. When they fight among themselves they make great use of the nose in the manner of hogs. They cannot travel faster than the slow walk of a man. They feed frequently while seated on the rump, using their fore paws and long claws somewhat like a squirrel. When sleeping they place the head beneath the breast, and become round, and look like a ball of earth. They clean their whiskers and body in the manner of Rats, Squirrels, etc.

The four which I kept alive never drank anything, though water was given to them. I fed them on potatoes, cabbages, carrots, etc. They tried constantly to make their escape by gnawing at the floor, but in vain. They slept wherever they found clothing, etc., and the rascals cut the lining of my hunting-coat all to bits, so that I was obliged to have it patched and mended. In one instance I had some clothes rolled up for the washerwoman, and, on opening the bundle to count the pieces, one of the fellows caught hold of my right thumb, with fortunately a single one of its upper incisors, and hung on till I shook it off, violently throwing it on the floor, where it lay as if dead; but it recovered, and was as well as ever in less than half an hour. They gnawed the leather straps of my trunks during the night, and although I rose frequently to stop their work, they would begin anew as soon as I was in bed again. I wrote and sent most of the above to John Bachman from St. Louis, after I had finished my drawing of four figures of these most strange and most interesting creatures.

And now to return to this day: When we reached Glasgow, we came in under the stern of the "John Auld." As I saw several officers of the United States army I bowed to them, and as they all knew that I was bound towards the mighty Rocky Mountains, they not only returned my salutations, but came on board, as well as Father de Smet.[1] They all of them came to my room and saw specimens and skins. Among them was Captain Clark,[2] who married the sister of Major Sandford, whom you all know. They had lost a soldier overboard, two had deserted, and a fourth was missing. We proceeded on until about ten o'clock, and it was not until the 2d of May that we actually reached Independence.

May 2. It stopped raining in the night while I was sound asleep, and at about one o'clock we did arrive at Independence, distant about 379 miles from St. Louis.[3] Here again was the "John Auld," putting out freight for the Santa Fé traders, and we saw many of their wagons.

[1] P. J. de Smet, the Jesuit priest, well known for his missionary labors among various tribes of Indians in the Rocky Mountains, on the Columbia River, and in other parts of the West. His work entitled "Oregon Missions and Travels over the Rocky Mountains in 1845-46" was published in New York by Edward Dunigan in 1847. On p. 39 of this book will be found mention of the journey Father de Smet was taking in 1843, when met by Audubon. — E. C.

[2] Captain Clark of the U. S. A.

[3] The distance of Independence from the mouth of the Missouri is about 376 miles by the Commission charts. In 1843 this town was still, as it long had been, the principal point of departure from the river on the Santa Fé caravan route. Trains starting hence went through Westport, Mo., and so on into the "Indian Territory." — E. C.

Of course I exchanged a hand-shake with Father de Smet and many of the officers I had seen yesterday. Mr. Meeks, the agent of Colonel Veras, had 148 pounds of tow in readiness for us, and I drew on the Chouteaux for $30.20, for we were charged no less than 12½ to 25 cts. per pound; but this tow might have passed for fine flax, and I was well contented. We left the "Auld," proceeded on our way, and stopped at Madame Chouteau's plantation, where we put out some freight for Sir William Stuart. The water had been two feet deep in her house, but the river has now suddenly fallen about six feet. At Madame Chouteau's I saw a brother of our friend Pierre Chouteau, Senr., now at New York, and he gave me some news respecting the murder of Mr. Jarvis. About twenty picked men of the neighborhood had left in pursuit of the remainder of the marauders, and had sent one of their number back, with the information that they had remained not two miles from the rascally thieves and murderers. I hope they will overtake them all, and shoot them on the spot. We saw a few Squirrels, and Bell killed two Parrakeets.

May 3. We ran all last night and reached Fort Leavenworth at six this morning. We had an early breakfast, as we had intended to walk across the Bend; but we found that the ground was overflowed, and that the bridges across two creeks had been carried away, and reluctantly we gave up our trip. I saw two officers who came on board, also a Mr. Ritchie. The situation of the fort is elevated and fine, and one has a view of the river up and down for some distance. Seeing a great number of Parrakeets, we went after them; Bell killed one. Unfortunately my gun snapped twice, or I should have killed several more. We saw several Turkeys on the ground and in the trees early this morning. On our reaching the landing, a sentinel dragoon came to watch that no one tried to escape.

After leaving this place we fairly entered the Indian country on the west side of the river, for the State of Missouri, by the purchase of the Platte River country, continues for about 250 miles further on the east side, where now we see the only settlements. We saw a good number of Indians in the woods and on the banks, gazing at us as we passed; these are, however, partly civilized, and are miserable enough. Major Mason, who commands here at present, is ill, and I could not see him. We saw several fine horses belonging to different officers. We soon passed Watson, which is considered the head of steam navigation.

In attempting to pass over a shallow, but a short, cut, we grounded on a bar at five o'clock; got off, tried again, and again grounded broadside; and now that it is past six o'clock all hands are busily engaged in trying to get the boat off, but with what success I cannot say. To me the situation is a bad one, as I conceive that as we remain here, the washings of the muddy sands as they float down a powerful current will augment the bar on the weather side (if I may so express myself) of the boat. We have seen another Turkey and many Parrakeets, as well as a great number of burrows formed by the "Siffleurs," as our French Canadians call all and every species of Marmots; Bell and I have concluded that there must be not less than twenty to thirty of these animals for one in any portion of the Atlantic States. We saw them even around the open grounds immediately about Fort Leavenworth.

About half-past seven we fortunately removed our boat into somewhat deeper water, by straightening her bows against the stream, and this was effected by fastening our very long cable to a snag above us, about 200 yards; and now, if we can go backwards and reach the deep waters along shore a few hundred yards below, we shall be able to make fast there for the night. Unfortunately it is now raining hard, the lightning is vivid, and the appearance of the night forbidding.

Thursday, May 4. We had constant rain, lightning and thunder last night. This morning, at the dawn of day, the captain and all hands were at work, and succeeded in removing the boat several hundred yards below where she had struck; but unfortunately we got fast again before we could reach deep water, and all the exertions to get off were renewed, and at this moment, almost nine, we have a line fastened to the shore and expect to be afloat in a short time. But I fear that we shall lose most of the day before we leave this shallow, intricate, and dangerous channel.

At ten o'clock we found ourselves in deep water, near the shore on the west side. We at once had the men at work cutting wood, which was principally that of ash-trees of moderate size, which wood was brought on board in great quantities and lengths. Thank Heaven, we are off in a few minutes, and I hope will have better luck. I saw on the shore many "Gopher" hills, in all probability the same as I have drawn. Bell shot a Gray Squirrel which I believe to be the same as our *Sciurus carolinensis.* Friend Harris shot two or three birds, which we have not yet fully established, and Bell shot one Lincoln's Finch[1] — strange place for it, when it breeds so very far north as Labrador. Caught a Woodpecker, and killed a Cat-bird, Water-thrush, seventeen Parrakeets, a Yellow Chat, a new Finch,[2] and very curious, two White-throated Finches, one White-crown, a Yellow-rump Warbler, a Gray Squir-

[1] This is the bird which Audubon first discovered in Labrador, in 1833, and named *Fringilla lincolnii* in honor of his young companion, Thomas Lincoln. It is described and figured under that name in Orn. Biogr. ii., 1834, p. 539, pl. 193, and as *Peucæa lincolnii* in B. of Am. iii., 1841, p. 116, pl. 177, but is now known as *Melospiza lincolni.* It ranges throughout the greater part of North America. — E. C.

[2] Apparently the very first intimation we have of the beautiful Finch which Audubon dedicated to Mr. Harris as *Fringilla harrisii,* as will be seen further on in his journal.

The other birds mentioned in the above text were all well-known species in 1843. — E. C.

rel, a Loon, and two Rough-winged Swallows. We saw Cerulean Warblers, Hooded Flycatchers, Kentucky Warblers, Nashville ditto, Blue-winged ditto, Red-eyed and White-eyed Flycatchers, Great-crested and Common Pewees, Redstarts, Towhee Buntings, Ferruginous Thrushes, Wood Thrush, Golden-crowned Thrush, Blue-gray Flycatcher, Blue-eyed Warbler, Blue Yellow-back, Chestnut-sided, Black-and-White Creepers, Nuthatch, Kingbirds, Red Tanagers, Cardinal Grosbeaks, common House Wren, Blue-winged Teals, Swans, large Blue Herons, Crows, Turkey-buzzards, and a Peregrine Falcon, Red-tailed Hawks, Red-headed, Red-bellied, and Golden-winged Woodpeckers, and Partridges. Also, innumerable "Gopher" hills, one Ground-hog, one Rabbit, two Wild Turkeys, one Whippoorwill, one Maryland Yellow-throat, and Swifts. We left the shore with a strong gale of wind, and after having returned to our proper channel, and rounded the island below our troublesome situation of last night, we were forced to come to under the main shore. Here we killed and saw all that is enumerated above, as well as two nests of the White-headed Eagle. We are now for the night at a wooding-place, where we expect to purchase some fresh provisions, if any there are; and as it is nine o'clock I am off to bed.

Friday, May 5. The appearance of the weather this morning was rather bad; it was cloudy and lowering, but instead of rain we have had a strong southwesterly wind to contend with, and on this account our day's work does not amount to much. At this moment, not eight o'clock, we have stopped through its influence.

At half-past twelve we reached the Black Snake Hills[1]

[1] Black Snake Hills (in the vicinity of St. Joseph, Mo.). "On the 24th we saw the chain of the Blacksnake Hills, but we met with so many obstacles in the river that we did not reach them till towards evening. They are moderate eminences, with many singular forms, with an alternation of open green and wooded spots." (Maximilian, Prince of Wied, "Travels in North America," p. 123.)

settlement, and I was delighted to see this truly beautiful site for a town or city, as will be no doubt some fifty years hence. The hills themselves are about 200 feet above the river, and slope down gently into the beautiful prairie that extends over some thousands of acres, of the richest land imaginable. Five of our trappers did not come on board at the ringing of the bell, and had to walk several miles across a bend to join us and be taken on again. We have not seen much game this day, probably on account of the high wind. We saw, however, a large flock of Willets, two Gulls, one Grebe, many Blue-winged Teals, Wood Ducks, and Coots, and one pair of mated Wild Geese. This afternoon a Black Squirrel was seen. This morning I saw a Marmot; and Sprague, a *Sciurus macrourus* of Say. On examination of the Finch killed by Harris yesterday, I found it to be a new species, and I have taken its measurements across this sheet of paper.[1] It was first seen on the ground, then on low bushes, then on large trees; no note was heard. Two others, that were females to all appearance, could not be procured on account of their extreme shyness. We saw the Indigo-bird, Barn Swallows, Purple Martin, and Greenbacks;[2] also, a Rabbit at the Black Snake Hills. The general aspect of the river is materially altered for the worse; it has become much more crooked or tortuous, in some places very wide with sand-banks naked and dried, so that the wind blows the sand quite high. In one place we came to a narrow and swift chute, four miles above the Black Snake

[1] The measurements in pen and ink are marked over the writing of the journal. As already stated, this bird is *Fringilla harrisii:* Aud. B. of Am. vii., 1844, p. 331, pl. 484. It had previously been discovered by Mr. Thomas Nuttall, who ascended the Missouri with Mr. J. K. Townsend in 1834, and named by him *F. querula* in his Man. Orn. 2d ed. i., 1840, p. 555. Its modern technical name is *Zonotrichia querula*, though it continues to bear the English designation of Harris's Finch. — E. C.

[2] That is, the Green-backed or White-bellied Swallow, *Hirundo bicolor* of Vieillot, *Tachycineta bicolor* of Cabanis, and *Iridoprocne bicolor* of Coues. — E. C.

Hills, that in time of extreme high water must be very difficult of ascent. During these high winds it is very hard to steer the boat, and also to land her. The settlers on the Missouri side of the river appear to relish the sight of a steamer greatly, for they all come to look at this one as we pass the different settlements. The thermometer has fallen sixteen degrees since two o'clock, and it feels now very chilly.

Saturday, May 6. High wind all night and cold this morning, with the wind still blowing so hard that at half-past seven we stopped on the western shore, under a range of high hills, but on the weather side of them. We took our guns and went off, but the wind was so high we saw but little; I shot a Wild Pigeon and a Whippoorwill, female, that gave me great trouble, as I never saw one so remarkably wild before. Bell shot two Gray Squirrels and several Vireos, and Sprague, a Kentucky Warbler. Traces of Turkeys and of Deer were seen. We also saw three White Pelicans, but no birds to be added to our previous lot, and I have no wish to keep a strict account of the number of the same species we daily see. It is now half-past twelve; the wind is still very high, but our captain is anxious to try to proceed. We have cut some green wood, and a considerable quantity of hickory for axe-handles. In cutting down a tree we caught two young Gray Squirrels. A Pewee Flycatcher, of some species or other, was caught by the steward, who ran down the poor thing, which was starved on account of the cold and windy weather. Harris shot another of the new Finches, a male also, and I saw what I believe is the female, but it flew upwards of 200 yards without stopping. Bell also shot a small Vireo, which is in all probability a new species[1] (to me at least). We saw a Goshawk, a Marsh

[1] The surmise proved to be correct; for this is the now well-known Bell's Vireo, *Vireo bellii* of Audubon: B. of Am. vii., 1844, p. 333, pl. 485. —E. C.

Hawk, and a great number of Blackbirds, but could not ascertain the species.[1] The wind was still high when we left our stopping place, but we progressed, and this afternoon came alongside of a beautiful prairie of some thousands of acres, reaching to the hills. Here we stopped to put out our Iowa Indians, and also to land the goods we had for Mr. Richardson, the Indian agent. The goods were landed, but at the wrong place, as the Agent's agent would not receive them there, on account of a creek above, which cannot at present be crossed with wagons. Our Sac Indian chief started at once across the prairie towards the hills, on his way to his wigwam, and we saw Indians on their way towards us, running on foot, and many on horseback, generally riding double on skins or on Spanish saddles. Even the squaws rode, and rode well too! We counted about eighty, amongst whom were a great number of youths of different ages. I was heartily glad that our own squad of them left us here. I observed that though they had been absent from their friends and relatives, they never shook hands, or paid any attention to them. When the freight was taken in we proceeded, and the whole of the Indians followed along the shore at a good round run; those on horseback at times struck into a gallop. I saw more of these poor beings when we approached the landing, perched and seated on the promontories about, and many followed the boat to the landing. Here the goods were received, and Major Richardson came on board, and paid freight. He told us we were now in the country of the Fox Indians as well as that of the Iowas, that the number about him is over 1200, and that his district extends about seventy miles up the river. He appears to be a pleasant man; told us that Hares[2]

[1] No doubt the species named Brewer's Blackbird, *Quiscalus brewerii* of Audubon, B. of Am. vii., 1844, p. 345, pl. 492, now known as *Scolecophagus cyanocephalus*. — E. C.

[2] The Prairie Hare, *Lepus virginianus* of Richardson, Fauna Boreali-Americana, i., 1829, p. 229, later described as *L. campestris* by Bachman,

COLUMBA PASSERINA, GROUND DOVE.

(Now Columbigallina passerina terrestri.)

FROM THE UNPUBLISHED DRAWING BY J. J. AUDUBON, 1838.

were very abundant — by the way, Harris saw one to-day. We are now landed on the Missouri side of the river, and taking in wood. We saw a Pigeon Hawk, found Partridges paired, and some also in flocks. When we landed during the high wind we saw a fine sugar camp belonging to Indians. I was pleased to see that many of the troughs they make are formed of bark, and that both ends are puckered and tied so as to resemble a sort of basket or canoe. They had killed many Wild Turkeys, Geese, and Crows, all of which they eat. We also procured a White-eyed and a Warbling Vireo, and shot a male Wild Pigeon. Saw a Gopher throwing out the dirt with his fore feet and not from his pouches. I was within four or five feet of it. Shot a Humming-bird, saw a Mourning Warbler, and Cedar-birds.

May 7, Sunday. Fine weather, but cool. Saw several Gray Squirrels and one Black. I am told by one of our pilots, who has killed seven or eight, that they are much larger than *Sciurus macrourus*, that the hair is coarse, that they are clumsy in their motions, and that they are found from the Black Snake Hills to some distance above the Council Bluffs.

We landed to cut wood at eleven, and we went ashore. Harris killed another of the new Finches, a male also; the scarcity of the females goes on, proving how much earlier the males sally forth on their migrations towards the breeding grounds. We saw five Sand-hill Cranes, some Goldfinches, Yellowshanks, Tell-tale Godwits, Solitary Snipes, and the woods were filled with House Wrens singing their merry songs. The place, however, was a bad one, for it was a piece of bottom land that had overflowed, and was sadly muddy and sticky. At twelve the

Journ. Philad. Acad. vii., 1837, p. 349, and then described and figured as *L. townsendii* by Aud. and Bach., Quad. N. A. i., 1849, p. 25, pl. 3. This is the characteristic species of the Great Plains, where it is commonly called "Jack-rabbit." — E. C.

bell rang for Harris, Bell, and me to return, which we did at once, as dinner was preparing for the table. Talking of dinner makes me think of giving you the hours, usually, of our meals. Breakfast at half-past six, dinner at half-past twelve, tea or supper at seven or later as the case may be. We have not taken much wood here; it is ash, but quite green. We saw Orchard Orioles, Blue-gray Flycatchers, Great-crested and Common Pewees, Mallards, Pileated Woodpeckers, Blue Jays, and Bluebirds; heard a Marsh Wren, saw a Crow, a Wood Thrush, and Water Thrush. Indigo-birds and Parrakeets plentiful. This afternoon we went into the pocket of a sand bar, got aground, and had to back out for almost a mile. We saw an abundance of Ducks, some White Pelicans, and an animal that we guessed was a Skunk. We have run about fifty miles, and therefore have done a good day's journey. We have passed the mouths of several small rivers, and also some very fine prairie land, extending miles towards the hills. It is now nine o'clock, a beautiful night with the moon shining. We have seen several Ravens, and White-headed Eagles on their nests.

May 8, Monday. A beautiful calm day; the country we saw was much the same as that we passed yesterday, and nothing of great importance took place except that at a wooding-place on the very verge of the State of Missouri (the northwest corner) Bell killed a Black Squirrel which friend Bachman has honored with the name of my son John, *Sciurus Audubonii.*[1] We are told that this species is not uncommon here. It was a good-sized adult male, and Sprague drew an outline of it. Harris shot another specimen of the new Finch. We saw Parrakeets and many small birds, but nothing new or very rare. This evening I wrote a long letter to each

[1] Not a good species, but the dusky variety of the protean Western Fox Squirrel, *Sciurus ludovicianus ;* for which, see a previous note. — E. C.

house, John Bachman, Gideon B. Smith of Baltimore, and J. W. H. Page of New Bedford, with the hope of having them forwarded from the Council Bluffs.

May 9, Tuesday. Another fine day. After running until eleven o'clock we stopped to cut wood, and two Rose-breasted Grosbeaks were shot, a common Blue-bird, and a common Northern Titmouse. We saw White Pelicans, Geese, Ducks, etc. One of our trappers cut one of his feet dreadfully with his axe, and Harris, who is now the doctor, attended to it as best he could. This afternoon we reached the famous establishment of Belle Vue[1] where resides the brother of Mr. Sarpy of St. Louis, as well as the Indian Agent, or, as he might be more appropriately called, the Custom House officer. Neither were at home, both away on the Platte River, about 300 miles off. We had a famous pack of rascally Indians awaiting our landing — filthy and half-starved. We landed some cargo for the establishment, and I saw a trick of the trade which made me laugh. Eight cords of wood were paid for with five tin cups of sugar and three of coffee — value at St. Louis about twenty-five cents. We have seen a Fish Hawk, Savannah Finch, Green-backed Swallows, Rough-winged Swallows, Martins, Parrakeets, Black-headed Gulls, Blackbirds, and Cow-birds; I will repeat that the woods are fairly alive with House Wrens. Blue Herons, *Emberiza pallida* — Clay-colored Bunting of Swainson — Henslow's Bunting, Crow Blackbirds; and, more strange than all, two large cakes of ice were seen by our pilots and ourselves. I am very much fatigued and will finish the account of this day to-morrow. At Belle Vue we found the brother-in-law of old Provost, who acts as clerk in the absence of Mr. Sarpy. The store is no great affair, and yet I am told that they drive a good trade with Indians on the Platte River, and others,

[1] Or Bellevue, in what is now Sarpy County, Neb., on the right bank of the Missouri, a few miles above the mouth of the Platte. — E. C.

on this side of the Missouri. We unloaded some freight, and pushed off. We saw here the first ploughing of the ground we have observed since we left the lower settlements near St. Louis. We very soon reached the post of Fort Croghan,[1] so called after my old friend of that name with whom I hunted Raccoons on his father's plantation in Kentucky some thirty-eight years ago, and whose father and my own were well acquainted, and fought together in conjunction with George Washington and Lafayette, during the Revolutionary War, against "Merrie England." Here we found only a few soldiers, dragoons; their camp and officers having been forced to move across the prairie to the Bluffs, five miles. After we had put out some freight for the sutler, we proceeded on until we stopped for the night a few miles above, on the same side of the river. The soldiers assured us that their parade ground, and so-called barracks, had been four feet under water, and we saw fair and sufficient evidence of this. At this place our pilot saw the first Yellow-headed Troupial we have met with. We landed for the night under trees covered by muddy deposits from the great overflow of this season. I slept soundly, and have this morning, May 10, written this.

May 10, Wednesday. The morning was fine, and we were under way at daylight; but a party of dragoons, headed by a lieutenant, had left their camp four miles distant from our anchorage at the same time, and reached the shore before we had proceeded far; they fired a couple of rifle shots ahead of us, and we brought to at once. The young officer came on board, and presented a letter from his commander, Captain Burgwin, from which we found that we had to have our cargo examined. Our cap-

[1] Vicinity of present Omaha, Neb., and Council Bluffs, Ia., but somewhat above these places. The present Council Bluffs, in Iowa, is considerably below the position of the original Council Bluff of Lewis and Clark, which Audubon presently notices. See "Lewis and Clark," ed. of 1893, p. 66. — E. C.

tain[1] was glad of it, and so were we all; for, finding that it would take several hours, we at once ate our breakfast, and made ready to go ashore. I showed my credentials and orders from the Government, Major Mitchell of St. Louis, etc., and I was therefore immediately settled comfortably. I desired to go to see the commanding officer, and the lieutenant very politely sent us there on horseback, guided by an old dragoon of considerable respectability. I was mounted on a young white horse, Spanish saddle with holsters, and we proceeded across the prairie towards the Bluffs and the camp. My guide was anxious to take a short cut, and took me across several bayous, one of which was really up to the saddle; but we crossed that, and coming to another we found it so miry, that his horse wheeled after two or three steps, whilst I was looking at him before starting myself; for you all well know that an old traveller is, and must be, prudent. We now had to retrace our steps till we reached the very tracks that the squad sent after us in the morning had taken, and at last we reached the foot of the Bluffs, when my guide asked me if I "could ride at a gallop," to which not answering him, but starting at once at a round run,

[1] The journals of Captain Joseph A. Sire, from 1841 to 1848, are extant, and at present in the possession of Captain Joseph La Barge, who has permitted them to be examined by Captain Chittenden. The latter informs us of an interesting entry at date of May 10, 1843, regarding the incident of the military inspection of the "Omega" for contraband liquor, of which Audubon speaks. But the inside history of how cleverly Captain Sire outwitted the military does not appear from the following innocent passage: "*Mercredi, 10 May.* Nous venons trés bien jusqu'aux côtes à Hart, où, à sept heures, nous sommes sommés par un officier de dragons de mettre à terre. Je reçois une note polie du Capt. Burgwin m'informant que son devoir l'oblige de faire visiter le bateau. Aussitôt nous nous mettons à l'ouvrage, et pendant ce temps M. Audubon va faire une visite au Capitaine. Ils reviennent ensemble deux heures après. Je force en quelque sorte l'officier à faire une recherche aussi stricte que possible, mais à la condition qu'il en fera de même avec les autres traiteurs." The two precious hours of Audubon's visit were utilized by the clever captain in so arranging the cargo that no liquor should be found on board by Captain Burgwin. — E. C.

I neatly passed him ere his horse was well at the pace; on we went, and in a few minutes we entered a beautiful dell or valley, and were in sight of the encampment. We reached this in a trice, and rode between two lines of pitched tents to one at the end, where I dismounted, and met Captain Burgwin,[1] a young man, brought up at West Point, with whom I was on excellent and friendly terms in less time than it has taken me to write this account of our meeting. I showed him my credentials, at which he smiled, and politely assured me that I was too well known throughout our country to need any letters. While seated in front of his tent, I heard the note of a bird new to me, and as it proceeded from a tree above our heads, I looked up and saw the first Yellow-headed Troupial alive that ever came across my own migrations. The captain thought me probably crazy, as I thought Rafinesque when he was at Henderson; for I suddenly started, shot at the bird, and killed it. Afterwards I shot three more at one shot, but only one female amid hundreds of these Yellow-headed Blackbirds. They are quite abundant here, feeding on the surplus grain that drops from the horses' troughs; they walked under, and around the horses, with as much confidence as if anywhere else. When they rose, they generally flew to the very tops of the tallest trees, and there, swelling their throats, partially spreading their wings and tail, they issue their croaking note, which is a compound, not to be mistaken, between that of the Crow Blackbird and that of the Red-winged Starling. After I had fired at them twice they became quite shy, and all of them flew off to the prairies. I saw then two Magpies[2]

[1] John Henry K. Burgwin, cadet at West Point in 1828; in 1843 a captain of the 1st Dragoons. He died Feb. 7, 1847, of wounds received three days before in the assault on Pueblo de Taos, New Mexico. — E. C.

[2] The question of the specific identity of the American and European Magpies has been much discussed. Ornithologists now generally compromise the case by considering our bird to be subspecifically distinct, under the name of *Pica pica hudsonica*. — E. C.

in a cage, that had been caught in nooses, by the legs; and their actions, voice, and general looks, assured me as much as ever, that they are the very same species as that found in Europe. Prairie Wolves are extremely abundant hereabouts. They are so daring that they come into the camp both by day and by night; we found their burrows in the banks and in the prairie, and had I come here yesterday I should have had a superb specimen killed here, but which was devoured by the hogs belonging to the establishment. The captain and the doctor — Madison[1] by name — returned with us to the boat, and we saw many more Yellow-headed Troupials. The high Bluffs back of the prairie are destitute of stones. On my way there I saw abundance of Gopher hills, two Geese paired, two Yellow-crowned Herons, Red-winged Starlings, Cowbirds, common Crow Blackbirds, a great number of Baltimore Orioles, a Swallow-tailed Hawk, Yellow Red-poll Warbler, Field Sparrow, and Chipping Sparrow. Sprague killed another of the beautiful Finch. Robins are very scarce, Parrakeets and Wild Turkeys plentiful. The officers came on board, and we treated them as hospitably as we could; they ate their lunch with us, and are themselves almost destitute of provisions. Last July the captain sent twenty dragoons and as many Indians on a hunt for Buffaloes. During the hunt they killed 51 Buffaloes, 104 Deer, and 10 Elks, within 80 miles of the camp. The Sioux Indians are great enemies to the Potowatamies, and very frequently kill several of the latter in their predatory excursions against them. This kind of warfare has rendered the Potowatamies very cowardly, which is quite a remarkable change from their previous valor and daring. Bell collected six different species of shells, and found a large

[1] No doubt Thomas C. Madison of Virginia, appointed Assist. Surg. U. S. A., Feb. 27, 1840. He served as a surgeon of the Confederacy during our Civil War, and died Nov. 7, 1866. — E. C.

lump of pumice stone which does float on the water. We left our anchorage (which means tied to the shore) at twelve o'clock, and about sunset we did pass the real Council Bluff.[1] Here, however, the bed of the river is utterly changed, though you may yet see that which is now called the Old Missouri. The Bluffs stand, truly speaking, on a beautiful bank almost forty feet above the water, and run off on a rich prairie, to the hills in the background in a gentle slope, that renders the whole place a fine and very remarkable spot. We tied up for the night about three miles above them, and all hands went ashore to cut wood, which begins to be somewhat scarce, of a good quality. Our captain cut and left several cords of green wood for his return trip, at this place; Harris and Bell went on shore, and saw several Bats, and three Turkeys. This afternoon a Deer was seen scampering across the prairies until quite out of sight. Wild-gooseberry bushes are very abundant, and the fruit is said to be very good.

May 11, Thursday. We had a night of rain, thunder, and heavy wind from the northeast, and we did not start this morning till seven o'clock, therefore had a late breakfast. There was a bright blood-red streak on the horizon at four o'clock that looked forbidding, but the weather changed as we proceeded, with, however, showers of rain at various intervals during the day. We have

[1] Council Bluff, so named by Lewis and Clark on Aug. 3, 1804, on which day they and their followers, with a number of Indians, including six chiefs, held a council here, to make terms with the Ottoe and Missouri Indians. The account of the meeting ends thus: "The incident just related induced us to give to this place the name of the Council-bluff; the situation of it is exceedingly favorable for a fort and trading factory, as the soil is well calculated for bricks, there is an abundance of wood in the neighborhood, and the air is pure and healthy." In a foot-note Dr. Coues says: "It was later the site of Fort Calhoun, in the present Washington Co., Neb. We must also remember, in attempting to fix this spot, how much the Missouri has altered its course since 1804." ("Expedition of Lewis and Clark," 1893, p. 65.)

now come to a portion of the river more crooked than any we have passed; the shores on both sides are evidently lower, the hills that curtain the distance are further from the shores, and the intervening space is mostly prairie, more or less overflowed. We have seen one Wolf on a sand-bar, seeking for food, perhaps dead fish. The actions were precisely those of a cur dog with a long tail, and the bellowing sound of the engine did not seem to disturb him. He trotted on parallel to the boat for about one mile, when we landed to cut drift-wood. Bell, Harris, and I went on shore to try to have a shot at him. He was what is called a brindle-colored Wolf,[1] of the common size. One hundred trappers, however, with their axes at work, in a few moments rather stopped his progress, and when he saw us coming, he turned back on his track, and trotted off, but Bell shot a very small load in the air to see the effect it would produce. The fellow took two or three leaps, stopped, looked at us for a moment, and then started on a gentle gallop. When I overtook his tracks they appeared small, and more rounded than usual. I saw several tracks at the same time, therefore more than one had travelled over this great sandy and muddy bar last night, if not this morning. I lost sight of him behind some large piles of drift-wood, and could see him no more. Turkey-buzzards were on the bar, and I thought that I should have found some dead

[1] This Wolf is to be distinguished from the Prairie Wolf, *Canis latrans*, which Audubon has already mentioned. It is the common large Wolf of North America, of which Audubon has much to say in the sequel; and wherever he speaks of "Wolves" without specification, we are to understand that this is the animal meant. It occurs in several different color-variations, from quite blackish through different reddish and brindled grayish shades to nearly white. The variety above mentioned is that named by Dr. Richardson *griseo-albus*, commonly known in the West as the Buffalo Wolf and the Timber Wolf. Mr. Thomas Say named one of the dark varieties *Canis nubilus* in 1823; and naturalists who consider the American Wolf to be specifically distinct from *Canis lupus* of Europe now generally name the brindled variety *C. nubilus griseo-albus*. — E. C.

carcass; but on reaching the spot, nothing was there. A fine large Raven passed at one hundred yards from us, but I did not shoot. Bell found a few small shells, and Harris shot a Yellow-rumped Warbler. We have seen several White Pelicans, Geese, Black-headed Gulls, and Green-backed Swallows, but nothing new. The night is cloudy and intimates more rain. We are fast to a willowed shore, and are preparing lines to try our luck at catching a Catfish or so. I was astonished to find how much stiffened I was this morning, from the exercise I took on horseback yesterday, and think that now it would take me a week, at least, to accustom my body to riding as I was wont to do twenty years ago. The timber is becoming more scarce as we proceed, and I greatly fear that our only opportunities of securing wood will be those afforded us by that drifted on the bars.

May 12, Friday. The morning was foggy, thick, and calm. We passed the river called the *Sioux Pictout,*[1] a small stream formerly abounding with Beavers, Otters, Muskrats, etc., but now quite destitute of any of these creatures. On going along the banks bordering a long and wide prairie, thick with willows and other small brush-wood, we saw four Black-tailed Deer[2] immediately on the bank; they trotted away without appearing to be much alarmed; after a few hundred yards, the two largest, probably males, raised themselves on their hind feet and pawed at each other, after the manner of stallions.

[1] Little Sioux River of present geography, in Harrison Co., Iowa: see "Lewis and Clark," ed. of 1893, p. 69.—E. C.

[2] Otherwise known as the Mule Deer, from the great size of the ears, and the peculiar shape of the tail, which is white with a black tuft at the tip, and suggests that of the Mule. It is a fine large species, next to the Elk or Wapiti in stature, and first became generally known from the expedition of Lewis and Clark. It is the *Cervus macrotis* of Say, figured and described under this name by Aud. and Bach. Quad. N. A. ii., 1851, p. 206, pl. 78, and commonly called by later naturalists *Cariacus macrotis.* But its first scientific designation is *Damelaphus hemionus,* given by C. S. Rafinesque in 1817.—E. C.

They trotted off again, stopping often, but after a while disappeared; we saw them again some hundreds of yards farther on, when, becoming suddenly alarmed, they bounded off until out of sight. They did not trot or run irregularly as our Virginian Deer does, and their color was of a brownish cast, whilst our common Deer at this season is red. Could we have gone ashore, we might in all probability have killed one or two of them. We stopped to cut wood on the opposite side of the river, where we went on shore, and there saw many tracks of Deer, Elk, Wolves, and Turkeys. In attempting to cross a muddy place to shoot at some Yellow-headed Troupials that were abundant, I found myself almost mired, and returned with difficulty. We only shot a Blackburnian Warbler, a Yellow-winged ditto, and a few Finches. We have seen more Geese than usual as well as Mallards and Wood Ducks. This afternoon the weather cleared up, and a while before sunset we passed under Wood's Bluffs,[1] so called because a man of that name fell overboard from his boat while drunk. We saw there many Bank Swallows, and afterwards we came in view of the Blackbird Hill,[2] where the famous Indian

[1] Wood's Bluff has long ceased to be known by this name, but there is no doubt from what Audubon next says of Blackbird Hill, that the bluff in question is that on the west or right bank of the river, at and near Decatur, Burt Co., Neb.; the line between Burt and Blackbird counties cuts through the bluff, leaving most of it in the latter county. See Lewis and Clark, ed. of 1893, p. 71, date of Aug. 10, 1804, where "a cliff of yellow stone on the left" is mentioned. This is Wood's Bluff; the situation is 750 miles up the river by the Commission Charts. — E. C.

[2] Blackbird Hill. "Aug. 11 [1804]. . . . We halted on the south side for the purpose of examining a spot where one of the great chiefs of the Mahas [Omahas], named Blackbird, who died about four years ago, of the small-pox, was buried. A hill of yellow soft sandstone rises from the river in bluffs of various heights, till it ends in a knoll about 300 feet above the water; on the top of this a mound, of twelve feet diameter at the base, and six feet high, is raised over the body of the deceased king, a pole about eight feet high is fixed in the centre, on which we placed a white flag, bordered with red, blue, and white. Blackbird seems to have been a person

chief of that name was buried, at his request, on his horse, whilst the animal was alive. We are now fast to the shore opposite this famed bluff. We cut good ash wood this day, and have made a tolerable run, say forty miles.

Saturday, May 13. This morning was extremely foggy, although I could plainly see the orb of day trying to force its way through the haze. While this lasted all hands were engaged in cutting wood, and we did not leave our fastening-place till seven, to the great grief of our commander. During the wood cutting, Bell walked to the top of the hills, and shot two Lark Buntings, males, and a Lincoln's Finch. After a while we passed under some beautiful bluffs surmounted by many cedars, and these bluffs were composed of fine white sandstone, of a soft texture, but very beautiful to the eye. In several

of great consideration, for ever since his death he has been supplied with provisions, from time to time, by the superstitious regard of the Mahas." ("Expedition of Lewis and Clark," by Elliott Coues, 1893, p. 71.)

"The 7th of May (1833) we reached the chain of hills on the left bank; . . . these are called Wood's Hills, and do not extend very far. On one of them we saw a small conical mound, which is the grave of the celebrated Omaha chief Washinga-Sabba (the Blackbird). In James' 'Narrative of Major Long's Expedition,' is a circumstantial account of this remarkable and powerful chief, who was a friend to the white man; he contrived, by means of arsenic, to make himself feared and dreaded, and passed for a magician. . . . An epidemical smallpox carried him off, with a great part of his nation, in 1800, and he was buried, sitting upright, upon a live mule, at the top of a green hill on Wakonda Creek. When dying he gave orders they should bury him on that hill, with his face turned to the country of the whites." ("Travels in North America," Maximilian, Prince of Wied.)

Irving, in chap. xvi. of "Astoria," gives a long account of Blackbird, based on Bradbury and Brackenridge, but places his death in 1802, incorrectly; and ends: "The Missouri washes the base of the promontory, and after winding and doubling in many links and mazes, returns to within nine hundred yards of its starting-place; so that for thirty miles the voyager finds himself continually near to this singular promontory, as if spell bound. It was the dying command of Blackbird, that his tomb should be on the summit of this hill, in which he should be interred, seated on his favorite horse, that he might overlook his ancient domain, and behold the backs of the white men as they came up the river to trade with his people."

places along this bluff we saw clusters of nests of Swallows, which we all looked upon as those of the Cliff Swallow, although I saw not one of the birds. We stopped again to cut wood, for our opportunities are not now very convenient. Went out, but only shot a fine large Turkey-hen, which I brought down on the wing at about forty yards. It ran very swiftly, however, and had not Harris's dog come to our assistance, we might have lost it. As it was, however, the dog pointed, and Harris shot it, with my small shot-gun, whilst I was squatted on the ground amid a parcel of low bushes. I was astonished to see how many of the large shot I had put into her body. This hen weighed $11\frac{3}{4}$ pounds. She had a nest, no doubt, but we could not find it. We saw a good number of Geese, though fewer than yesterday; Ducks also. We passed many fine prairies, and in one place I was surprised to see the richness of the bottom lands. We saw this morning eleven Indians of the Omaha tribe. They made signals for us to land, but our captain never heeded them, for he hates the red-skins as most men hate the devil. One of them fired a gun, the group had only one, and some ran along the shore for nearly two miles, particularly one old gentleman who persevered until we came to such bluff shores as calmed down his spirits. In another place we saw one seated on a log, close by the frame of a canoe; but he looked surly, and never altered his position as we passed. The frame of this boat resembled an ordinary canoe. It is formed by both sticks giving a half circle; the upper edges are fastened together by a long stick, as well as the centre of the bottom. Outside of this stretches a Buffalo skin without the hair on; it is said to make a light and safe craft to cross even the turbid, rapid stream — the Missouri. By simply looking at them, one may suppose that they are sufficiently large to carry two or three persons. On a sand-bar afterwards we saw three more Indians, also with a canoe frame, but we only interchanged the common yells usual on such occasions. They looked as destitute and as hungry as if they had not eaten for a week, and no doubt would have given much for a bottle of whiskey. At our last landing for wood-cutting, we also went on shore, but shot nothing, not even took aim at a bird; and there was an Indian with a flint-lock rifle, who came on board and stared about until we left, when he went off with a little tobacco. I pity these poor beings from my heart! This evening we came to the burial-ground bluff of Sergeant Floyd,[1] one of the companions of the never-to-be-forgotten expedition of Lewis and Clark, over the Rocky Mountains, to the Pacific Ocean. A few minutes afterwards, before coming to Floyd's Creek, we started several Turkey-cocks

[1] "Aug. 20th, 1804. Here we had the misfortune to lose one of our sergeants, Charles Floyd. . . . He was buried on the top of the bluff with the honors due to a brave soldier; the place of his interment was marked by a cedar post, on which his name and the day of his death were inscribed." ("Expedition of Lewis and Clark," by Elliott Coues, p. 79.)

"On the following day [May 8, 1833] we came to Floyd's grave, where the sergeant of that name was buried by Lewis and Clark. The bank on either side is low. The left is covered with poplars; on the right, behind the wood, rises a hill like the roof of a building, at the top of which Floyd is buried. A short stick marks the place where he is laid, and has often been renewed by travellers, when the fires in the prairie have destroyed it. ("Travels in North America," p. 134, Maximilian, Prince of Wied.) — M. R. A.

Floyd's grave became a landmark for many years, and is noticed by most of the travellers who have written of voyaging on the Missouri. In 1857 the river washed away the face of the bluff to such an extent that the remains were exposed. These were gathered and reburied about 200 yards further back on the same bluff. This new grave became obliterated in the course of time, but in 1895 it was rediscovered after careful search. The bones were exhumed by a committee of citizens of Sioux City; and on Aug. 20 of that year, the 91st anniversary of Floyd's death, were reburied in the same spot with imposing ceremonies, attended by a concourse of several hundred persons. A large flat stone slab, with suitable inscription, now marks the spot, and the Floyd Memorial Association, which was formed at the time of the third burial, proposes to erect a monument to Floyd in a park to be established on the bluff. — E. C.

from their roost, and had we been on shore could have accounted for more than one of them. The prairies are becoming more common and more elevated; we have seen more evergreens this day than we have done for two weeks at least. This evening is dark and rainy, with lightning and some distant thunder, and we have entered the mouth of the Big Sioux River,[1] where we are fastened for the night. This is a clear stream and abounds with fish, and on one of the branches of this river is found the famous red clay, of which the precious pipes, or calumets are manufactured. We will try to procure some on our return homeward. It is late; had the weather been clear, and the moon, which is full, shining, it was our intention to go ashore, to try to shoot Wild Turkeys; but as it is pouring down rain, and as dark as pitch, we have thrown our lines overboard and perhaps may catch a fish. We hope to reach Vermilion River day after to-morrow. We saw abundance of the birds which I have before enumerated.

May 14, Sunday. It rained hard and thundered during the night; we started at half-past three, when it had cleared, and the moon shone brightly. The river is crooked as ever, with large bars, and edged with prairies. Saw many Geese, and a Long-billed Curlew. One poor Goose had been wounded in the wing; when approached, it dived for a long distance and came up along the shore. Then we saw a Black Bear, swimming across the river, and it caused a commotion. Some ran for their rifles, and several shots were fired, some of which almost touched Bruin; but he kept on, and swam very fast. Bell shot at it with large shot and must have touched

[1] Which separates Iowa from South Dakota. Here the Missouri ceases to separate Nebraska from Iowa, and begins to separate Nebraska from South Dakota. Audubon is therefore at the point where these three States come together. He is also just on the edge of Sioux City, Iowa, which extends along the left bank of the Missouri from the vicinity of Floyd's Bluff to the Big Sioux River. — E. C.

it. When it reached the shore, it tried several times to climb up, but each time fell back. It at last succeeded, almost immediately started off at a gallop, and was soon lost to sight. We stopped to cut wood at twelve o'clock, in one of the vilest places we have yet come to. The rushes were waist-high, and the whole underbrush tangled by grape vines. The Deer and the Elks had beaten paths which we followed for a while, but we saw only their tracks, and those of Turkeys. Harris found a heronry of the common Blue Heron, composed of about thirty nests, but the birds were shy and he did not shoot at any. Early this morning a dead Buffalo floated by us, and after a while the body of a common cow, which had probably belonged to the fort above this. Mr. Sire told us that at this point, two years ago, he overtook three of the deserters of the company, who had left a keel-boat in which they were going down to St. Louis. They had a canoe when overtaken; he took their guns from them, destroyed the canoe, and left them there. On asking him what had become of them, he said they had walked back to the establishment at the mouth of Vermilion River, which by land is only ten miles distant; ten miles, through such woods as we tried in vain to hunt in, is a walk that I should not like at all. We stayed cutting wood for about two hours, when we started again; but a high wind arose, so that we could not make headway, and had to return and make fast again, only a few hundred yards from the previous spot. On such occasions our captain employs his wood-cutters in felling trees, and splitting and piling the wood until his return downwards, in about one month, perhaps, from now. In talking with our captain he tells us that the Black Bear is rarely seen swimming this river, and that one or two of them are about all he observes on going up each trip. I have seen them swimming in great numbers on the lower parts of the Ohio, and on the Mississippi. It is said that at times, when the common Wolves are extremely hard pressed for food, they will eat certain roots which they dig up for the purpose, and the places from which they take this food look as if they had been spaded. When they hunt a Buffalo, and have killed it, they drag it to some distance — about sixty yards or so — and dig a hole large enough to receive and conceal it; they then cover it with earth, and lie down over it until hungry again, when they uncover, and feed upon it. Along the banks of the rivers, when the Buffaloes fall, or cannot ascend, and then die, the Wolves are seen in considerable numbers feeding upon them. Although cunning beyond belief in hiding at the report of a gun, they almost instantly show themselves from different parts around, and if you wish to kill some, you have only to hide yourself, and you will see them coming to the game you have left, when you are not distant more than thirty or forty yards. It is said that though they very frequently hunt their game until the latter take to the river, they seldom, if ever, follow after it. The wind that drove us ashore augmented into a severe gale, and by its present appearance looks as if it would last the whole night. Our fire was comfortable, for, as you know, the thermometer has been very changeable since noon. We have had rain also, though not continuous, but quite enough to wet our men, who, notwithstanding have cut and piled about twelve cords of wood, besides the large quantity we have on board for to-morrow, when we hope the weather will be good and calm.

May 15, Monday. The wind continued an irregular gale the whole of the night, and the frequent logs that struck our weather side kept me awake until nearly daybreak, when I slept about two hours; it unfortunately happened that we were made fast upon the weather shore. This morning the gale kept up, and as we had nothing better to do, it was proposed that we should walk across the bottom lands, and attempt to go to the prairies, distant about two and a half miles. This was accordingly done; Bell, Harris, Mr. La Barge[1] — the first pilot — a mulatto hunter named Michaux, and I, started at nine. We first crossed through tangled brush-wood, and high-grown rushes for a few hundreds of yards, and soon perceived that here, as well as all along the Missouri and Mississippi, the land is highest nearest the shore, and falls off the farther one goes inland. Thus we soon came to mud, and from mud to muddy water, as *pure* as it runs in the Missouri itself; at every step which we took we raised several pounds of mud on our boots. Friend Harris very wisely returned, but the remainder of us proceeded through thick and thin until we came in sight of the prairies. But, alas! between us and them there existed a regular line of willows — and who ever saw willows grow far from water? Here we were of course stopped, and after attempting in many places to cross the water that divided us from the dry land, we were forced back, and had to return as best we could. We were mud up to the very middle, the perspiration ran down us, and at one time I was nearly exhausted; which proves to me pretty clearly that I am no longer as young, or as active, as I was some thirty years ago. When we reached the boat I was glad of it. We washed, changed our clothes, dined, and felt much refreshed. During our excursion out, Bell saw a Virginian Rail, and our sense of smell brought us to a dead Elk, putrid, and largely consumed by Wolves, whose tracks were very numerous about it. After dinner we went to

[1] This is Captain Joseph La Barge, the oldest living pilot on the Missouri, and probably now the sole survivor of the "Omega" voyage of 1843. He was born Oct. 1, 1815, of French parentage, his father having come to St. Louis, Mo., from Canada, and his mother from lower Louisiana. The family has been identified with the navigation of the Western rivers from the beginning of the century, and in 1850 there were seven licensed pilots of that name in the port of St. Louis. Captain Joseph La Barge still lives in St. Louis, at the age of eighty-two, and has a vivid recollection of Audubon's voyage of 1843, some incidents of which he has kindly communicated through Captain H. M. Chittenden, U. S. army.

the heronry that Harris had seen yesterday afternoon; for we had moved only one mile above the place of our wooding before we were again forced on shore. Here we killed four fine individuals, all on the wing, and some capital shots they were, besides a Raven. Unfortunately we had many followers, who destroyed our sport; therefore we returned on board, and at half-past four left our landing-place, having cut and piled up between forty and fifty cords of wood for the return of the "Omega." The wind has lulled down considerably, we have run seven or eight miles, and are again fast to the shore. It is reported that the water has risen two feet, but this is somewhat doubtful. We saw abundance of tracks of Elk, Deer, Wolf, and Bear, and had it been anything like tolerably dry ground, we should have had a good deal of sport. Saw this evening another dead Buffalo floating down the river.

May 16, Tuesday. At three o'clock this fair morning we were under way, but the water has actually risen a great deal, say three feet, since Sunday noon. The current therefore is very strong, and impedes our progress greatly. We found that the Herons we had killed yesterday had not yet laid the whole of their eggs, as we found one in full order, ripe, and well colored and conditioned. I feel assured that the Ravens destroy a great many of their eggs, as I saw one helping itself to two eggs, at two different times, on the same nest. We have seen a great number of Black-headed Gulls, and some Black Terns, some Indians on the east side of the river, and a Prairie Wolf, dead, hung across a prong of a tree. After a while we reached a spot where we saw ten or more Indians who had a large log cabin, and a field under fence. Then we came to the establishment called that of Vermilion River, [1] and met Mr. Cerré, called usually Pascal, the agent of the

[1] Vermilion is still the name of this river, and also of the town at its mouth which has replaced old Fort Vermilion, and is now the seat of Clay

Company at this post, a handsome French gentleman, of good manners. He dined with us. After this we landed, and walked to the fort, if the place may so be called, for we found it only a square, strongly picketed, without port-holes. It stands on the immediate bank of the river, opposite a long and narrow island, and is backed by a vast prairie, all of which was inundated during the spring freshet. He told me that game was abundant, such as Elk, Deer, and Bear; but that Ducks, Geese, and Swans were extremely scarce this season. Hares are plenty — no Rabbits. We left as soon as possible, for our captain is a pushing man most truly. We passed some remarkable bluffs of blue and light limestone, towards the top of which we saw an abundance of Cliff-Swallows, and counted upwards of two hundred nests. But, alas! we have finally met with an accident. A plate of one of our boilers was found to be burned out, and we were obliged to stop on the west side of the river, about ten miles below the mouth of the Vermilion River. Here we were told that we might go ashore and hunt to our hearts' content; and so I have, but shot at nothing. Bell, Michaux, and I, walked to the hills full three miles off, saw an extraordinary quantity of Deer, Wolf, and Elk tracks, as well as some of Wild Cats. Bell started a Deer, and after a while I heard him shoot. Michaux took to the top of the hills, Bell about midway, and I followed near the bottom; all in vain, however. I started a Woodcock, and caught one of her young, and I am now sorry for this evil deed. A dead Buffalo cow and calf passed us a few moments ago. Squires has seen one other, during our absence. We took at Mr. Cerré's establishment two *engagés* and four Sioux Indians. We are obliged to keep bright eyes upon them, for they are singularly light-fingered. The woods are filled with wild-

County, South Dakota. On the opposite side of the Missouri is Dixon Co., Nebraska. The stream was once known as Whitestone River, as given in "Lewis and Clark." — E. C.

gooseberry bushes, and a kind of small locust not yet in bloom, and quite new to me. The honey bee was not found in this country twenty years ago, and now they are abundant. A keel-boat passed, going down, but on the opposite side of the river. Bell and Michaux have returned. Bell wounded a large Wolf, and also a young Deer, but brought none on board, though he saw several of the latter. Harris killed one of the large new Finches, and a Yellow-headed Troupial. Bell intends going hunting to-morrow at daylight, with Michaux; I will try my luck too, but do not intend going till after breakfast, for I find that walking eight or ten miles through the tangled and thorny underbrush, fatigues me considerably, though twenty years ago I should have thought nothing of it.

May 17, Wednesday. This was a most lovely morning. Bell went off with Michaux at four A. M. I breakfasted at five, and started with Mr. La Barge. When we reached the hunting-grounds, about six miles distant, we saw Bell making signs to us to go to him, and I knew from that that they had some fresh meat. When we reached them, we found a very large Deer that Michaux had killed. Squires shot a Woodcock, which I ate for my dinner, in company with the captain. Michaux had brought the Deer — Indian fashion — about two miles. I was anxious to examine some of the intestines, and we all three started on the tracks of Michaux, leaving Squires to keep the Wolves away from the dead Deer. We went at once towards a small stream meandering at the foot of the hills, and as we followed it, Bell shot at a Turkey-cock about eighty yards; his ball cut a streak of feathers from its back, but the gobbler went off. When we approached the spot where Michaux had opened the Deer, we did so cautiously, in the hope of then shooting a Wolf, but none had come; we therefore made our observations, and took up the tongue, which had been forgotten. Bell joined us, and as we were returning to Squires we saw flocks of the Chestnut-collared Lark or Ground-finch, whose exact measurement I have here given, and almost at the same time saw Harris. He and Bell went off after the Finches; we pursued our course to Squires, and waited for their return. Seeing no men to help carry the Deer, Michaux picked it up, Squires took his gun, etc., and we made for the river again. We had the good luck to meet the barge coming, and we reached our boat easily in a few minutes, with our game. I saw upwards of twelve of Harris' new Finch (?) a Marsh Hawk, Henslow's Bunting, *Emberiza pallida*, Robins, Wood Thrushes, Bluebirds, Ravens, the same abundance of House Wrens, and all the birds already enumerated. We have seen floating eight Buffaloes, one Antelope, and one Deer; how great the destruction of these animals must be during high freshets! The cause of their being drowned in such extraordinary numbers might not astonish one acquainted with the habits of these animals, but to one who is not, it may be well enough for me to describe it. Some few hundred miles above us, the river becomes confined between high bluffs or cliffs, many of which are nearly perpendicular, and therefore extremely difficult to ascend. When the Buffaloes have leaped or tumbled down from either side of the stream, they swim with ease across, but on reaching these walls, as it were, the poor animals try in vain to climb them, and becoming exhausted by falling back some dozens of times, give up the ghost, and float down the turbid stream; their bodies have been known to pass, swollen and putrid, the city of St. Louis. The most extraordinary part of the history of these drowned Buffaloes is, that the different tribes of Indians on the shores, are ever on the lookout for them, and no matter how putrid their flesh may be, provided the hump proves at all fat, they swim to them, drag them on shore, and cut them to pieces; after which they cook and eat this loathsome and abominable flesh, even to the marrow found in the bones. In some instances this has been done when the whole of the hair had fallen off, from the rottenness of the Buffalo. Ah! Mr. Catlin, I am now sorry to see and to read your accounts of the Indians *you* saw[1]—how very different they must have been from any that I have seen! Whilst we were on the top of the high hills which we climbed this morning, and looked towards the valley beneath us, including the river, we were undetermined as to whether we saw as much land dry as land overflowed; the immense flat prairie on the east side of the river looked not unlike a lake of great expanse, and immediately beneath us the last freshet had left upwards of perhaps two or three hundred acres covered by water, with numbers of water fowl on it, but so difficult of access as to render our wishes to kill Ducks quite out of the question. From the tops of the hills we saw only a continual succession of other lakes, of the same form and nature; and although the soil was of a fair, or even good, quality, the grass grew in tufts, separated from each other, and as it grows green in one spot, it dies and turns brown in another. We saw here no "carpeted prairies," no "velvety distant landscape;" and if these things are to be seen, why, the sooner we reach them the better. This afternoon I took the old nest of a Vireo, fully three feet above my head, filled with dried mud; it was attached to two small prongs issuing from a branch fully the size of my arm; this proves how high the water must have risen. Again, we saw large trees of which the bark had been torn off by the rubbing or cutting of the ice, as high as my shoulder. This is accounted for as

[1] As Audubon thus gently chides the extravagant statements of George Catlin, the well-known painter and panegyrist of the Indian, it may be well to state here that his own account of the putridity of drowned buffalo which the Indians eat with relish is not in the least exaggerated. Mr. Alexander Henry, the fur-trader of the North West Company, while at the Mandans in 1806, noticed the same thing that Audubon narrates, and described it in similar terms.

follows: during the first breaking up of the ice, it at times accumulates, so as to form a complete dam across the river; and when this suddenly gives way by the heat of the atmosphere, and the great pressure of the waters above the dam, the whole rushes on suddenly and overflows the country around, hurling the ice against any trees in its course. Sprague has shot two *Emberiza pallida*, two Lincoln's Finches, and a Black and Yellow Warbler, *Sylvicola* [*Dendrœca*] *maculosa*. One of our trappers, who had gone to the hills, brought on board two Rattlesnakes of a kind which neither Harris nor myself had seen before. The four Indians we have on board are three Puncas[1] and one Sioux; the Puncas were formerly attached to the Omahas; but, having had some difficulties among themselves, they retired further up the river, and assumed this new name. The Omahas reside altogether on the west side of the Missouri. Three of the Puncas have walked off to the establishment of Mr. Cerré to procure moccasins, but will return to-night. They appear to be very poor, and with much greater appetites than friend Catlin describes them to have. Our men are stupid, and very superstitious; they believe the rattles of

1 "The Puncas, as they are now universally called, or as some travellers formerly called them, Poncaras, or Poncars, the Pons of the French, were originally a branch of the Omahas, and speak nearly the same language. They have, however, long been separated from them, and dwell on both sides of Running-water River (L'Eau qui Court) and on Punca Creek, which Lewis and Clark call Poncara. They are said to have been brave warriors, but have been greatly reduced by war and the small-pox. According to Dr. Morse's report, they numbered in 1822 1,750 in all; at present the total number is estimated at about 300." ("Travels in North America," Maximilian, Prince of Wied, p. 137.)

"Poncar, Poncha, Ponca or Ponka, Punka, Puncah, etc. 'The remnant of a nation once respectable in point of numbers. They formerly [before 1805] resided on a branch of the Red River of Lake Winnipie; being oppressed by the Sioux, they removed to the west side of the Missouri on Poncar River . . . and now reside with the Mahas, whose language they speak.' ("Lewis and Clark," p. 109, ed. 1893.

snakes are a perfect cure for the headache; also, that they never die till after sunset, etc. We have discovered the female of Harris's Finch, which, as well as in the White-crowned Finch, resembles the male almost entirely; it is only a very little paler in its markings. I am truly proud to name it *Fringilla Harrisii*, in honor of one of the best friends I have in this world.

May 18, Thursday. Our good captain called us all up at a quarter before four this fair morning, to tell us that four barges had arrived from Fort Pierre, and that we might write a few letters, which Mr. Laidlow,[1] one of the partners, would take to St. Louis for us. I was introduced to that gentleman and also to Major Dripps,[2] the Indian agent. I wrote four short letters, which I put in an envelope addressed to the Messieurs Chouteau & Co., of St. Louis, who will post them, and we have hopes that some may reach their destination. The names of these four boats are "War Eagle," "White Cloud," "Crow-feather," and "Red-fish." We went on board one of them, and found it comfortable enough. They had ten thousand Buffalo robes on the four boats; the men live entirely on Buffalo meat and pemmican. They told us that about a hundred miles above us the Buffalo were by thousands, that the prairies were covered with dead calves, and the shores lined with dead of all sorts; that Antelopes were there also, and a great number of Wolves, etc.; therefore we shall see them after a while. Mr. Laidlow

[1] Wm. Laidlow was a member of the Columbia Fur Company at the time of its absorption by the Western Department of the American Fur Company, his service with the latter being mainly at Fort Pierre. With the exception, perhaps, of Kenneth McKenzie, also of the Columbia Fur Company, Laidlow was the ablest of the Upper Missouri traders.

[2] This is Andrew Dripps, one of the early traders, long associated with Lucien Fontenelle, under the firm name of Fontenelle and Dripps, in the Rocky Mountain Fur Trade. In later years he was appointed Indian Agent, and was serving in that capacity during the "Omega" voyage of 1843.—E. C.

told me that he would be back at Fort Pierre in two months, and would see us on our return. He is a true Scot, and apparently a clean one. We gave them six bottles of whiskey, for which they were very thankful; they gave us dried Buffalo meat, and three pairs of moccasins. They breakfasted with us, preferring salt meat to fresh venison. They departed soon after six o'clock, and proceeded rapidly down-stream in Indian file. These boats are strong and broad; the tops, or roofs, are supported by bent branches of trees, and these are covered by water-proof Buffalo hides; each has four oarsmen and a steersman, who manages the boat standing on a broad board; the helm is about ten feet long, and the rudder itself is five or six feet long. They row constantly for sixteen hours, and stop regularly at sundown; they, unfortunately for us, spent the night about two miles above us, for had we known of their immediate proximity we should have had the whole of the night granted for writing long, long letters. Our prospect of starting to-day is somewhat doubtful, as the hammering at the boilers still reaches my ears. The day is bright and calm. Mr. Laidlow told us that on the 5th of May the snow fell two feet on the level, and destroyed thousands of Buffalo calves. We felt the same storm whilst we were fast on the bar above Fort Leavenworth. This has been a day of almost pure idleness; our tramps of yesterday and the day previous had tired me, and with the exception of shooting at marks, and Sprague killing one of Bell's Vireo, and a Least Pewee, as well as another female of Harris's Finch, we have done nothing. Bell this evening went off to look for Bats, but saw none.

May 19, Friday. This has been a beautiful, but a very dull day to us all. We started by moonlight at three this morning, and although we have been running constantly, we took the wrong channel twice, and thereby lost much of our precious time; so I look upon this day's travel as a very poor one. The river was in several places inexpressibly wide and shallow. We saw a Deer of the common kind swimming across the stream; but few birds were killed, although we stopped (unfortunately) three times for wood. I forgot to say yesterday two things which I should have related, one of which is of a dismal and very disagreeable nature, being no less than the account given us of the clerks of the Company having killed one of the chiefs of the Blackfeet tribe of Indians, at the upper settlement of the Company, at the foot of the great falls of the Missouri, and therefore at the base of the Rocky Mountains, and Mr. Laidlow assured us that it would be extremely dangerous for us to go that far towards these Indians. The other thing is that Mr. Laidlow brought down a daughter of his, a half-breed of course, whom he is taking to St. Louis to be educated. We saw another Deer crossing the river, and have shot only a few birds, of no consequence.

May 20, Saturday. We have not made much progress this day, for the wind rose early, and rather ahead. We have passed to-day Jacques River,[1] or, as I should call it, La Rivière à Jacques, named after a man who some twenty or more years ago settled upon its banks, and made some money by collecting Beavers, etc., but who is dead and gone. Three White Wolves were seen this morning, and after a while we saw a fourth, of the brindled kind, which was trotting leisurely on, about 150 yards distant from the bank, where he had probably been feeding on some carrion or other. A shot from a rifle was quite enough

[1] This is the largest river which enters the Missouri thus far above Big Sioux River, coming from the north through South Dakota. The origin of the name, as given by Audubon, is known to few persons. *Jacques* is French for "James," and the stream has oftener been known as James River. Another of its names was Yankton River, derived from that of a tribe of the Sioux. But it is now usually called Dakota River, and will be found by this name on most modern maps. — E. C.

to make him turn off up the river again, but farther from us, at a full gallop; after a time he stopped again, when the noise of our steam pipe started him, and we soon lost sight of him in the bushes. We saw three Deer in the flat of one of the prairies, and just before our dinner we saw, rather indistinctly, a number of Buffaloes, making their way across the hills about two miles distant; after which, however, we saw their heavy tracks in a well and deep cut line across the said hills. Therefore we are now in what is pronounced to be the "Buffalo country," and may expect to see more of these animals to-morrow. We have stopped for wood no less than three times this day, and are fast for the night. Sprague killed a *Pipilo arcticus*, and Bell three others of the same species. We procured also another Bat, the *Vespertilio subulatus* of Say, and this is all. The country around us has materially changed, and we now see more naked, and to my eyes more completely denuded, hills about us, and less of the rich bottoms of alluvial land, than we passed below our present situation. I will not anticipate the future by all that we hear of the country above, but will continue steadily to accumulate in this, my poor journal, all that may take place from day to day. Three of our Indian rascals left us at our last wooding-ground, and have gone towards their miserable village. We have now only one Sioux with us, who will, the captain says, go to Fort Pierre in our company. They are, all that we have had as yet, a thieving and dirty set, covered with vermin. We still see a great number of Black-headed Gulls, but I think fewer Geese and Ducks than below; this probably on account of the very swampy prairie we have seen, and which appears to become scarce as we are advancing in this strange wilderness.

May 21, Sunday. We have had a great deal that interested us all this day. In the first place we have passed no less than five of what are called rivers, and their names are as follows:[1] Manuel, Basil, L'Eau qui Court, Ponca Creek; and Chouteau's River, all of which are indifferent streams of no magnitude, except the swift-flowing L'Eau qui Court,[2] which in some places is fully as broad as the Missouri itself, fully as muddy, filled with quicksands, and so remarkably shallow that in the autumn its navigation is very difficult indeed. We have seen this day about fifty Buffaloes; two which we saw had taken to the river, with intent to swim across it, but on the approach of our thundering, noisy vessel, turned about and after struggling for a few minutes, did make out to reach the top of the bank, after which they travelled at a moderate gait for some hundreds of yards; then, perhaps smelling or seeing the steamboat, they went off at a good though not very fast gallop, on the prairie by our side, and were soon somewhat ahead of us; they stopped once or twice, again resumed their gallop, and after a few

[1] It is not difficult to identify these five streams, though only one of them is of considerable size. See "Lewis and Clark," ed. of 1893, pp. 106–108.

1st. "Manuel" River is Plum Creek of Lewis and Clark, falling into the Missouri at Springfield, Bonhomme Co., S. D. It is Wananri River of Nicollet and of Warren; to be found on the General Land Office maps as Emanuel Creek, named for Manuel da Lisa, a noted trader on the Missouri in early days.

2d. "Basil" River is White Paint Creek of Lewis and Clark, falling in on the Nebraska side, a little below the mouth of the Niobrara, at the 935th mile point of the Missouri. The modern name is variously spelled Bazile, Basille, Bozzie, etc.

3d. L'Eau qui Court is of course the well-known Niobrara River.

4th. Ponca River falls in a mile or two above the Niobrara, on the same side of the Missouri.

5th. Chouteau Creek is present name of the stream next above, on the other side of the Missouri, at the 950th mile point. — E. C.

[2] L'Eau qui Court River has been called Rapid River, Spreading Water, Running Water, and Quicourt. "This river rises in the Black Hills, near the sources of Tongue River, and discharges itself into the Missouri about 1,000 miles from its mouth. The mouth is said to be 150 paces broad, and its current very rapid. There are said to be hot springs in this neighborhood, such as are known to exist in several places on the banks of the Missouri." ("Travels in North America," Maximilian, Prince of Wied, p. 141.)

diversions in their course, made to the hill-tops and disappeared altogether. We stopped to wood at a very propitious place indeed, for it was no less than the fort put up some years ago by Monsieur Le Clerc. Finding no one at the spot, we went to work cutting the pickets off his fortifications till we were loaded with the very best of dry wood. After we left that spot, were found several *Pipilo arcticus* which were shot, as well as a Say's Fly-catcher. The wind rose pretty high, and after trying our best to stem the current under very high cliffs, we were landed on Poncas Island, where all of us excepting Squires, who was asleep, went on shore to hunt, and to shoot whatever we might find. It happened that this island was well supplied with game; we saw many Deer, and Bell killed a young Doe, which proved good as fresh meat. Some twelve or fourteen of these animals were seen, and Bell saw three Elks which he followed across the island, also a Wolf in its hole, but did not kill it. Sprague saw a Forked-tailed Hawk, too far off to shoot at. We passed several dead Buffaloes near the shore, on which the Ravens were feeding gloriously. The *Pipilo arcticus* is now extremely abundant, and so is the House Wren, Yellow-breasted Chat, etc. We have seen this day Black-headed Gulls, Sandpipers, and Ducks, and now I am going to rest, for after my long walk through the deep mud to reach the ridge on the islands, I feel somewhat wearied and fatigued. Three Antelopes were seen this evening.

May 22, Monday. We started as early as usual, *i. e.*, at half-past three; the weather was fine. We breakfasted before six, and immediately after saw two Wild Cats of the common kind; we saw them running for some hundreds of yards. We also saw several large Wolves, noticing particularly one pure white, that stood and looked at us for some time. Their movements are precisely those of the common cur dog. We have seen five or six this day. We began seeing Buffaloes again in small gangs, but this afternoon and evening we have seen a goodly number, probably more than a hundred. We also saw fifteen or twenty Antelopes. I saw ten at once, and it was beautiful to see them running from the top of a high hill down to its base, after which they went round the same hill, and were lost to us. We have landed three times to cut wood, and are now busy at it on Cedar Island.[1] At both the previous islands we saw an immense number of Buffalo tracks, more, indeed, than I had anticipated. The whole of the prairies as well as the hills have been so trampled by them that I should have considered it quite unsafe for a man to travel on horseback. The ground was literally covered with their tracks, and also with bunches of hair, while the bushes and the trunks of the trees, between which they had passed, were hanging with the latter substance. I collected some, and intend to carry a good deal home. We found here an abundance of what is called the White Apple,[2] but which is anything else but an apple. The fruit grows under the ground about six inches; it is about the size of a hen's egg, covered with a woody, hard pellicle, a sixteenth of an inch thick, from which the fruit can be

[1] "'Cedar' is the name which has been applied by various authors to several different islands, many miles apart, in this portion of the river. . . . We reached an island extending for two miles in the middle of the river, covered with red cedar, from which it derives its name of Cedar Island." ("Lewis and Clark," ed. of 1893.)

"Cedar Island is said to be 1075 miles from the mouth of the Missouri. On the steep banks of this long, narrow island which lies near the southwest bank, there were thickets of poplars, willows, and buffalo-berry; the rest of the island is covered with a dark forest of red cedars, of which we immediately felled a goodly number. The notes of numerous birds were heard in the gloom of the cedar forest, into which no ray of sun could penetrate. Here, too, we found everywhere traces of the elks and stags, and saw where they had rubbed off the bark with their antlers." ("Travels in North America," Maximilian, Prince of Wied, p. 144.)

[2] Translating the usual French name (*pomme blanche*) of the *Ps[illegible]ea esculenta.*

drawn without much difficulty; this is quite white; the exterior is a dirty, dark brown. The roots are woody. The flowers were not in bloom, but I perceived that the leaves are ovate, and attached in fives. This plant is collected in great quantities by the Indians at this season and during the whole summer, and put to dry, which renders it as hard as wood; it is then pounded fine, and makes an excellent kind of mush, upon which the Indians feed greedily. I will take some home. We found pieces of crystallized gypsum; we saw Meadow Larks whose songs and single notes are quite different from those of the Eastern States; we have not yet been able to kill one to decide if new or not.[1] We have seen the Arkansas Flycatcher, Sparrow-hawks, Geese, etc. The country grows poorer as we ascend; the bluffs exhibit oxide of iron, sulphur, and also magnesia. We have made a good day's run, though the wind blew rather fresh from the northwest. Harris shot a Marsh Hawk, Sprague a Nighthawk, and some small birds, and I saw Martins breeding in Woodpeckers' holes in high and large cotton-trees. We passed the "Grand Town"[2] very early this morning; I did not see it, however. Could we have remained on shore at several places that we passed, we should have made havoc with the Buffaloes, no doubt; but we shall have enough of that sport ere long. They all look extremely poor and shabby; we see them sporting among themselves, butting and tearing up the earth, and when at a gallop they throw up the dust behind them. We

[1] This is Audubon's first mention of the Western Meadow Lark, which he afterward decided to be a distinct species and named *Sturnella neglecta*, B. of Am. vii., 1844, p. 339, pl. 487. It is interesting to find him noting the difference in the song from that of the Eastern species before he had had an opportunity of examining the bird itself. — E. C.

[2] "Grand Town" is perhaps the large prairie-dog village which once covered several acres on the right bank of the Missouri, in the vicinity of the butte known as the Dome, or Tower, between Yankton and Fort Randall. — E. C.

saw their tracks all along both shores; where they have landed and are unable to get up the steep cliffs, they follow along the margin till they reach a ravine, and then make their way to the hills, and again to the valleys; they also have roads to return to the river to drink. They appear at this season more on the west side of the Missouri. The Elks, on the contrary, are found on the islands and low bottoms, well covered with timber; the common Deer is found indifferently everywhere. All the Antelopes we have seen were on the west side. After we had left our first landing-place a few miles, we observed some seven or eight Indians looking at us, and again retiring to the woods, as if to cover themselves; when we came nearly opposite them, however, they all came to the shore, and made signs to induce us to land. The boat did not stop for their pleasure, and after we had fairly passed them they began firing at us, not with blank cartridges, but with well-directed rifle-balls, several of which struck the "Omega" in different places. I was standing at that moment by one of the chimneys, and saw a ball strike the water a few feet beyond our bows; and Michaux, the hunter, heard its passing within a few inches of his head. A Scotchman, who was asleep below, was awakened and greatly frightened by hearing a ball pass through the partition, cutting the lower part of his pantaloons, and deadening itself against a trunk. Fortunately no one was hurt. Those rascals were attached to a war party, and belong to the Santee tribes which range across the country from the Mississippi to the Missouri. I will make no comment upon their conduct, but I have two of the balls that struck our boat; it seems to be a wonder that not one person was injured, standing on deck as we were to the number of a hundred or more. We have not seen Parrakeets or Squirrels for several days; Partridges have also deserted us, as well as Rabbits; we have seen Barn Swallows, but no more Rough-winged. We have yet plenty of Red-headed Woodpeckers. Our captain has just sent out four hunters this evening, who are to hunt early to-morrow morning, and will meet the boat some distance above; Squires has gone with them. How I wish I were twenty-five years younger! I should like such a tramp greatly; but I do not think it prudent now for me to sleep on the ground when I can help it, while it is so damp.

May 23, Tuesday. The wind blew from the south this morning and rather stiffly. We rose early, and walked about this famous Cedar Island, where we stopped to cut large red cedars [*Juniperus virginianus*] for one and a half hours; we started at half-past five, breakfasted rather before six, and were on the lookout for our hunters. *Hunters!* Only two of them had ever been on a Buffalo hunt before. One was lost almost in sight of the river. They only walked two or three miles, and camped. Poor Squires' first experience was a very rough one; for, although they made a good fire at first, it never was tended afterwards, and his pillow was formed of a buck's horn accidentally picked up near the place. Our Sioux Indian helped himself to another, and they all felt chilly and damp. They had forgotten to take any spirits with them, and their condition was miserable. As the orb of day rose as red as blood, the party started, each taking a different direction. But the wind was unfavorable; it blew up, not down the river, and the Buffaloes, Wolves, Antelopes, and indeed every animal possessed of the sense of smell, had scent of them in time to avoid them. There happened however to be attached to this party two good and true men, that may be called hunters. One was Michaux; the other a friend of his, whose name I do not know. It happened, by hook or by crook, that these two managed to kill four Buffaloes; but one of them was drowned, as it took to the river after being shot. Only a few pieces from a young bull, and its tongue, were brought on board, most of the men being too lazy, or too far off, to cut out even the tongues of the others; and thus it is that thousands multiplied by thousands of Buffaloes are murdered in senseless play, and their enormous carcasses are suffered to be the prey of the Wolf, the Raven and the Buzzard. However, the hunters all returned safely to the boat, and we took them in, some tired enough, among whom was friend Squires. He had worn out his moccasins, and his feet were sore, blistered, and swollen; he was thirsty enough too, for in taking a drink he had gone to a beautiful clear spring that unfortunately proved to be one of magnesia, which is common enough in this part of our country, and this much increased his thirst. He drank four tumblers of water first, then a glass of grog, ate somewhat of a breakfast, and went to bed, whence I called him a few minutes before dinner. However, he saw some Buffaloes, and had hopes of shooting one, also about twenty Antelopes. Michaux saw two very large White Wolves. At the place where we decided to take the fatigued party in, we stopped to cut down a few dead cedars, and Harris shot a common Rabbit and one Lark Finch. Bell and Sprague saw several Meadow-larks, which I trust will prove new, as these birds have quite different notes and songs from those of our eastern birds. They brought a curious cactus, some handsome well-scented dwarf peas, and several other plants unknown to me. On the island I found abundance of dwarf wild-cherry bushes in full blossom, and we have placed all these plants in press. We had the misfortune to get aground whilst at dinner, and are now fast till to-morrow morning; for all our efforts to get the boat off, and they have been many, have proved ineffectual. It is a bad spot, for we are nearly halfway from either shore. I continued my long letter for home, and wrote the greatest portion of another long one to John Bachman. I intend to write till a late hour this night, as perchance we may reach Fort Pierre early next week.

May 24,[1] *Wednesday.* We remained on the said bar till four this afternoon. The wind blew hard all day. A boat from Fort Pierre containing two men passed us, bound for Fort Vermilion; one of them was Mr. Charity, one of the Company's associate traders. The boat was somewhat of a curiosity, being built in the form of a scow; but instead of being made of wood, had only a frame, covered with Buffalo skins with the hair on. They had been nine days coming 150 miles, detained every day, more or less, by Indians. Mr. Charity gave me some leather prepared for moccasins — for a consideration, of course. We have seen Buffaloes, etc., but the most important animal to us was one of Townsend's Hare.[2] We shot four Meadow-larks [*Sturnella neglecta*] that have, as I said, other songs and notes than ours, but could not establish them as new. We procured a Red-shafted Woodpecker, two Sparrow-hawks, two Arkansas Flycatchers, a Blue Grosbeak, saw Say's Flycatcher, etc. I went on shore with Harris's small double-barrelled gun, and the first shot I had was pretty near killing me; the cone blew off, and passed so near my ear that I was stunned, and fell down as if shot, and afterwards I was obliged to lie down for several minutes. I returned on board, glad indeed that the accident was no greater. We passed this afternoon bluffs of sulphur, almost pure to look at, and a patch that has burnt for two years in succession. Alum was found strewn on the shores. A toad was brought, supposed to be new by Harris and Bell. We landed for the night on an island so thick

[1] May 24 is the date given by Audubon, B. Amer. viii., p. 338, as that on which Mr. Bell shot the specimen which became type of *Emberiza Le Conteii*, figured on plate 488. This bird is now *Ammodramus* (*Coturniculus*) *lecontei*; it long remained an extreme rarity. — E. C.

[2] The common Prairie Hare, *Lepus campestris*, for which see a previous note. — E. C.

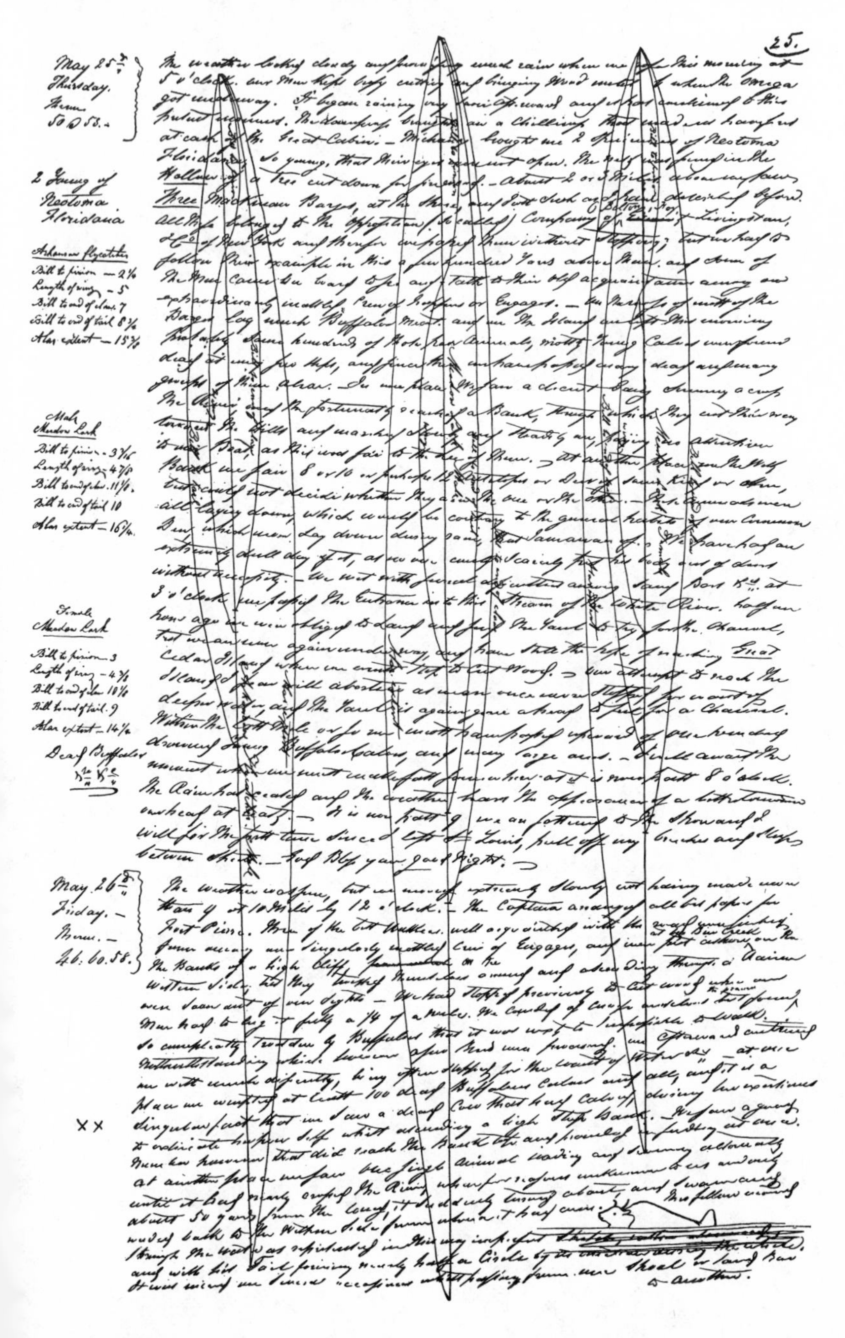

FACSIMILE OF A PAGE OF THE MISSOURI RIVER JOURNAL.

REDUCED ONE THIRD.

with underbrush that it was no easy matter to walk through; perhaps a hundred Buffalo calves were dead in it, and the smell was not pleasant, as you may imagine. The boat of Mr. Charity went off when we reached the shore, after having escaped from the bar. We have seen more White Wolves this day, and few Antelopes. The whole country is trodden down by the heavy Buffaloes, and this renders the walking both fatiguing and somewhat dangerous. The garlic of this country has a red blossom, otherwise it looks much like ours; when Buffalo have fed for some time on this rank weed, their flesh cannot be eaten.

May 25, Thursday. The weather looked cloudy, and promised much rain when we rose this morning at five o'clock; our men kept busy cutting and bringing wood until six, when the "Omega" got under way. It began raining very soon afterwards and it has continued to this present moment. The dampness brought on a chilliness that made us have fires in each of the great cabins. Michaux brought me two specimens of *Neotoma floridana*, so young that their eyes were not open. The nest was found in the hollow of a tree cut down for firewood. Two or three miles above us, we saw three Mackinaw barges on the shore, just such as I have described before; all these belonged to the (so-called) Opposition Company of C. Bolton, Fox, Livingstone & Co., of New York, and therefore we passed them without stopping; but we had to follow their example a few hundred yards above them, for we had to stop also; and then some of the men came on board, to see and talk to their old acquaintances among our extraordinary and motley crew of trappers and *engagés*. On the roofs of the barges lay much Buffalo meat, and on the island we left this morning probably some hundreds of these poor animals, mostly young calves, were found dead at every few steps; and since then we have passed many dead as well as many groups of living. In one place we saw a large gang swimming across the river; they fortunately reached a bank through which they cut their way towards the hills, and marched slowly and steadily on, paying no attention to our boat, as this was far to the lee of them. At another place on the west bank, we saw eight or ten, or perhaps more, Antelopes or Deer of some kind or other, but could not decide whether they were the one or the other. These animals were all lying down, which would be contrary to the general habit of our common Deer, which never lie down during rain, that I am aware of. We have had an extremely dull day of it, as one could hardly venture out of the cabin for pleasure. We met with several difficulties among sand-bars. At three o'clock we passed the entrance into the stream known as White River;[1] half an hour ago we were obliged to land, and send the yawl to try for the channel, but we are now again on our way, and have still the hope of reaching Great Cedar Island[2] this evening, where we must stop to cut wood. — *Later.* Our attempt to reach the island I fear will prove abortive, as we are once more at a standstill for want of deeper water, and the yawl has again gone ahead to feel for a channel. Within the last mile or so, we must have passed upwards of a hundred drowned young Buffalo calves, and many large ones. I will await the moment when we must make fast somewhere, as it is now past eight o'clock. The rain has ceased, and the weather has the appearance of a better day to-morrow, overhead at least. Now it is

[1] La Rivière Blanche of the French, also sometimes called White Earth River, and Mankizitah River; a considerable stream which falls into the right bank of the Missouri in Lyman Co., South Dakota, at the 1056 mile point of the Commission charts. — E. C.

[2] So called from its size, in distinction from the Cedar Island already mentioned on p. 505. This is Second Cedar Island of Warren's and Nicollet's maps, noticed by Lewis and Clark, Sept. 18, 1804, as "nearly a mile in length and covered with red cedar." It was once the site of an establishment called Fort Recovery. The position is near the 1070th-mile point of the Missouri. — E. C.

after nine o'clock; we are fastened to the shore, and I will, for the first time since I left St. Louis, sleep in my cabin, and between sheets.

May 26, Friday. The weather was fine, but we moved extremely slowly, not having made more than ten miles by twelve o'clock. The captain arranged all his papers for Fort Pierre. Three of the best walkers, well acquainted with the road, were picked from among our singularly mixed crew of *engagés*, and were put ashore at Big Bend Creek, on the banks of a high cliff on the western side; they ascended through a ravine, and soon were out of sight. We had stopped previously to cut wood, where our men had to lug it fully a quarter of a mile. We ourselves landed of course, but found the prairie so completely trodden by Buffaloes that it was next to impossible to walk. Notwithstanding this, however, a few birds were procured. The boat continued on with much difficulty, being often stopped for the want of water. At one place we counted over a hundred dead Buffalo calves; we saw a great number, however, that did reach the top of the bank, and proceeded to feeding at once. We saw one animal, quite alone, wading and swimming alternately, till it had nearly crossed the river, when for reasons unknown to us, and when only about fifty yards from the land, it suddenly turned about, and swam and waded back to the western side, whence it had originally come; this fellow moved through the water as represented in this very imperfect sketch, which I have placed here, and with his tail forming nearly half a circle by its erection during the time he swam. It was mired on several occasions while passing from one shoal or sand-bar to another. It walked, trotted, or galloped, while on the solid beach, and ultimately, by swimming a few hundred yards, returned to the side from whence it had started, though fully half a mile below the exact spot. There now was heard on board some talk about the *Great Bend*, and the captain asked me whether I would like to go off and camp, and await his arrival on the other side to-morrow. I assured him that nothing would give us more pleasure, and he gave us three stout young men to go with us to carry our blankets, provisions, etc., and to act as guides and hunters. All was ready by about five of the afternoon, when Harris, Bell, Sprague, and I, as well as the three men, were put ashore; and off we went at a brisk walk across a beautiful, level prairie, whereon in sundry directions we could see small groups of Buffaloes, grazing at leisure. Proceeding along, we saw a great number of Cactus, some Bartram Sandpipers, and a Long-billed Curlew. Presently we observed a village of prairie Marmots, *Arctomys* [*Cynomys*] *ludovicianus*, and two or three of our party diverged at once to pay them their respects. The mounds which I passed were very low indeed; the holes were opened, but I saw not one of the owners. Harris, Bell, and Michaux, I believe, shot at some of them, but killed none, and we proceeded on, being somewhat anxious to pitch our camp for the night before dark. Presently we reached the hills and were surprised at their composition; the surface looked as if closely covered with small broken particles of coal, whilst the soil was of such greasy or soapy nature, that it was both painful and fatiguing to ascend them. Our guides assured us that such places were never in any other condition, or as they expressed it, were "never dry." Whilst travelling about these remarkable hills, Sprague saw one of Townsend's Hare, and we started the first and only Prairie Hen we have seen since our departure from St. Louis. Gradually we rose on to the very uppermost crest of the hills we had to cross, and whilst reposing ourselves for some minutes we had the gratification of seeing around us one of the great panoramas this remarkable portion of our country affords. There was a vast extent of country beneath and around us. Westward rose the famous Medicine Hill, and in the opposite direction were the wanderings of the Missouri for many miles, and from the distance we were then from it, the river appeared as if a small, very circuitous streamlet. The Great Bend was all in full view, and its course almost resembled that of a chemist's retort, being formed somewhat like the scratch of my pen thus:—

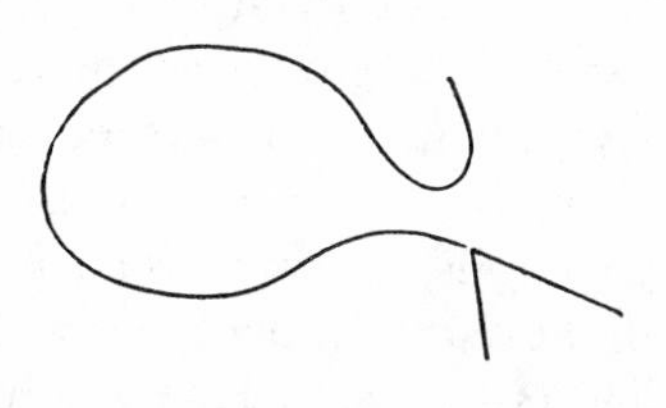

The walk from our landing crossing the prairies was quite four miles, whilst the distance by water is computed to be twenty-six. From the pinnacle we stood on, we could see the movements of our boat quite well, and whilst the men were employed cutting wood for her engines, we could almost count every stroke of their axes, though fully two miles distant, as the crow flies. As we advanced we soon found ourselves on the ridges leading us across the Bend, and plainly saw that we were descending towards the Missouri once more. *Chemin faisant*, we saw four Black-tailed Deer, a shot at which Michaux or Bell, who were in advance, might perhaps have had, had not Harris and Sprague taken a route across the declivity before them, and being observed by these keen-sighted animals, the whole made off at once. I had no fair opportunity of witnessing their movements; but they looked swiftness itself, combined with grace. They were not followed, and we reached the river at a spot which evidently had been previously camped on by Indians; here we made our minds up to stop at once, and arrange for the night, which now promised to be none of the fairest. One man remained with us to prepare the camp, whilst Michaux and the others started in search of game, as if blood-hounds. Meantime we lighted a large and glowing fire, and began preparing some supper. In less than half an hour Michaux was seen to return with a load on his back, which proved to be a fine young buck of the Black-tailed

Deer. This produced animation at once. I examined it carefully, and Harris and Sprague returned promptly from the point to which they had gone. The darkness of the night, contrasting with the vivid glare of our fire, which threw a bright light on the skinning of the Deer, and was reflected on the trunks and branches of the cottonwood trees, six of them in one clump, almost arising from the same root, gave such superb effect that I retired some few steps to enjoy the truly fine picture. Some were arranging their rough couches, whilst others were engaged in carrying wood to support our fire through the night; some brought water from the great, muddy stream, and others were busily at work sharpening long sticks for skewers, from which large pieces of venison were soon seen dropping their rich juices upon the brightest of embers. The very sight of this sharpened our appetites, and it must have been laughable to see how all of us fell to, and ate of this first-killed Black-tailed Deer. After a hearty meal we went to sleep, one and all, under the protection of God, and not much afraid of Indians, of whom we have not seen a specimen since we had the pleasure of being fired on by the Santees. We slept very well for a while, till it began to sprinkle rain; but it was only a very slight shower, and I did not even attempt to shelter myself from it. Our fires were mended several times by one or another of the party, and the short night passed on, refreshing us all as only men can be refreshed by sleep under the sky, breathing the purest of air, and happy as only a clear conscience can make one.

May 27, Saturday. At half-past three this morning my ears were saluted by the delightful song of the Red Thrush, who kept on with his strains until we were all up. Harris and Bell went off, and as soon as the two hunters had cleaned their rifles they followed. I remained in camp with Sprague for a while; the best portions of the Deer, *i. e.*, the liver, kidneys, and tongue, were cooked for

VIEW ON THE MISSOURI RIVER, ABOVE GREAT BEND.

FROM A WATER-COLOR DRAWING BY ISAAC SPRAGUE.

breakfast, which all enjoyed. No Wolves had disturbed our slumbers, and we now started in search of quadrupeds, birds, and adventures. We found several plants, all new to me, and which are now in press. All the ravines which we inspected were well covered by cedars of the red variety, and whilst ascending several of the hills we found them in many parts partially gliding down as if by the sudden effects of very heavy rain. We saw two very beautiful Avocets [*Recurvirostra americana*] feeding opposite our camp; we saw also a Hawk nearly resembling what is called Cooper's Hawk, but having a white rump. Bell joined the hunters and saw some thousands of Buffalo; and finding a very large bull within some thirty yards of them, they put in his body three large balls. The poor beast went off, however, and is now, in all probability, dead. Many fossil remains have been found on the hills about us, but we saw none. These hills are composed of limestone rocks, covered with much shale. Harris thinks this is a different formation from that of either St. Louis or Belle Vue — but, alas! we are not much of geologists. We shot only one of Say's Flycatcher, and the Finch we have called *Emberiza pallida*,[1] but of which I am by no means certain, for want of more exact descriptions than those of a mere synopsis. Our boat made its

[1] Audubon probably refers to the brief description in his own Synopsis of 1839, p. 103, a copy of which no doubt accompanied him up the Missouri. He had described and figured what he supposed to be *Emberiza pallida* in the Orn. Biogr. v., 1839, p. 66, pl. 398, fig. 2; B. Amer. iii., 1841, p. 71, pl. 161, from specimens taken in the Rocky Mts. by J. K. Townsend, June 15, 1834. But this bird was not the true *pallida* of Swainson, being that afterwards called *Spizella breweri* by Cassin, Pr. Acad. Philad., 1856, p. 40, The true *pallida* of Swainson is what Audubon described as *Emberiza shattuckii*, B. Amer. vii., 1844, p. 347, pl. 493, naming it for Dr. Geo. C. Shattuck, of Boston, one of his Labrador companions. He speaks of it as "abundant throughout the country bordering the upper Missouri;" and all mention in the present Journal of the "Clay-colored Bunting," or "*Emberiza pallida*," refers to what Audubon later named Shattuck's Bunting — not to what he gives as *Emberiza pallida* in the Orn. Biog. and Synopsis of 1839; for the latter is *Spizella breweri*. — E. C.

appearance at two o'clock; we had observed from the hill-tops that it had been aground twice. At three our camp was broken up, our effects removed, our fire left burning, and our boat having landed for us, and for cutting cedar trees, we got on board, highly pleased with our camping out, especially as we found all well on board. We had not proceeded very far when the difficulties of navigation increased so much that we grounded several times, and presently saw a few Indians on the shore; our yawl was out sounding for a passage amid the many sand-bars in view; the Indians fired, not balls, but a salute, to call us ashore. We neared shore, and talked to them; for, they proving to be Sioux, and our captain being a good scholar in that tongue, there was no difficulty in so doing. He told them to follow us, and that he would come-to. They ran to their horses on the prairie, all of which stood still, and were good-looking, comparatively speaking, leaped on their backs without saddles or stirrups, and followed us with ease at a walk. They fired a second salute as we landed; there were only four of them, and they are all at this moment on board. They are fine-looking fellows; the captain introduced Harris and me to the chief, and we shook hands all round. They are a poor set of beggars after all. The captain gave them supper, sugar and coffee, and about one pound of gunpowder, and the chief coolly said: "What is the use of powder, without balls?" It is quite surprising that these Indians did not see us last night, for I have no doubt our fire could have been seen up and down the river for nearly twenty miles. But we are told their lodges are ten miles inland, and that may answer the question. I shall not be sorry now to go to bed. Our camp of the *Six Trees* is deserted and silent. The captain is almost afraid he may be forced to leave half his cargo somewhere near this, and proceed to Fort Pierre, now distant fifty miles, and return for the goods. The Indians saw nothing of the three men who were sent yesterday to announce our approach to Fort Pierre.

Sunday, May 28. This morning was beautiful, though cool. Our visiting Indians left us at twelve last night, and I was glad enough to be rid of these beggars by trade. Both shores were dotted by groups of Buffaloes as far as the eye could reach, and although many were near the banks they kept on feeding quietly till we nearly approached them; those at the distance of half a mile never ceased their avocations. A Gray Wolf was seen swimming across our bows, and some dozens of shots were sent at the beast, which made it open its mouth and raise its head, but it never stopped swimming away from us, as fast as possible; after a while it reached a sand-bar, and immediately afterwards first trotted, and then galloped off. Three Buffaloes also crossed ahead of us, but at some distance; they all reached the shore, and scrambled up the bank. We have run better this morning than for three or four days, and if fortunate enough may reach Fort Pierre sometime to-morrow. The prairies appear better now, the grass looks green, and probably the poor Buffaloes will soon regain their flesh. We have seen more than 2,000 this morning up to this moment — twelve o'clock.

We reached Fort George[1] at about three this afternoon. This is what is called the "Station of the Opposition line;" some Indians and a few lodges are on the edge of the prairie. Sundry bales of Buffalo robes were brought on board, and Major Hamilton, who is now acting Indian agent here until the return of Major Crisp, came on board also. I knew his father thirty-five years ago. He pointed out to us the cabin on the opposite shore,[2] where a part-

[1] Situated on the right bank of the Missouri, in Presho Co., South Dakota. See "Lewis and Clark," ed. of 1893, p. 127. — E. C.

[2] This "cabin on the opposite shore" was somewhere in the vicinity of Rousseau, at or near the mouth of present Little Medicine Creek (formerly East Medicine Knoll River, originally named Reuben's Creek by Lewis and Clark, after Reuben Fields, one of their men). — E. C.

ner of the "Opposition line" shot at and killed two white men and wounded two others, all of whom were remarkable miscreants. We are about thirty miles below Fort Pierre. Indians were seen on both sides the river, ready to trade both here and at Fort Pierre, where I am told there are five hundred lodges standing. The Indian dogs which I saw here so very closely resemble wild Wolves, that I feel assured that if I was to meet with one of them in the woods, I should most assuredly kill it as such. A few minutes after leaving Fort George, we stopped to sound the channel, and could not discover more than three and a half feet of water; our captain told us we would proceed no farther this day, but would camp here. Bell, Harris, and Sprague went off with guns; Squires and I walked to Fort George, and soon met a young Englishman going towards our boat on a "Buffalo Horse" at a swift gallop; but on being hailed he reined up. His name was Illingsworth; he is the present manager of this establishment. He welcomed us, and as he was going to see Captain Sire, we proceeded on. Upon reaching the camp we found a strongly built log cabin, in one end of which we met Mr. Cutting, who told me he had known Victor [Audubon] in Cuba. This young gentleman had been thrown from his horse in a recent Buffalo chase, and had injured one foot so that he could not walk. A Buffalo cow had hooked the horse and thrown the rider about twenty feet, although the animal had not been wounded. We also met here a Mr. Taylor, who showed me the petrified head of a Beaver, which he supposed to be that of a Wolf; but I showed him the difference in the form at once. I saw two young Wolves about six weeks old, of the common kind, alive. They looked well, but their nature was already pretty apparently that of the parents. I saw an abundance of semi-wolf Dogs, and their howlings were distressing to my ear. We entered the lodge of a trader attached to our company, a German, who is a clever man; has considerable knowledge of botany, and draws well. There were about fifteen lodges, and we saw a greater number of squaws and half-breed children than I had expected. But as every clerk and agent belonging to the companies has "a wife," as it is *called*, a spurious population soon exhibits itself around the wigwams. I will not comment upon this here. We returned before dark to our boat, and I am off to bed.

Monday, May 29. I was up early, and as soon as breakfast was over, Major Hamilton and myself walked to Fort George. We found the three gentlemen to whom I showed the plate of quadrupeds, and afterwards I went to their store to see skins of Wolves and of the Swift Fox. I found a tolerably good Fox skin which was at once given me; I saw what I was assured were two distinct varieties (for I cannot call them species) of Wolves. Both, however, considering the difference in size, were old and young of the same variety. They both had the top of the back dark gray, and the sides, belly, legs, and tail, nearly white. When I have these two sorts in the flesh, I may derive further knowledge. I looked at the Indian Dogs again with much attention, and was assured that there is much cross breeding between these Dogs and Wolves, and that all the varieties actually come from the same root.

Harris now joined us, and found he had met a brother of Mr. Cutting in Europe. The gentlemen from the fort came back to the boat with us; we gave them a luncheon, and later a good substantial dinner, the like of which, so they told us, they had not eaten for many a day. Mr. Illingsworth told us much about Buffaloes; he says the hunting is usually more or less dangerous. The Porcupine is found hereabouts and feeds on the leaves and bark as elsewhere, but not unfrequently retires into the crevices of rocks, whenever no trees of large size are to be found in its vicinity. Elks, at times, assemble in groups of from fifty to two hundred, and their movements are as regular as those of a flock of White Pelicans, so that if the oldest Elk starts in any one direction, all the rest follow at once in his tracks. Where he stops, they all stop, and at times all will suddenly pause, range themselves as if a company of dragoons, ready to charge upon the enemy; which, however, they seldom if ever attempt. After dinner Mr. Illingsworth told me he would go and shoot a Buffalo calf for me — we will see. Bell, Harris, Squires, and myself went off to shoot some Prairie-dogs, as the *Arctomys ludovicianus* is called. After walking over the hills for about one mile, we came to the "village," and soon after heard their cries but not their barkings. The sound they make is simply a "chip, chip, chip," long and shrill enough, and at every cry the animal jerks its tail, without however erecting it upright, as I have seen them represented. Their holes are not perpendicular, but oblique, at an angle of about forty degrees, after which they seem to deviate; but whether sideways or upwards, I cannot yet say. I shot at two of them, which appeared to me to be standing, not across their holes, but in front of them. The first one I never saw after the shot; the second I found dying at the entrance of the burrow, but at my appearance it worked backwards. I drew my ramrod and put the end in its mouth; this it bit hard but kept working backwards, and notwithstanding my efforts, was soon out of sight and touch. Bell saw two enter the same hole, and Harris three. Bell saw some standing quite erect and leaping in the air to see and watch our movements. I found, by lying down within twenty or thirty steps of the hole, that they reappeared in fifteen or twenty minutes. This was the case with me when I shot at the two I have mentioned. Harris saw one that, after coming out of its hole, gave a long and somewhat whistling note, which he thinks was one of invitation to its neighbors, as several came out in a few moments. I have great doubts whether their cries are issued at the appearance of danger or not. I am of opinion that they are a mode of recognition as well as of amusement. I also think they feed more at night than in the day. On my return to the boat, I rounded a small hill and started a Prairie Wolf within a few steps of me. I was unfortunately loaded with No. 3 shot. I pulled one trigger and then the other, but the rascal went off as if unhurt for nearly a hundred yards, when he stopped, shook himself rather violently, and I saw I had hit him; but he ran off again at a very swift rate, his tail down, stopped again, and again shook himself as before, after which he ran out of my sight between the hills. Buffalo cows at this season associate together, with their calves, but if pursued, leave the latter to save themselves. The hides at present are not worth saving, and the Indians as well as the white hunters, when they shoot a Buffalo, tear off the hide, cut out the better portions of the flesh, as well as the tongue, and leave the carcass to the Wolves and Ravens. By the way, Bell saw a Magpie this day, and Harris killed two Black-headed Grosbeaks. Bell also saw several Evening Grosbeaks to-day; therefore there's not much need of crossing the Rocky Mountains for the few precious birds that the talented and truth-speaking Mr. —— brought or sent to the well-paying Academy of Natural Sciences of Philadelphia! The two men sent to Fort Pierre a few days ago have returned, one this evening, in a canoe, the other this afternoon, by land.

May 30, Tuesday. We had a fine morning, and indeed a very fair day. I was called up long before five to receive a Buffalo calf, and the head of another, which Mr. Illingsworth had the goodness to send me. Sprague has been busy ever since breakfast drawing one of the heads, the size of nature. The other entire calf has been skinned, and will be in strong pickle before I go to bed.

Mr. Illingsworth killed two calves, one bull, and one cow. The calves, though not more than about two months old, as soon as the mother was wounded, rushed towards the horse or the man who had struck her. The one bull skinned was so nearly putrid, though so freshly killed, that its carcass was thrown overboard. This gentleman, as well as many others, assured us that the hunting of Buffaloes, for persons unaccustomed to it, was very risky indeed; and said no one should attempt it unless well initiated, even though he may be a first-rate rider. When calves are caught alive, by placing your hands over the eyes and blowing into the nostrils, in the course of a few minutes they will follow the man who performs this simple operation. Indeed if a cow perchance leaves her calf behind during a time of danger, or in the chase, the calf will often await the approach of man and follow him as soon as the operation mentioned is over. Mr. Illingsworth paid us a short visit, and told us that Mr. Cutting was writing to his post near Fort Union to expect us, and to afford us all possible assistance. We made a start at seven, and after laboring over the infernal sand-bars until nearly four this afternoon, we passed them, actually cutting our own channel with the assistance of the wheel. Whilst we were at this, we were suddenly boarded by the yawl of the "Trapper," containing Mr. Picotte, Mr. Chardon, and several others. They had left Fort Pierre this morning, and had come down in one hour and a half. We were all duly presented to the whole group, and I gave to each of these gentlemen the letters I had for them. I found them very kind and affable. They dined after us, being somewhat late, but ate heartily and drank the same. They brought a first-rate hunter with them, of whom I expect to have much to say hereafter. Mr. Picotte promised me the largest pair of Elk horns ever seen in this country, as well as several other curiosities, all of which I will write about when I have them. We have reached

Antelope River,[1] a very small creek on the west side. We saw two Wolves crossing the river, and Harris shot a Lark Finch. We have now no difficulties before us, and hope to reach Fort Pierre very early to-morrow morning.

Fort Pierre,[2] *May 31, Wednesday.* After many difficulties we reached this place at four o'clock this afternoon, having spent the whole previous part of the day, say since half-past three this morning, in coming against the innumerable bars — only *nine miles!* I forgot to say last evening, that where we landed for the night our captain caught a fine specimen of *Neotoma floridana,* a female. We were forced to come-to about a quarter of a mile above Fort Pierre, after having passed the steamer "Trapper" of our Company. Bell, Squires, and myself walked to the Fort as soon as possible, and found Mr. Picotte and Mr. Chardon there. More kindness from strangers I have seldom received. I was presented with the largest pair of Elk horns I ever saw, and also a skin of the animal itself, most beautifully prepared, which I hope to give to

[1] Or Antelope Creek, then as now the name of the small stream which falls into the Missouri on the right bank, about 10 miles below the mouth of the Teton. It has also been known as Cabri Creek, Katota Tokah, and Highwater Creek, the latter being the designation originally bestowed by Lewis and Clark, Sept. 24, 1804. It runs in Presho Co., S. Dak. — E. C.

[2] The *old* fort of this name was three miles above the mouth of the Teton River; this was abandoned, and another fort built, higher up, on the west bank of the Missouri. The Prince of Wied reached this fort on the fifty-first day of his voyage up the Missouri, and Audubon on the thirty-third of his; a gain in time which may possibly be attributed both to better weather and to the improvement in steamboats during ten years. The Prince says: "Fort Pierre is one of the most considerable settlements of the Fur Company on the Missouri, and forms a large quadrangle surrounded by pickets. Seven thousand buffalo skins and other furs were put on board our boat to take to St. Louis. . . . The leather tents of the Sioux Indians, the most distinguished being that of the old interpreter, Dorion (or Durion), a half Sioux, who is mentioned by many travellers, and resides here with his Indian family. His tent was large, and painted red; at the top of the poles composing the frame, several scalps hung." ("Travels in North America," p. 156, Maximilian, Prince of Wied.)

my beloved wife. I was also presented with two pairs of moccasins, an Indian riding-whip, one collar of Grizzly Bear's claws, and two long strings of dried white apples, as well as two Indian dresses. I bought the skin of a fine young Grizzly Bear, two Wolf skins, and a parcel of fossil remains. I saw twelve young Buffalo calves, caught a few weeks ago, and yet as wild, apparently, as ever. Sprague will take outlines of them to-morrow morning, and I shall draw them. We have put ashore about one-half of our cargo and left fifty of our *engagés*, so that we shall be able to go much faster, in less water than we have hitherto drawn. We are all engaged in finishing our correspondence, the whole of the letters being about to be forwarded to St. Louis by the steamer "Trapper." I have a letter of seven pages to W. G. Bakewell, James Hall, J. W. H. Page, and Thomas M. Brewer,[1] of Boston, besides those to my family. We are about one and a half miles above the Teton River, or, as it is now called, the Little Missouri,[2] a swift and tortuous stream that finds its source about 250 miles from its union with this great river, in what are called the Bad Lands of Teton River, where it seems, from what we hear, that the country has been at one period greatly convulsed, and is filled

[1] W. G. Bakewell was Audubon's brother-in-law; James Hall, brother of Mrs. John W. Audubon; J. W. H. Page, of New Bedford. Thomas Mayo Brewer, who became a noted ornithologist, edited the 12mo edition of Wilson, wrote Part I. of the "Oölogy of North America," which was published by the Smithsonian Institution in 1857, and was one of the authors of Baird, Brewer, and Ridgway's "History of North American Birds." He died in Boston Jan. 23, 1880, having been born there Nov. 21, 1814. He is notorious for his mistaken zeal in introducing the English Sparrow in this country. — E. C.

[2] The Teton, or Bad River, has long ceased to be known as the Little Missouri, — a name now applied to another branch of the Missouri, which falls in from the south much higher up, about 23 miles above present Fort Berthold. Teton River was so named by Lewis and Clark, Sept. 24, 1804, from the tribe of Sioux found at its mouth: see the History of the Expedition, ed. of 1893, p. 131, and compare p. 267. The Indian name was Chicha, Schicha, or Shisha. — E. C.

with fossil remains. I saw the young Elk belonging to our captain, looking exceedingly shabby, but with the most beautiful eyes I ever beheld in any animal of the Deer kind. We have shot nothing to-day. I have heard all the notes of the Meadow Lark found here and they are utterly different from those of our common species. And now that I am pretty well fatigued with writing letters and this journal, I will go to rest, though I have matter enough in my poor head to write a book. We expect to proceed onwards some time to-morrow.

June 1, Thursday. I was up at half-past three, and by four Sprague and I walked to the Fort, for the purpose of taking sketches of young Buffalo calves. These young beasts grunt precisely like a hog, and I would defy any person not seeing the animals to tell one sound from the other. The calves were not out of the stable, and while waiting I measured the Elk horns given me by Mr. Picotte. They are as follows: length, 4 feet 6½ inches; breadth 27 to 27½ inches; circumference at the skull 16 inches, round the knob 12 inches; between the knobs 3 inches. This animal, one of the largest ever seen in this country, was killed in November last. From seventeen to twenty-one poles are necessary to put up a lodge, and the poles when the lodge is up are six or seven feet above the top. The holes at the bottom, all round, suffice to indicate the number of these wanted to tighten the lodge. In time Sprague made several outline sketches of calves, and I drew what I wished. We had breakfast very early, and I ate some good bread and fresh butter. Mr. Picotte presented me with two pipe-stems this morning, quite short, but handsome. At eleven we were on our way, and having crossed the river, came alongside of the "Trapper," of which Mr. John Durack takes the command to St. Louis. The name of our own captain is Joseph A. Sire. Mr. Picotte gave me a letter for Fort Union, as Mr. Culbertson will not be there when we arrive. One of

Captain Sire's daughters and her husband are going up with us. She soled three pairs of moccasins for me, as skilfully as an Indian. Bell and Harris shot several rare birds. Mr. Bowie promised to save for me all the curiosities he could procure; he came on board and saw the plates of quadrupeds, and I gave him an almanac, which he much desired.

After we had all returned on board, I was somewhat surprised that Sprague asked me to let him return with the "Omega" to St. Louis. Of course I told him that he was at liberty to do so, though it will keep me grinding about double as much as I expected. Had he said the same at New York, I could have had any number of young and good artists, who would have leaped for joy at the very idea of accompanying such an expedition. Never mind, however.

We have run well this afternoon, for we left Fort Pierre at two o'clock, and we are now more than twenty-five miles above it. We had a rascally Indian on board, who hid himself for the purpose of murdering Mr. Chardon; the latter gave him a thrashing last year for thieving, and Indians never forget such things — he had sworn vengeance, and that was enough. Mr. Chardon discovered him below, armed with a knife; he talked to him pretty freely, and then came up to ask the captain to put the fellow ashore. This request was granted, and he and his bundle were dropped overboard, where the water was waist deep; the fellow scrambled out, and we heard, afterward, made out to return to Fort Pierre. I had a long talk with Sprague, who thought I was displeased with him — a thing that never came into my head — and in all probability he will remain with us. Harris shot a pair of Arkansas Flycatchers, and Squires procured several plants, new to us all. Harris wrote a few lines to Mr. Sarpy at St. Louis, and I have had the pleasure to send the Elk horns, and the great balls from the stomachs of

Buffalo given me by our good captain. I am extremely fatigued, for we have been up since before daylight. *At* 12 *o'clock of the night.* I have got up to scribble this, which it is not strange that after all I saw this day, at this curious place, I should have forgotten. Mr. Picotte took me to the storehouse where the skins procured are kept, and showed me eight or ten packages of White Hare skins, which I feel assured are all of Townsend's Hare of friend Bachman, as no other species are to be met with in this neighborhood during the winter months, when these animals migrate southward, both in search of food and of a milder climate.

June 2, Friday. We made an extremely early start about three A. M. The morning was beautiful and calm. We passed Cheyenne River at half-past seven, and took wood a few miles above it. Saw two White Pelicans, shot a few birds. My hunter, Alexis Bombarde, whom I have engaged, could not go shooting last night on account of the crossing of this river, the Cheyenne, which is quite a large stream. Mr. Chardon gave me full control of Alexis, till we reach the Yellowstone. He is a first-rate hunter, and powerfully built; he wears his hair long about his head and shoulders, as I was wont to do; but being a half-breed, his does not curl as mine did. Whilst we are engaged cutting wood again, many of the men have gone after a Buffalo, shot from the boat. We have seen more Wolves this day than ever previously. We saw where carcasses of Buffaloes had been quite devoured by these animals, and the diversity of their colors and of their size is more wonderful than all that can be said of them. Alexis Bombarde, whom hereafter I shall simply call *Alexis*, says that with a small-bored rifle common size, good shot will kill any Wolf at sixty or eighty yards' distance, as well as bullets. We passed one Wolf that, crossing our bows, went under the wheel and yet escaped, though several shots were fired at it. I had a specimen of *Arvicola pennsylvanicus*[1] brought to me, and I was glad to find this species so very far from New York. These animals in confinement eat each other up, the strongest one remaining, often maimed and covered with blood. This I have seen, and I was glad to have it corroborated by Bell. We are told the Buffalo cows are generally best to eat in the month of July; the young bulls are, however, tough at this season. Our men have just returned with the whole of the Buffalo except its head; it is a young bull, and may prove good. When they reached it, it was standing, and Alexis shot at it twice, to despatch it as soon as possible. It was skinned and cut up in a very few minutes, and the whole of the flesh was brought on board. I am now astonished at the poverty of the bluffs which we pass; no more of the beautiful limestone formations that we saw below. Instead of those, we now run along banks of poor and crumbling clay, dry and hard now, but after a rain soft and soapy. Most of the cedars in the ravines, formerly fine and thrifty, are now, generally speaking, dead and dried up. Whether this may be the effect of the transitions of the weather or not, I cannot pretend to assert. We have seen more Wolves to-day than on any previous occasions. We have made a good day's work of it also, for I dare say that when we stop for the night, we shall have travelled sixty miles. The water is rising somewhat, but not to hurt our progress. We have seen young Gadwall Ducks, and a pair of Geese that had young ones swimming out of our sight.

June 3, Saturday. Alexis went off last night at eleven o'clock, walked about fifteen miles, and returned at ten this morning; he brought three Prairie Dogs, or, as I

[1] Wilson's Meadow Mouse. This is the name used by Aud. and Bach. Quad. N. Am. i., 1849, p. 341, pl. 45, for the *Arvicola riparius* of Ord, now known as *Microtus riparius*. But the specimen brought to Audubon can only be very doubtfully referred to this species. — E. C.

call them, Prairie Marmots. The wind blew violently till we had run several miles; at one period we were near stopping. We have had many difficulties with the sand-bars, having six or seven times taken the wrong channel, and then having to drop back and try our luck again. The three Marmots had been killed with shot quite too large, and not one of them was fit for drawing, or even skinning. Sprague and I have taken measurements of all their parts, which I give at once. [*Here follow forty-two measurements, all external, of the male and female.*] I received no further intelligence about the habits of this species, except that they are quite numerous in every direction. We passed four rivers to-day; the Little Chayenne,[1] the Moroe, the Grand, and the Rampart. The Moroe is a handsome stream and, I am told, has been formerly a good one for Beaver. It is navigable for barges for a considerable distance. Just before dinner we stopped to cut drift-wood on a sand-bar, and a Wolf was seen upon it. Bell, Harris, and some one else went after it. The wily rascal cut across the bar and, hiding itself under the bank, ran round the point, and again stopped. But Bell had returned towards the very spot, and the fellow was seen swimming off, when Bell pulled the trigger and shot it dead, in or near the head. The captain sent the yawl after it, and it was brought on board. It was tied round the neck and dipped in the river to wash it. It smelled very strong, but I was heartily glad to have it in my power to examine it closely, and to be enabled to take very many measurements of this the first Wolf we have actually procured. It was a male, but rather poor; its general color a grayish yellow; its measurements are

[1] This is spelt thus in the Journal, and also on Tanner's map of 1829: see also Lewis and Clark, ed. of 1893, p. 152. The "Moroe" River of the above text is present Moreau River, falling into the Missouri from the west in Dewey Co., S. Dak. Grand River was also known by its Arikara name, Weterhoo, or Wetarhoo. Rampart River is about two miles above Grand River; it was also called Maropa River.—E. C.

as follows [*omitted*]. We saw one Goose with a gosling, several Coots, Grebes, Blue Herons, Doves, Magpies, Red-shafted Woodpeckers, etc. On a sand-bar Bell counted ten Wolves feeding on some carcass. We also saw three young whelps. This morning we saw a large number of Black-headed Gulls feeding on a dead Buffalo with some Ravens; the Gulls probably were feeding on the worms, or other insects about the carcass. We saw four Elks, and a large gang of Buffaloes. One Wolf was seen crossing the river towards our boat; being fired at, it wheeled round, but turned towards us again, again wheeled round, and returned to where it had started. We ran this evening till our wood was exhausted, and I do not know how we will manage to-morrow. Good-night. God bless you all.

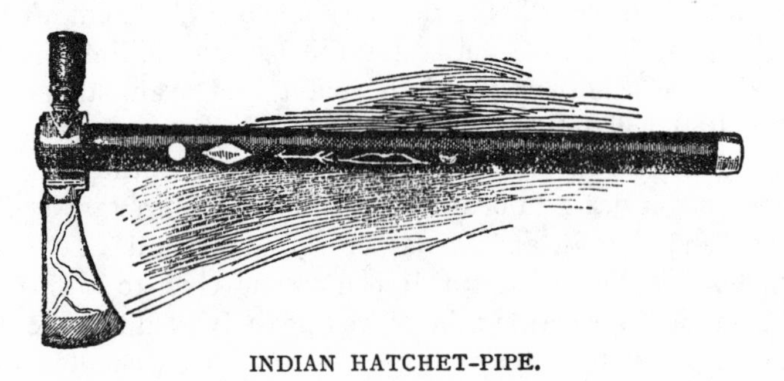

INDIAN HATCHET-PIPE.

Carried by Audubon during many of his journeys.

A CATALOG OF SELECTED

DOVER BOOKS

IN ALL FIELDS OF INTEREST

A CATALOG OF SELECTED DOVER BOOKS IN ALL FIELDS OF INTEREST

TWENTY-FOUR ART NOUVEAU POSTCARDS IN FULL COLOR FROM CLASSIC POSTERS, Hayward and Blanche Cirker. Ready-to-mail postcards reproduced from rare set of poster art. Works by Toulouse-Lautrec, Parrish, Steinlen, Mucha, Cheret, others. 12pp. 8¼× 11. 24389-3 Pa. $2.95

READY-TO-USE ART NOUVEAU BOOKMARKS IN FULL COLOR, Carol Belanger Grafton. 30 elegant bookmarks featuring graceful, flowing lines, foliate motifs, sensuous women characteristic of Art Nouveau. Perforated for easy detaching. 16pp. 8¼ × 11. 24305-2 Pa. $2.95

FRUIT KEY AND TWIG KEY TO TREES AND SHRUBS, William M. Harlow. Fruit key covers 120 deciduous and evergreen species; twig key covers 160 deciduous species. Easily used. Over 300 photographs. 126pp. 5⅜ × 8½. 20511-8 Pa. $2.25

LEONARDO DRAWINGS, Leonardo da Vinci. Plants, landscapes, human face and figure, etc., plus studies for Sforza monument, *Last Supper*, more. 60 illustrations. 64pp. 8¼ × 11⅛. 23951-9 Pa. $2.75

CLASSIC BASEBALL CARDS, edited by Bert R. Sugar. 98 classic cards on heavy stock, full color, perforated for detaching. Ruth, Cobb, Durocher, DiMaggio, H. Wagner, 99 others. Rare originals cost hundreds. 16pp. 8¼ × 11. 23498-3 Pa. $3.25

TREES OF THE EASTERN AND CENTRAL UNITED STATES AND CANADA, William M. Harlow. Best one-volume guide to 140 trees. Full descriptions, woodlore, range, etc. Over 600 illustrations. Handy size. 288pp. 4½ × 6⅜. 20395-6 Pa. $3.95

JUDY GARLAND PAPER DOLLS IN FULL COLOR, Tom Tierney. 3 Judy Garland paper dolls (teenager, grown-up, and mature woman) and 30 gorgeous costumes highlighting memorable career. Captions. 32pp. 9¼ × 12¼. 24404-0 Pa. $3.50

GREAT FASHION DESIGNS OF THE BELLE EPOQUE PAPER DOLLS IN FULL COLOR, Tom Tierney. Two dolls and 30 costumes meticulously rendered. Haute couture by Worth, Lanvin, Paquin, other greats late Victorian to WWI. 32pp. 9¼ × 12¼. 24425-3 Pa. $3.50

FASHION PAPER DOLLS FROM GODEY'S LADY'S BOOK, 1840-1854, Susan Johnston. In full color: 7 female fashion dolls with 50 costumes. Little girl's, bridal, riding, bathing, wedding, evening, everyday, etc. 32pp. 9¼ × 12¼. 23511-4 Pa. $3.95

THE BOOK OF THE SACRED MAGIC OF ABRAMELIN THE MAGE, translated by S. MacGregor Mathers. Medieval manuscript of ceremonial magic. Basic document in Aleister Crowley, Golden Dawn groups. 268pp. 5⅜ × 8½. 23211-5 Pa. $5.00

PETER RABBIT POSTCARDS IN FULL COLOR: 24 Ready-to-Mail Cards, Susan Whited LaBelle. Bunnies ice-skating, coloring Easter eggs, making valentines, many other charming scenes. 24 perforated full-color postcards, each measuring 4¼ × 6, on coated stock. 12pp. 9 × 12. 24617-5 Pa. $2.95

CELTIC HAND STROKE BY STROKE, A. Baker. Complete guide creating each letter of the alphabet in distinctive Celtic manner. Covers hand position, strokes, pens, inks, paper, more. Illustrated. 48pp. 8¼ × 11. 24336-2 Pa. $2.50

READY-TO-USE BORDERS, Ted Menten. Both traditional and unusual interchangeable borders in a tremendous array of sizes, shapes, and styles. 32 plates. 64pp. 8¼ × 11. 23782-6 Pa. $3.50

THE WHOLE CRAFT OF SPINNING, Carol Kroll. Preparing fiber, drop spindle, treadle wheel, other fibers, more. Highly creative, yet simple. 43 illustrations. 48pp. 8¼ × 11. 23968-3 Pa. $2.50

HIDDEN PICTURE PUZZLE COLORING BOOK, Anna Pomaska. 31 delightful pictures to color with dozens of objects, people and animals hidden away to find. Captions. Solutions. 48pp. 8¼ × 11. 23909-8 Pa. $2.25

QUILTING WITH STRIPS AND STRINGS, H.W. Rose. Quickest, easiest way to turn left-over fabric into handsome quilt. 46 patchwork quilts; 31 full-size templates. 48pp. 8¼ × 11. 24357-5 Pa. $3.25

NATURAL DYES AND HOME DYEING, Rita J. Adrosko. Over 135 specific recipes from historical sources for cotton, wool, other fabrics. Genuine premodern handicrafts. 12 illustrations. 160pp. 5⅜ × 8½. 22688-3 Pa. $2.95

CARVING REALISTIC BIRDS, H.D. Green. Full-sized patterns, step-by-step instructions for robins, jays, cardinals, finches, etc. 97 illustrations. 80pp. 8¼ × 11. 23484-3 Pa. $3.00

GEOMETRY, RELATIVITY AND THE FOURTH DIMENSION, Rudolf Rucker. Exposition of fourth dimension, concepts of relativity as Flatland characters continue adventures. Popular, easily followed yet accurate, profound. 141 illustrations. 133pp. 5⅜ × 8½. 23400-2 Pa. $3.00

READY-TO-USE SMALL FRAMES AND BORDERS, Carol B. Grafton. Graphic message? Frame it graphically with 373 new frames and borders in many styles: Art Nouveau, Art Deco, Op Art. 64pp. 8¼ × 11. 24375-3 Pa. $3.50

CELTIC ART: THE METHODS OF CONSTRUCTION, George Bain. Simple geometric techniques for making Celtic interlacements, spirals, Kellstype initials, animals, humans, etc. Over 500 illustrations. 160pp. 9 × 12. (Available in U.S. only) 22923-8 Pa. $6.00

THE TALE OF TOM KITTEN, Beatrix Potter. Exciting text and all 27 vivid, full-color illustrations to charming tale of naughty little Tom getting into mischief again. 58pp. 4¼ × 5½. (USO) 24502-0 Pa. $1.75

WOODEN PUZZLE TOYS, Ed Sibbett, Jr. Transfer patterns and instructions for 24 easy-to-do projects: fish, butterflies, cats, acrobats, Humpty Dumpty, 19 others. 48pp. 8¼ × 11. 23713-3 Pa. $2.50

MY FAMILY TREE WORKBOOK, Rosemary A. Chorzempa. Enjoyable, easy-to-use introduction to genealogy designed specially for children. Data pages plus text. Instructive, educational, valuable. 64pp. 8¼ × 11. 24229-3 Pa. $2.50

Prices subject to change without notice.

Available at your book dealer or write for free catalog to Dept. GI, Dover Publications, Inc., 31 East 2nd St. Mineola, N.Y. 11501. Dover publishes more than 175 books each year on science, elementary and advanced mathematics, biology, music, art, literary history, social sciences and other areas.